CARRIAGES AT ELEVEN

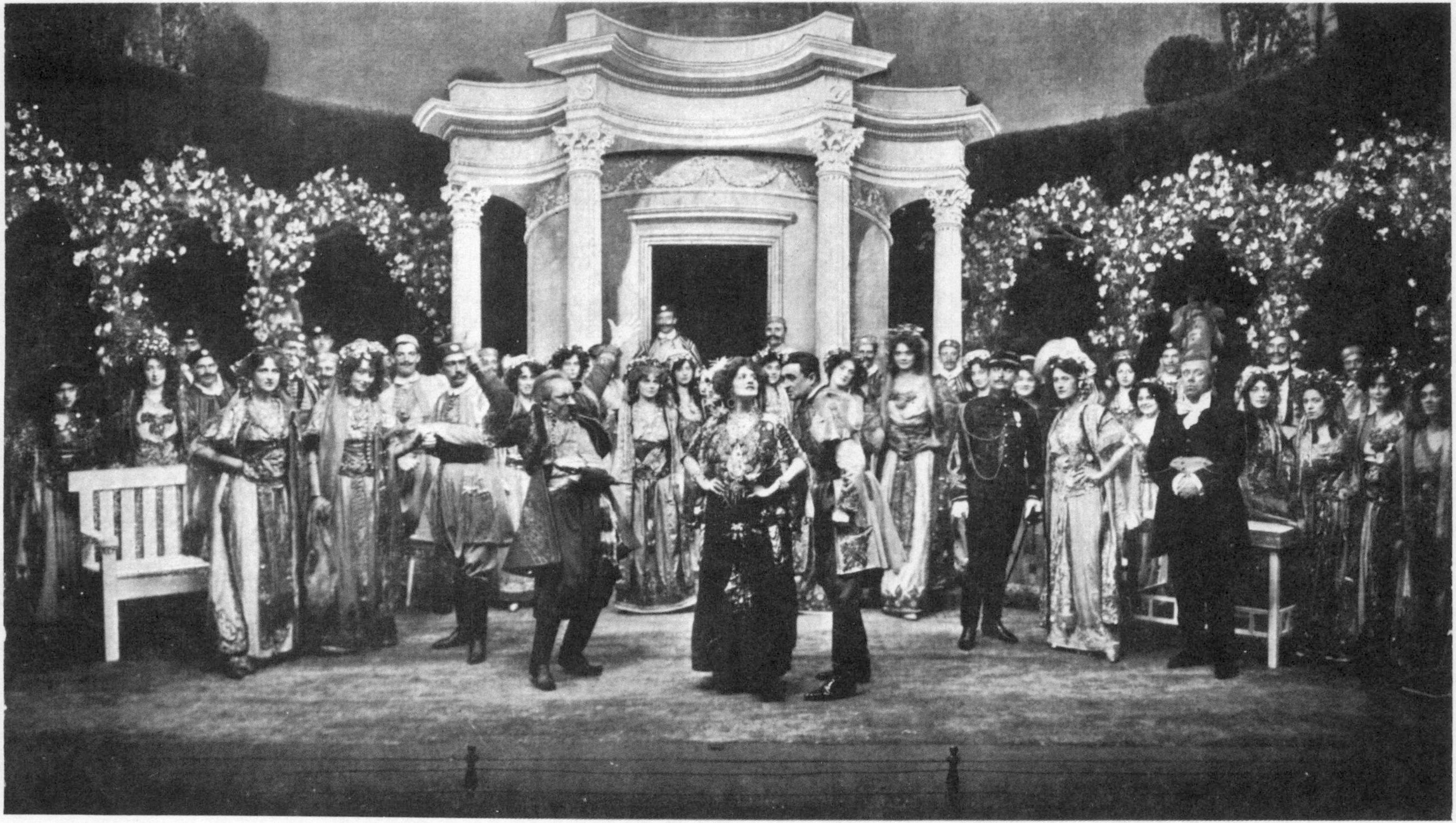

'THE MERRY WIDOW' AT DALY'S

CARRIAGES AT ELEVEN

The Story of the Edwardian Theatre

By

W. MACQUEEN-POPE

With 43 Illustrations

KENNIKAT PRESS
Port Washington, N. Y./London

TO

MOYA AND BILL

WHO WERE NOT BORN WHEN WE RODE IN

CARRIAGES AT ELEVEN

CARRIAGES AT ELEVEN

First published in 1947
Reissued in 1970 by Kennikat Press
Library of Congress Catalog Card No: 72-102849
SBN 8046-0759-1

Manufactured by Taylor Publishing Company   Dallas, Texas

CONTENTS

LIST OF ILLUSTRATIONS

The illustrations showing scenes in the following plays are from the
Raymond Mander and Joe Mitchenson collection : *The King of
Cadonia ; Captain Drew on Leave ; The Scarlet Pimpernel ; A Message
from Mars ; The Christian ; Antony and Cleopatra ; Penelope ; John
Chilcote, M.P. ; King Henry VIII ; Caesar and Cleopatra*

CHAPTER I

The Doors Open

LONDON IN THE DAYS OF KING EDWARD VII WAS A CITY OF SMILES, THE habitation of wealth, of peace, of security, and of power. London was an English city, speaking its own language, conscious that it was the centre of the whole world, that it called the tune and held the balance as the capital of the greatest Empire ever known. And that word Empire then meant what it said.

Those were the days of dignity, and of stability. Home life flourished. The great majority were householders, and as such had a stake in the country. Flats were gradually becoming popular, but they were still not considered to be quite 'homes'—they were looked upon as being a little foreign, a little insecure. A flat dweller had not the same moral standing as the master of a house.

Life moved at a more leisurely pace. Although the tempo was already quickening, it was still a gentle amble, and not a breakneck gallop. Sixty miles an hour in a railway train was fast enough for most people, and too fast for many. Distance still existed, and with it the sense of romantic adventure and the lure of far-off things. The telephone was a luxury of the few, or a thing of business. If you wanted to communicate with your friends, you wrote them a long letter. If they lived near by, you called round, or attended the 'At Home Day' on 'The Third Thursday' or whatever afternoon the lady of the house decreed. There were plenty of good conversationalists, and conversation was looked upon as a pleasure, and was not just a jumbled bunch of scraps and witticisms —or the latest jokes from the radio.

If you visited friends, you did so in some state, and you dined. You did not invade the house, drink cocktails by the dozen, and throw cigarette ends about the floor. You showed good breeding and good manners, and it was always 'Ladies First.' For the home was the hub of the wheel of life, for all save that small section called 'The Smart Set.' Responsibility was one of the ordinary tasks of existence, a thing to be shouldered in the natural course of events. There was time for many things, there was leisure for the enjoyment of beauty, for pictures (not the moving variety), for poetry, for the countryside, and the River Thames.

Things were stable, for the home was the anchor. Progress was going on all round, but nobody paid much attention to it. Every year brought some new wonder, which disturbed nobody, for man was still master of the machine. The new marvels were discussed, though scarcely understood. The frame of mind towards them was, 'What will they be up to next?' Nobody looked upon the new internal combustion engine or the determined attempts of men to fly as something which would bring danger and destruction to mankind. A century of peace had made us oblivious of war, except as something far away to be dealt with by a small, professional army, which was always triumphant. Even the recent Boer War had failed to really shake us. England had not yet become Great Britain in our speech ; we were still insular, still sure of ourselves with the

7

deepest confidence. We still regarded Canada, New Zealand, Australia, as Colonies. The Empire was our god and Kipling was its prophet.

We were, we knew, *fin de siècle* and that rather thrilled us. But the changes were coming leisurely, in the good old British way, and we had no reason to suppose that the twentieth century would not be the same as the nineteenth.

The Edwardian days were not just confined to the short reign of King Edward, they started earlier than that, immediately after the Diamond Jubilee, that greatest (almost the only) boost the Empire ever had, the last time the almost legendary old Royal recluse, Queen Victoria, showed herself in state to her awe-struck but worshipping people from all over the globe. And showed herself to them in London.

That was really the beginning of the Edwardian era, and it extended, with very little difference, after that King's death and the accession of his son, King George V. The Edwardian times really mean from 1897 —if not a few years before—right up to the coming of the First World War in 1914, when the whole world changed and with it our world of London. For up to then all had been secure, all had been peaceful and, for the great majority, comfortable ; money was cheap and plentiful. There was Society, and there was the Middle Class (that solid backbone) and there were the working classes, the firm substantial feet upon which everything stood.

Although the motor-car was creeping in—King Edward drove in them—the taxi was competing and beating the hansom, tube railways were burrowing underground, and 'flying machines' invading the air —the social life of London was divided sharply into two halves—'Carriage Folk' and 'Non-Carriage Folk.'

That was why you observed upon so many theatre programmes the phrase, 'Carriages at Eleven.'

For the Theatre was part of our social life. Except for the not quite respectable music hall, it had no competitor in the realm of entertainment. It stood alone, the undoubted aristocrat. And, as it is one of the duties of the Theatre to reflect the life passing around it, the Theatre itself, in the Edwardian days, was as stable and secure as the life of its patrons. It was—far more than it is to-day—a true microcosm of London. It had its division socially just as had the life outside. There was a sharp cleavage between the pit and the stalls quite apart from the wooden barrier between them. It was conducted with a dignity and a courtesy not understood at all to-day. It disregarded the outside march of progress and it had nothing to do with rush or vulgar clamour. It was run as were the homes of the people, with stately decorum and good manners. It had distinction with stability, and this was bestowed upon it by the actor-managers, whose theatres were their homes.

It had taken that shape under Queen Victoria ; it did not change under King Edward, it changed little under King George until all that it stood for fell in ruins, blown to pieces by the guns of 1914. It took a world upheaval to alter it.

The Victorian phrases continued under Edward, and even when George V ruled, programmes still stated 'Carriages at Eleven,' even though that carriage had become an electric brougham and later a limousine. Ladies were earnestly requested to remove their hats and bonnets, long after even elderly ladies had banished the bonnet into the limbo of forgotten things. Still these polite fictions held on, although the carriage had become a car, roaring motor buses had pushed the horse-drawn vehicle off the road, the honk of the taxi had drowned the tinkle of the hansom, and sometimes, to our vast excitement, an aeroplane zoomed overhead. And although the telephone had become a necessity, women were in business and demanding a vote, family circles were breaking up, and men were no longer too old at forty, still the Theatre remained the same, stately, dignified, slow to change. Even to-day it still calls the uniformed official outside, who opens the doors of the cars and will do his best to get a taxi, 'The Linkman'—a thing he has not been since the time when men and boys lit Londoners home by links, when street lighting was hardly known.

It was the actor-manager who bestowed this stability upon the Edwardian Theatre. In his theatre he sold branded goods. You knew what to expect in nearly every London playhouse. Each had a settled policy and abided by it. There were a few who were not so consistent, but mostly they stuck to their own line. And one actor-manager seldom, if ever, poached on the preserves of another. He did not have to, for he was selling himself in the best possible manner. And each had his own standard, below which he must not fall. They vied with each other in this, it is true, and so kept everything at a high level.

And you knew where to find them. Like the general public, they seldom moved from their established home. A very few were nomadic, but they only travelled short distances, with long terms of residence in between. But the truly great ones moved only about once or twice in their careers, like the British householders whom they served. So you always knew where your friend, the actor-manager, lived, and you knew exactly what he would offer you when you called. For the spirit of home life was prevalent in the Theatre, too.

When you paid them a visit, these great men were your hosts, and, like all good hosts, your obedient servants. They did their utmost to make your stay with them an agreeable one. They placed their best at your disposal. And you, on your part, as a playgoer, visited them in the same spirit. You made it an occasion of some formality. If by reason of your social standing, or your purse (and in Edwardian days this was becoming almost the same thing) you occupied the boxes, stalls or dress circle, you wore evening dress. You would not have dreamt of doing otherwise—and if you had, you would not have been admitted. If you were a still honoured, but not top-table guest, well, there was the pit or the gallery to suit your pocket and your wardrobe, or that curious, class-conscious part of the house, the upper circle, for what might be described as the lower middle class of playgoers, those who did not aspire to or could not afford the expensive parts, but who disdained to wait outside for the doors to open. And, still clinging to the past it hated to relinquish, many theatres called this part of the theatre 'The Upper Boxes,' many years after the partitions had been swept away.

But your position in the theatre made no difference to the actor-manager. Provided you had executed that little formality at the box office or paybox, you were equally his honoured guests no matter where you sat. It was presumed that he had no knowledge of the unfortunate but necessary financial transaction which made you his guest, the curtain, the proscenium arch, and the footlights cut him off from worldly affairs. And the smallness of the box office window made the proceeding as secret as possible, a mere affair between you and the 'evening dressed' official inside.

Indeed, to make up for the distance that you, in the cheaper parts, were away from him, he would frequently 'play' to you, so as to let you know that he was conscious of your presence below the salt and that it made no difference to him. And also because he knew full well that you would show your appreciation of his efforts as host more exuberantly than the guests at the top table. You liked this, and so did he.

Sometimes, and it happened not infrequently, you did not agree with him over the quality of the entertainment he offered you. Well, it was a pity, and both you and he felt regretful. But that did not stop you, as a patron of the pit or gallery, from booing him at the end of the show. The stalls might applaud, half-heartedly, but the patrons of the unreserved seats showed their lack of reserve vocally. The demonstration was more in sorrow than in anger. The boos were for the play and for the author, rather than for the actor-manager. But you included him, for you considered he had been guilty of a lack of taste and discernment. He knew all about that.

He would show his regret by withdrawing the play after a short run. There would be a few remarks by him in the *Daily Telegraph* on a Thursday, and in the *Referee* on a Sunday, to the effect that the production had 'failed to attract'—he never admitted failure of quality or acting—and an announcement of a new play. That suited everyone. He saved his face by outwardly keeping up a show of faith in his rejected offering, and you felt that your judgment was confirmed. You felt convinced he had done his best, even in the present disagreeable circumstances, and that he would do much better next time. Everyone —even an actor-manager—was liable to make a mistake. So even when there was a real first-night storm, like that caused by Pinero's *Wife Without a Smile*—there was no ill-will afterwards. For you knew and admired the actor-manager, and what is more, you respected him. You felt friendly disposed towards a man who had given you so many happy evenings, so many pleasant memories, you looked upon him as a friend. And this although ninety per cent of you had never met him, would never meet him, and had hardly ever seen him off the stage.

For the actor-manager lived a life apart from the general play-going public, and therein lay much of his strength. He was exclusively West End ; he was not seen about all over the place. His was the dignity of distance and aloofness—you had to pay to see him and that gave him much value. He was never alluded to in the newspapers other than by his full patronymic or title ; he did not suffer from being casually addressed by his Christian name by one of those super-intimate friends, a B.B.C. interviewer or compère, whilst millions listened to the familiarity. No, he lived in his own world, the world of the Theatre.

And if, perchance, you happened to be in the West End—which

really was the West End then—and came upon him face to face in Piccadilly, Pall Mall, or Bond Street, or perhaps crossing Leicester Square en route for the Green Room Club or the more cloistral calm of the Garrick Club, you would have raised your hat to him as a personality of eminence worthy of salute, and you would have met with a similar courtesy on his part. It would all have been very polite and charming, and you would have experienced a pleasant thrill, and told them all about it when you got home.

You would never have accosted him as 'Herbert,' Cyril,' 'George,' 'Charlie' or 'Arthur,' and have demanded his autograph, thrusting upon him a somewhat dirty piece of paper, bearing your own name and address, and insisting that he should send you his signed photograph at his own expense, and with all possible speed. Yet that is commonly done to-day by young people, who seldom go to the theatres but who invest a few coppers each week in a visit or visits to the cinema, and thereby consider the stars subservient to their lightest whim and command. Maybe that is the right attitude, for the great actors of old would protest that they were the obedient humble servants of the public. But one wonders what sort of a reception these pushing young folk would have received, if they had tried their familiar tricks upon Garrick, Macready, Mrs. Siddons, Kean, Kemble, Irving, Wyndham, Hawtrey, Maude, Tree or any of them? We remember Tree's reply to the suffragette who knocked off his tall hat and then complained that he was no gentleman. "Madame," replied that great man, "how can you know if I am no gentleman when you deprive me of the means of behaving as one?" To-day, one presumes, the proper reply would be a good hard shove and the command : "Say, sister, scram, and cut out the rough stuff." But in the days when we ordered our carriages at eleven, we spoke pure English. It was not necessary for a performer to adopt an American accent to attain popularity. If we had an accent, at least it was an English one, and if we used slang, at least it was native. But then, of course, the man you met would have looked the celebrity he undoubtedly was. He would have worn his tall hat and frock coat with an air, and would, in nearly every case, have been clean-shaven in an age of moustaches. He would have had a mysterious something about him which proclaimed his calling. You would spot him as an actor anywhere. Never, even in the desert spaces of August in London, when nobody was supposed to be in Town (and very frequently the actor-manager was not either), never, even in those summer days would he have been seen in Town in a sports coat and flannel trousers. And that applied to nearly all actors of standing as well. It was the rule of the Theatre to 'dress well, on and off.' It was even in the contracts. Nowadays, actors look like everyone else. From their own point of view it is a pity. That stamp of romance, that hall mark of mystery, has gone. On a summer's day recently, one of the best actor-managers of to-day, one of the few remaining, perhaps the only one, who still retains, in the theatre, anything of the air of the Edwardian days, was seen proceeding towards his playhouse dressed in a shirt open at the neck, an old coat slung over his shoulder, flannel trousers, and as he went, he was eating an ice cream cornet. Other times, other manners.

The great Edwardian personages took the eye at once. Even if you had never entered a theatre in your life, you would have known they were 'somebodies.' Sir Squire Bancroft, one of the few moustached actors, was an unforgettable figure, his silver hair, his bearing, his monocle with its broad black ribbon, his grey frock coat and topper—a universal celebrity ; so was Sir Charles Wyndham, with his beautifully brushed hair, his mobile, handsome face with its actor's mouth, and his air of complete but unconscious distinction. Sir George Alexander, utterly immaculate, tremendously respectable, carrying with him the very essence of St. James's ; Sir John Martin-Harvey, quite unable at any time or place, or in any style of clothing, to disguise the aura of romance surrounding him, or the fact that he was an actor. You might have met a frock-coated figure with a beautiful, scholarly and ascetic face, matching perfectly the golden voice he possessed. It would have been Sir Johnstone Forbes Robertson, but you would never have mistaken him for a professor, he was undoubtedly a Thespian. If you had seen an alert, striding figure, with a rather wide mouth and strong jaw, you would have recognized Lewis Waller at once, for always there was the shadow of a cloak and sword, thigh boots and spurs superimposed on Savile Row, whilst Cyril Maude, so neat, so dapper, so fresh-complexioned and so distinctly the cultured English gentleman of breeding, had yet twinkling from his eyes and radiating from his entire person the creative force which is distinctive to a fine actor—and he has it yet, this young man in his eighties, with eye, bearing, wit and talent alike undimmed by the passing years.

Another man with a moustache, probably less formally dressed than some of the others, yet attired with all the care, smartness and valeting of an exclusive clubman, with the perfect *savoir-faire* and assurance of a man-about-town, but still unmistakably an actor, would have been Sir Charles Hawtrey, the light comedian *par excellence* and a much better actor than he ever cared, or dared, to show. Or you might have met, and you can still meet, the quick, alert, ever-youthful figure of Seymour Hicks (now a knight), actor, theatre proprietor, playwright and wit, who has written, produced, and performed in more plays than any living man, and still has that mischievous eye and dominant nose. The exploits of his youth were prodigious, throwing those of Noel Coward into insignificance, but then Seymour was living amongst giants and his amazing versatility and output was regarded as nothing abnormal.

Towering above them all, you might have seen the tall figure of Sir Herbert Tree, wrapt in thought, aloof from the world, living partly in the past and partly in the future, but keenly alive to the present all the same, proceeding—for one can never say he walked—down the Haymarket to his 'beautiful theatre.' So great was the veneration in which he was held by playgoers that Leslie Bloom, who has for years been the President of the Gallery First Nighters, proudly admits that he once followed Sir Herbert, to him the embodiment of the Theatre, down that ancient thoroughfare, taking care to place his feet exactly where Sir Herbert had trod. Mr. Bloom had been, on occasions, amongst those 'gods' who had booed Sir Herbert in the aforesaid 'beautiful theatre' but his respect and admiration for the great personality were always uppermost. Also, he would probably boo him again and still abate nothing of his regard.

And, in the early days of the period, you could still have caught a glimpse, though a rare one, of the pale, compelling, *pince-nez*-ed and characteristic features of a man who looked what he was, a great, a very great actor, not only of his day but of all time, and leader of the profession for which he had done so much—Sir Henry Irving himself.

There were many more, and all distinctive : large and burly Arthur Bourchier, a mixture of Oxford, White's Club and the stage, with the latter predominating ; Sir John Hare, who might have been a family solicitor but for the greyhound look of vitality about him which denoted the eminent actor ; Fred Terry, whose family charm radiated strongly, and others who will be met in their homes, for the theatres in which they played were their homes, one and the same thing to them. They lived, with their work, in their playhouses and did not operate from suites of offices with large staffs of assistants and secretaries. Mass production was unknown to them, these men were like the craftsmen of old, working on their creations with their own brains and their own hands.

The great Edwardian actresses, too, were women of the Theatre and not of Society. They lived a life cut off from the rest of the world by the proscenium arch. It was an unusual thrill to see them off the stage. And they, in their wisdom, seldom put themselves on view. Yet, perhaps, one might catch a fleeting glance in Bond Street, or in one of the great shops where dresses were created—a vision of regal beauty which was—and is—Julia Neilson, that vivid, large-eyed darkness and distinction which is Irene Vanbrugh, that intensely alive and vital piece of femininity, with its quick, small eyes, and sweeping walk which was Marie Tempest, the cultured distinction and poise of Violet Vanbrugh and Lena Ashwell, the elusive, mordant-witted and lovely Mrs. Patrick Campbell, that charming and gracious womanhood of Winifred Emery, the direct, well-dressed challenge of Ellis Jeffreys—such a typical Englishwoman of her time ; Constance Collier, Lily Hanbury, Ethel Irving—a host of other goddesses who were worshipped from afar. And there was the intriguing cavalcade of the musical stage as well, women who really possessed that misused word 'glamour'—like Evie Greene, Marie Studholme, Edna May, Isobel Jay, Ruth Vincent, Adrienne Augarde, Ellaline Terriss (as beautiful now as then), Mabel Love—and two mere children, Zena and Phyllis Dare, who still sparkle with brilliance, talent and charm. And, of course, Gertie Millar and Lily Elsie . . . all allure, beauty, poise and lovely to look at, and all of them, beyond a shadow of doubt, of the Stage.

All these great folk were real, they could be seen in the flesh. Their actual voices could be heard by playgoers, in tones and modulations of their own, not distorted by mechanical amplification. A young playgoer of to-day, if whisked back to Edwardian times, would look in vain for microphones destroying the stage atmosphere. They were unknown. A player who could not be heard would not be seen either—the stage had no place for them. You had your actors and actresses at first hand —no need to advertise the fact that the performance was not a picture but an actual appearance. So very naturally, with a feast of greatness' in store, a visit to the theatre was an event, and an important event, too.

If you were playgoers of moderate means, that visit to the play was something to plan, to talk about and to anticipate with eagerness.

Carriage folk of course went everywhere, to all plays. They had their seats booked, many of them ran credit accounts with the 'Libraries' and if they were landed gentry and lived in the country they relied on the 'Library' they patronized to arrange their play-going for them when they came to Town. The play-going of the carriage folk was easy, and they differed very little from their descendants of to-day. They arrived late and a visit to the play was sandwiched between a dinner and a supper. They disturbed the house by their late arrival, they trooped out in the interval—the men, not the women, for ladies in those days did not go into the bar and never smoked in public—and often they left before the fall of the curtain.

But with the playgoers of the more humble parts, play-going was something to be savoured to the full. Not a moment of that visit was to be lost or wasted, every bit of it was enjoyable, from the setting out to the arrival home, with the programme to cherish as a memento of a wonderful evening.

Often it was quite a journey, for there was not that network of tubes, and the buses were neither so frequent nor so large, also they were horse-drawn for a great part of the time. Yet they managed to do the journey just as fast as the monster machines of to-day, for traffic jams were unusual, and what was looked upon as congestion then would have been a clear road to-day. So, if you lived in an outlying suburb, you took the train to your terminus, and you got on a bus to the nearest stopping point to the theatre you wished to visit. You hurried to the pit or gallery door and you commenced a vigil. You might have to wait two, three or four hours, according to the strength of the attraction you had chosen, and to the power of the actor-manager on whom you were going to call. There were no stools then to be hired outside the theatre, to make a reserved seat for you and on which, when booked, you had no need to sit for more than the last ten minutes of your wait ; there were no reserved pits and galleries to give you the comfort of a stall at your own price. In the earlier days there were no queues, but just a glorious rough-and-tumble crowd who pushed, shoved, shouted and screamed when the doors opened, and fought desperately to get a good seat to see a play. We were a tough generation and the battle was to the strong.

When the queue system was introduced, wealthier playgoers poached. They hired District Messenger boys to queue up for them, and arrived only shortly before the doors opened. These patrons who deserted the higher priced seats and saved a few shillings by the messenger employment were resented by the regular pit patron, but on the whole good-naturedly. They often had to stand some chaff and wisecracks, as the phrase goes to-day, and if they could be manœuvred out of position when the rush began, you may be sure it was done.

The regular cheap price playgoers, having got into position, began to enjoy themselves. They all had food, for that is an essential part of theatre-going. Many of them came equipped with reading matter.

Some read novels, Marie Corelli, Frankfort Moore, Seton Merriman, Anthony Hope, Conan Doyle, Hall Caine, W. W. Jacobs, and the many paper-covered editions of popular books which flooded the market. Others had magazines and periodicals—*Pearson's, The Wide World, The Strand, The Windsor, The Penny Pictorial, Pictorial Comedy, M.A.P., T.P.'s Weekly* and the like. But mostly they talked. And they talked about the Theatre, plays and performers. There were discussions into which those near them would be drawn. Many a friendship was made in the pit and gallery queue, and many a marriage, too. There were, of course, the few who, at the beginning, would attempt to impress their neighbours with their own importance, would mention loudly the fact that they had been unable to secure stalls, in which, of course, they usually sat, and would pretend to treat this as an exciting piece of slumming. The regular queue-ers had little time for them, and were unimpressed and unamused. A few well-chosen words would silence the pretenders, who later would be sure to condemn themselves out of their own mouths by their know-ledge of the regular queue routine. If the queue was for a Saturday matinée, you would find that quite a number were going to dash from that afternoon show to another theatre at night. These were the cream of playgoers and were treated with respect. It showed what a hold the Theatre had upon its public ; but then the appetite had not been sated with a bi- or tri-weekly dropping in at the pictures.

And whilst you waited, and ate and talked, there were the 'buskers' to entertain you. These had not then reached the elaboration which showed itself just before the last war, when every moment of waiting time was filled with kerb-side entertainment, working on a regular programme, and often with quite an elaborate show—and even company —to present. In Edwardian days this theatre of the gutter was a scratch affair and frowned on by the police. But there was quite a lot of it not-withstanding the fact that it had to be somewhat furtive and intermittent on account of the minions of the law. Always there would be a blind man who would be led along the queue by, one supposes, a female relative, who moaned a request, on a rising scale : "Buy a box of matches orf the BLIND, please." The top of the scale was reached on the word 'Blind,' and fell sharply on the 'please.' The tinkle of a coin into the enamelled mug led to 'Thang-Gyou' with the accent on the first word. The blind man himself might have been dumb as well. He never spoke. He just proffered a somewhat shop-soiled box of matches. One trembles to think what would have happened if the giver of a coin had taken that box in exchange. They never did !

The blind man would be succeeded by entertainers. They were of three kinds, vocal, instrumental and, shall we say, elocutionists. Woe-begone-looking women wailed old ballads, of which neither words nor tunes were apparent. One small old man, white-haired but chubby, with an entrancing smile, would sing 'A Farmer's Boy.' Perhaps the word 'sing' is not right, he delivered himself of it in a very loud voice, without a vestige of melody, but with much gusto and the queue were always on tip-toe when he got to the end of each of the numberless verses and reached out for the topmost 'B-o-o-o-y.' His amusement value was in inverse ratio to his musical ability, but he always reaped a shower of coppers.

So well did he do, that he elaborated the act and later appeared with a wheezy and broken-down harmonium, worked by a handle, which he wheeled about on an equally decrepit pram. He still sang only of the glories of being a farmer's boy, but the more musically inclined of the listening playgoers were of the opinion that the accompaniment on the harmonium was 'The War March of the Priests.' But it made no difference.

One of the star attractions was two small but enterprising boys. They were duettists, intermittent duettists. They established themselves facing the queue but some distance apart. Then, having glanced right and left, they began their entertainment. As they sang, unaccompanied, of course, their heads turned in every direction, to watch for their natural enemy, the London policeman. In the middle of a song, one would suddenly shout "Copper"—and they would fly for their lives, to reappear as soon as the leisurely moving officer of the law, trying to establish by his expression that he was totally unaware of the very existence of such things as boys in the scheme of life, had proceeded on his beat. Then they would reappear and start all over again. So well did this go, and so many laughs did it secure, and such a harvest of 'coppers' of a more welcome kind, that they would spring many false alarms. Their repertoire consisted of three songs popular on the 'halls' at that time. They never achieved more than a verse and chorus of each, sometimes only a chorus. One concerned a man who went into a bootmaker's shop, tried on a pair of boots, went out again and then :

"I never stopped running till I got home, I got home, I got home
I never stopped running till I got home
And that's how I saved the army." ('Copper.')

The second effort was of a different kind, but full of worldly philosophy :

"Don't you wish you had a wife like mine ?
Take my word, she's all right
She don't argue, she don't fight
When you want to go to bed each night
Bung her in the dustbin, hang her on the line
Don't you wish you had a wife like mine ?"

And the closing number included a dance. It went :

"Oh, I owe
I don't know how much money I owe
Oh, I owe
I'll pay you in the morning
Oh, I owe
I don't know what I owe heigho
But when I pay the money I owe . . ."

They both did a double shuffle and came round with their caps, gathering a considerable harvest to liquidate the supposed astronomic debts. Whether the financial appeal of the last song had anything to do with their placing it immediately before the collection, nobody knows. If so, it proves them to have been showmen. No doubt well off long since and retired. Or else moving picture magnates.

There was another singer of music hall songs, but an adult performer this time. He reaped a rich reward by being topical at the time of King Edward VII's coronation, and did not change his repertoire for years afterwards. His voice was husky and redolent of many pints, his face was red and shining and his manner of the tavern and hearty. But in Coronation Year he earned the price of many gallons by singing :

> "There'll be no War-er
> So long as we've a King like good King Hedward
> There'll be no war-er
> 'E 'ates that sort of thing
> Mothers, don't worry
> So long as we've a king like good Hedward
> Peace wiv Honner his 'is motter
> SO—(removing hat) Gawd Save the King."

That never failed. He also regaled us with a Coronation song immensely popular in that far-off year of 1902 :

> "On Coronation Day, on Coronation Day
> We'll all be merry
> Drinking whisky, wine and sherry
> We'll all be merry
> On Coronation Day."

His listeners might wonder if that mixture of drinks was really conducive to merriment but they cashed up after he had delivered himself, with the frankness of open-hearted confession, of the following :

> "Oh I'm pore, but I'm prahd and I'm partikuler
> I don't like work and never did
> And there's lots of millionaires wot wear the same sized 'at as I do
> Wot never went to work, so why should I ?"

And his audience contributed many reasons why he should never soil his hands by manual labour.

But by far the greater portion of the queue entertainers were shabby, disreputable-looking men who, nevertheless, imposed themselves upon the audience they found at their mercy. By some strange chance, according to them, each had been a member of Sir Henry Irving's company. When Irving died, it became 'the late Sir 'Enry Hirving.' By another coincidence each of them had, by an unspecified accident, 'over which,' they hastened to assure you, 'they had no control,' been deprived of the right of earning their living on the boards of the theatre, so had to turn to this method of getting a crust of bread. Some went even further and hinted at professional jealousy amongst the 'high-ups.' But at any rate, there they were, forced to perform outside the theatre instead of inside, and there were the playgoers, unable to take to flight. They announced what they were about to do in loud, harsh voices. Sometimes it was an excerpt from Shakespeare, sometimes an impression of a scene from Dickens, sometimes a popular poem, but always, as delivered by them, quite unrecognizable in every way. One of them, a pale-faced man, with a cunning expression, a waxed moustache, a sombrero hat and a foxy cast of countenance, did none of these things. His lead-in was the same, but he recited a poem, of which presumably he was the author, for a careful research by one interested playgoer failed to find the original. It went on for a long time. It began :

> "I was spending some time at Monaco
> That hotbed of gambling and vice
> Where you win twenty thou in a moment
> And lose it again, in a trice . . ."

B

The reciter hissed the words 'vice' and 'trice' and went on during what seemed æons with a long story of an unlucky gambler saved by some kind of good Samaritan, for it ended :

> "The golden words he uttered were
> A friend in need, is a friend indeed . . ."

and immediately came the peroration : "And I 'ope, ladies and gentle-men, that I shall find amongst you many friends indeed to 'elp this friend in need. I'm a member of the late Sir Henry Irving's company, ladies and gents, who on account of a haccident over which I 'ad no control am now reduced to hentertaining you in this manner outside the theatre hinstead of hinside, as his my right. But 'opin' that my hefforts 'ave served to w'ile away some weary moments of waitin', I thank you hin hadvance, for bein' friends indeed."

All these men got support. Most of the unwilling listeners must have known they were frauds but perhaps they thought that, the profession being notoriously precarious, there might be a grain of truth somewhere and few had the moral courage to refuse the proffered greasy hat. An intelligent foreigner, if amongst them, must have formed a very low opinion of the 'support' with which Irving surrounded himself, and put it down, doubtless, to the popular legend that actor-managers would not tolerate any other stars in the company (which was the exact opposite of the truth).

There were paper tearers, and a 'chapeaugraphist.' This gentleman, by the aid of a circular piece of felt, with a round hole in the middle, became Wellington, Nelson, Napoleon and a Nun in turns, according to the angle of the 'chapeau.' He became a 'Nun' by the simple expedient of placing the circle of felt around his face and assuming a dreamy expression whilst gazing heavenward, with one finger supporting his series of chins, which would have incurred the wrath of any self-respecting Mother Superior and been conducive of severe penance. Chapeaugraphy seems to be a lost and unregretted art.

But now the queue has closed up. Those nearest the door have heard sounds inside the theatre. Books, newspapers and magazines are pocketed or put in handbags with what remains of the refreshments. There is an air of being 'greyhounds in the slips, straining the start.' But those inside are not anxious to open. There is seemingly a routine to be gone through, for you heard the fireman conversing by shouts with someone apparently in the Antipodes, and the chink of money as the paybox man got ready his change. Then a pause, some more muffled conversation, and then, the eagerly awaited rattle of chains and clattering of woodwork, as at long last, the doors are thrown open and the playgoers surge forward, to plank down their half-crown or shilling, snatch up their checks, rush up or down stairs, according to whether they are pittites or gallery-goers, and at last into the empty auditorium. A race down the centre aisle, if any, for the best seats, a more frenzied rush round for the seats at the ends, the gradual filling up of the whole place as the queue gets in and accommodates itself. Then you would settle down, and if you had been early comers, congratulate yourself on the excellent position you had got 'just as good as a stall.' You would get a programme, and in the most eminent actor-managers' theatres, these were given you free (and all programmes should be free). Not only were they given you, but they bore in large type a prayer—almost an entreaty—from the management that you would give no gratuities to the attendants. But you did not read the programme yet, that was a joy still to come. You probably had half an hour to wait still, before the show commenced, but the first fine careless rapture of your joy was upon you, for you were Inside a Theatre to see a play.

CHAPTER II

'Curtain-Raiser'

WHEN YOU HAD SETTLED IN YOUR PLACE, YOU LOOKED AT YOUR programme. It was then that the tremendous politeness and desire to please the public on the part of the Edwardian Theatre and its actor-managers became apparent.

Firstly, at a great number of theatres, especially at those in which the actor-managers held sway, the programmes were free. Certain theatres, under the control of managers who did not act themselves, had already farmed out this concession, along with the bars and cloak-rooms, to catering firms, but the actor-managers made all this part of their service to their guests. They did not give you free drinks, of course, but you were not expected to pay sixpence to find out the necessary details of what you had already paid to see. Nor were you expected to pay another sixpence to have your coat and hat looked after whilst you saw the play, and to be detained when it was over whilst crowds pushed and fought around the cloakroom window and were embarrassed by the sight of a saucer containing a decoy half-crown or some odd coins, by which the attendants, already paid for the job, showed their expectation of largesse on your part. No, these things were not for the actor-manager in Edwardian days. Your programme bore ample evidence of it, and of the desire on the part of your host to make you comfortable. He did not command, he did not instruct you in what you should do. He requested you—and often, he earnestly requested you, to observe the rules of his household made for your comfort and convenience. He besought you not to give gratuities to the staff and told you that if you forgot yourself in this respect, you might get the person you had tipped instant dismissal. He had taken your money to see his play, he was not going to put you to further expense. And also, he was going to give you fair measure and no short weight. Whatever you had paid, you would get your money's worth. In fact, he did everything he could for your comfort except greet you in person. That, by reason of his acting, he could not do, but he had his representative in the front of the house, his manager, whom you would find the pink of politeness, of tact and diplomacy. This gentleman, the manager, wore, of course, faultless evening dress, to which he added a top hat, to show he was the manager. In the afternoon he wore a morning coat, but no top hat, although one or two wore it, even then, so that you should know them. Apart from his technical managerial duties—and he had a large say in matters in those days, as the link between actor and public—as soon as the doors opened, he was your deputy host. His name was on the programme, of course, and you were invited to make any complaints you might have direct to him. And, what is more, if you did so, you would find that he attended to them personally. He was your servant, he could not do too much for you. He knew all the regular patrons, he would welcome them personally and express his pleasure at their presence. ^ This delighted them, and gave them a pleasant feeling of prestige in front of their friends, and of superiority over other members of the audience not so favoured. Those house managers, men like Henry Dana, at His Majesty's ; C. T. Hunt Helmsley at St. James's and elsewhere ; Horace Watson at the Haymarket, and others, did much to make their theatres prosperous and popular.   They were part of the undertaking, their handling of the people meant a great deal, and they were allowed to use their judgment and initiative. They were in the councils of their chiefs, and were usually his friend as well.   Their advice was sought and taken.   For in the Edwardian Theatre the personal touch meant everything. It gave each theatre its own atmosphere, it gave a feeling of comfort and security to the playgoer.   And each manager was a personality, not a mere figure-head to receive instructions from a head office issuing mass production rules, not a mere clerk to check the 'returns' and pay a few salaries, but a man whose judgment and experience were relied upon.

You were, of course, not allowed to smoke in the Edwardian Theatre. But there was no arbitrary order such as 'No Smoking.' Your attention was drawn to the facilities offered for smoking between the acts. On a programme of *The Gay Lord Quex* produced at the old Globe Theatre in 1899, it says : 'Notice.   Gentlemen are earnestly requested not to light cigarettes in any part of the Theatre except the Smoking Room.' A special smoking room, you notice, and of course, no mention of ladies in this, for ladies in those days did not smoke in public, and seldom in private either. You will also observe that only cigarettes are mentioned. Men who smoked cigars in those days would never have thought of wasting a good one in the short interval, when only half at most could be consumed, and no gentleman ever dreamed of smoking a pipe in the West End, in or out of a theatre. That request to confine smoking to the special room (for it would appear that the vestibule and corridors were excluded), was very necessary in the case of this particular theatre, which was a ramshackle affair and, with the Opera Comique, its neighbour, was known as one of the 'Ricketty Twins.' Few people desired to smoke during the progress of a play in those days, they did not worry about it. Perhaps they were far more theatre-minded, perhaps the plays and the acting were good enough to take their minds off a craving for nicotine. That is a matter of personal opinion.   But the same programme also proclaims in large type 'No Fees of Any Kind,' and you are invited to address all enquiries or complaints to the General Manager, Mr. C. T. H. Helmsley^ The Globe had an actor-manager then in John Hare.   The programme was free. Doors opened at seven-thirty. It began at eight and carriages were at eleven.

A programme of the Vaudeville, when *Alice in Wonderland* was being played there by Seymour Hicks and Ellaline Terriss in 1900, announces

'Large Smoking Room and Balcony on First Floor.' But mostly, smoking is not mentioned ; as a theatre problem, it did not arise. The management are at pains to assure you that all refreshments supplied are of the best quality. An announcement from a programme of *The Likeness of the Night*, presented by Mr. and Mrs. Kendal at St. James's in 1901, when George Alexander had let them the theatre, serves as an example of all the rest. It says : 'No Fees. No Charge for Programme or Cloak Room Attendance. No Fees.' It adds : 'The Attendants are strictly forbidden to accept gratuities, and are liable to instant dismissal should they do so. Visitors to the Theatre are earnestly begged to assist the Management in carrying out a regulation framed for their comfort and convenience.' It also prints the enticing announcement : 'Ladies and Gentlemen are invited to avail themselves of the New Lounge above the Vestibule where Tea and Coffee can be procured during the Entr'actes.' And a further touch of personal service is the note that theatre attendants will book you tables at the adjacent Dieudonne Restaurant. That the restaurant paid for an advertisement in the programme is beside the point. You could. and did, reserve a table whilst at the theatre without the slightest trouble.

There was another thing the Theatre did for you in those days. In the West End the early door system which obtained in the provinces and the suburbs (for every suburb of note had its theatre) was not considered the correct thing. For those early doors cost extra and the actor-manager was always for a square deal. So you find that at the Criterion Theatre, and elsewhere, on wet nights, the doors opened half an hour earlier. The Lyric let you in fifteen minutes earlier if the weather was inclement.

That, of course, was a gesture on the part of the theatre to the cheap playgoer. Bad weather outside the theatre did not concern those who ordered their carriages at eleven. Nor, to any extent, did the question of cloakroom fees, or the lounge over the vestibule, or for the matter of that, the special smoking-room, interest the people in the pit, gallery and even the upper circle when they read their programmes. But the actor-manager had not forgotten them. He knew they had waited a long time to see him. He knew they were happy to go to a theatre and he determined to do all he could for them. One thing he never did, and that was to give short weight. In the 'between wars' period, plays often began at nine p.m. and were over by, and sometimes before, eleven. A baker, or a coal merchant who served out his goods that way would have been prosecuted. But the below-salt guests of the actor-manager soon found that he was thinking of them.

He gave them music, real music. No panatropes—they were unknown, true, but he would not have used them if they had been there. He supplied a quartette, or quintette, sometimes a sextette of excellent musicians, often conducted by a man of note, like Ernest Bucalossi, who before the curtain rose and in what were then called the entr'actes, discoursed sweet music. These little orchestral concerts were all part of the show. That portion of the audience which had arrived early, really listened to them, and applauded ; it was quite a feature of the visit. It had its place in the evening out, and it prepared people for what was to come, it got them in the right mood. It had its place on the programme also as part of the show and it was treated as such. There was no swing, no jazz, for they were in the loom of the future. Usually it was selected in accordance with the type of play, and the type of theatre, too. It was never unduly classic, it was light, it was charming and it was well played.

Here is a typical example, from the St. James's. It began twenty minutes before the curtain rose, by the way :

SELECTION	..	..	'Messenger Boy'	*Caryll*
ENTR'ACTE	..	..	'Melodie'	*Paderewski*
			'Toreador and Andalouse' ..	*Rubinstein*
			'Hungarian Dances'	*Michaels*
SELECTION	..	..	'The Mikado'	*Sullivan*
MARCH	..	..	'Young England'	*Farban*

Quite an acceptable, well chosen little orchestral concert, which would do credit to the B.B.C.

And here is another, from the Lyceum, when William Gillette appeared as 'Sherlock Holmes' in 1901.

OVERTURE	.. ..	'Zampa'	.. ..	*Herold*
SALTARELLO	.. .. ..	..	.. ..	*Gounod*
SPANISH DANCES	.. ..	..	.. ..	*Moskowski*
PAS DES FLEURS	.. ..	..	.. ..	*Delibes*
VALSE BLEU	.. .. ..	..	.. ..	*Margis*

and the orchestra was conducted by Raymond Roze.

At the Globe under Hare, and beneath the baton of Haydn Waud, for *The Gay Lord Quex,* they gave even a wider selection :—

OVERTURE	..	'Morning, Noon and Night' ..	*Suppé*
SELECTION	..	.. 'A Runaway Girl'	*C. Godfrey*
XYLOPHONE SOLO	.. ..	.. .. ..	*Kavanagh*
SPANISH DANCE	.. ..	.. ..	*Moszkowski*
CZARDAS (No. VI)	.. ..	.. *Gustav Michiels*	*(Gansegrinne)*
SELECTION	..	'The Belle of New York' ..	*Godfrey*

It should be explained that the spelling of the composers' names is as on the programme, and that C. Godfrey arranged, not composed, the selections. There was something for everybody, as you can see.

The programmes did not carry much advertising, as they used to up to the wartime paper economy rule. Nor were such things as the Magazine Programme known, although Sir Charles Wyndham at the theatre bearing his name had something of the kind as early as 1900. For the programme of *Mrs. Dane's Defence* you got quite a lot, but you paid sixpence for it. A light blue cover bore the legend 'Wyndham's Theatre' in copperplate script in dark blue. There were six pages of advertisements, mostly referring to the goods on sale at the bars (which you were assured were under the direct control of the management) but Macmillan's advertised the plays of Henry Arthur Jones, and a firm of bookmakers, who did a big trade in those days, named Topping and Spindler, also had a space. But you had to send your bets to Flushing. There were four pages of 'Gossip' paragraphs. The first two had a literary flavour, and smacked a little of advertising, another is a dissertation on the custom of Christmas, two deal with items of interest in the history of the Comédie Française, then there is another literary one and another concerning the *Fin de Siècle*, which was of course a great topic. No doubt those playgoers who crowded to see Mr. Wyndham (he had not then received the accolade) lapped it up before they saw *Mrs. Dane's Defence*, the cast of which included Alfred Kendrick, Alfred Bishop, E. W. Garden, Lena Ashwell, Marie Illington (what an actress) and Mary Moore. And, of course, Mr. Wyndham himself. The play began at the odd hour of eight-twenty, but there was a lavish programme of music including Beethoven, Mascagni, Gounod, and Leoncavallo . . . selections from both 'Cav' and 'Pag' being included. It is also of interest that at Wyndham's, then, the upper circle was called 'The Family Circle.'

But the actor-manager did more for the clients of his cheaper parts than merely to give them music. Very often, more often than not, he provided a curtain-raiser. This was a one-act play, seen only by the early comers. It would play to empty boxes, half empty upper circle, to a gradually filling stalls and dress circle, but to an attentive, grateful and appreciative pit and gallery. Often these plays were little gems. They deserved much better treatment than they got, but those who saw them delighted in them. They served a really useful purpose. They gave young dramatists a chance. Not that they were always the work of beginners. Practised hands like Keble Howard, Jerome K. Jerome, Anthony Hope and W. W. Jacobs, to say nothing of Seymour Hicks, Val Prinsep, A.R.A., B. C. Stephenson, Frederick Fenn, F. D. Bone, and many others, did not disdain them. They also served to give young actors and actresses a chance to win their spurs. Sometimes a well-known actor appeared, if he were in the main piece, but mostly the cast was drawn from the understudies and, as a rule, the stage manager played as well. How much better for those understudies than spending the whole evening in the dressing-room and hardly ever getting a chance of appearing except when they know everyone is disappointed at not seeing the star, whereas in the curtain-raiser they were welcome for their own sakes. The stalls and boxes lost much by missing the curtain-raiser, but to them dinner was more important. The 'unreserved' adored them, for from their point of view, the play was the thing. And the more they got the better they were pleased.

One does not include, as curtain-raisers, the one-act plays of J. M. Barrie, which were a thing apart and a feature of the show. Nor the one-act plays of W. S. Gilbert, which usually formed part of a 'triple bill,' a thing never seen nowadays, so much has the Theatre altered. Nor can Tree's great performances in *The Van Dyck* nor *The Man Who Came Back*, nor Irving's *Waterloo* be classed in this way. They were masterpieces on their own.

But the ordinary curtain-raiser was always enjoyable and often supremely good. *Pride of Regiment*, by F. D. Bone, was a complete drama in one act, a tensely written and gripping play. *Compromising Martha* was a delightful comedy by Keble Howard, about a curate and the daughter of the squire who met clandestinely in the cottage of a very old woman called 'Martha' and eventually won her over to their cause. Played at the Haymarket, it often took several curtains. Keble Howard even wrote a second act to it. *Her Dearest Friend* was another excellent curtain-raiser, so was *The Convict on the Hearth*, whilst that fine actor, Louis

Calvert, gave one of his very best performances in another one-acter called *The Nelson Touch*. *The Peacemaker* was a delightful comedy, but perhaps the supreme one-act play (in two scenes) was *The Monkey's Paw*—the best Grand Guignol thriller ever written and by that master-humorist, W. W. Jacobs, at that, for he had a nice turn for the macabre when he chose. The same author's *That Brute Simmonds* was also a big success as a first piece.

Sometimes, instead of a play, a concert party was provided. That clever troupe, 'The Grotesques,' did much to popularize 'Little Grey Home in the West' when playing the audience in at Wyndham's Theatre. And sometimes we had an entertainer at the piano—who was always first-class. Tom Clare, Ernest Hastings, Dorothy Varick, Barclay Gammon, Nelson Jackson, Helen Marr were the best known, and perhaps Miss Marr did more than any of them to entertain the real playgoers.

This pre-main-show performance was a piece of evolution. It was a link with the days when theatres opened really early and you went in half price at nine o'clock and still had what would to-day be a full evening's entertainment. In those days one had a burletta to start with, a big play, either Shakespeare, classic comedy or new drama, and then a farce. It was quite the thing, in the 'fifties, to go to the Haymarket after the opera, to see the celebrated comedian, Wright, in a farce to finish the bill. This man never appeared much before midnight, and got £30 per week, but as much as £100 per week was taken at the doors after midnight to see him. Playgoers got some four and a half hours of entertainment for their money. Those were the days, indeed, when you received full measure and brimming over. The Edwardian managements did not go so far as that, but they gave ample return. The gradual reduction of playing time, in return for the same admission charge, was one of the reasons why the Theatre lost its grip in later years. When the talkies arose to make it face its first really serious opposition, it put up no sort of fight. It gave less instead of more. So it lost the battle.

But there were no talkies—and hardly any moving pictures—in the days of Good King Edward, although they were peeping in at the music halls, as last turn, under the name of The Bioscope, and in some places shops had been converted into cinemas. There was, as yet, no sort of decision as to how this word was pronounced. Some said Kinema, but most of them called it either the Bioscope or the moving pictures. They had not yet become part of the daily life of the people. They had not yet created Hollywood, and led to the greatest infiltration and bloodless conquest of ideals and language in the history of the world. But they were there, just round the corner. The actor-manager, however, lost no sleep over them. He gave his patrons, or his guests, a full evening's entertainment. From the time you entered, until the time you left, there was something doing. You only had about eight or ten minutes in which to settle down, read your programme and start eating chocolates, before entertainment started.

That did not stop you eating chocolates—or other things. For it is a curious fact in British play-going that no playgoer can support a couple of hours or so at the theatre without almost constant nourishment. It has almost always been so. Probably, in Tudor days, the 'groundlings' chewed as they stood and watched the performance. Apples were plentiful in playgoers' pockets in the reign of Charles I, for some benighted and progressive French actors, at the Blackfriars, who dared to include women in their ranks, found that these 'forward hussies' were, in a contemporary phrase, 'pippin pelted' off the stage for their unwomanly and immoral behaviour in daring to appear before the public in a masculine monopoly. They did not wear masculine attire or do anything outrageous, they just played the parts written for women, but always in England played by boys. The London playgoers would not stand it, and these Eves, so far from picking apples for presentation to unsuspecting Adams, received apples in plenty from the outraged descendants of Adam in the audience. It may have been Man's Revenge on Woman for the Fall, but it certainly proved that Carolian playgoers refreshed themselves at the theatre.

When Drury Lane, the first real theatre, opened, it had its refreshment contractor in the person of 'Orange Moll,' whose girls did not only sell oranges, but cakes and confectionery as well. She was not allowed to sell them to the rough people in the upper gallery who used them to combine sustenance with missiles. But downstairs and up to the second gallery, playgoers munched as they do to-day. Is not a smell of orange peel part of the authentic theatre atmosphere? Did not the patrons of the old Surrey Theatre make it a feature of the Boxing Night revels there, by pelting the occupants of the pit and boxes with orange peel? No Boxing Night—and few others—was complete without it. When Mr. Wopsle played *Hamlet* was there not 'a peck of orange peel'? according to Joe Gargery, and was not another performance of this tragedy, seen by Herbert and Pip, notable by the fact that 'the general indignation took the form of nuts'? Food again, carried by playgoers, you see. One passes over the throwing of rotten eggs. These could not be consumed, but they were food all the same. But when Robert Baddeley, the Drury Lane actor, died, how did he gain immortality in that theatre? Not by endowing a charity, or leaving a memorial plaque, but by making a little fund to bake a cake to be eaten annually on Twelfth Night in his honour. True he had been a pastry cook, but he knew that eating a cake in a theatre was a time-honoured tradition and would please people more than anything else.

The theatres of the actor-manager had banished oranges, though at certain of them you could still smell them, and see them being consumed, in the galleries. Especially at Christmas time. Nuts, too, were not encouraged and seldom eaten, although popcorn was chewed and at the end of the period, pea-nuts got in. However, there were abundant selections of chocolates with which to regale yourself, and the young ladies who showed you to your place carried trays of enticing-looking boxes, which they sold freely. That of course will start all over again when sweets come off the ration imposed by war. It was extremely bad form, if you were one of the carriage folk, to take your chocolates into the theatre with you. It was not the thing at all. You bought them off the attendants, and the sight of a man or woman coming into the stalls with a box of chocolates under the arm was almost as bad as brown boots with a frock coat. This was, of course, all part of the general politeness. You knew, full well, that part of the profit on that chocolate would eventually find its way into the pocket of the actor-manager. But both he and you pretended that you did not, and you, as guest, would not be guilty of the solecism of bringing food into your host's house.

The cheap parts had no such qualms. They would, it is true, often buy chocolates in the theatre, there was no difference in the price, but they wanted to eat whilst standing in the queue and so came amply provided. What was not eaten outside, was consumed inside. Only when they ran out did they purchase from the attendants. And they often ran out. A most popular brand was one which consisted of about two dozen little slabs of chocolate (neapolitaines is the trade description), all nicely wrapped in silver paper, and contained in a convenient cardboard carton, oblong in length and fitting nicely into the pocket. The carton was rich purple and the lettering gold. With one or two of these in hand, a young man and his 'best girl' who got good seats in the pit or gallery considered themselves in heaven. So great was the appetite for chocolates, and sweets out of paper bags, that the rustling caused by making a selection in the dark often offended the few who were more intent on the play than eating and a good deal of 'shushing' would ensue. Matinée tea-trays, always a nuisance to those who don't want them, were then in vogue, as now, but the attendants in the Edwardian theatre would never have dared to open the doors before the curtain fell on each act, and pile their trays outside for quick service. Such an interruption would have infuriated players and playgoers alike.

There was the same coming and going to the bars in the interval. That will never stop. At one time when W. K. Haselden did the cartoons for the *Daily Mirror*, there was an outcry against the crowding in the bars, with its consequent bad service, and especially against the brands of whisky sold. That was not quite true. You could have any brand you liked to ask for, within reason, but if you just asked for 'Scotch,' well, you got what was known as the 'Theatre' whisky, a lesser known brand which showed a greater profit. The racket, when the bars eventually passed out of the hands of the actor-managers into the hands of contractors, was in the sodas. They made you buy a big one, and used up what was left for other customers. But even that was not true of all firms. Nor was the congestion at the bars the fault of the hard-working barmaids. Bars were small, of necessity, and everyone wanted serving at once. But even so, the crush was not so great then as now, for women never went to the bar. To-day they outnumber the men.

When, in the later part of their careers, the more conservative of the actor-managers parted with the control of their bars to the enterprise of contractors, they did so at the call of commercialism, which was beginning to affect even them. It was better, they found, to have a regular weekly income from this source than to take the risk themselves. For opposition was beginning to tell, and the worst form was the week-end habit and the car. The weekly rental paid for the bar, cloakroom and programme concession of an average theatre not in the habit of presenting musical plays, was £40. Those who staged musical shows demanded and got more. For music cultivated thirst and the habituées were of a more light-minded kind. Seeing that a programme could be made easily to produce £20 a week revenue from its advertisements alone, and then sold for sixpence, and that the matinée tea never showed less than sixty-six and two-thirds profit, the contractors were on a good thing. But some actor-managers never parted with these rights, even to the end ; they compromised by charging for programmes.

But those programmes of the Edwardian days which did carry advertisements have some nostalgic memories. There is the advertisement for 'Tatcho,' for instance, a hair restorer discovered by George R. Sims, the most famous columnist of the day, who wrote under the pen-name of 'Dagonet' in the *Referee* and who could make a restaurant or a commodity, or a hotel, by a paragraph. Although ladies' lingerie was still a secret, a firm advertised 'H.S. Corsets' with illustrations, which had a graded cost of from 3s. 11d. to 21s. per pair. These were the days of whalebone and waists. The *Ladies' Gazette* proclaimed itself a sixpenny magazine for twopence. Hinde's hair curlers introduced themselves and left it at that for they were necessities in these pre-bob and shingle days, when all but the richest women 'did' their own hair and would rather have died than comb it in a theatre—indeed, you could not comb the elaborate and towering mass of hair which adorned the heads. 'Pick-me-Up' cigarettes offered themselves for threepence for twelve and sixpence for twenty-five. Stagg and Mantle's offered three-quarter length coats with ornate trimmings for six and a half guineas. The Manchester Hotel, in Aldersgate Street, drew attention to its five hundred bedrooms, its 2s. 6d. luncheons and special five-course table d'hôte dinners at 3s. 6d.—and stated that it was within a shilling cab fare and one penny omnibus ride from the theatre. You could obtain an electric corset for the small sum of 6s. 6d. which cured you whilst you wore it, whilst a firm of electric light contractors assured you that they worked for the Marquis of Salisbury, the Marquis of Ripon, the Houses of Parliament and the London County Council. How could you resist such an overpowering combination ? A bicycle called 'The Advance' which said it held all the British records begged you to send a post card for a catalogue (it did not disclose its price) whilst a tubeless tyre declared that 'a simple child can detach it' but said nothing about putting it on again.

'My Valet' cleaning and dyeing firm promised you clothes pressed and repaired within twenty-four hours for 12s. 6d. per month and made no restriction as to quantity. The Charing Cross Bank and the Birkbeck Bank placed themselves at your disposal, and Mr. Sandow, the strong man, offered you, in his own words, the opportunity to 'give you strength to fight your battles of life for years to come' for the small sum of 12s. 6d. One machine, it added, was enough for a whole family. The Villa Villa Hotel lured you with the promise of a special theatre supper for 2s. (and it contained a whole week's rations and more), whilst you could lunch there for 1s. 6d. or dine for 2s. 6d.—and at scores of other places in Soho—and very well too. A firm of outfitters offered you the best fitting double fold collar, worn either as a 'straight up' or 'double fold,' for 3s. 3d. the half dozen. There were plenty of bargains on those programmes, from brandy at 66s. per dozen, to stockbrokers who charged no commission. Evidently philanthropists.

But quite apart from all this, from the curtain-raiser and the excellent theatre orchestra, there was also the sight of the stalls audience to look at. These good folk, who came by carriage, were mostly late arrivals, and caused annoyance by that means. But they were well-dressed scoundrels, all the same. The men all wore evening dress—white waistcoats and tails, for dinner-jackets were never worn if you were escorting a lady. They carried tall hats or those opera hats which crushed up and could be put under the seat, tall hats of corded silk, which you never see to-day. The women were also in full evening dress, as it was then understood. There was always a rustle of satin or swish of silk as they moved. Their hair was elaborate—maybe some of it was added, but the effect was superb, for woman had not then shed her crowning glory. Their shoes were of satin and high heeled, and their gowns were lovely. They sparkled, they shone, they were jewelled creatures of another world to the denizens of the pit, who watched them and commented on them. Their skirts were long and they had figures. They moved with care and grace. And they did not all look alike. For although they were the slaves of fashion, yet each struck her own personal note. Their dresses might be of the same style but each was individual. They carried fans, they wore long gloves. Their complexions may or may not have been their own—mostly they were—but no woman in those days would have dreamed of 'doing her face' in public. She would have been asked to leave. If they wore rouge, it was skilfully applied in privacy and with care. Make-up was not respectable. A little powder, also discreetly and secretly put on, was permissible ; some indulged in what was called 'lip salve'—also put on at home. For a woman obviously made up was a woman of what was then known as 'a certain class.' The line was very definite. But they brought charm and femininity with them, those carriage folk. They made the stalls a mass of colour and richness. What would have happened if, as was seen the other day in a West End theatre, a woman had come striding into the stalls wearing a yellow pullover, no hat, a pair of jodhpurs much the worse for wear and carrying a riding whip, one can only conjecture. She would never have got by the attendants' scandalized protests, of course. As it was, the only comment on the young Amazon was : "Has she left the horse in the cloakroom ?"

The gentleman attending on the lady or ladies would have comported himself with the utmost politeness. He would foresee her slightest wish, he would never suggest she should have a drink. Perhaps he might supply, per the attendant, a cup of coffee in the interval, or see to it that she got a Neapolitan ice, if she required one. And when that carriage came at eleven, he would have asked her permission to smoke. He would be attentive to her every whim. She was a woman, and something to be taken care of. He would rather have died than to have let her pay for anything. If she was wearing flowers they were probably his gift.

These people from a world apart came into the stalls. You resented them from the pit, if they obscured your gaze when you wanted to see the stage, by their late arrival, their leisurely manner of sitting down, and their frequent rearrangement of seats if in a party. But you gazed at them with real interest when the curtain was down and the lights up. They, too, were part of the show, these rich playgoers who came at their ease, in their own time, whose clothes forbade them to walk, whose carriages would be there at eleven.

Perhaps you were a little envious. Many a young man assured the girl sitting beside him on the pit bench, or craning her neck over the gallery rail, that the time would come when he, too, would escort her to a stall and she should be one of those semi-goddesses. No doubt, sometimes, that came true. And anyway, anticipation was half the pleasure. For these young people knew nothing of having a car—to say nothing of a carriage. They went by train, by bus, by tram, and later by tube. Sometimes they ran to a 'hansom' or in later days a taxi (never so charged with romance). But they were not envious. Life was different, class distinctions were sharp and understood.

The people in the upper circle looked down too. They did not wear evening dress. They wore, however, their best clothes for the occasion. The young man, or the married man with his wife, would have his Sunday suit on (there were Sunday suits in those days). They felt that they were almost of the same class, for they had reserved seats. But they were conscious, in their hearts, of the difference. The women wore their 'best' blouse and had taken much care over their appearance—and they would wear gloves too, and very likely flowers which their escort had provided. They were being regaled by boxes of chocolates bought from the theatre attendants, and also with ices. They were having a fine time. None of these young ladies wore rouge, and few of them much powder. And their applause would be louder than the stalls and boxes, but not quite so noisy as that of the 'unreserved.' But they would cry at the wrongs and sufferings of the hero or heroine, quite unaffectedly, for in spirit they were far more akin to the pit and gallery than the stalls.

But whatever the part of the house you sat in, you were the 'paying guest' of that man who ran the house, whose power and presence had summoned you. You would discuss him, his company and the play in which he had appeared before you, for some time afterwards, and you would remember it, too. You had read what you called a 'critique' when it was first produced. And that 'critique' had probably occupied a whole column and sometimes a column and a half of well-written, closely-printed matter with no sensational headlines. It had been written by a critic who knew his job, who understood what he was called upon to criticize, who was learned in theatre lore, and who knew what he was writing about. He was dealing with a matter of some importance, for a new play was an event. He did not just report it in a short paragraph, he went into the whole matter, he weighed it up, he gave reasons. He criticized the thing as a whole, play, idea, presentation, and acting. He took into consideration the standing of the actor-manager and his standard as well. He drew attention to any shortcoming. He gave praise when praise was due. Sometimes he offended and a dignified correspondence ensued. Sometimes he pleased. No actor-manager ever liked real criticism—it was good criticism when it praised, bad when it blamed. But then the actor-manager knew the trouble he had taken, the care he had exercised, in presenting that offering to his public. For he did take care. Plays were read, not by typists and secretaries, but by experienced people. He, in turn, considered those passed to him as being worthy. He commissioned the best dramatists to write him plays and they knew how to fit him as well as his tailor. Everything was of the best, he would endure nothing second-rate. That is why there was space for criticism, for one thing. The dignity and standing of these men of the Theatre made them important and with them, the Theatre. The amount of space given to films to-day as compared with the Theatre has nothing to do, as so many people imagine, with the amount of advertising given to the Press. It is simply because the film industry has made itself more important than the Theatre, and has a wider public appeal. One day, when the Theatre decides to make itself important, or someone arises who will do that for it, space will come back and criticism again be detailed. But never to quite the same extent, for to-day people read headlines and look at pictures. They haven't the time to give to detail. And that is a curse of modernity.

The actor-manager did not get his long 'notices' and his full houses by advertising. He did very little of that, as it is known to-day. His theatre announcement appeared in the usual columns, and also 'Under the Clock' where that facility was provided. That was a column in certain newspapers which bore a clock at its top. Underneath were a list of the shows, giving the entire cast appearing, a thing you never get to-day. He had some posters, and they were as individual as he was. You knew at a glance to which theatre they referred. He did not display his goods in the window. He kept them inside. He never told you that his was the best show on earth, that you would die with laughing, that there were sixty laughs per minute, that it was London's greatest success. He never boosted himself or his company as the finest ever seen. He never shouted at you. It was not a clamant age. It was not a vulgar age, and shouting was decidedly vulgar.

Like those exclusive West End shops which eschewed window display because they knew the customers who were on their books, so he too knew his own power of attraction. He had built it up. He had made his home a place where you got good quality, the best quality, of the line he supplied, in its right atmosphere, where you were treated as someone he was glad to see, and for whom he had a regard. He presented his attraction. It was for you to say if you approved or not. He knew that no clamour, in those days, would make a good play of a bad one. But he knew, too, that it had to be a very bad play, or a very bad part for him, which would not run for about two months. He had his regular customers who always came to worship at his shrine. But the public was not to be hoodwinked. That was an affair of the showground. He did not believe in that. His showmanship, and he had plenty, was more subtle. Its keynote was quality, and of the supreme art of selling himself. You had given him that power by your appreciation. All he had to do was to keep up his standard. And seldom, very seldom, did he fall below it. And you, on your part, were not saturated by entertainment. To you an evening at the theatre was an event. You went prepared to like it. And one must admit that even the failures always had something of merit to remember, a lovely scene, or a real bit of acting to treasure in the memory. And also there was always the actor-manager himself to gaze at—that alone was worth the money. That was why you did not resent his occasional lapses but always forgave them. For he was an integral part of the theatre.

That was why you were now seated in the playhouse, listening to that orchestra, enjoying the curtain-raiser, waiting for the big moment when the last strains would die away, the lights would die down and there would be a momentary pause before the curtain swept up and—the real play began.

That was what you had come for. The moment had arrived and you were happy, completely happy because—you were in a theatre . . . you had partaken of your *hors d'œuvres*—now came the feast.

CHAPTER III

'My Beautiful Theatre'

'I TAKE IT THAT THE ENTIRE BUSINESS OF THE STAGE IS . . . ILLUSION.' So said Herbert Beerbohm Tree in his book, *Thoughts and Afterthoughts*.

He lived up to it, and he created stage illusions which have become realities of memory, and set a tradition which will always endure in the history of the British Theatre.

He created something else, something which he delighted to call his 'beautiful theatre,' and he was right in so calling it. For he himself created that theatre—now His Majesty's Theatre, and it was the very essence of the Edwardian Theatre, as he was the very embodiment of the actor-manager.

There is nothing to-day comparable to the work done by that man in that theatre which he made so great. He wrote a page which nothing can expunge. He and his theatre were the very zenith of the actor-manager's rule, so much attacked in its day, but the lack of which is so sadly felt since the first World War swept it away.

He built that theatre in the Haymarket, on the corner of King Charles II Street, out of the money he made as an actor-manager at the Haymarket Theatre opposite, and mostly out of the profits of his production of *Trilby* and his own performance of 'Svengali' therein. So Her Majesty's, as it was called when he opened it in 1897, was in every sense the home of the actor-managerial system, built by one out of his earnings as such. Could anything have been more fitting?

It was Diamond Jubilee year when he opened it, at once the crowning glory and swan song of the Victorian age, and the beginning of the Edwardian days.

That night of 29th April 1897 was a red letter one in British Theatre annals, marking the apex of an era, the continuation of a reign which was to succeed Irving, and which had begun quietly at the Comedy Theatre, had grown up to lusty youth at the Haymarket and now, in its full manhood, displayed its grandeur of work, imagination and achievement at this new theatre, the last word in everything theatrical at that time. For on that night Herbert Beerbohm Tree threw open the doors of his own home to his guests, the public, and a period of greatness, of which our stage can always be proud, had begun.

Well might he call it 'My Beautiful Theatre.' It was beautiful in every respect, but it also contained dignity, efficiency, comfort, consideration and magnificent acting and production. And all these things Tree gave it.

He did more. He gave it atmosphere at its very first performance. This playhouse is unique in this respect. Most of them have to spend years in accumulating that tradition which gives the true theatre atmosphere, but not Her Majesty's. It became great at once, because of the greatness of its creator. His own terrific personality and power, his high ideals, his insistence on beauty and perfection, stamped itself at once on the playhouse. The others—even Garrick—only added their greatness to theatres already famous. They made them more illustrious, it is true, and sometimes they changed the luck of an unfortunate theatre. But Tree achieved it all in a new theatre as soon as he opened it. His own force and command, his own sweeping power, made this a great theatre overnight. It was a thing almost without parallel.

In the theatre he loved, and indeed practically lived in, he gave us productions which gleam in the memory, stage settings which were a veritable National Gallery of scenic art, acting which has never been bettered, and a company which was, to all intents and purposes, a stock company from which sprang those who were to be the leaders of their profession in the next generation. They themselves, the people who worked there, called Her—or His—Majesty's 'The First Theatre in the Greatest Empire the World Has Ever Seen.' That is what they thought about it, and they were quite right. Yet these people who thought, said and believed this, were the very folk whom the critics of the actor-manager system said were being belittled and robbed of their chances by it. Well, they did not think so. They acknowledged their Chief by reason of his knowledge, his flair, his genius and his personality, which made him tower above them. You might as well say that Oxford and Cambridge dwarf their undergraduates. For His Majesty's was the University for actors, and those who passed out from there had every right to add M.A. to their names, for at His Majesty's they did indeed become masters and mistresses of their art.

Tree made his theatre the stronghold for Shakespeare. Since his time our greatest cultural possession has only been allowed fleeting appearances. But Tree gave us Shakespeare in all his glory, not only in that terrific orchestra of word-music but in settings in which the author himself would have revelled. No need to bewail here the attempt to bring forth great objects on a scaffold. Shakespeare at His Majesty's meant great acting in great stage pictures. Nor did anyone save those who will always find fault cavil at it. To-day we hear much about elaborate scenic settings swamping the actor. Perhaps at His Majesty's the actors were of a stature to stand up to the scenery.

Was *Henry VIII* any less the play which Shakespeare wrote because of that marvellous banqueting hall bestowed on it by Tree? Why should not that wood near Athens in *A Midsummer Night's Dream* really look like a wood, with bluebells and rabbits in it? Why should not *Twelfth Night* show us a dream garden of loveliness? The memory of those and many more scenes endures with those privileged to see them, and when they hear or read the words spoken therein, that is how they conjure up the scene. That 'Coast of Wales' in *Richard II*, and the pro-

BILLIE BURKE

MAURICE FARKOA

HAYDEN COFFIN

GABRIELLE RAY

GERTIE MILLAR AS 'MITZI'
AND EDMUND PAYNE AS
'MAX MODDELKOPF' IN
'THE GIRLS OF GOTTENBERG'

SOME GAIETY GIRLS
(*Left to right*) Misses Desmond, Chesney,
Forsythe, Beresford, Heath, Hamilton

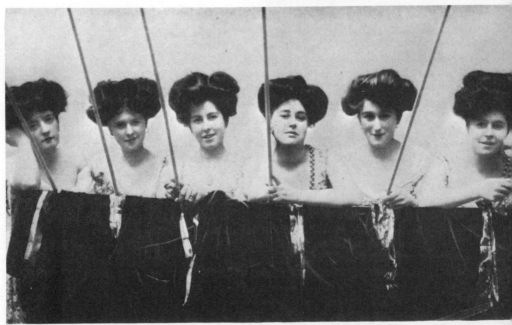

cession through London. Did they not live? *Julius Cæsar* at Tree's theatre enabled us to gaze at the grandeur of Rome. And in no case did the acting suffer, for one remembers it vividly to-day.

Shakespeare drew all London to His Majesty's. The Annual Festival at Eastertide was looked forward to eagerly. The gay abandon of the dance of the entire company of *The Merry Wives of Windsor* before the curtain, after it had fallen on the massive Falstaff in Windsor Park, confronted and defied by the tiniest of tiny imps, drew such enthusiasm as is seldom seen in the theatre to-day, and sent the audience forth delighted, happy and laughing—which is surely the duty of the Theatre. We had really seen Merry England. And the tragedies were treated as tragedies should be, the production, the acting and the settings were like the swell of a mighty organ.

The actor-managers, and Tree amongst them, have been accused of always taking the limelight and the centre of the stage. That is not true. Very often they contented themselves with small parts. In *The War God*, in *Joseph and His Brethren*, in *False Gods*, Tree played quite small parts. Sometimes he would do a play which he thought ought to be seen even if there were no part for him—as witness *Drake* and *Marie Odile*. His casts were always star-studded. One recalls with delight his *Merry Wives* when Mrs. Kendall and Ellen Terry played those two delightful women to Tree's 'Falstaff.' One remembers with gratitude his *School for Scandal* which contained Marie Lohr, Ellis Jeffreys, Suzanne Sheldon, Dagmar Wiehe, Robert Loraine, Basil Gill, Henry Neville, Lionel Brough, Edward Terry, Herman Vezin, H. V. Esmond, Charles Quartermaine, and Godfrey Tearle. Was that 'pinching the limelight' in a show, despite the fact that Tree played 'Sir Peter'?

But of course, habitually, the actor-manager played the lead. He was the star, he was the man the public wanted to see, he was the attraction for which they paid. The public made his popularity, he did not impose it on them. Many actors ventured into management to find that, however much the public liked them as spokes in the wheel of the theatre, they did not regard them as axles. What would film fans say if Betty Grable, Humphrey Bogart, Bing Crosby or any of the gods and goddesses of the celluloid, were kept in the background? Yet there is no outcry about that. The public never complained, only the pedants amongst critics and some disappointed actors. And it was the public which mattered then, as always. The public could not have too much of the star.

Tree really used His Majesty's as a Repertory Theatre in the grandest sense of the word. He eschewed long runs, he did not like them. His creative mind rebelled against them. Profits and gain arising therefrom did not interest him. He wanted to use his theatre for plays, plays, acting and more plays, and he did it. When he was unable, because of public demand, to take off his production of *Henry VIII* when he desired to do so, he referred to it as 'an obstinate success.' It was his longest run, from 1st September 1910 until 8th April 1911—just over seven months. And he was sick of it, cross with it, he wanted to get on and do other things. The second longest run was *Drake*, Louis N. Parker's Pageant play, which was there for six and a half months, but in which Tree did

C

not appear. He produced it. But he played in the revival of it in August 1914, immediately after the outbreak of war.

Sir Herbert Tree did not count success from the number of performances, but from the applause and the genuine pleasure and admiration drawn from his audiences. Having shown them a beautiful piece of work, he did not rest until he had another ready for them. All this was good for the theatre, for the players and for the audience. Yet, new plays or revivals, new productions of Shakespeare, or reproductions of those he had staged before, each was put on with the same meticulous care, the same grandeur, the same superb casting.

The Seats of the Mighty, *The Silver Key*, *Ragged Robin*, *The Musketeers*, *Carnac Sahib*, *Rip Van Winkle*, *King John*, *Julius Cæsar*, *A Midsummer Night's Dream*, *Herod*, *Twelfth Night*, *The Last of the Dandies*, *Ulysses*, *The Eternal City*, *The Resurrection*, *Richard II*, *The Darling of the Gods*, *The Tempest*, *Much Ado About Nothing*, *Business is Business*, *Oliver Twist*, *Nero*, *Colonel Newcome*, *The Winter's Tale*, *Antony and Cleopatra*, *The Mystery of Edwin Drood*, *The Beloved Vagabond*, *The Merchant of Venice*, *Faust*, *The School for Scandal*, *False Gods*, *Beethoven*, *The O'Flynn*, *Henry VIII*, *Orpheus in the Underground*, *Pinkie and the Fairies*, *Macbeth*, *Othello*, *Drake*, *The Happy Island*, *Joseph and His Brethren*, *Pygmalion*, *David Copperfield*, *Marie Odile*, *The Right to Kill*, *Mavourneen*, a complete list of his major productions at this theatre in the eighteen years of his reign there—that speaks for itself. The average run was about three months. It would make the senses of a manager to-day reel. And interspersed were big revivals, Shakespeare Festivals at which he invited guests such as Lewis Waller, Benson, and other great ones to bring along their companies to his stage. Also such special productions as *Ariadne in Naxos* and *The Perfect Gentleman* (put on just for a month but perfect in every way), *The War God*, by Zangwill, for a few performances because he thought it ought to be seen ; *Hansel and Gretel* as a curtain-raiser to *The Beloved Vagabond* ; *Beethoven* as part of a triple bill with *A Russian Tragedy* and *The Lethal Hotel ;* a revival of *The Ballad Monger* reinforced by *Flodden Field* (by Alfred Austin) and Kipling's *The Man Who Was* ; a mimed play by Catulle Mendes as makeweight for *The Seats of the Mighty ; Katherine and Petruchio* (Garrick's version of *The Taming of the Shrew*) as pendant for a revival of *The Silver Key* ; *The First Night* in one act, with *Captain Swift*, and *The Van Dyke* thrown in now and again. If that was not making full use of a theatre, then nothing was. If that was not presenting the Drama, then there has never been such a thing.

The annual Festival of Shakespeare entailed the production of six plays, all with magnificent casts. That was what one of the decried actor-managers did in the Edwardian Theatre. Nobody has done as much before or since. Incidentally, it was real repertory. No wonder the Theatre was important, no wonder we got good acting, no wonder we talked about the Theatre and thrilled to go to it. To-day such methods would be looked upon as the highroad to bankruptcy. Theatrical managers of modern times would regard it as madness. But it was Theatre in excelsis, such as nobody sees to-day. And no wonder Sir Herbert Tree became a knight and no wonder that the members of that company became the stars of the next generations. They were full graduates.

Simply to go to His Majesty's was a thrill. As soon as you entered it, you sensed its atmosphere. It did not matter what part of the house, you felt that this was an important place, where things happened. Its main entrance can be seen to-day, but in Tree's time, it was graced by footmen in powdered wigs and liveries. Paintings hung on the walls, of Tree himself, and other great ones, good pictures by celebrated artists. Everything was in tone, nothing cheap, nothing vulgar. There were no noisy advertisements of the show, no assurances of the pleasures to be seen within, no 'edited' quotations from newspapers or eulogies with the unconvincing caption 'vide Press.' This was a home of the best quality, and it spoke for itself. Nothing second-rate could happen. There might perhaps be plays you did not like (there were) but they would be done in a manner of distinction. This was the home of a great man who dealt in greatness. It was the same all over the theatre. And Tree, mindful of the pockets of his poorer friends, gave them a large upper circle, in which you could get a front seat for four shillings, and many rows at the humble price of two shillings. Neither he, nor any other actor-manager, dreamed of increasing the prices for a first night. For two shillings you could, from a reserved seat, see the best the English Theatre could offer you. It was astounding. And the staff, from the highest to the lowest, were quiet-voiced, good-mannered, courteous and soft-footed. Nobody slammed a door, nobody ever interrupted during a performance. That was left to unmannerly guests, who might do so if they pleased. The staff, like the theatre, was first-class. There was a pit, of course, and a gallery, for the actor-manager believed in these parts of the house. It was only after the first World War, when inflated incomes led to a rush on the stalls, that short-sighted managements thought the days of the cheaper seats were over and built theatres, and altered existing ones, to make them pitless. And then had to 'job' the back seats for whatever they could get, reducing the theatre to a bargain basement.

From that 2s. upper circle, from every seat in the house, at His Majesty's, from the gallery to the boxes, you could see the whole of the stage and hear every word spoken. Its dark red, its cream and gold were the right decorations for a theatre. There was nothing tawdry, nothing meretricious anywhere, front or back. It was, indeed, a Temple of the Drama. The brochures of the current attraction, giving details of times, prices, matinées and cast, were quite little works of art, its small bills for the 'libraries' and hotels were worth framing. One of Buchel's, for *Macbeth*, was very effective, and the same artist's poster and cards for *Richard II* had the quality of an old missal. You took them home and kept them with æsthetic pleasure. Nobody ran about, there was unhurried calm and an air of confidence.

If you went to a First Night—if you were lucky enough to get seats —then indeed you saw what the Edwardian Theatre really meant. Everyone in the stalls, dress circle and boxes were real celebrities. It was not a case of Burke and Debrett, but of the peerage, the law, medicine, all the arts, the Army, the Navy, yes, and the Church as well. Whilst the hidden orchestra played to you, you craned forward to see all the rank, style and brains that London could offer you. There are no such first nights now. The black and white of the men, all in full rig, set off the bright dresses, the furs, the flashing jewels of the women. The programmes were as dignified as the audience, printed on what looked like parchment, in black and red, with a crown surmounting the name of the theatre ; they were as distinctive as everything else about His Majesty's, and were indeed a trademark. Even when, in later and leaner years, contractors took them over, no change in form, type or size was permitted.

You read the cast, which equalled the audience in brilliance. You watched the arrival of the top-table guests, pointing out those you knew by sight. There were always the Rutland family, all quite beautiful to see. J.J. Shannon, Sargent, Alma Tadema, Arnold White, F. E. Smith, before he became Lord Birkenhead, a young man called Winston Churchill, Lloyd George, Sir Anderson Critchett, Major 'Hoppy' Davis, and a good sprinkling of minor royalties leap to the mind as 'regular' first nighters.

All these people had come because it was an occasion not to be missed, not because it was just part of the social game. They would have to discuss it later everywhere they went. And they really wanted to see what Tree was offering, because it was the best. On first night programmes there was usually a foreword by Tree explaining the motive of the production, and to assist the critics who might have to get their 'stuff' in early.

A first night at 'H.M.T.,' as it was affectionately called, was a real first night before it was a social occasion. It became a social occasion because it was a Tree first night in the Theatre. The theatre came first. The social side afterwards. Nowadays that is not so.

And then, as the hour approached, the lights dimmed slowly down—they never went out with a snap, as it were—there was a momentary rustle and then complete silence as the great crimson curtain swept up, and disclosed a perfect stage picture to the view.

Then you would see an evening of wonderful 'theatre'—the best of everything. And at the end, after all the 'calls' had been taken, the figure of Sir Herbert would come before the curtain. He would grasp the fold of it in his right hand, and he would stand to receive your applause. Then he would make a 'curtain speech' which would be a model of what such things should be, make his final bow, and you would go home, with your mind full of wonderful sights and sounds. But even with Tree, this picture had its reverse side. Sometimes the play did not please. Then, Sir Herbert or no Sir Herbert, Tree got 'the bird.' He probably knew he deserved it long before he got it, but he never flinched. He got it badly over a play called The O'Flynn, even though this romantic drama was written by Justin Huntly McCarthy. It was fustian stuff, despite the fine cast, which could not save it. The fault was largely Tree's who had miscast himself, a thing he was apt to do on occasions. He played the part of a gay, swashbuckling Irish 'D'Artagnan,' which was not 'up his street' at all. And Henry Ainley played a swarthy, black-a-vised villain. The trouble started almost at once or, at least, as soon as Tree made his entrance. He had to appear down a chimney, an odd sort of idea for a romantic hero anyway. He did not like this sort of thing, he never felt quite happy even on an ordinary rostrum, so why he put himself in this position must be his own secret. To make it more realistic, for he was nothing if not realistic, he was lowered down the chimney by thick ropes of elastic which were tested to take his weight for the descent and then allow him to gain his feet. His appearance down the chimney was heralded by a heavy fall of bricks—there should have been soot but realism stopped at this. The bricks made a good entrance. Not so Sir Herbert. For something went wrong with that ingenious elastic idea. Instead of depositing him on his feet it jerked him up in the air again, and he bounced, literally, several times before he got his balance. It was not only undignified, it was unromantic. Neither Tree nor the play ever recovered from it. Thereafter all the incidents which should have been exciting became ridiculous, and even a desperate duel between Tree as hero and Ainley as villain was not taken seriously. The gallery found the sight of Tree seated on a table, nonchalantly parrying deadly thrusts of the villain's rapier and even doing so with a wine glass instead of his sword, extremely amusing. At the end there was a storm of 'boos.' Tree bowed to the storm. On went the Shakespeare Festival and all was well again.

Nor did a play called *The Right to Strike* fare much better, and one called *The Happy Island* even worse. Save for one moment in the first act, when, suddenly plunging the stage in darkness, Tree recited from Isaiah, this offering had little to recommend it. It went from bad to worse. We ended up on a tropical island, a truly lovely scene and worthy of a better cause. Eric Maturin was some sort of a settler there, and there was a crowd of 'natives' led by Fisher White. They were always prostrating themselves and moaning "Tabu, tabu," and it got on the nerves of the gallery who began to join in and say it for them. Sir Herbert himself, in red shirt, riding breeches and top boots (a costume which did not suit him), tied to an altar and about to be sacrificed, led only to hilarity, which turned into ironic cheers when Phyllis Neilson-Terry burst through the brakes of bamboo to the rescue, at the head of the essential party of British sailors. There was no Union Jack, but all the other trappings of transpontine melodrama were there. Again, Tree got the bird.

These, it is true, were isolated instances, but they go to show that even the great ones partook of Homer's weakness, and occasionally nodded. They were always promptly told of it by their audiences, but there was no rancour, no ill-feeling. It was just a misunderstanding, that was all, as between gentlemen. After all, tastes differ, and one man's meat is another man's poison. So the actor-manager, who found himself in possession of the 'bird,' tried again and always found ready appreciation his just reward.

Those few black spots simply serve to throw up into bright relief the rest of the glory. Also it raises the question of Tree as an actor. About this there were two schools of thought, always. You were either anti or violently pro-Tree. And there were more 'pro' than anti. But he did have that trick of playing parts for which he was not suited in the least. Sometimes he got away with it by the greatness of his production and the sheer power of his own personality, plus some purple patches which he could nearly always supply in any part. But candour compels the admission that even his most violent fans did not like his 'Antony' in

Antony and Cleopatra, his 'Hamlet' (of which a critic said that it was funny without being vulgar), his 'Macbeth' (although it had some fine moments) —and other heroic or romantic parts. Yet his 'Antony' in *Julius Cæsar* was fine, and his famous oration a masterpiece of delivery and stagecraft. How the mob responded, how the passion rose, how the crowd swayed, shouted and bawled as he won them over.

But when he got into his own line, he was without equal. His 'Demetrius' in *The Red Lamp*, his 'Falstaff' (one of the truly great performances of all time), his 'Malvolio,' his 'Fagin' (never equalled), his 'Colonel Newcome,' his 'Micawber' (it was that man come to life, stepping straight from the book and how Dickens would have loved it), his crook in *The Van Dyke*, his eerie, magnificent performance in *The Man Who Was*, his 'Bottom' in *The Dream*, his 'Zakkuri' in *The Darling of the Gods* and above all his 'Svengali' in *Trilby*—this is a gallery of portraits which no other actor ever eclipsed. Then he rose to terrific heights. Yet he imperilled his 'Micawber' (only it was too wonderful) by doubling 'Dan'l Peggotty' (in which he was bad). And only in slightly lesser success to his great *tours-de-force* were his 'Beethoven,' his 'Jasper' in *Edwin Drood*, his 'Gringoire' in *The Ballad Monger*, his 'Count d'Orsay' in *The Last of the Dandies*, his 'Sir Peter Teazle' and his 'Paragot' in *The Beloved Vagabond*. The truth about Tree was that he was a great character actor, who excelled in comic or horrific parts, where strong character delineation was required. This he could do better than any of his contemporaries or successors. And he was, at heart, a comedian, who loved his joke and who adored a laugh. His 'Wolsey' was a dignified effort, but 'Othello' was not so good. Nevertheless, his production of *Henry VIII* gave unforgettable memories of perfect staging, of Ainley's golden voice as 'Buckingham,' of a marvellous 'Katherine' from Violet Vanbrugh, a great Henry VIII from Bourchier, and an altogether adorable 'Anne Bulléyn' from Laura Cowie. The spacious times of Tudor England lived again. Every part was perfectly cast, with actors like A. E. George, Edward Sass, Gerald Lawrence, and others of equal standing in quite minor parts.

His *Othello* was another wonderful production, and had the great advantage of Laurence Irving as 'Iago,' a most memorable performance by that actor, whose genius was never fully appreciated when his sad and tragic end came. Phyllis Neilson-Terry, then a young girl, was the 'Desdemona,' and pretty Alice Crawford the 'Emilia,' Philip Merivale the 'Cassio.'

He was an impressive and somewhat terrifying 'Mephistopheles' in his staging of *Faust*—a most beautiful production. Ainley played 'Faust' and nobody could wish a better, Rosina Fillipi was the Nurse, Godfrey Tearle the 'Valentine' and Marie Lohr, then, like Phyllis Neilson-Terry, at the very beginning of her career, was 'Marguerite'—and a lovely, charming, innocent, heart-wringing Marguerite this fine actress gave us, although only a girl. The version was by Stephen Phillips, and one remembers the figure of Tree as 'Mephisto' at the end of the prologue, proclaiming :

"Mother, still crouching on the bounds of light
With face of sea and hair of tempest
Still huddled in huge and immemorial hate
Behold thy son, and some vast aid extend."

and the gradually increasing mutter and roll of thunder which followed the appeal.

But the list could go on forever. Two memories of Dickens, however, must be recorded. They were stupendous. Often stage versions of Dickens do not succeed. But in *Oliver Twist* and *David Copperfield* Tree gave us the perfect stage forms. His 'Oliver Twist' prepared by Comyns Carr was in every way remarkable. Again, a stupendous cast. George Shelton a real 'Mr. Grimwig,' J. Fisher White an equally real 'Mr. Brownlow,' Nellie Bowman the most gentle and appealing of 'Olivers,' Lettice Fairfax as 'Rose Maylie' and Basil Gill a romantic 'Harry Maylie.' That supreme stage villain, W. L. Abingdon, as 'Monks,' a performance to remember. One can hear, echoing down the years from 1905, his admonition to 'Rose' about 'Oliver' : "If you have any affection for this child—and women's fancies are sometimes oddly placed—tend the bastard well, young lady, tend the bastard well." It was a real thrill as he delivered it. Every part, however tiny, was superbly played, even 'Mrs. Bedwin' was in the hands of Jennie Lee, an actress who had, in her time, made all London weep at her 'Jo' in *Bleak House*. But standing out in high relief are three performances, Lyn Harding as 'Bill Sikes,' Constance Collier as 'Nancy,' and Tree as 'Fagin.' Harding, always a magnificent actor and one of His Majesty's towers of strength, was wonderful as the brutal 'Sikes,' it was a truly great performance. And so was the tragedy of 'Nancy' as presented us by Constance Collier. This pair was impeccable. Tree rose to his greatest heights as 'Fagin.' This was a character after his own heart. He ran the whole gamut. The comic genius which peeped through the evil as he presided over his boys in the Thieves Kitchen, when Frank Stanmore as 'The Artful Dodger,' Charles Hanbury as 'Charlie Bates,' and the rest put Oliver through his first paces in crime ; his incredible menace in his little lullaby over putting 'Oliver' to bed, his grim, silent acting when, candle in hand in a dark stage, he listened to the blows which meant the bludgeoning of Nancy (and Constance Collier's screams were something to hear for weeks afterwards) and the blowing out of that candle as a heavy thud announced the dropping of the corpse by Sikes—and the tense, demented terror of the man when we saw our glimpse of him in the Condemned Cell—this was the greatest of great acting. His *David Copperfield* was the truest stage version ever shown. All the atmosphere of the book was recaptured. Save perhaps for Tree's own performance as 'Dan'l Peggoty' it was without flaw. Here again was a marvellous cast and beautiful acting. Agnes Thomas was everyone's idea of 'Betsy Trotwood,' H. Gill had all the requisites for 'Steerforth,' Fred Ross used his remarkable voice with effect as 'Ham,' Nigel Playfair gave a splendid etching of 'Mr. Dick' (kite and all), every part was right out of the pages of the masterpiece. Outstanding, however, were the beauty and grace of Evelyn Millard as 'Agnes,' the embodiment of 'Em'ly' by Jessie Winter, the absolute life-like 'David' of Owen Nares and the arch villainy, never overdone for a moment, of 'Uriah Heep,' by that fine actor Charles Quartermaine. Sydney Fairbrother's 'Mrs. Micawber' matched Tree's 'Wilkins Micawber' and one cannot say more. For 'Micawber' was 'Tree' and he was 'Micawber.' With what unction did he roll out his advice, with what dignity did he make his speeches, with what tremendous aplomb did he assist at the unmasking of 'Heep'—and with what joy did he, in the last scene, prepare to make the famous punch. But the scene which lingers most is that in which David entertained the Micawbers to supper, whilst the evil 'Littimer' (played beautifully by Croker King) waited upon them. Tree's assumption of being used to it all, his efforts to hide the fork with which he had been toasting the sausage, his apparently impaling himself with it by sticking it in his shirt front, his efforts at easy dignity—this was the high light of truly comic acting. A memory of the Edwardian Theatre to cherish forever.

Perhaps the high spot of his career at His Majesty's was, quite naturally, his knighthood. The evening he received it he was playing 'Malvolio.' His reception was enormous, for everyone felt proud of his honour, as if they themselves had received it. But when he came to the lines, which seemed so apposite : "Some are born great, others achieve greatness, and some have greatness thrust upon them," well, he stopped the show. The audience stood and cheered for minutes.

Tree was in every way a remarkable man and a remarkable manager. Tall, with a curious walk, a habit of bending one knee in upon the other whilst standing still, his left arm akimbo, his right hand wandering in the air, he was full of mannerisms which, nevertheless, we accepted as part of Tree. His eyes were pale blue and gazed into the future. His voice was flat and curiously guttural at times, but quite unmistakable. Nor did you ever miss a word of what he said. But his personality was overpowering at short range, and he was every inch the embodiment of Theatre and the leader of his profession. Incidentally he was the last, up to now. His mantle was too large for other wearers, it would have smothered them. One person only could have worn it, Seymour Hicks, but he preferred to have fun, and maybe he was right.

Tales about Tree are endless. Some are true, some not. But his sense of humour was so strong, his desire to have a lark so terrific, that he kept all those in his theatre on their toes with suspense. And in this respect, he got away with murder. His wit, more often than not quite spontaneous, was devastating. Sometimes, however, he would think up a joke and wait for the right moment to crack it. But if it came to repartee, he was crushing. He did the most unexpected things without turning a hair, for his own amusement. When in the mood, he often dried up his entire company. For instance, in *The Darling of the Gods*, his first entrance as the villain 'Zakkuri' was on top of a rostrum before which stood over ninety people, calling on his name, their hands raised in supplication, their backs to the audience. One afternoon the scene went as clockwork, but there was no 'Zakkuri' to face the imploring crowd. They shouted, they howled, they called his name. Then, quietly, from downstage behind them, a quiet voice said in unmistakable tones: "Were you looking for somebody ?" Tree had altered his business, and entered downstage behind the crowd, just to see what they would do in that predicament.

He did a similar thing in *Edwin Drood*. In the last scene he, as 'Jasper,' should have been found in the tomb by the searchers who broke in. Stanley Bell, his stage manager, watching the scene one afternoon from the corner, saw Tree enter the tomb and the doors close, saw the searchers arrive and start operations with a crowbar and then became conscious of someone standing behind him. Turning he found to his horror that it was the Chief, who was watching the stage with the greatest interest. "Chief," he gasped out, "you ought to be in the tomb." "I know, I know," answered Tree dreamily. "But, Chief," demanded the anxious and frightened Bell, "what will they do when they break in and find you not there?" "That's just what I want to see," said Tree, with a chuckle.

At rehearsals of *Macbeth* he made some famous cracks. He had real Guardsmen for the armies in the battle scene. These men entered into the spirit of the fight with gusto and laid about them so heartily that their swords chopped pieces off the scenery and smacked against the backcloth. "Soldiers, soldiers," shouted Tree, "listen to me. Never hit a backcloth when it's down." And later, when an over-zealous soldier had inflicted a slight flesh wound on his stage opponent, he declared : "I make a ruling. Any one soldier found killing any other soldier will be fined." He would have jokes with members of his company. One was Hubert Carter, a most robust actor with the loudest voice on the stage. Stentor should have been his name, the Bull of Bashan must have been an ancestor, and Boanerges might have fathered him. At a rehearsal of Brieux' *False Gods*, in which he played 'Pharaoh,' to his immense surprise Tree, seated in the stalls, called out : "Hubert, speak up." Carter spoke up, letting his magnificent voice roll out like an organ peal. "Louder, louder," demanded Tree. Somewhat amazed, Hubert was much, very much louder. He would have topped a barrage at its height. "No, no," cried Tree, "louder, louder still." Carter took a breath, and made the scenery shake and the theatre re-echo with his mighty voice. "Better, better," said Tree, "but still not loud enough." Carter, baffled and stunned, tried again. This time the whole theatre shook as if a gale had struck it. His veins stood out, his eyes started, and sweat broke out on his brow with his terrific effort of sound. The speech over, breathless, he gazed at Tree. "Could you hear that, Chief?" he queried. "Oh, yes, yes," replied Tree, gently. "I can hear you, Hubert, but there's a man in Trafalgar Square who can't."

Ion Swinley, who, like so many more, started his career with Tree, played 'Donalbain' in *Macbeth*. It is a small part and he finished early. He did not want to wait about in the theatre and go on in the battle at the end. So he read all there was to find out about Donalbain, discovered that he had left Scotland, settled in Ireland and never returned, and put this sedulously round the theatre so that it could reach Sir Herbert's ears. He knew Tree was a stickler for accuracy. Sure enough, one day at rehearsal Tree said : "Swinley, what's all this about Donalbain going to Ireland?" "It's right, Chief," said Swinley, "he did and never returned. I thought you ought to know because if I appeared again, someone would spot it and write in." "Yes, yes," said Tree, in a far-away voice, "very right, very thoughtful. Yes, yes, accuracy at all costs. But you will come on in the battle scene—and wear a beard !" You could not hoodwink Sir Herbert.

One of Tree's failings was a liability to forget his lines. This nearly always occurred for several performances and sometimes there came a play in which certain lines would always escape him. Mostly it was got over by judicious prompting. Indeed, Cecil King, one of his great stage managers, learnt all his Chief's parts and would go on with the crowd to give him a quiet prompt and reminder. Once, however, this was not possible. The elusive lines occurred when Tree was on with only one other character, and at a moment when he was farthest from the corner. So a brilliant idea occurred to the stage management. They would write the lines very large on a board, the call boy should go down into the orchestra pit, out of sight of the audience, hold up the board and Tree could glance down and read them off. Tree approved highly. The next performance the boy was duly in the pit with the board. The moment came, Tree dried up. He strolled down to the footlights, gazed idly into the pit, stared, smiled, stared again, shrugged his shoulders and then walked to the prompt corner. "What's the line?" he hissed. "But, Chief," whispered Stanley Bell, "the boy's down in the pit with it all written on a board." "I know, I know," replied Tree *sotto voce*, "but he's holding it upside down." And that call boy was Claude Rains, now a great star himself.

Sometimes the joke was against Tree, but he never cared. During the rehearsals of *False Gods*, in which Ainley and Mrs. Patrick Campbell played the leads, Brieux, the author, had come to rehearsals and there had been some friction. That did not daunt Tree. After the triumphant first night, he gave his usual supper party in the Dome above the theatre, where he held court amidst the Gothic surroundings of a baronial hall. He invited Brieux. The famous French dramatist had not come. Tree sent his valet to find him. After an absence the man returned. "Well, well, well," said Tree, "is he coming?" "Sir," said the valet, "Mr. Brieux said you were a monkey." "I know, I know," said Tree, quite unconcerned, "but is he coming to my party?" Brieux came all right.

Again, during rehearsals of this play, the representative of Saint-Saëns, who had composed the music, came down to see how things were. A play by Brieux with incidental music by such a composer, that was how Tree did things. This man was French and spoke bad English. He got very excited and found fault with the orchestra which, under Tree's musical director, Adolf Smidt, an Austrian, was playing off stage. Mostly he complained that the flutes played too loudly. He had them 'piano,' then more 'piano,' then 'pianissimo,' until they were hardly heard at all. Still he shouted that it would not do. "De flutes, de flutes," he yelled, "more soft, more soft." The annoyed and baited Smidt came on to the stage, and down to the footlights. "How is the flutes play more softly as they can?" he demanded. "They do, they do," shouted the excited Frenchman. And on top of this display of murdered English came the quiet voice of Tree. "Half an hour off for everyone," he said. There was really no other comment possible.

Tree was not the only person whom Stanley Bell found behind him unexpectedly in the prompt corner at H.M.T. Once in the production of *Antony and Cleopatra* during a scene on the banks of the Nile which was a marvel of colour, pageantry, and—shall we say—want of costume —he was conscious that someone was behind him. He turned, and saw a figure of a man, in evening dress, wearing a black dress overcoat, tall hat on head, and in his moustached and bearded mouth, a large and obviously good cigar. It was no less a person than King Edward VII. "I just came through the stage door," said the King. "I was so impressed by this scene when I visited the play, I wanted to see it again. Do you mind?" Bell hastily found him a seat and there the King sat and watched the scene, asking lots of questions. Then suddenly through the pass door came an agitated usher. "Mr. Bell, Mr. Bell," he said, "what's the matter, please? Mr. Dana has sent me round to know if the theatre's on fire." Then Stanley Bell realized that the smoke from the King's cigar, which he puffed heartily, was creeping round the edge of the proscenium arch. But the curtain fell before any trouble occurred. That was something which could only have occurred in the Edwardian Theatre.

Tree was merciless in riposte or in dealing with people who annoyed him. A man he hardly knew gate-crashed his dressing-room. Tree gazed at him blankly. The man introduced himself effusively. "Pardon me," said Tree. "I did not recognize you in my make-up."

One young and impatient actor at His Majesty's did not think he was making fast enough progress. He went to see Tree and airily told him so, suggesting that Sir Herbert might write to Frank Benson, and suggest the young man should join his company to get more varied experience. Tree agreed gravely. Nothing happened for some time, so the young and impulsive man again sought Tree. "Excuse me, Chief," he said, "but did you write to Benson about me?" "Write!" said Tree. "My dear boy, I wired."

It was his spirit of mischief that made him shout, on getting out of the train on his almost State visit to Moscow: "Stanley, Stanley, what a lot of foreigners"—and his dignified sense of rebuke that made him say to some students he was addressing, and who showed a disposition to 'rag,' "Excuse me, gentlemen, I have a few more pearls to cast."

Contrast that with his action when a ragged old woman outside the stage door curtsied and offered a rather faded bunch of violets for sale. Tree took the flowers, gave the old girl five shillings, raised his hat, made a deep bow, and then passed on. Said the man with him: "I can understand the five bob, Chief, but why the bow?" "Commerce, commerce," murmured Tree, "she represents commerce. I don't understand commerce, and I always salute what is beyond me!" He was not very pleased when, by an accident, Frances Dillon, playing one of the Weird Sisters in *Macbeth* and flying through the air on a wire, got off her course and landed with all her weight (and she was what was known as 'a fine woman') on his chest, but when he cut some lines in the 'Banquo's' ghost scene and gave a cue too soon, which caused the electrician to light up the 'transparency' some minute too early, thereby showing the Ghost with its gown held in both hands running hastily to get into position, nobody laughed more heartily than he. But perhaps the most curious trick he ever did was in *Henry VIII*. Again it was a matinée, and whilst he as Wolsey waited in the wings, Arthur Bourchier as the King came off the stage, cursing heartily. "Herbert," said the aggrieved Bourchier, "we are all being insulted. There's a man in the front row reading the paper all the time. Have him turned out." "Leave him to me," said Sir Herbert. A towering figure in his scarlet robes and long train, imposing and dignified to a degree, he swept on to the stage. Spotting the offending man immersed in the latest news, he swept down to the footlights. The man was oblivious. So Tree knelt down, and leaned over, gazing straight at the reader. This man sensed something wrong, looked up and found himself staring straight into Tree's enquiring blue eyes. "Tell me," said the great actor, with every appearance of interest, "what won the two-thirty?" The guilty desecrater of His Majesty's knew not where to look. He crammed the paper in his pocket, scarlet in face as Tree's Cardinal's robes, but made no reply. Sir Herbert rose to his full height, over six feet. He gazed all round at the amazed and breathless audience. With a great gesture, he pointed at the now terribly embarrassed and frightened man. "He doesn't know," he informed them. Then, with a burst of applause, he stepped back—and went on with the scene. Nobody but a great man could have done that —and held his audience. But Tree was a very great man.

Lord of the beautiful theatre he had built, he was master of his own world. The very soil beneath the playhouse was hallowed, for on it had once stood the theatre built by Sir John Vanbrugh, which had become the King's Opera House and then the Italian Opera House. Now it was—and is—His Majesty's Theatre. He was beloved by his staff and by his companies. His public were faithful to him. Even those who professed to dislike his acting crowded in to see his epoch-making productions. Irving, whose mantle he wore with ease, had not liked him at all—had called him 'that mummer.' But Tree gloried in being a mummer, for he was entirely of the Theatre—it was no insult to him.

He treated everyone with great courtesy, and he was lavish with those marks of esteem which the actor-managers presented to their guests— the souvenirs of the plays in which they performed. These beautiful and often costly gifts were things of merit and value. Beautifully bound and printed, well written as to letterpress, they contained either coloured plates of the scenes and artists, or well produced photographs, and every member of the audience was given one free, no matter where he sat, usually on the hundredth, but often, with Tree, on the fiftieth performance. Everyone in the audience on the first night of *David Copperfield* received a bound copy of the novel with lovely illustrations of the company by Frank Reynolds and Buchel. It was Christmas Eve and an inscription read : 'A Christmas Gift from Sir Herbert Tree to each member of the audience at the first performance of *David Copperfield* at His Majesty's Theatre on Christmas Eve, 1914.' It was the last souvenir of this great host and the last of such things before the war swept them away almost entirely. Might not such a courtesy be practised by managements to-day? Those souvenirs were sought after and treasured. Those of us who got them have them still as memories of great Edwardian days, links which stretched across the footlights and treasured thoughts of great nights at the theatre and of great actor-managers, the like of whom we shall never see again. And the greatest theatre of Edwardian times was His Majesty's, and the greatest actor-manager Sir Herbert Beerbohm Tree. As he said, the business of the stage might be illusion, but he made it very real, and enduring.

CHAPTER IV

'The Idol of the Ladies'

IT WAS GEORGE GROSSMITH (THEN 'JUNIOR') WHO USED TO SING TO US ABOUT that 'Archie' who was 'the idol of the ladies and the envy of the men.' Except for the fact that the hero of the song was of a very light-hearted and frolicsome disposition, the phrase exactly fitted Sir George Alexander, even in the days when he was just 'Mr. Alexander.' For this great actor-manager was indeed the idol of the ladies and the envy of the men. The ladies' idolatry was caused by his good looks, his air of distinction and his charm. The men envied his perfect tailoring, in which they followed his lead. There were very few women who did not possess a photograph of him, to gaze at admiringly. In the earlier days, it would be a 'cabinet' purchased from Ellis and Walery, and later on picture postcards, not one but many. For he was one of the picture postcard kings. Not a tall man, but over the middle height, he was the very essence of respectability in its most genteel and refined form. He was 'good form' in a day when bad form was almost crime. He looked, and was, the 'perfect gentleman' (in the best sense of that misused word) both on and off the stage. You never saw him otherwise than immaculate. His hair was perfectly done, his suits the perfection of cut, his linen spotless, his boots (we seldom wore shoes then in Town) highly polished, his gloves just the right shade and material, his umbrella perfectly rolled, his stick gold-mounted and fashionable (for there were fashions in walking-sticks then).

On the stage he was the same. He was not a great actor but he was a very good one indeed and he was always conscious of his limitations. Unlike Tree, he never 'miscast' himself.

And on and off the boards, in the theatre or outside, he was un-mistakably the actor—which accounted for much of his charm with the public. If Tree succeeded Irving, Alexander carried on the work of the Bancrofts. His line was Comedy, in the real sense of the word. Some-times he gave us Shakespeare, and it was always first class. Sometimes he gave us Romance, and it was always romantic. But mostly it was real Comedy at the St. James's Theatre.

That playhouse was the ideal setting for Alexander. It had an atmosphere which his brilliant and successful management much in-creased. For he was in the very spirit of that royal district of St. James's —when you thought of St. James's Street, you thought of him. And his theatre had something of the feeling of one of the very best clubs in that district of clubland, of which only 'the best people' were members. In a subtle way, he conveyed this to you, his guests or audiences. He conveyed to you the idea that you were of 'the best people' or you would not have come to call on him. He gave you credit for having the same taste and good judgment that he himself possessed, and he certainly had both. The atmosphere of the St. James's Theatre was one of extreme good breeding and all that it stood for. It was not so vast and spacious, nor so tremendously vital as His Majesty's. It was more sedate, leisurely

—it was as a beautiful porcelain or china tea-set might be to a gold dinner service—but at the same time, it was the best of its kind. Its staff was like a set of well-trained servants—it was, in fact, the essence of St. James's, of clubland, quiet, restful and a place where you went to meet nice people and hear good conversation. And at Alexander's theatre you always did both.

He himself had been with Irving. He had played 'Valentine' and, later, the title role in *Faust* with that great man, amongst other things. So he had learned in the best school. Neither he nor Tree came of theatrical stock— few of the actor-managers did so. His real name was George Alexander Gibb Samson, and he began life as a clerk. His detractors spread the rumour that he had been a shopwalker, which was totally and completely untrue. But what a performance he would have given as such and how the sales would have mounted. But he started in commerce and he was a good business-man and remained so all his life. He never lost his head. Strangely enough, his introduction to the stage was one of those co- incidences which happen in real life, for his firm got up some amateur theatricals in aid of a hospital and played at the St. James's Theatre— and young Gibb was in the cast. Perhaps he made up his mind, then, that one day he would rule there. At any rate, the stage claimed him and he graduated through touring companies and local 'stocks,' to the Kendals and then to Irving. No training could have been better. He did not start his actor-managerial career at the St. James's but at the old Avenue (now the Playhouse), but he did not remain there long. For in 1890 he transferred his production, *Sunlight and Shadow*, from the Avenue to the St. James's and his career as a great actor-manager, who was to do so much for his profession and for every branch of it, had begun.

The career of the St. James's, up to that time, was a very chequered one. It was already an old theatre. It had been built in 1835 by John Braham, the famous tenor, who sank all his savings in it and lost every penny, having to start all over again at the age of sixty-four. It was built on the site of an old inn dating back to the Restoration in King Street, St. James's. It was, and still is, the most westerly of the real West End theatres, if the Victoria Palace, an ex-music hall, and the modern Westminster be omitted. That was against its early success and against it too in the earlier days of George Alexander. It said much for his power that he drew all London there. Before he came, there had been chopping and changing. Everything had been tried, and every- thing had failed. The only glimmer of success had been a season of performing animals. For many years it was devoted to French plays and players. But always there was a hoodoo. This was broken for the first time when, in 1879, John Hare and Mrs. Kendal went there in management. They showed that good plays, well produced, with brilliant acting could make an unlucky theatre into a good one, and they remained there for eight years. When they left, they were all at the very top of their profession. But the theatre slipped back again into failure, until its real tenant arrived, the man whose fate it was to make this one of the famous theatres of London, of the whole country, if not of Europe as well.

His first step was to make it a comfortable house, and he installed electric light, a great innovation. His first new play was *The Idler*, by

Haddon Chambers, and although it got a mixed Press, it succeeded all the same. Alexander and the St. James's were now launched on a career of success which was to last until his death in 1918. He was only fifty-nine then, and he had achieved so much.

From the very start he impressed his views, his methods and his personality on his theatre and it became like himself. He made it a place which you were delighted to visit. It gave you a sense of well-being. Members of the public who aspired no higher than the pit or the gallery, when visiting the St. James's always had a feeling that they were moving in the best circles—and, indeed, they were, in the very best theatre circles. From the general manager down to the cloakroom attendant, politeness and restraint reigned. The little man who had charge of an obscure cloakroom somewhere in the depths beneath the stalls once had a disagreement with a customer over a hat. He was reported to the manager, who had him 'on the carpet.' His case was that the gentleman who had done him the honour to entrust the hat into his keeping was a bad-tempered, crotchety, unreasonable old man. But he did not express it in that way. In reply to the manager's question he said : "Sir, I found the gentleman somewhat austere." That was the true St. James's spirit. The housekeeper, who kept the place like a new pin, knew every patron and their tastes. And she knew all about Royalty, for whose visits to the Royal Box she kept a special tea-set with a solid silver tea and coffee pot. On one occasion, being told that Her Royal Highness the Princess Royal (the Duchess of Fife) was coming to the matinée, and that a nice tea was to be served, she replied : "Rightly speaking, sir, Her Royal Highness does not partake of tea—she prefers coffee." That, again, was real St. James's. In her black silk dress and gold chains, she pervaded the theatre and nothing escaped her eagle eye.

The box office manager, Arnold, was a character, and part of the place, too. He and Leverton, of the Haymarket, shared seniority amongst the men who sat at the receipt of custom. Arnold always wore a tall hat on duty and had a smile on his large, fresh-complexioned face, which no matter what the state of the weather, always looked as if he had just washed it with meticulous care. Probably he had, for his day always began—right up to very mature years—with a plunge in his local swimming bath. For years he had an assistant whose very name was right for the theatre, for it was De Courcy. Even the tickets at the St. James's were different. They were not of paper but of pasteboard, and had something of the appearance of a railway ticket. True, they assured you of a pleasant journey for the evening, or the afternoon, as the case might be. The politeness which was so much a part of the theatre even extended to the refusal of applications for free seats. The manager would not say to Arnold, when handing him a stamped and addressed envelope, "Regret this one"—the usual managerial formula for turning down an application and posting a printed form whereby 'Sir George Alexander regrets that, owing to public demand, he is unable to comply with your request at the moment.' No ; he would say : "Send him Box C." This was a polite fiction, for there was no Box C in the theatre. Arnold understood what to do. But if, because it was near the end of a run, there happened to be room for a *bona fide* member of the profession, and the request was granted, then you were sent, not the usual theatre ticket stamped 'Complimentary' but a special ticket, a paper one, larger in size than the one sold for cash, showing clearly what it was, placing the recipient apart from the cash customers, and carrying instructions to the effect that you must wear evening dress, or you would not be admitted. It stated in large type, impossible to be overlooked, 'Evening Dress Compulsory.' Alexander was not going to have the tone of his stalls or dress circle let down by a non-paying guest. Nor did he desire to let his paying guests know that some were in 'on the nod.' But it mattered little, for in Edwardian days nobody would have dreamed of entering the stalls or circle unsuitably attired. But no chances were taken. It was probably a desire to inculcate his own good manners into the late arriving stallites, whose noisy entrances so often disturbed the house, which caused Alexander to 'ring up' on *The Second Mrs. Tanqueray* at the odd hour of 8.10 p.m. If so, it was unsuccessful, for nothing will make some playgoers punctual.

People entered the service of the St. James's and stayed there. They became not servants but retainers, and behaved as such. The service was perfect. Outside the theatre they had no interests, nor did they want them. They served a good master, they were part of the outfit. They knew little and cared less of what life was like in less sheltered theatres. They knew the ways of St. James's and nothing else mattered. They lived in a little world of their own, a pleasant backwater of London, and were like the staff of a country mansion in the days of the Stately Homes of England.

When Alexander died and the regime changed, the man who had been for many years treasurer of the theatre came into contact with a life he did not know, with conditions he had no idea existed. He told a friend he had no notion that so many cut-throats infested the theatrical profession. He was never the same again. But by that time the Edwardian Theatre had vanished. The ways of the actor-managers were no more, the walls were down, the castles were tenements open to all comers and the rough blast of the very commercial world beat upon those who had led a leisurely, comfortable life.

Do not think, however, that the St. James's was not a 'commercial' theatre. It was, but in comparison with the commercial theatre of to-day it was as different as chalk is from cheese. There one man held sway ; his taste, his judgment, his methods were the correct way of life. He had his high standards which he supported in his own way. All of which his theatre reflected. But after his time, then each incoming tenant had ways of his own, the Theatre was but a brief resting place—a place in which as much money was to be made as possible, or if lost, then the sooner he was out, the better for everyone.

Alexander was, compared to Tree, a commercial manager. He did not believe in short runs and constant change. His idea was that each play should run as long as possible. Like Tree, he took the same pains over each production, he never ceased in his endeavour to find the best ; but having found it, he was content for it to run its full and entire course. He was, of course, selling a different line of goods. They were the Alexander brand which he sold himself on his own personality and

CRBERT CAMPBELL AND DAN LENO

BERTRAM WALLIS AND ISOBEL JAY IN
'THE KING OF CADONIA'

LENA ASHWELL

LILY BRAYTON

MARY MOORE AS 'MISS MILLS,' SIR CHARLES WYNDHAM AS 'CAPTAIN DREW'
AND VANE TEMPEST AS 'ERNEST WHITE' IN 'CAPTAIN DREW ON LEAVE'

JULIA NEILSON, A. KENDRICK, M. CHERRY, FRED TERRY, AND HORACE HODGE
IN 'THE SCARLET PIMPERNEL'

drawing power. But he took care that they should be as good a fit a his clothes, he took care to have nothing second-hand, that there should be no creases except in the right place, and that those who surrounded him should be of the front rank.

He had plays written for him, thereby encouraging dramatists. If he had the star part, it was because that was his job and that was what the public wanted. On his own scale and within the limitations of Comedy, his productions were just as brilliant as Tree's. It was, naturally, the drawing-room against the Forum at Rome, but then both can be right and perfect, and both were.

Alexander gave chances to young actors and actresses. He taught them their jobs, he gave them their first big break, and it was an ideal school in which to learn. At His Majesty's they learnt breadth, at the St. James's they learned manners and restraint. He was, too, a great master of the difficult art of casting. It was he who selected an almost unknown young actress to play a part in what was a bombshell of its period, which started a new line of play, when he entrusted the difficult part of 'Paula Tanqueray' to Mrs. Patrick Campbell. And how right his judgment was. It was he who, in search of the perfect romantic actor, went down to inspect the Benson Company, the great training ground of those days. And how it is missed now. He wanted someone to play 'Paolo' in his forthcoming *Paolo and Francesca*. It must be some-one who was just right. The choice at the finish lay between two young actors. One was called Matheson Lang and the other Henry Ainley. After deliberation, Alexander chose Ainley. His wisdom was apparent as soon as young Harry, as 'Paolo,' stepped upon the stage. There was an audible gasp of admiration from the whole theatre, from men and women alike. Indeed, Ainley looked like something out of a stained-glass window, or an Old Master. He was the incarnation of romantic manly beauty; nothing effeminate—on the contrary, real masculine vigour and virility, added to the pictorial charm of Cinquecento costume and appeal. To his amazing handsomeness, of both face and figure, he had the additional gift of a wonderful voice. He swept all London off its feet. It may not have been a perfect performance, for Ainley was young and inexperienced, but his appearance and appeal were enough. Evelyn Millard brought her talent and great beauty to the part of 'Francesca.' She and Ainley made a picture, framed in Alexander's beautiful setting, that it was a joy to gaze upon. Also the play was in verse, by Stephen Phillips. One wonders if any manager would take such a risk to-day? Alexander, the wicked actor-manager who was always supposed to grab the plums, played the part of 'Giovanni,' the husband. The part was unsympathetic but his performance was out-standing. It ran for 133 performances, and is a lovely memory of a time when the stage—and the actor-managers—put beauty in the van of their endeavour.

Never did Alexander wish to shine unduly brightly or to twinkle on his own. He was always one of a veritable milky way of stars, but the pivot and crux of the whole thing, nevertheless. True, his judgment of a play was bounded by the possibility of being suitable for his theatre or not. But in that he was right. He was catering for his own clientele in

D

his own theatre. What had he to do with other goods, however excellent they might be? In that attitude was his strength and the strength of the Theatre of his time. Yet he would do things like *Paolo and Francesca, As You Like It, If I Were King, The Prisoner of Zenda, Rupert of Hentzau, Old Heidelberg, Much Ado About Nothing,* and others which by no means fitted the drawing-room dramas and comedies which people believed to be the staple St. James's fare. In that list are two Shakespearean plays, whilst *Paolo and Francesca* was, as has been stated, a poetic drama of mediæval Italy ; *The Prisoner of Zenda and Rupert of Hentzau* dashing romances of 'Ruritania' ; *If I Were King,* the story of François Villon in the days of Louis XI of France ; and *Old Heidelberg,* a nostalgic romance of that great University and a young German princeling. And let it be said that all of these were amongst his real successes. His variety in them dispels the idea that he could only play characters who wore fault-less evening dress and frock coats. For he was 'Orlando' in *As You Like It,* 'Benedict' in *Much Ado,* 'Giovanni Malatesta,' a middle-aged, rough, soldier tyrant, in *Paolo and Francesca,* the dashing 'Rudolf Rassendyl' in *The Prisoner of Zenda* and its Hentzau-ian sequel, and a charming young, shy and gauche princeling in *Old Heidelberg.* In *If I Were King* he played 'Villon,' a dirty, bearded, desperate rascal in the first act, a handsome romantic figure in the rest of the play. And what is more, he dashed on the St. James's stage on a white horse, and wearing full armour.

But whether it was poetry, Shakespeare, romantic drama or comedy, it became a St. James's play by the way in which he handled and pro-duced. His method of treating his guests the audience cannot be better shown than by an extract from one of his programmes :

'Mr. George Alexander would respectfully request those ladies who frequent the St. James's Theatre intent on viewing the performance to recollect the similar purpose in those who sit behind them. If therefore every large hat were left in the Cloak Room (for which there is no charge) the lady so doing would confer a great benefit on her immediate neighbours.'

That is from the programme of *The Tree of Knowledge,* by R. C. Carton, produced at the St. James's in 1897. It is a complete summary of the method by which the Edwardian Theatre was run. Note the careful phrasing, the terrific politeness which is without any trace of servility, the courtesy and dignity of the whole thing. In a few lines it sums up the entire spirit of the times. Note also that it was quite evident that ladies frequented the theatre—they did not merely visit it. There is a subtle compliment to them there. It is a host speaking to familiar but valued friends. Note that they are 'intent on viewing the perform-ance,' not merely seeing the play. It is a well-bred appeal to well-bred people. And that was the essence of the Edwardian Theatre.

It is to be feared that the appeal often fell on stony ground, and that the majority of the ladies did not comply with the respectful request. There is little doubt that they would have liked to do so, also that some number, moved by it and their conscience, would indeed remove those hats. And no doubt all of them felt the urge, after reading it. The difficulty was two-fold. First the hat, and then their hair. A woman's coiffure then was something at which a girl of to-day would stand amazed. Hair, of course, was worn long. It was piled on top of the head, in a most ornate style, and, it may be whispered, reinforced by extra curls and what were known as 'switches.' It had an artificial foundation on which it was piled, which served two purposes, one to support that hair and the other to form something through which hatpins could be run, so as to keep the hat secure. And, as hats ran to size, this was no light matter. The hats were kept on the head by the aforesaid hatpins, long and dangerous affairs, and several pins went to the hat. Often the pins were quite ornate. The ordinary one was adorned with a plain, round jet knob, but you could get them with silver or gold or even jewelled hilts like daggers. And they were almost as lethal as those weapons. It was not the taking off of the hat which mattered so much, it was the putting it on again. This was an undertaking which required care ; the charm of the hat, and the part in the feminine picture of loveliness lay in its perfect adjustment. The common enquiry, as between woman and woman, was : "Is my hat on straight?" For if it was askew, every-thing was out of focus. That was why the matinée-goer (hats were never worn in the evening, of course, except in the unreserved parts)—often refrained from removing her hat. To get it on again she required time, room and a large mirror. She wanted time because it had to go 'just so' and also, if those pins were put in hurriedly, the lady of the Edwardian Theatre ran a grave risk of wounding herself by driving them into her scalp, a painful and unpleasantly bloody experience. If and when, how-ever, she did surrender to the politely whispered request of the lady or gentleman in the stall behind her, or to the loud and irate shout of : "Take that hat off," from someone in the pit, she either had to hold it on her lap all the afternoon (and its size was such that it would occupy the entire space) or pin it on the back of the seat in front of her. Frequent were the loud squeaks of pain when one of those hatpins penetrated the back of the seat into the back of the occupant thereof, and profuse the apologies. In the pit and gallery, women mostly took off their hats as soon as asked (though seldom before). If not, they had to endure sarcastic and very pointed remarks all the time, which spoilt their enjoyment and that of the people near them.

There is a programme note (in dealing with the price of seats) which, in quoting the price of the upper circle, says in brackets—'Bonnets allowed.' That, of course, raised the vexed question amongst the occupants of that midway plane of "When is a hat a bonnet ?" It also put the occupants in their correct social precedence.

In spite of all the politeness, earnest and respectful requests, few women left their hats in those specially provided and free cloakrooms. You see, the hat was the high spot of the whole costume effect. In the days of the Edwardian Theatre women did not all wear the same sort of hats. Not a bit of it. Their hats were all different, and bought specially to go with certain dresses and to suit the wearer—there was no massed hat production such as we see to-day (if we see hats at all) or such as struck us in the days of the 'cloche,' for instance, when all women looked alike. The Edwardian women theatre-goers—or perhaps we should say, ladies who frequented the theatre intent on viewing the performance—were determined to look as different from their sisters as possible, whilst still remaining 'in the framework'—as is the phrase of to-day—of fashion.

Two women who wore the same model of hat at the same time and place were immediately potential enemies. In Edwardian days, theatres and audiences alike believed in individuality.

It was not only to his audiences that Alexander showed such consideration and politeness. It was the same with his companies. He never overworked them at rehearsals. Not for him those driving hours of repetition, lasting until the small hours of the morning. For one thing, he studied the play and worked out everything before he called the first rehearsal, and secondly he knew that you got better work and results out of people who were fresh than people who were weary. He was a stickler for punctuality, however, and if a rehearsal was called for eleven a.m. that was when it began, not at eleven-fifteen. But he always gave them the afternoon to themselves—and in their short rehearsal they accomplished more than companies to-day achieve in treble the time, because the actor-manager knew exactly what he wanted. Also, those actor-managers gave the players credit for having brains as well and of knowing their business. A play was not just the repetition of the personality of the producer, but the expression of the chosen players' personalities and talents within the frame of the play. He would tell them the reasons why such things were to be, and sometimes alter intonations and 'readings' of certain lines, in view of something to happen later on. But he never made them stock figures of his own ideas. And, although he showed them every consideration, he never spared himself.

It was the same with the dramatists. If he wanted a playwright to write him a play, he would have a conference with him about it, when the dramatist would tell Alexander his idea and working out of a story. The actor-manager would suggest, discuss and go into every detail with the dramatist, so that, when the finished article came out, it was according to measure and it fitted the frame of his theatre. Much time, heartbreak and argument were thereby saved. And the polish provided made the whole thing—for always the play is the thing—gleam like a jewel. With men like the actor-managers in possession of the theatre, there was a good reason for playwrights to write plays. There were stable managements to produce them, there was a constant demand. For every actor-manager had not one, but several plays ready. He was never, or very seldom, caught napping. He always had a programme prepared well ahead. The dramatists who provided plays for the St. James's were the cream of their day. R. C. Carton, Haddon Chambers, Henry Arthur Jones, H. V. Esmond, Anthony Hope, John Oliver Hobbes, Sydney Grundy, Stephen Phillips, Justin Huntly McCarthy, Alfred Sutro, G. Bernard Shaw, E. Temple Thurston, A. E. W. Mason, Henry Bernstein, Rudolf Besier, C. B. Fernald, H. A. Vachell, Louis N. Parker, they are all in the St. James's tapestry, to say nothing of distinguished writers who contributed the many curtain-raisers of fine quality which Alexander, like the other actor-managers, put in for good entertainment weight. Are there as many first-class dramatists to-day?

But two names shine out like beacons from this distinguished management—the names of Oscar Wilde and Arthur Wing Pinero, the latter, like Alexander, and largely because of his work at the same theatre, received the honour of knighthood.

From Oscar Wilde, Alexander had *Lady Windermere's Fan* and *The Importance of Being Earnest*—probably the greatest success of both actor and playwright. For this play became Alexander's 'stand-by.' If ever he wanted a break between new productions, if ever he was at a loss whilst new plays were being prepared, a revival of *The Importance* would always fill the theatre. This masterpiece provided him with one of his best parts, in 'John Worthing,' and he had a wonderful foil in Allan Aynesworth as 'Algernon Moncrieffe.' The history of the first production of that play almost requires a book by itself. Wilde made trouble at rehearsals and Alexander politely but firmly turned him out of the theatre. Wilde retaliated by inviting Alexander and Aynesworth to supper. They thought it discreet to accept and went with a good deal of trepidation. Wilde welcomed them and said : "My dear Aleck and my dear Tony. I have only one thing to say to you. You are neither of you my favourite actor. We will now go to supper." Wilde attended the first night, and went round to see Alexander afterwards. He told the actor-manager that he thought the play charming, quite charming, and that from time to time it bore some resemblance to a play he had once written which had the same title. That was his revenge for being ejected from rehearsals. But the initial success was blighted by the trial of Wilde and the great scandal resultant therefrom brought it to a premature end. When all this had blown over, its revival was a triumph, again and again.

But amongst the St. James's dramatists, Pinero is the great name. Altogether he wrote seven plays for the St. James's, including *Playgoers* in one act. This may not seem a big proportion when one considers that (including one-act plays) Alexander presented in all eighty-two productions (revivals also included). But the Pinero's were plays of such quality that they stand out. The first Pinero at the St. James's was the ever-famous *The Second Mrs. Tanqueray*. That was as far back as 1893, but it started something new and marked an era in the drama. The others were *The Princess and the Butterfly* in 1897 ; *His House in Order* in 1906 ; *The Thunderbolt* in 1908 ; *Mid Channel* in 1909 ; *Playgoers*, in one act, in 1913 ; and *The Big Drum* in 1915. Alexander appeared in all of these except *Mid Channel* and *Playgoers*. Pinero was the dramatist who is most typical of the Edwardian Theatre. He understood his job, he was as great a craftsman as he was a story teller, and it is the combination of the two which makes the successful dramatist. These dramatists of the Edwardian and late Victorian epochs did not bother their heads about messages, or mental and moral uplift. They had a story to tell and they told it in expert manner. They knew their people, and they fitted them perfectly. They always gave Alexander and one or two of the other actor-managers a big speech at the end of the second or third acts (it depended upon how many acts) because that was when the big stuff had to be put over and that was the crucial moment when the actor-manager could do it. They could all deliver long speeches, and hold the audience spellbound. Alexander excelled at this. His diction, audibility, timing and phrasing were perfect, even if his mouth always seemed to sag a little at the right-hand corner.

The plays of interjection, of words of one syllable, where no speech is more than two lines long, would have been no good to the actor-manager nor to the audience. They would have felt cheated. Nor would a man like Pinero have written them. All of his plays, successful or not, were wonderful pieces of craftsmanship. Machine-made, if you like, but running like a Rolls Royce engine. Every phrase, every line, every speech, every bit of action advanced the story, there was no padding. They were perfectly timed. And they were always about something— not just a thin story bolstered up. The play lasted the whole while. And Pinero was a great draughtsman when it came to character studies. And, furthermore, he always had something to say, all of his plays had 'meat' in them. ☉ Perhaps his most perfect sample of this type of Edwardian Theatre was *His House in Order*. It provided Alexander with an ideal part. It had a fine, arresting story. It raised a problem and dealt with it. It was full of observation, of drama, of comedy, and its characters were real flesh and blood people. Its memory is imprinted on those who saw it at the St. James's as a perfect evening at the theatre, a most satisfying slice of The Drama. How one recalls 'Hilary's' rebuke to 'Nina' when she had attired herself in pink to go to what was regarded, by the family into which she had married, as a solemn occasion. He said he must go and dress. "To put on your black, I suppose?" she sneered. "No," came the reply, "not black—nor pink." Hilary was Alexander, Nina was Irene Vanbrugh. And that scene where 'Nina' showed 'Hilary' the letters she had found, which proved that the Annabelle Mary, the first wife of sainted memory, had feet of clay, that she had a lover, and that the son was that lover's son. The tenseness, the nervous strain of the two as they read them ! You could have heard a pin drop. What a play and what a cast ! Herbert Waring, Irene Vanbrugh, Nigel Playfair, Dawson Milward, Iris Hawkins as the little son, Lyall Swete, Bella Pateman, C. M. Lowne, Beryl Faber, Marcelle Chevalier. It showed the care that Alexander took so that not even ovals should go into round holes. *His House in Order* was Alexander's biggest success. He was perfectly suited, and Irene Vanbrugh has never been better, great actress though she be. Milward, that tall, military-looking man, was the right 'Major Maureward,' Herbert Waring the complete prig as 'Filmer Jesson,' the second husband, Lyall Swete, heavy, ponderous, bearded, presented the epitome of the mid-Victorian man of wealth and pillar of the Church or Chapel, Bella Pateman, severe, acid and respectable as the black-silk-clad matron, C. M. Lowne superb as the caddish son, 'Pryce Ridgeley'—these three members of the 'Ridgeley' family were quite real, and absolute representations of what the perky little 'Mayor' of Nigel Playfair described as 'The Sanctimonious Set,' nor could Beryl Faber have been improved upon as the icy 'Geraldine.' Even Mdlle. Marcelle Chevalier as the French governess (a small part) and little Iris Hawkins as the boy could not have been better. This was an evening in the theatre to be remembered always. And an actor-manager provided it.

It was one of many. Alexander had few real flops. True, a play called *The Conquerors*, by Paul M. Potter, was speedily removed, but mostly the attraction of Alexander and his company, and the prestige of his theatre, gave them a run.

Alexander did not appear in *Mid Channel*, a very powerful Pinero play. Despite fine performances by Lyn Harding, Nina Sevening, Eric Maturin and Irene Vanbrugh (magnificent as always) it was too gloomy. But in the last scene there were two small parts, two upholsterers working on the furniture. One of those two was Owen Nares. In his production of *As You Like It*, in which the one and only Julia Neilson played 'Rosalind,' a handsome young man played 'Amiens' (with song). His name was Bertram Wallis. C. Aubrey Smith played the small part of the Usurping Duke, whilst his Grace in exile was James Fernandez, a famous actor. H. H. Vincent was the 'Jacques,' whilst H. V. Esmond was 'Touchstone.' That veteran of to-day, Vincent Sternroyd, was 'Le Beau.' A young actor called H. B. Irving played the almost minor role of 'Oliver,' and Alexander himself was 'Orlando.' The actor-manager of the St. James's was supreme in his choice of actresses. In this production we find Julie Opp ('Hymen'), Fay Davis ('Celia'), Ellis Jeffreys ('Phoebe'), and Kate Phillips as 'Audrey.' The 'Rosalind' was Julia Neilson, that grand actress and great lady, our Queen of the Stage to-day, still as lovely, as regal and charming as ever. That production was in 1898.

Alexander's leading ladies want a volume to themselves. Their names are another rebuttal of the selfishness of the actor-manager. For in his long reign there, amongst them were Ada Neilson, Marion Terry, Maud Millett, Lily Hanbury, Evelyn Millard, Violet Vanbrugh, Fay Davis, and of course Mrs. Patrick Campbell, Julia Neilson, Irene Vanbrugh and as a very young leading lady indeed, beautiful Lilian Braithwaite, now a Dame of the British Empire. Mrs. Patrick Campbell burst into glory there in *The Second Mrs. Tanqueray*. She was no less alluring and wonderful when she played *Bella Donna* there, years later. Of Julia Neilson there is so much to be said that space forbids, except to enshrine her amongst the great ones of this great theatre. Irene Vanbrugh, whose distinction, whose large dark and expressive eyes, and whose mobile, sensitive face gripped and held you then as now, is perhaps the ideal St. James's leading lady. Lilian Braithwaite got her first really great chance there, when as a young and beautiful girl she showed she was also a beautiful actress in *If I Were King*. She was another to whom Alexander gave a chance. H. B. Irving gained much useful knowledge with him, Robert Loraine made an early appearance as 'Jacques du Bois' in that memorable *As You Like It*. And for a portion of the run Dorothea Baird was the 'Phoebe.' Henry Ainley, Eric Maturin, Owen Nares and a host of others stepped on the ladder of fame. In their younger days Matheson Lang and Godfrey Tearle added to their increasing laurels under his management. But the list is endless.

For years his stage manager was E. Vivian Reynolds, not only a fine stage manager, but a fine actor, who often played as well as being 'in the corner.' He was as distinguished to look at as any member of this distinguished theatre and company. A gentle-mannered man, with a scholarly face, he knew his business and was a grand first lieutenant. Men like Robert V. Shine and C. T. H. Helmsley were business managers, and Walter Slaughter was for years musical director. Alexander had the best around him.

He had a trade mark too. For many years his programmes and

posters bore the figure of a Beefeater, a Yeoman of the Guard. By that
you knew it was a St. James's production. This figure of something so
typically British, so much of the State, the mark of good service, the
personal guard of monarchs, was the best possible device for Alexander
and the St. James's.

Like his brother actor-managers, Alexander practically lived in the
theatre. All his business was done from there. And often, on special
occasions, he would transform the stage and give parties to which everyone who was anyone was glad to be invited. His wife was the perfect
hostess, as he was the perfect host. Indeed, she was not only hostess but
helpmate and kept her eye on details of the stage productions which
needed feminine touch and taste. She still works tirelessly for charity.

Alexander's dressing-room was in the front of the house, but quite
distinct and apart from it. The actual dressing-room was a cubicle, all
mirrors and lights, which was in a corner of what was a typical Victorian
drawing-room, absolutely redolent of the atmosphere of St. James's,
theatre and district. There he did his work, ran his business, planned his
productions and made his theatre a landmark in London. He received
his knighthood in 1911, the year of King George's Coronation. In the
general world, the Edwardian era had passed, but inside the theatre it
was to remain for three more years. The honour gave general delight
and he was overwhelmed with congratulations. His title became him and
he became it. Alexander had, at one time, political aspirations. He wanted
to contest a seat in the Conservative interest. Finally he relinquished the
idea and it was as well. A popular public servant like an actor should
have no visible politics. But he did become a member of the London
County Council, and performed excellent work as such.

His first nights were as brilliant as Tree's, if not so tremendously big
and breath-taking. But on a first night the St. James's boasted a house
full of celebrities of all kinds, and gossip writers of to-day would have
needed all their space. They would not only have had to chronicle the
names of popular members of the profession (whose presence there showed
that they were, in the polite stage phrase, 'resting') but Royalty, medicine,
art, literature, and holders of ancient titles.

There were, in those days, no floodlights thrown on the real celebrities
as they entered, no rude and dirty boys dashed about with autograph
books, no B.B.C. commentator spoke into a microphone to tell the world
that the best of it was seeing the play, and no pushing men with candid
cameras caused miniature storms of lightning so that readers of 'Society'
papers might see glimpses of playgoers looking deathly pale and a little
stunned and blinking, as they went to their seats.

Such things then did not matter. The Theatre was of sufficient
importance to draw these people, without publicity thrown in. Indeed,
such things would have been considered vulgar. It was pre-eminently a
select company of guests coming to be entertained by their host. It was
much more brilliant than anything of its kind to-day. It did not need
artificial floodlight—it was bright enough by itself.

Amongst other things, Alexander popularized the soft, double-fold
collar such as everyone wears to-day. Then, of course, everyone wore
stiff linen collars. And even when Alexander wore a soft collar on the

stage, he did so in a scene portraying a country house. He would never have dreamt of wearing one in the West End. Nowadays nobody dreams of wearing anything else—even at a wedding or funeral—the last two functions which make any attempt at ceremony. Only at Court would they think of assuming the linen collar. They even wear the soft ones with evening dress.

On one occasion Sir George attempted the impossible. In a play by E. Temple and Katherine Cecil Thurston it was necessary to have a double. The title of the play was *John Chilcote, M.P.* London was searched, the country was searched. But how could there be another Alexander? His whole strength was his individuality. Eventually a man was found who bore a superficial resemblance. He was the editor of a 'glossy' monthly called *The Smart Set.* But he was not an actor, and he was not an Alexander. The play failed. But it did something to life all the same, it made an impact. For that was the play in which Alexander appeared in a soft collar.

Alexander treated his company as his friends, and with the same courtesy as he treated his public. But he expected them to remember always that they were appearing with him at the St. James's. That entailed certain duties, certain restraints, certain methods of life and of dress. One afternoon, two young members of his company were walking down Bond Street. They were young, they were handsome, they were on the ladder of success, they were at the St. James's in *If I Were King.* They were Henry Ainley and Lilian Braithwaite. They had been to tea together. They were dressed in an informal manner, Lilian Braithwaite in a 'costume,' as it was then called, and Ainley in a somewhat flamboyant manner for those days, a soft hat, tweeds, and possibly a Norfolk jacket—the equivalent of that we now call a sports coat. It was summer time in London, when the Season was something which mattered and life was good. Suddenly they came face to face with George Alexander. He wore a silk hat, a morning coat and the formal accessories, and looked as if he had been poured into them. They saluted him respectfully. He returned the salute and stopped. They stopped too. "I am pleased," he said, "that two young members of my company should be friendly. It is what I desire, what I like. But I would ask you to remember that this is Bond Street and that you are members of the St. James's Theatre company. That requires social obligations in dress. I am sure I need not say more." He smiled gravely, saluted them, and passed on. They never forgot it.

King Street, St. James's, on a night in the Edwardian era would show a phase of London you could not see to-day. Nine people out of ten whom you passed in the street, if the night were fine, would be men in evening dress. There would be hardly any women pedestrians. This was man's part of London. Motors would be so few as to be remarkable if one passed. But in their place, broughams, smart, shiny and immaculate, flashed by, drawn by a well-matched pair of high-stepping horses. They were driven by a coachman in livery in a cockaded hat and by his side sat a liveried footman as well, his arms folded in an unnatural attitude. Hansoms would tinkle along and, like the broughams, the occupants would be in full dress. Those which contained a woman as well as a man

—or we should say a lady as well as a gentleman—would, if not bound for a dinner party or ball, be going to the St. James's Theatre. These were the people who ordered their carriages at eleven. The brougham would stop at the theatre entrance. The footman would leap down, open the door and remove the fur rug from the knees of the wealthy, leisured people inside. He would stand to attention whilst they got out. If it were a damp or muddy night, the theatre's linkman put a strange curved basket, never seen to-day, over the carriage wheel, so that by no means could a spot of mud get near her ladyship's silks or his lordship's dress trousers. As they went in, he saluted, as did the footman, and the coachman brought his whip smartly to an upright position, and that couple, who left the linkman to tell the footman to tell the coachman to have the carriage there at eleven, walked up the few steps into the softly lit and tasteful vestibule of the theatre itself.

Those who had no carriage to call at eleven, and who could not afford a hansom, but who had been drawn by Alexander to his theatre from outlying districts had bussed it from Victoria, Charing Cross, Liverpool Street, or King's Cross according to where they lived. When that magic hour of eleven approached they had to think of getting home, they had to think of last trains and long journeys. The St. James's was not in a convenient position for them, but they had to go there. But that was why suburban playgoers, except at matinées, seldom saw the last few minutes of a St. James's play. That is why probably the programme of *As You Like It* contains the following strange note : 'The Audience is earnestly requested to remain seated until the conclusion of the Epilogue spoken by "Rosalind" at the end of the play.' But even that earnest request was mostly disregarded. Nobody wanted to go. Was not that Epilogue spoken by our own Julia Neilson ? Would we willingly have missed one word she said, one moment of the chance of gazing at her whom we loved so much? But the demand of that last train was imperative. We could not earnestly request it to wait. It would pay no heed, it was not an actor-manager. So we had to pour out, and run down Piccadilly towards Hyde Park Corner to catch our bus before the crowds around Piccadilly filled it up. But once in it as we jogged towards our destination, we closed our eyes and we dreamed of the glorious hours we had spent in the St. James's Theatre, of the beauty we had seen, of the acting, of the staging and—always—of our esteemed and revered host— Sir George Alexander. We had been in another world. We just lived to go there again. No need to 'earnestly request' us to do that.

CHAPTER V

The Home of English Comedy

"NO, THE HAYMARKET ONLY WILL TEMPT US," SAID MR. BANCROFT, WHEN desiring to leave the small Prince of Wales's Theatre (now the Scala) which he and his wife had made so famous, for a bigger stage and field. He said that in Victorian times, but he would have said the same in Edwardian days—and he would have said the same to-day.

To-day, the Haymarket is the only theatre in London where you can recapture the feeling of Edwardian days. You can do this because the Haymarket is the only theatre left which has real atmosphere (if one excludes Drury Lane which holds the life and glory of centuries in its walls). It is the second oldest theatre in London, and it has an indefinable 'something' about it which sets it apart from all other playhouses. Redecorated and altered several times, it still retains that atmosphere which it had when the Georges reigned, when Queen Victoria held sway and when King Edward VII was known as 'The Peacemaker.' It has never changed, so it enables you to feel what an Edwardian theatre was like. It has its own traditions, it stands aloof from the modern hurry and scurry. It makes no concessions to a machine age, its air is still that of earnestly requesting that bonnets should be removed and that carriages should be called at eleven. Yet it is as up-to-date as any other theatre in presentation and equipment—if it was slow to change from gas to electricity, having made the change, it keeps apace of time. But it is gracious, courteous, and smiling—preferring its old world manners to the slap-dash methods of to-day. That is why a visit to the Haymarket is always worth while, and has always been worth while. You would never be surprised if you met, on its staircase leading to the dress circle, a man in silken attire with a powdered wig and a sword. If the occupant of the stall next to you had a frilled shirt-front and whiskers, it would occasion no amazement. If, on leaving, you stood next to a lady with a wonderful coiffure surmounted by a tiara, long gloves, a perfect dress with a wasp waist and flowing train, whilst her escort wore a high, starched collar to his dress clothes, rather short tails and patent boots with kid tops, it would seem quite in order. For of all theatres, the Haymarket combines the ages. It is still an Edwardian theatre, it is still a Victorian theatre, it is still a Regency theatre, it is still a Georgian theatre—the first George was on the throne when it arose, next door to its present site, a little theatre built by a carpenter named John Potter in the year 1720 on the site of an old tavern. And when it moved one door down the street, to be rebuilt in bigger and grander style, that old site once more became a tavern—a more modern one, with a bar which was almost a club and a restaurant which had as fine a clientele and cuisine as any in London.

The Haymarket has a list of memories which is stupendous. It has been, pre-eminently, an actor-manager's house, and more than that, a dramatist-manager's house as well. Fielding is its first great name. He is followed by the amazing Samuel Foote, actor-manager-dramatist, who got it a Patent as Theatre Royal by the sacrifice of his own leg. George Colman, Benjamin Webster, John Baldwin Buckstone (whose ghost haunts it), the Bancrofts, Herbert Beerbohm Tree, and then, in Edwardian times, the very pick of the actor-managerial combination in Cyril Maude and Frederick Harrison. For nine years those two men controlled the house and made it the very drawing-room of theatres. Something which savoured of style, distinction, and again of the best people. Not so majestic as their neighbour, His Majesty's, not quite so formal and austere as the St. James's. But something of a real English household, with a jolly, good-natured, smiling host, where you came to enjoy yourself in a light-hearted way sure of your welcome, and sure of your fare, and where you would meet the right people and never be embarrassed.

The Haymarket, in the days of Maude and Harrison, never let you down. Some plays pleased better than others, but it was a wonderfully high level, with that prince of light comedians and perfect player of 'elderly' parts, Cyril Maude, on the stage, his delightful wife, Winifred Emery, beside him, a most talented and finished actress—and the pick of the English comedy actors and actresses around them. Once again, taste, good style, and the best of everything that a theatre could supply. Again, in the staff there were the real retainers. The florid, rather long face of W. H. Leverton framed in the box office window, clean-shaven, a little quizzical maybe, but kindly and courteous and attentive to the public demand. He always wore an old-fashioned 'choker' collar, straight up and tall, with the tie kept in place by little golden clips, almost the last man to wear this neck furniture. His hair waved about his forehead from a central parting, for he parted his hair in the middle, and always about the corners of his mouth and the middle of his eyes there lurked a little smile. If you saw him coming down the Haymarket, with his characteristic, rather stiff-kneed walk, you would say to yourself : 'Ah, a family solicitor of the old school.' Yet he fitted exactly into that box office window although there was nothing apparently theatrical about him at all. He should have fitted it, too, for he sat there for over fifty years and was the doyen of the box office managers. He knew everyone. And he knew his place. He was never perturbed, never out of temper.

When Tree left the Haymarket for his 'beautiful theatre' opposite he wanted Leverton to go with him. But Leverton stayed at the Haymarket, he was already part of the fixtures. And in his later days he would actually sit in the theatre and see the play on a first night, a most unusual thing for a box office man to do. But Leverton was part of the Haymarket and part of the Edwardian Theatre, as he had also been part of the Victorian Theatre. The Haymarket seems to specialize not only in long service but long life. You cannot get really old in a place which is eternally young. That is probably why the chiefs of the theatre find it easy to retain the 'atmosphere'—for H. G. Chippendale, who was for forty-five years the electrician, the very first electrician there and who indeed conducted the change over from gas to electric light, is still alive, although retired. And why Mrs. Charlotte Pitcher, its housekeeper, kept it spotless and immaculate for over forty years, and why Charles La Trobe, a real man of the theatre who handles productions with the same skill that he handled Edwardian ones, has been at the Haymarket in charge of the stage for thirty years. And there are many in that theatre who remember the time when carriages came at eleven, and still remain the same efficient servants as ever.

During the Maude-Harrison regime the manager was Horace Watson, a great figure in the theatre managers' cavalcade. A rather severe-looking man with a firm chin and a square face, a little heavy-eyed but extremely sound and reliable. He looked what he was, a first-class business man who knew his job. He had the manners of a diplomat and the aura of a cabinet minister. There was no nonsense about him, and he was not the sort of man with whom anyone would take a liberty. He was of his generation, the epitome of the solid and substantial theatre of the Edwardian days and he ran the Haymarket as it should be run Nobody was surprised, when Frederick Harrison died, that Watson was appointed to carry on the Haymarket tradition. He did so with distinction, and with enterprise. Whilst the Green Room remained there, and it has only recently become a dressing-room, it was Mr. Watson's habit, every matinée day, to take tea with the ladies and gentlemen of the company, a delightful function which might well be copied nowadays—if there were Green Rooms in which to do it. The Haymarket never sought publicity, it always considered it a bit vulgar. It was aware of the Press, but it expected it to keep its place. It employed a Press representative, when such things became necessary to the smooth running of the theatre, but his name was not to be found on the programmes, as at more pushing and modern theatres. Mr. Watson had no personal contact with the 'boys' of Fleet Street, he lived the aloof life of the Edwardian Theatre. When Frederick Harrison died, the Press representative was told that Mr. Watson would, on this occasion, meet the representatives of the Fourth Estate and that they were to be summoned to the theatre. They came. Mr. Watson addressed them. "Gentlemen," he said, "it is with the deepest regret that I have to inform you that Mr. Frederick Harrison has passed away. Good morning." There was no 'story,' no details, no 'follow up.' But it was felt to be a very important occasion, as indeed it was. The Haymarket of to-day is lucky inasmuch as a Watson is still in charge, Mr. Stuart Watson, son of Horace Watson, a charming, courteous gentleman, who keeps the theatre as true to its traditions and atmosphere as any of his predecessors. One hopes that there will always be a Watson at the Haymarket. Then it will always be the Haymarket.

For it is a landmark of London. Its dignified frontage with the pillars facing on the Haymarket, to be seen in its full glory it must be approached from King Charles II Street. As you emerge from St. James's Square, there it is before you, a real theatre holding the essence of the London Theatre of the past two centuries secure in its keeping.

The Haymarket's highest spot in Edwardian times was that management of Cyril Maude and Frederick Harrison. Both were men of culture, of social standing, and had the best interests of the Theatre at heart. They both had ideals and lived up to them. Harrison had been at Trinity, Cambridge, and had graduated there. He was destined for the Church but here, as is so often the case, the stage stepped in and the Church lost a distinguished son. After a battle with his family he joined Frank Benson. And, indeed, he was quite a good actor. Had he lived a little longer, he would have been knighted for his stage services. But death intervened.

Cyril Maude has amongst his ancestors that knight Tracy who was one of the men who killed Thomas à Becket, and comes of a very old family indeed. His father was a soldier in the Indian Army, and he has many soldier relatives, one of them a V.C. He himself is a Londoner by birth, having first seen the light in St. George's Square, Pimlico—over eighty years ago. His school was Charterhouse. As a small boy he made up his mind either to be a clergyman or an actor. His family inclined to the Army but the stage won. Not without a struggle with relatives, who told him, as did his friends, how he would lose caste if he became an actor. But Maude could never lose caste—he is caste itself—and instead he conferred caste on the profession which, although he says he has retired—he still adorns. He had a distinguished stage career before he joined hands with Harrison at the Haymarket and he had married Winifred Emery, who was of real stage tradition, for the Emerys go back far in theatrical history and their names shine. She added much lustre for she was one of the very best actresses of her generation. Is it to be wondered at that the Haymarket was so brilliant even in the brilliant Edwardian days of the Theatre? With two men like Maude and Harrison, and the ideal leading lady, it had to be good. For both Maude and Harrison detested anything cheap or second class, it had no part in their scheme of things. Both were what is called 'gentlemen' in days when this mattered a good deal, and both put the stamp of their breeding and education on the theatre they controlled. There was nothing snobbish about it—anything less snobbish than Maude it would be impossible to imagine. And Harrison did not know what the word meant either. As an illustration of this, a young actress after a job was seen coming down the Haymarket stairs from his office smiling happily. Her friend who was waiting jumped to conclusions. "You've got the part. I can see it in your face," she cried. "No," said the smiling girl, "but he was so nice about it that I feel just as happy as if I had succeeded." That is a story which Leverton loved to tell of his chief—of a man who treated everyone, whatever their position, with the same consideration and kindliness.

It was just that these two men were of their generation, a generation which abhorred cheapness and only wanted quality. To buy an article because it was cheap, to stage a play because it was inexpensive, that was beyond their comprehension. The era of Woolworth's was not yet. One bought goods to last—one produced plays to have every chance of success—so everything must be of the best.

Maude and his wife had decided to go into management and were indeed treating for the Garrick Theatre when Harrison, who was running the Lyceum with Forbes Robertson and not doing too well, told him that if they joined hands they could get the Haymarket when Tree left it. Harrison had for some time been business manager for Tree. Maude naturally agreed, for the Haymarket was a prize worth having. So they got the theatre, did some redecorating (their tastes clashed over the wall-paper), and they started in 1896, with *Under the Red Robe*, a dramatized version of Stanley Weyman's famous novel. Harrison wanted to play 'Richelieu' in this, but Maude talked him out of it. That production began a nine years' association which gave them twenty-three successful productions. Harrison did the business side, with Horace Watson as manager ; Maude looked after the stage and played most of the leading parts. His wife was leading lady.

Twenty-three plays in nine years might seem a lot to-day, but in Edwardian days it was not usual for a play to run for a couple of years, as so many do nowadays. Despite the fact that there were fewer forms of entertainment and that 'pictures' were unknown, in Edwardian days people were not so bitten with the idea of entertainment. Transport was not so easy, young people did not earn so much money, and the 'home' had greater calls. But, on the other hand, a play could run for one hundred performances and make a larger profit than would amass to-day in three times that career. You went to the theatre as often as you could, but it was something to look forward to, not a weekly habit, except for the few mad fanatics who spent their lives there. And you looked forward to it, and remembered it always. It was not immediately wiped out by a visit to a film or another play.

That production of *Under the Red Robe* was first class. One wonders if Stanley Weyman is read to-day? He should be, for he was a grand story-teller of tales of cloak and sword—and knew all about Romance. He was a Victorian and Edwardian best seller.

Although Maude was the actor-manager of the outfit, he did not play the lead in that opening play. The hero was played by Herbert Waring and Winifred Emery played the leading woman's role. Sydney Valentine was 'Richelieu,' Holman Clark (what an actor) played 'Clon,' the dumb man, and made a terrific success, and Granville Barker played a small part. Maude contented himself with quite a little comedy part. And a pretty young actress also in the cast was Eva Moore.

The second production was by Sydney Grundy (adapted from the French). It was called *The Marriage of Convenience*. They had the great advantage of the presence of William Terriss in the cast with them. The furniture was real Louis Quinze. Holman Clark and Sydney Valentine, two real Edwardian actors of quality, remained on from the last play. Winifred Emery was, of course, the leading lady. Maude had a better part this time, and the scene was one of the most perfect 'interiors' that the Theatre, even the Haymarket, has ever seen. That was in 1897, when the Edwardian era really commenced. And its great progenitor liked *The Marriage of Convenience*. He came to see it several times. And on one of the occasions he sent for Mr. and Mrs. Maude and Terriss to come to his box. They went, and felt very nervous, for it was not so usual for actors and actresses to be sent for in those days. When Edward became King, he did so frequently. Not only did they face the Heir to the Throne, then a king in all but name, but Princess Maud (later Queen of Norway) as well. The conversation languished and they stood in a row feeling very afraid and hardly knowing what to say. They just answered questions and the position was a trying one. But Terriss, who was breeziness personified, could not keep quiet for long. He burst out, "We all hope Persimmon is going to win the Gold Cup to-morrow. Yes, sir, we've all put our shirt on it." The Prince of Wales was delighted, he roared with laughter, promised to do his best, and thereafter everyone was at their ease. For it was Ascot time, the height of the Season, when a Royal horse first past the post was an occasion which gave the whole country delight—and thrilled the Edwardian Theatre as it thrilled Edwardian London. For Edward loved and patronized the playhouse as he did the Turf.

An outstanding event in the Haymarket annals was the production of *The Little Minister*. Barrie dramatized the famous novel himself and came to all rehearsals. Sir Alexander Mackenzie wrote the incidental music. That was how they did things at the Haymarket. He refused a fee, so Maude and Harrison gave him a huge silver bowl—that, again, was how they did things. And they gave the play a wonderful cast. Winifred Emery as 'Babbie,' and she had never been better, W. G. Elliot was 'The Earl of Rintoul,' C. M. Hallard 'Captain Halliwell,' Brandon Thomas, Mark Kinghorne, F. H. Tyler, E. Holman Clark 'the Elders,' Sydney Valentine was 'Rob Dow,' Sydney Fairbrother was 'Micah Dow,' Mrs. E. H. Brooke was 'Nanny Webster,' and Cyril Maude played 'Rev. Gavin Dishart,' the Little Minister himself. The play was an enormous success and Maude was a success as a young lover, he who usually played old men and played them supremely well.

Like other actor-managers, Harrison and Maude gave their friends the public a beautiful souvenir of this play, with portraits of the cast by Phil May—and wonderful portraits too. They were contained in a red portfolio with the programme inside the cover, and included a photo of the theatre with large queues outside—playgoers waiting to see the play. Looking at it to-day, one is struck by the fact that little has changed save the buildings on the left of the picture and a certain absence of traffic in the road—probably accounted for by the fact that the photographer had tipped the police to hold it up for a moment. But when one looks at the costumes worn by those ladies and gentlemen who are 'eager to frequent' the Haymarket Theatre, one is back again in more spacious times.

Here, again, the programmes strike the note of politeness. It is not so amazingly dignified as the St. James's, but then, the fare is lighter and the personality of the leading man entirely different. But, again, there is an insistence that No Fees shall be given to the attendants, and it adds, 'The Management trusts that the public will co-operate with them in sustaining this rule.' Not so fulsome as the St. James's, you see. It informs them that the Refreshment Bars are under direct control and that all wines and spirits are of the best quality. It adds 'Fuller's Sweets.' Those white boxes with the red autograph of Fuller's thereon are a nostalgic memory of Edwardian days. You always gave the lady 'Fuller's.'

Its prices were : Boxes, £1 1s. 0d. to £5 5s. 0d. ; Stalls, 10s. 6d. ; Balcony Stalls, 7s. ; Balcony (Bonnets allowed), 5s. ; Upper Boxes (reserved), 2s. ; Pit Circle, 2s. 6d. ; Gallery, 1s. There was, of course, no entertainment tax. At the Haymarket, it will be observed, the dress circle was 'Balcony Stalls.' The upper circle (where bonnets were allowed) was called The Balcony. The pit circle and upper boxes, reserved at the humble price of 2s. 6d. and 2s., are noteworthy. This part of the house was the result of the Bancrofts having abolished the pit at the Haymarket which led to a riot on their opening night.

But that pit circle and upper boxes at the Haymarket were wonderful value. You got a comfortable seat with a perfect view, and it remains the same to-day. In the later period, just before the First World War, at the very end of the Edwardian Theatre, there was another attraction in that part of the house, for young gentlemen who frequented the Haymarket, intent on viewing the performance. That was the prettiest girl who ever sold programmes. She was dark, petite, with a delightful figure and a most devastating pair of eyes in her pretty face. She was a serious rival to the show from the young men's point of view. Despite the warning on the programme one is certain that boxes of chocolates, flowers and other small offerings were lavished upon her. Yet, with all her beauty, she fitted perfectly into the Haymarket frame, for she was demure, discreet and had perfect manners and deportment. Her name was Marjorie Jones and she afterwards went on the stage herself. The upper boxes were never quite the same afterwards, and no doubt the memory of her lingers in the hearts of playgoers, now in middle age.

Looking at that programme of *Under the Red Robe*, one is struck by the number of names apart from those already mentioned which afterwards became famous—but were then attached to small parts—J. L. Mackay, Bernard Gould, Dawson Milward, Clarence Blakiston, Cosmo Hamilton (to become a widely read novelist) and Annie Saker. Again under the actor-manager, perfect acting. A great landmark for the Maude-Harrison management was *The Second in Command*, produced there in 1900. The Boer War was still dragging along, and this was what we should now call a war play. But what a difference! For this war was still a gentlemen's war, and this play was a play about that small, professional Army of those days—those soldiers of the Queen who always won—commanded by officers and gentlemen. Perhaps they were greater gentlemen than they were officers—the amount of disasters entailed on the Army in that war would lead one to think so. But in Robert Marshall's play (and he was Captain Robert Marshall, too) war and its business became the affair of gentlemen. The uniforms were supplied not by a theatrical costumier, but by Hawkes & Co., the great military tailors. We had a glimpse of rankers, and a true and genuine glimpse, too. But all the people who mattered were officers—and most assuredly, gentlemen. It was a good play, a typically good play of its period. It was a real comedy, it held its audience, this tale of the Dragoon Guards, and the delightful little Second in Command, 'Major Christopher Bingham,' who finally won the Victoria Cross, being invested with it whilst in bed in hospital by a General Officer (and undoubtedly a minor Royalty, as played), in a scene which lingers in the memory. One can recall the lovable little man—was he not played by Cyril Maude and could he fail to be otherwise?—gazing at the Cross and saying, "I wish—I wish—I was worth it." We, his enchanted audience, knew that he was and our thunders of applause testified the same. The play ran for 278 performances. Not even the death of the old Queen, which entailed a week's closure, affected the business. What made it the more poignant was the fact that at the first reading of the play, just after the words quoted had been spoken, there was an urgent call for Mr. Maude. He went downstairs to hear the news that his uncle, Colonel Francis Maude, V.C., had just died. It was a real coincidence and a bit of real 'theatre' as it happened. What a company Messrs. Harrison and Maude provided for that play—Allan Aynesworth, Herbert Sleath, A. Vane Tempest (a real Edwardian type and fine actor), Wilfred Forster, Sybil Carlisle, Fanny Coleman and Muriel Beaumont. And, of course, Cyril Maude. Winifred Emery was not in it at first, for a happy event was expected—and that happy event was John Maude, now a great legal luminary.

What productions and what acting Maude and Harrison gave us at

E

the Haymarket, what finish and what taste ! The whole list of plays is redolent of it. *The Manœuvres of Jane*, by Henry Arthur Jones, when the author fell foul of Maude for the business he introduced into the character of 'Lord Bapchild,' and used to chase him up and down Rotten Row during their early morning rides ; lovely revivals of *She Stoops to Conquer* and *The School for Scandal* (with Winifred Emery a model 'Lady Teazle,' and Maude the finest 'Sir Peter' of his generation), a revival of *Caste* (another triumph for them both—'Eccles' might have been written for Maude), *Cousin Kate*, a delightful Hubert Henry Davies comedy, which they feared would fail but which was a triumph, with Graham Browne, Rudge Harding, Master Cyril Smith, Carlotta Addison, Beatrice Ferrar (a Haymarket stalwart), Pamela Gaythorne and that perfect actress, Ellis Jeffreys. There was a curtain-raiser too—the Haymarket was famous for them—called *The Shades of Night*, by Robert Marshall. And always a delightful orchestra played in the intervals—on this occasion discoursing Mozart, Strauss, Sullivan, Raff, and a little thing by the Haymarket's musical director, Paul Graener.

Joseph Entangled was memorable for a fire backstage on the first night, and the electric light failed. With *Frocks and Frills*, Maude touched another Haymarket high spot also with *The Clandestine Marriage*, and his perfor-mance of 'Lord Ogleby,' a play written by a man who had in his time run the Haymarket, George Colman, and the part which Maude played had been intended for his collaborator, David Garrick. But Garrick let King play it and missed a chance. Maude was superb. *Beauty and the Barge*, another big Maude success, was originally produced at the New Theatre, for the Haymarket was undergoing alterations. It transferred there, however, when the theatre was ready. This play, by Louis N. Parker and W. W. Jacobs, gave to the stage the whole of the atmosphere which Jacobs, that great humorist, had been able to get into his books. As 'Captain Barley,' the skipper of the barge, Maude was perfectly suited. This old man was right up his street ; it was a masterpiece of make-up, of observation (he studied the type at first hand) and of performance. The scene where the barge is moored alongside the water meadow will always be remembered, and so will the scene in the Inn, with Mary Brough as the typical barmaid of the period, Lennox Pawle as the Mate, and little E. M. Robson as the man who did the chucking out. Edmund Maurice was a fiery colonel—and 'what a performance,' as a comedian of note to-day would remark—Kenneth Douglas a real juvenile lead (we don't seem to have them to-day), and Jessie Bateman the ideal heroine. Just to make a full evening, Maude gave us another Jacobs play, *The Monkey's Paw*, as curtain-raiser. This, as already stated, was the ideal thriller—a piece of rising horror which was masterly. You never saw the Thing so dreaded—but through Maude's inspired performance (he appeared in both plays) your imagination gave it full colour and terror. *The Ghost of Jerry Bundler* was another Jacobs one-acter at the Haymarket, and other notable little plays were *Compromising Martha*, *The Nelson Touch*, and *Charlie The Sport*, in which those two good actors, Hugh Buckler and E. W. Tarver, both appeared.

In 1905 they did *Everybody's Secret*—with Henri de Vries, the Dutch actor, playing seven parts all by himself, as curtain-raiser in a sketch called *A Case of Arson*, and it was terrific. And then they revived *The Cabinet Minister*, the Pinero play.

In 1905 that partnership which had been so splendid and so brilliant —which had kept the Haymarket in its true sphere as the home of English comedy—was dissolved. There had been misunderstandings and rows, so very common in the Theatre, which had grown and widened until the breach was complete between the two men who made that theatre such a shining light in a shining time—and they agreed to separate. Maude went off on his own, to the Playhouse, which is another story. Harrison remained at the Haymarket. So often, when two men who have done so much together split up, bad luck comes to both. But this was not the case in this instance, which was a good thing for both of them, for the Haymarket and for the Theatre in general.

Those nine years may not have given the stage great plays—they did not. Save *The Little Minister*, few would be worth reviving. But they were just what was wanted then. For the Haymarket was the home of comedy. That note was struck with great precision by the very act drop which bore a beautiful representation of *The School for Scandal*, the model English comedy. Just to be in the Haymarket, to listen to the orchestra playing the overture and to look at that curtain was well worth while. But if the plays laid no claim to greatness, nobody cared. One went to the Haymarket to be amused, and one was. For they were all the work of men who knew their business, who had a story to tell which they told well and clearly. The plays bore no message, they made no demands on one's intellect—intellects were 'not quite the thing' then, either—they were designed to amuse, and they did. But they had wit, clarity, were written with good speeches and plenty of good, new, fresh epigrams, and were spoken by people who knew how to do it, people who were perfectly dressed, and represented their generation to perfection, just as their audiences did. There were no great flights of virtue, and no black villainy. If villain there were, it was because he was a 'cad.' And in Edwardian days—and at the Haymarket—that was villainy enough. And always there was Cyril Maude to smile, to sparkle and to display the true art of the comedian. If George Grossmith Junior gave us a song-picture (unwittingly, it is true) of Alexander, he gave us one of Cyril Maude with intent. For Grossmith was a pioneer of revue and understood topicality spiced with wit. He had a song in *The Spring Chicken* at the Gaiety, which he sang dressed as Shakespeare, and hit at the follies of the day. It was just at the time when the split between Maude and Harrison was becoming known. He sang :

> "Maude, Maude, it's 'Everyone's Secret'
> You're fine though you're not very large
> But stick to your duty for you are the Beauty
> Who steered the old Haymarket barge
> Whilst you're Our Little Minister
> We shall be there to applaud
> As neat as a squirrel
> Is our little Cyril
> Come into the Garden, Maude."

Not great verse, but a perfect word picture and tribute to Cyril Maude. The fact that no Official Recognition was ever given to him is, in the words of a great Haymarket Victorian character, 'Lord Dundreary,' "one of those things which no fellah can understand."

The Haymarket tradition went on, although one missed Maude. But then he could be seen at his own theatre, doing things just as well. Right through the Edwardian era and beyond it, the guidance of Harrison kept the Haymarket at his top level. Everyone will remember that glorious adventure which was *Bunty Pulls the Strings*—when a company of unknown Scots actors, mostly of the same family, came to that great theatre with a play written by one of them—Graham Moffat—played in the broadest of Scots dialect. Disaster was prophesied, triumph was attained. London flocked to the Haymarket for 617 performances. Herbert Trench had leased it and his tenancy was remarkable. Not only Bunty, but a striking production of *King Lear*—with Norman McKinnel as 'Lear'—struck a note of greatness. McKinnel was not a great Lear, but it was a wonderful production and there was fine acting by Dawson Milward as 'Edmund,' Charles Quartermaine as 'Edgar,' H. R. Hignett as 'The Fool,' and Marie Polini as 'Regan.' To say nothing of James Hearn and C. V. France, two magnificent actors of that time. What a remarkable array of these men the stage then possessed. They were not stars—but they were wonderful. To-day, they would have been acclaimed. Then we took them in our stride.

During this period the Haymarket presented two perfect comedies, both by that fine dramatist, Rudolf Besier. They were *Don* and *Lady Patricia*. *Don* was very nearly the perfect comedy; it even preserved the 'Unities.' It was a thrilling social problem, and perfectly played by a perfect cast which included Ellen O'Malley, Miss Granville, Frances Ivor, James Hearn, Norman McKinnel (strong, grim and arresting as a Plymouth Brother of fanatical mood intent on murder), Christine Silver, Dawson Milward and Charles Quartermaine, who played 'Don.' Nobody who saw it will forget the typical Colonel of Milward, his disgust at the length of the idealistic Don's hair, his horror at the mere mention, in mixed company, of an indecent photograph ('Have you taken leave of your senses, sir?') and his correction, when reading a letter, of the name of the writer, as to which he had been wrongly informed. That a disaster of the first magnitude threatened was as nothing to him. The point was that the name was 'Tomsett," NOT 'Thompson.' Nor will they forget the scene between Don and the supposedly outraged husband, the Plymouth Brother whom Don beat at the pistol point.

Lady Patricia was of a different texture. This was artificial comedy at its zenith. Mrs. Patrick Campbell was the infuriating but wholly charming, inconsequential 'Lady Patricia.' It was something to cherish, that performance. Two young people in the case were Charles Maude and Athene Seyler (fresh from the Royal Academy of Dramatic Art). There were superb performances irom Eric Lewis and C. V. France, who played a whole scene in which he had nothing to do but light Chinese lanterns and fix them on a tree. He had one remark only : "These little candles burn uncommon fast—uncommon fast they do," but he played that scene with such artistry and comedy that he held us spellbound for some seven or eight minutes. Real talent—real acting.

There was another Haymarket night to remember when Trench gave us *The Blue Bird*, so beautifully staged and played that stout, middle-aged, prosperous playgoers, whom one would have thought incapable of emotion, cried like children and cheered at the end as if for victory. Outstanding were Ernest Hendry as 'The Dog' and Norman Page as 'The Cat.' One will never forget 'Tyltyl's' triumphant shout of "There are No Dead" as a tense audience saw the graves open and clusters of beautiful lilies arise.

One does not forget, either, Phyllis Neilson-Terry's beautiful performance (practically her début) in *Priscilla Runs Away*, nor Marie Lohr's girlish charm and cleverness, with a background of delightful comedy from A. E. Matthews, Fred Lewis and Aubrey Smith in *My Wife*.

But there was another page of glory, contributed by Laurence Irving. He gave us *The Pretenders* and showed us that he was a truly great actor, a fitting son of his father. In this William Haviland as the 'Bishop' gave us a death scene which triumphed over death, for its memory is immortal. It was a veritable *tour-de-force* of acting. Then Laurence Irving, so soon to be drowned so tragically but so heroically, produced *Typhoon*, in which, as a Japanese, he gave us a glimpse into the real character of those people to whom we were then allied. And he gave us more. He gave us what many playgoers consider one of the finest performances the English stage has ever seen. The only word to describe it is gigantic. In spite of it all, his own magnificence and lovely acting from his wife, Mabel Hackney, Charles Quartermaine and Arthur Whitby, the play languished, and one lovely May night in 1913, when the era was drawing to its close, we went to the Haymarket to see *Within the Law*—and to witness a triumph by a young lady previously only known in musical comedy—Mabel Russell. The play was produced by Sir Herbert Tree, who took a call and made a speech. And thereby hangs a tale.

For Irving had desired to make a speech at the close of *Typhoon*, and how we clamoured for it. But all he did was to bow and touch his lips. Laurence Irving believed in *Typhoon* and transferred it to the Queen's Again a triumph and this time a speech. Stepping forward, the younger Irving said : "Ladies and gentlemen, this occasion gives me the greatest pleasure, the more so since I can address you. Our play has been welcomed again. Produced with acclamation at the Haymarket, it entered into a period of what Doctor Johnson called inspissated gloom, and I was compelled to withdraw from there to make way for a play to be produced by Sir Herbert Tree. On the occasion of its first production at the Haymarket, you were good enough to demand a speech of me. I was unable to reply to it because I was informed that it was the rule of the Haymarket that no speeches must be made from the stage. Whether that law was one of the Medes and Persians I do not know, but judge my astonishment when I read that Sir Herbert Tree had, a few nights ago, made a speech from that very stage, nor do I find that in so doing he left his coat tails in the hands of a baffled and protesting management. Now it is a fine thing to be Sir Herbert Tree and it is a fine thing to have a play produced by Sir Herbert Tree, but I think it just as fine to be the second son of old Sir Oliver. In that capacity I thank you, my friends, and so does my wife. Behind this curtain, before which I speak, are a few sandwiches and a bottle or two of champagne. If any of you, from the gallery to the stalls, care to come round and see us, we shall be proud to welcome you as our friends and the refreshment, such as it is, is at your disposal." This quite unprecedented first night speech was a bombshell. But we went round, we ate those sandwiches and drank that champagne. We congratulated Irving—more, we thanked him for his magnificent performance. And shortly after we mourned our host and the great loss the stage had suffered when he sank beneath the icy Canadian waters with *The Empress of Ireland*—on his way home. Laurence Irving, in whom burned the true genius, was always belligerent. He threatened a New York critic publicly with a thrashing—in a curtain speech—for having made remarks about the legs of Mabel Hackney. It is a good thing for the critic that Irving did not find him, for he was a man of action.

But do not think that every Haymarket first night was a triumph. Oh, dear, no! As at His Majesty's and also the other theatres, the Edwardian playgoer showed his displeasure in no set terms when the plays were not up to sample. One recalls a terrible first night—when boos, hisses and cat-calls drove a comedy called *Love Watches* from the stage, despite the fact that lovely, delightful and charming Billie Burke had come back amongst us to play the lead. We loved her but we hated the play and showed our displeasure in the usual manner of those days. We felt affronted that such things should be at the Haymarket.

There was an even worse first night than this. The play was called *All That Matters*. It had a grand cast. Norman Trevor, Lyall Swete, C. V. France, Helen Haye, Charles Maude, Fisher White, and Phyllis Neilson-Terry. It was in 1911, and it was lovely Phyllis's second part at the Haymarket. She had been so delightful in *Priscilla* that we went with high hopes. The first act was promising but long, very long. Nor had we got very far. Then, in the second act, one of those little things happened which are tragedies in the theatre. It was, of course, in the days of long skirts, when lingerie was shocking, never mentioned and never seen—except in corset advertisements. Beneath the skirt of an actress appeared a length of pink ribbon. It began to trail on the stage and increase its length. The house began to titter. It was in a long scene between that fine actress, C. V. France, and Lyall Swete (on this occasion miscast). As the scene progressed, the ribbon got longer and longer. The actress, probably unaware, could have done nothing about it anyway. The house began to laugh. It never settled down again. The play did not improve and the manners of the audience worsened. There was a scene in a cave by the seaside, with waves dashing up at the back. The gallery—and one regrets, the upper boxes, too, took sides about this. Some held that it was *The Forty Thieves* and their opponents were certain it was *Aladdin*. The point was discussed loudly and with argument, what time the players struggled on the stage. The last act was quite out of control. But one actor nearly saved the day. It was Fisher White. As an old countryman (philosophically inclined as are all stage old countrymen) he began a long speech. That was the main trouble about *All That Matters*, it was too long in every way (even the ribbon had been that). And Fisher White, in the part, had something of a catchword—'Thank the Lord.' The house was noisy and unruly when he began. He fought that audience.

He made his speech. So well did he play, with such artistry and command did he deliver that long oration, that he got the upper hand of the restless, jeering house and stilled them into silence. He had almost finished, and the house was hushed. Pausing in his flood of words, he walked up to the door. He turned to deliver his final peroration. "One more word only," he said impressively, and a quiet voice from the gods said with great distinctness : "Thank the Lord." A yell of laughter followed. It was all over. *All That Matters* was not for us—or the Haymarket.

Strife, that great play of Galsworthy's, was a Haymarket triumph and that same actor, Fisher White, triumphed in it, so did Norman McKinnel in as good a performance as will ever be seen there or else-where. But the figure which must stand for the lovely Haymarket—that theatre of all the charms and graces, which to know is to love—in the great Edwardian days, is the figure of Cyril Maude. In himself he possessed the Haymarket charm. He was of its calibre. He was perfectly dressed and groomed, one never doubted that his polished boots were made to measure. But you were not so conscious of this as you were of Alexander's sartorial splendour. For the personality of Maude was of a different kind. It sparkled crisply, it was a delight to see and to be aware of. It was the essence of British comedy, of good tone, of tradition, of country houses and the best drawing-rooms. Maude was in private life—he is still for that matter—the perfect host. So he was in the theatre. There was a touch of Victorianism about Alexander. There was the brilliance and more care-free note of the Edwardian with Cyril Maude. Here was still the real English character, but one felt that the freedom and youth which the Edwardian days brought to this country, when the shadow of eternal mourning in high places had been swept away, was perfectly expressed in this grand actor. He exuded friendliness, he does to-day. His fresh complexion, his bright, slightly protruding eyes, his dapper, neat manner, his mastery of his art was all-compelling and joyous. His dressing-room was a place which the cream of the land, of society, art and letters, delighted to visit. Great artists drew pictures on its walls, poets inscribed verse—and these things are still preserved there —for at the Haymarket change is not welcomed—tradition still holds sway. Even John Baldwin Buckstone, in ghostly form, still visits his dressing-room, as can be vouched. for by many who have occupied it. Maude has a board on which the great people who called on him wrote their names. On it is a short and plain signature, contrasting greatly with the many flourishes of others—it is just 'George P'—the man who was to be our sovereign George V. That was what Maude meant to the Haymarket. And one little thing known to few. A young, almost unknown dramatist wrote a play for the Haymarket and for Maude. It went into rehearsal but it aroused such argument and such quarrels that it was never produced there. It was a thousand pities. For that young dramatist was George Bernard Shaw and the play was, *You Never Can Tell*. Maude was to play 'William the waiter.' What a performance that would have been—and still may be—for an enterprising management longs to lure Cyril Maude from his Devonshire retirement to let us see what would be a masterpiece, a crowning glory to a great career.

And one afternoon, in 1942, on his eightieth birthday, young Mr.

Cyril Maude came up from Devonshire to play once more at the Haymarket Theatre. The great ones of the profession rallied round to give their help to make this birthday a great occasion and to aid the ever-youthful actor to raise well over four figures for the R.A.F. Benevolent Fund. Cyril Maude, at eighty, was giving performances for the troops in Devon, even playing shows all by himself, and doing volunteer coastguard duties at night. That afternoon he gave us the quarrel scene from *The School for Scandal* with Vivien Leigh as 'Lady Teazle.' Once again we saw the perfect 'Sir Peter.' Age had not withered the art of the actor. Custom had not staled his energy or his acting. He gave us a delightful one-act comedy, in which as an amorous old gentleman, he got off with a young lady in the Park, to discover she was to be the new housemaid at his house. He showed the youngsters the true meaning of comedy acting. His partner was just as perfect—she was Irene Vanbrugh. At the end, he made the perfect speech, crisp, humorous, informal, and as charming and friendly as he is himself. And the great ones of to-day stood by and applauded with tears in their eyes. Sir Kenneth Barnes gave him a vast laurel wreath, and for the first time Maude showed emotion. It was a stirring and a wonderful occasion.

Not only players had come to welcome him, but in the auditorium were his old friends, his old public. On sticks, on helpers' arms, even in bath-chairs, came these elderly playgoers to whom he had given so much happiness. They were going to have one more sight of the man they adored, and one more opportunity to applaud and acclaim him. And their youth came back to match his as they did so. It was a moving experience. One girl, born after Edwardian days, said, moist-eyed : "This afternoon, I have seen greatness." Her father replied : "You have seen my youth, my dear." It was true. For there was Maude, as young as ever, and there was the Haymarket Theatre, his frame, as young and as everlasting as ever too. Long may they both remain so.

CHAPTER VI

Daly's, the Delectable

THE NAME OF THE THEATRE MIGHT HAVE BEEN DALY'S BUT ITS GREATNESS came from George Edwardes, who built it and eventually made it an immortal landmark in London's theatreland. Except to give his name to this playhouse, run a few plays there very well, especially when Shakespearean, and give us wonderful Ada Rehan, Augustin Daly means little to the English Theatre. The whole achievement of Daly's was the work of one man, George Edwardes. He was not an actor-manager but he was a Manager, with a capital M, and he did everything but act. He gave something to those of us who remember Victorian and Edwardian days which can never fade—a memory which is golden and which, like gold, is inviolate from the rust of time. There is nothing in London to-day which can come within measurable distance of the Edwardian days of Daly's when George Edwardes—the Guv'nor—showed us what the musical stage should be like and what musical comedy really was.

It was a golden centre of a golden age. It stood in Leicester Square, then a spot enchanted. For the Square was the heart of London's pleasure-land, the centre of its night life, and its very name was a world-wide synonym for naughtiness. Leicester Square even held its own with Paris in that respect. For when Edwardian gentlemen winked and Edwardian ladies raised their hands in deprecation at the mention of the Gay City, they did just the same when Leicester Square cropped up in conversation.

To-day, it is just a square in London, cosmopolitan, a bit passé, without a thrill. Then it was very different. One's eyes brightened and one's step lightened as one strolled into it. Leicester Square, the very bullseye of the gaiety of the land. The centre of all that was masculine pleasure —for the ladies 'who frequented Leicester Square' were 'intent' on one purpose only.

Leicester Square was an adventure in itself.

But do not imagine that Daly's was a place where you saw naughty entertainments. Oh, dear no, quite the reverse. It was, under Edwardes, in the time of its true greatness, a place of dignity. It might present musical comedies but they were not naughty affairs. They were productions of great taste, and of the highest class. Their mounting, their music, their presentation, their casts, were all of the finest quality. Vulgarity could not live there. It was not allowed. 'Dirt' and salacity had no part in the fare provided—the women could charm and the men amuse without that. For a genius controlled those shows, who employed only the best workmen and who saw to it that Daly's and its atmosphere of real music with real comedy, was kept immune from smut and bad taste. It is perhaps a little difficult to describe the atmosphere of Daly's to a young playgoer of to-day. The whole place had the texture of the finest velvet, the sheen, the gloss, and the richness of pile of that material at its best. It did not blaze, it glowed. It did not compel attention, it just attracted you with the certainty of a magnet drawing a piece of steel. You could not resist it. For of its kind and of its day, it was the best in the world. It knew it, and you knew it. It was Daly's—and there was no more to be said.

Few theatres in London have had such a short life and made such a tremendous impact. It stood for only forty-four years. The reign of George Edwardes was considerably less. Yet in that time—between 1895 and 1915, when he died, in twenty short years—he did such terrific things, that he made Daly's a place of world-wide renown. He made it a theatre of quality such as may never come again. He made it an integral part of the London of its age, indeed of the whole country—for his tentacles in the shape of touring companies of real Daly's quality, took something of his theatre's charm to the great cities of the provinces. They did more, they trained and groomed the men and girls who were to become Daly's stars in their turn. But he could never send the real thing that was Daly's on tour, for that stood in those four walls in Leicester Square, a place quite unique and so distinct as to retain its shape and its atmosphere for as long as those who remember it remain alive. For the now ageing Victorians and Edwardians who pass the Warner Cinema in Leicester Square to-day, do not see it. They see that grey stone theatre, with its name in facsimile copperplate over its little balcony, its unimposing but characteristic façade, its window boxes, and if it is night, they see its soft lights, its smart audience streaming out of their carriages, its tall-hatted men escorting its silken women, its stage door with its lovely girls passing in to dazzle them from its stage— and they are blind to the whirl and clamour of motor buses, the honk and jangle of taxis, the milk bars, the girls in trousers, the hatless youths and the prevalence of American accents around them. To them, there stands Daly's—and all that it meant. A piece of gold cradled in velvet—with a great magician whose one aim it was to give them a glorious evening of taste, glamour, and twenty carat quality in a theatre which typified its age.

The history of Daly's is really the history of the Edwardian period. For Edwardes only lived one year after the commencement of the war which changed the world. Daly's went on, it is true. It did some great shows whilst his presence lingered and whilst those who knew his ways carried on. But then Big Business came into the Theatre—and Daly's did not understand Big Business any more than Big Business understood Daly's. For Daly's was a Theatre—and a Theatre is never—and never can be—business. The two do not mix. Daly's became Daly's in name only.

Augustin Daly, who gave his name to this theatre, was an American manager of courage, ideas, drive and enterprise. He had been a journalist (as had our own John Hollingshead), a dramatist and an author, and he was the foremost American manager of his time. He was the first American manager to have a theatre in London. He wanted a London home but none was available. The astute George Edwardes undertook to build a theatre, and let it to Daly for a term of years at £5,000 per annum. Daly agreed, and so the theatre was built. Although it bore Daly's name, the building, the scheme and the inspiration were all those of George Edwardes, and it is entirely to him that Daly's owed its greatness. It was opened in 1893. Augustin Daly presented Shakespeare with Ada Rehan as leading lady—*The Taming of the Shrew*. He gave all sorts of plays and many young English actors and actresses gained advancement there. He even did a play by Tennyson, *The Foresters*, which failed, but made history by being the first production to use electric light on the stage. But although a new and beautiful theatre bore his name, Daly was not destined to become a London institution himself. The clever man, the genius, who had built that theatre was waiting his chance and in 1894, Edwardes showed London Humperdinck's *Hansel and Gretel* for the first time. This was his first production in what was to be his ancestral home and it ran for 161 performances. George Edwardes knew what he was about. He struck the musical note, where Daly had played Shakespeare—it was not a case of Shakespeare and the musical glasses but Shakespeare versus musical plays, and musical plays won.

Still there was a hiatus during which such people as Duse, Ellen Terry, and Bernhardt appeared there. And with the latter came Guitry the elder. And, strange as it may seem to-day, Forbes Robertson, William Terriss and Arthur Bourchier all appeared at Daly's.

In 1895, right on the threshold of the Edwardian period, George Edwardes started that cavalcade of music at Daly's which was destined to make it glorious. He began with *An Artist's Model*, with music by Sidney Jones and a cast which contained many names which were to shine right through and beyond the Edwardian era. For that company included Letty Lind, Lottie Venne, Leonora Braham, Marie Tempest, Eric Lewis, J. Farren Soutar, Maurice Farkoa, William Blakeley and Hayden Coffin. It ran for 405 performances. The real Daly's was born. In fifteen years it only needed eleven plays—a remarkable record which speaks for itself. Although George Edwardes is dead, Augustin Daly long forgotten by the public, and Daly's Theatre itself swept away, those plays which gave it such brilliant life still sing their music to us—we remember and love them like old friends and their melody brings back our youth.

It is probable that *The Geisha* is an enduring classic in this respect—linked with Marie Tempest as 'O Mimosa San' and the music of Sidney Jones—who has far too little credit and memory given to him. *San Toy* will not be forgotten either—again Sidney Jones's music. Perhaps *A Greek Slave* is not so well remembered. Yet that was in the Edwardian Theatre period and it was Sidney Jones's music, too. Its cast was another example of George Edwardes at Daly's in his true form—Marie Tempest, Hilda Moody, Gladys Homfrey, Maggie May, Elizabeth Kirby, Letty Lind, Huntley Wright, Scott Russell, Frank Boor (to be a great front-of-house manager next door at the Hippodrome), Rutland Barrington and Hayden Coffin. Could one assemble a cast like that to-day?

Despite what is said in sneers at the Edwardian Theatre and its actor-managers—so far as musical comedy is concerned the stars of to-day hug the centre of the stage far more than they did then. They are, of course, fewer in number and the shows are much more 'personality shows' than those of Edwardes. He knew better. He had his own formula, his own method. He made a show and put the stars in it. He took care to suit them, but it was a case of the show being the all-important thing. The show carried the stars, not the stars the show. And that is why we remember them.

With Edwardes everything must be in focus. There must be no gigantic figures in the foreground with everything else tailing off in perspective. It was not enough just to give the one or two stars a couple of good numbers and dances and let the chorus jump around. The musical comedies were as carefully made and constructed as any play by Pinero ; a perfect mixture of song, music and story. There was no assault on the senses by a mass of lightly clad girls 'hoofing' and performing acrobatics. If our senses were assailed by force, it was an attack to which we readily surrendered and which carried us away, for it was done not by means of massed physical effort but by music—music delightfully written, expertly scored and beautifully sung, and it occurred at the end of the first act. For then one had a musical finale, which was the link between the fading days of light opera and the growing days of musical comedy. That first act finale was something to hear and remember. It was always encored and it was worth it. Perhaps it was the keynote of the difference between the Georgian musical show and the Edwardian. For the Georgian musical show is largely an appeal to the eye. The Edwardian musical show appealed to the eye but it appealed also and most importantly to the ear. It never forgot that it was a musical comedy. To-day one wonders why they are not called Dansical comedies or costumical comedies.

They needed no microphones at Daly's. They had never heard of them. They would not have been allowed. For George Edwardes had no use for people who could not be heard. Their place was not in the theatre. All of his artistes knew their job, were trained in it, and understood music. They were primarily singers, and, just a short head behind, they were actors and actresses. Marie Tempest, for instance, to leave him in *San Toy*, became the Queen of the Stage and was regarded as our finest actress. She was just as good an actress whilst she was at Daly's as ever she was later. And how she could sing, too. Rutland Barrington knew how to point every word, and how to sing a song with the best of them. He had learnt all that in Gilbert and Sullivan. If Hayden Coffin was a little stiff, he had masculine glamour and a delightful voice. And when he played a naval officer, as he so often did, one realized why every nice girl loved a sailor. Huntley Wright, the comedian who was Daly's fun personified, was a nimble dancer and an expert singer. And when it came to *A Country Girl* we had the greatest leading lady of musical comedy our stage has ever seen—Evie Greene. Here was a lovely woman, with a lovely voice, who was a truly accomplished actress. For she could sing, she could, if needs be, clown, and she could play a dramatic scene with the best of the 'legitimate actresses.' Her only counterpart to-day is Mary Ellis.

It would perhaps be right to place *San Toy* as the first of the Edwardian shows at Daly's. It was produced on 21st October 1899. The Victorian era outside the Theatre was drawing to its close under the shadow of the Boer War. Here was Edwardes at his best, presenting a mixture provided by masters of their arts. Here were scenic settings by Joseph Harker, and costumes by Percy Anderson. Here was a book by Edward Morton. And here was a cast which glittered—Marie Tempest, Hayden Coffin, Rutland Barrington, Colin Coop, Hilda Moody, Gracie Leigh, Maidie Hope, Scott Russell, Lionel Mackinder, Fred Kaye, Topsy Sinden, and Huntley Wright. Many playgoers always claimed that *San Toy* was the Guv'nor's best effort. It certainly ranks with the best. It challenged *The Geisha*. It had a lighter touch, an added air of gaiety. It was a piece of sunshine with all the colour of the East in it. It gave us memorable songs. Who will forget 'Rhoda and Her Pagoda'? Who will forget 'Chinee Soldier Man, he Wavee Piecee Fan' as described by Huntley Wright? And Hayden Coffin's song, 'Motherland.' We were patriotic then and not ashamed of it. Times have indeed changed. The Chinese Soldier Man of to-day waves something more deadly than a fan, and has waved it most effectively against his enemy, the Jap. Those two Daly's plays—*The Geisha* and *San Toy*—were Japan versus China. And China, as represented by *San Toy*, won, for it ran one week longer— 768 performances against 760 of *The Geisha*. A close thing, but a victory. And don't think there was no dancing. Not by any means. But this was, in general effect, a background. A company of lovely girls in beautiful dresses moving gracefully and in time to the music, nothing sensational, but just a perfect piece of the wonderful jig-saw contrived and fitted into place by Willie Warde, who knew all there was to be known about the dancing in those days and who could act and sing as well.   We always had a *pas seul*, and in *San Toy* it was given us by Topsy Sinden, the very incarnation of grace.   We had just enough, not too much.   The time was to come, after the First World War, when the chorus of musical shows were to dance the principals off the stage, when their evolutions, a mixture of the jungle and the barrack square, were the high spot, when they got the 'notices' and the glory.   That was either a lack of command on the part of the stars or a falling off in public taste— probably a bit of both.   It would never have been allowed by George Edwardes.   It meant lack of balance, it meant weakness somewhere, and that was something he would never have tolerated.

San Toy was to mark changes at Daly's.   Marie Tempest left during the run.   The battle was with Edwardes.   He wanted her, as a Chinese boy, to wear Chinese trousers.   Marie Tempest wanted shorts as being more becoming.   She won, but she left.   She was replaced by Florence Collingbourne.   And during the run, Gracie Leigh was replaced by Ethel Irving.   That replacement was not permanent, for Gracie came back to Daly's afterwards and was with Edwardes for years.   Marie Tempest never did.   But when Ethel Irving was in *San Toy* a sketch was put in, written by Harry Grattan, another Edwardes stalwart at the Gaiety.   It was a little gem of drama, with a tragic ending, played by Huntley Wright and Ethel Irving.   Both showed then that in after years they were to be stars of the straight stage as well as the musical.   It was received with great favour and applause, but when Edwardes took a second look at it, he cut it out.   It was magnificent, but it was not Daly's. He was undoubtedly right.

Daly's was indeed a training ground for the legitimate theatre.   So many of its people, both men and women, afterwards shone in straight plays—Huntley Wright, Hayden Coffin, Marie Tempest, Ethel Irving, Lennox Pawle, Sybil Arundale, Rutland Barrington, Tom Walls, to mention only a few.   No wonder we had something unique in the Daly's musical plays.   *San Toy* marked an epoch.   It added the final touch to the greatness of Daly's.   It drew all the smartest of the smart.   It made it a different theatre to any other playhouse.   And it gave the name to the most successful racehorse Edwardes ever had.

The terrific figure of George Edwardes, the Guv'nor, has dwarfed so many of his lieutenants, who were themselves giants.   And nobody has suffered more in this respect than Sidney Jones.   That gifted and essentially British composer gave us music which was truly first class.   He was always in the picture.   He was always the perfect purveyor of songs for the people who had to sing them.   His musical comedies stand in a class by themselves.   *The Geisha*, *An Artist's Model*, *A Greek Slave*, and *San Toy*, those were his Daly's plays.   They form a perfect gallery of what musical comedy should be, as regards scores.   They stand as an achievement which since his day has never been bettered, if indeed it has been equalled.   To his credit also are *A Gaiety Girl*, *My Lady Molly* and *The King of Cadonia*, but they were not at Daly's.   But Jones can stand for the music of Daly's—which was, and still in part is, the music of our lighter stage *in excelsis*.   It was certainly the best music of the Edwardian Theatre.

George Edwardes, if he had not actually invented musical comedy, had certainly made it into a coherent thing. The whole pattern and texture was woven by him. Others may have supplied the threads but he made it into a whole. And he exported it to America, which was glad to get it. Nowadays, we import wholesale, we export very little. That is because the stars come before the play. It was not so with Edwardes.

He saw no reason why musical comedy should not have a definite shape—as definite as a straight play. Many of the best songs arose directly from the plot. All were part of it. There was no sudden alteration of 'locale' just for the sake of throwing in an exotic song from overseas. No, it was home-made and it was team-made, the team working as one man. It did not need half a dozen authors and composers. It got its strength from that. It flowed smoothly and it was like the velvet which was so symbolic of Daly's. Having got his cast—and it was to all intents and purposes a stock company—his scenic artists and designers, his author and his lyric writer, Edwardes set the pattern. He lived in his theatre, he was his theatre. His offices were there. His huge room, entered from Lisle Street, was like himself. It was a sanctum where sport and drama mixed. Like all great men he had great people round him. And he knew how to use them. Money meant little to him—he was often financially on the rocks. But achievement meant much. He did not disdain detail. A man of the theatre of to-day often tells his staff : "Don't bother me with details, those are your affair." That man has never and never will occupy a niche anywhere near Edwardes. For to Edwardes, detail mattered. He knew it was the correctness of detail, in its quality and placing, which made the complete whole. A single ill-fitting dress, a pair of shoes, never escaped his notice. A halting lyric, a poor melody or refrain, a weak situation or piece of dialogue, he knew all about it. And to get it right, he would have a real expert called in, and then either pass or condemn the result. Sometimes this led to complications. Edwardes had many failings, amongst which was a bad memory for names. He would get them all mixed up. So once during a rehearsal, he said to those around him, in that curious sleepy and sometimes slightly fretful voice : "No, no, it's all wrong, it won't do at all. We must have it altered. Send for Eustace Miles." His lieutenants stared. They knew the Guv'nor's flair, they knew how he would always pick on the right man. But Eustace Miles—what did he want him for ? Eustace Miles was, in those days, the champion tennis player and the arch exponent of vegetarianism. He had indeed a restaurant in Chandos Street devoted to vegetarian food which was quite a sensation in its day. What on earth could the Guv'nor want him for ? But the duty of the lieutenants was clear. Theirs not to reason why, theirs but to do or die. The Guv'nor had spoken, he must be obeyed. So one of them went off to Chandos Street post haste. He found Eustace Miles. He told him George Edwardes wanted him urgently at Daly's. Mr. Miles was polite but unimpressed. He was very busy, he would come over some time. That would not do for the Edwardesian ambassador. The Guv'nor was waiting. He insisted politely, but, oh, so firmly, that Mr. Miles came at once. After a good deal of pressure, Eustace Miles went across to Daly's. He went in a hansom, which the lieutenant had kept waiting.

He knew no more than the other man why Edwardes should want him —but the magic of the name prevailed. They entered the stalls of Daly's. There sat Edwardes, conducting the rehearsal. He gave a glance in their direction, but took not the slightest notice of the great tennis-vegetarian. The rehearsal went on. Miles waited a little and then began to fidget. The Edwardesian emissary never left his side. "Look here," said Miles, after a bit. "I cannot wait here all day. Does Mr. Edwardes want to see me or does he not? I've come over at great inconvenience, so please ask him to see me at once or I must go." Nor could the emissary placate him. So at last this man sidled up to the Guv'nor who was intent on the business of the stage. He coughed politely. "He's here, Guv'nor," he said. "Who's here?" demanded Edwardes. "Eustace Miles," said the man. "Eustace Miles?" shouted Edwardes. "Eustace Miles? What's he doing here?" "You said you wanted him," explained the worried lieutenant. "I said so? I said so?" said Edwardes. "What do you mean, my boy? I don't want Eustace Miles. Fetch me Leslie Stiles." Tableaux. But Eustace Miles took it all in good part, for Edwardes apologized for the seeming absurdity of his underlings.

He watched every point. He missed nothing. At a dress rehearsal of *A Country Girl* he gave orders to cancel the entire last act scenery. It was not what he wanted. A new set must be made. A new set was made. It took a long time to fix on the first night, for it had only just been delivered. There was a bit of restiveness in the gallery, but the show survived to be a triumph.

Edwardes knew it all. He would show them how to act and how to sing, though he could do neither himself. Yet somehow he conveyed just what was wanted. On one occasion he showed Adeline Genee herself how to dance. It was a scene never to be forgotten by those who were privileged to witness it. She had joined the cast of *The Little Michus*, not a very strong Daly's offering, in 1905. There was a little difficulty over a few steps which led up to someone else's entrance. The great ballerina could not get it to the satisfaction of the Guv'nor. It was not that she did not do it perfectly in her own way, but it was not just what he wanted. "I'll show you, my dear," he said from his place in the stalls. All the theatre folk stood with bated breath as he made his way through the pass door. Then in his frock coat and with his silk hat crammed firmly on the back of his head, he himself showed Genee how he wanted those steps done. He could not dance one step, it was an elephant instructing a butterfly. But somehow he conveyed to the great Genee just what was in his mind. And she did it. "That's it, that's it, Adeline," panted Edwardes, "just what I want, my dear. I knew I had only to show you," and he went back to the stalls, as if nothing untoward had happened, and the theatre breathed again. For, you see, George Edwardes knew all about it. When one of his horses ran, the whole theatre was on it, stars, chorus, stage hands and call boy. He was conducting a rehearsal just before leaving for Kempton Park. It was 'Jubilee' Day and 'San Toy' was running. The theatre hoped for a tip, if not from the horse's mouth, at least from the Guv'nor's, for Edwardes was generous that way. Quite early in the proceedings he called to J. A. E. Malone, his right-hand man. "Look here, Malone," he said, "you carry on. I've got to go to Kempton Park." Everyone waited. He turned and addressed the company. "Now, boys and girls, ladies and gentlemen," he said. "I expect you want to know about 'San Toy' which is running in the Jubilee. Well, all I can tell you is that he is trying. He's going to do his best. I don't say he will win, but he is out to try. Do what you like about it. I think we shall get a place. So if you like, back it both ways. I don't think you'll lose. Good morning." To the shouts of good luck from all concerned, he took his departure. The rehearsal was held up. Everyone was scribbling out bets. They were backing 'San Toy' to win, for a place, each way, doubled up and down with other fancies—every man jack of them, players, carpenters, firemen, props, electricians, the whole of Daly's. Alfred, the call boy, rushed out with a perfect snowstorm of paper slips around him, to get the money on. And get it on he did. The company rehearsed, it is true, but its collective mind was at Kempton Park, with the Guv'nor and 'San Toy.' Upstairs in the offices, the great ones of Daly's—Emilie Reed (Edwardes's wonderful secretary), E. J. Biggs (who kept the accounts), G. Edwards Minor, the manager, Garrett Todd, the stage manager, Arthur Cohen (whose duties were never defined but who was a person of great importance), possibly Anderson from the box office with his inevitable tall hat, Blackman, the other stage manager —and, as the time came for the 'Off,' doubtless Malone himself—gathered round the tape machine which was an important part of the Daly's fixtures. The whole theatre waited on tenterhooks. Then came the result. 'San Toy' had won—at twenty-five to one. And every street bookmaker within half a mile of Daly's was completely broke when it came to paying out.

One thing only did Edwardes care for as much as the Theatre. That was the Turf. There he was just as great a figure. The whole profession followed him, and when he won, took personal pleasure. In their hearts they had a proprietary right in his horses.

If Edwardes was generous with racing tips, he was equally generous in other ways. That is why he was so often financially embarrassed. He never considered the value of money personally. And he had a soft heart for those in trouble. Sometimes he would sack some members of the chorus whom he thought had passed their prime and were not quite up to the standard he required any longer. It is perhaps not correct to say he sacked them. He never did such things himself. He would instruct Malone to do so. Malone would give those girls their 'notice.' They would be broken-hearted. They would waylay the Guv'nor as he approached the theatre and with tears in their eyes, plead their cause. Edwardes always gave in. "Tell Malone to cancel those girls' notice," he would say, "why did he sack them? I never said so. It's all a mistake." So Malone would put them back and gradually dispose of them elsewhere as occasion arose. And their admiration for the Guv'nor was thus never dimmed.

Indeed, nearly everyone who served him had a saying : "God bless George Edwardes." They said this sincerely. And they meant it. For at the end of every run, at the end of every tour, it was quite a common thing for the actors to keep the clothes which he had provided for them to wear. So when you congratulated a theatrical friend on a smart suit,

CHARLES HAWTREY (*right*) IN 'A MESSAGE FROM MARS'

MATHESON LANG AS 'JOHN STORM,' GRACE LESTER AS 'BLACK MEG,'
AND MARJORIE DAY AS 'JENNIE' IN 'THE CHRISTIAN'

BEERBOHM TREE

MARTIN HARVEY

OSCAR ASCHE

H. B. IRVING AS 'LESURQUES' IN
'THE LYONS MAIL'

he smiled, raised his hat, and said : "God bless George Edwardes."
Actors then wore tall hats and frock or morning coats when on business.
Sometimes, indeed quite often, his generosity was taken advantage of.
This was very marked when, on the last night of *Kitty Grey*, to mark its
success, he told the company they could have their props. In that last
scene was a large table covered with wedding presents, as required in
the play. They were all genuine silver articles, hired at considerable
expense from a well-known firm. But the curtain had hardly fallen
when they all vanished. The company had taken him at his word. And
on another occasion, he himself drew the line. Someone had at some
time or another presented him with a very costly and very beautiful
cabinet of oriental workmanship. It had been delivered to Daly's. It
had never got any further. Edwardes was always going to take it home,
but never did. Eventually it found its way into a dressing-room. At
that time there were two members of Daly's Theatre Company who were
inveterate card players. They would stop and play after the show with
their friends, sometimes all night long. On one occasion the session
lasted over Saturday night well into Sunday morning. Then the two
men prepared to go home. And they prepared for something else as
well. They had designs on that cabinet which stood in their dressing-
room. So they had hired a barrow on which to remove it. With infinite
labour and in the Sunday hush of Lisle Street, they got that cabinet
down the stairs and were loading it on the barrow when a familiar voice
broke on their ears. "Oh, no, boys, oh, no," it said in the unmistakable
soft drawl, "not that. I don't mind your pinching the wardrobe, I don't
mind you pinching the props ; but I draw the line at the furniture.
Put it back now, like good boys, put it back." So those shamefaced and
apologetic actors took the cabinet off the barrow and carted it back
into the dressing-room, under the amused and watchful eye of the
Guv'nor, who had come down to the theatre on some business of his
own. Not another word was said, nobody ever referred to it again. But
no further furniture-removing jobs were ever attempted at Daly's.

Two of the regulars at Daly's were Fred Kaye and Lennox Pawle.
They were a couple of amazing men. They had amazing ways—they
were characters such as do not exist to-day, in or out of the Theatre.
They were sworn friends. They would visit each other's dressing-rooms
to partake of liquid hospitality. Sometimes, after a few visits they would
conceive a dislike for the play in which they were appearing, or perhaps
they thought their parts therein were not good enough. So, leaning out
of the window, they would shout to the waiting queues : "Don't come
in, it's a rotten play." And they would feel they had done their duty.
Not that the crowd took the slightest notice. But on one occasion, they
went further. During the first act they decided that the play which they
were gracing at the moment was not such as they could endure with
composure. They both agreed on this with the greatest dignity. Their
prestige was suffering, they concluded. They must make a very emphatic
protest. So in the interval both of them shed their stage clothes, assumed
their ordinary attire and, arm in arm, walked out of the theatre without
a word to anyone. Inside, when their absence was discovered, confusion
reigned. Understudies were rapidly dressed and pushed on—the play

proceeded. It was reported to the Guv'nor. He sent for the culprits. They duly appeared 'on the carpet.' What he said to them is not known. One was forgiven forthwith, the other suspended for a short time. But it never happened again. Edwardes knew how to handle them, and he knew their value as part of Daly's as well. Nor did the frequent absences of a young and promising actor escape his notice. This young man's failure to turn up at the theatre coincided with important race meetings and sporting events. The Guv'nor had a fellow feeling. So he would send for the young man. "Oh, Tom," he would say, "I've got a little mare down at Ogbourne I'd like your opinion about. Go down there, will you, and give her a gallop. Let me know what you think." The young man, flattered and proud, would do so and make his report. "Thank you, thank you," Edwardes would say ; "and look here, don't go missing performances. It's bad, you know, it won't do at all. So don't do it, will you ? There's a good boy." And for a long time young Tom would not do it. But he achieved what the Guv'nor never did. He owned and trained a Derby winner, and his name is Tom Walls. He was part of Daly's, too.

For some years the acting manager of Daly's was George Edwards, too. He had no final 'e' on his name but it was felt that one George Edwardes was enough, 'e' or no 'e.' So the 'e'-less one became Edwards Minor, and was so called on the programmes. He was succeeded by T. J. Courtly, of whom it was said with truth, that he was 'courtly by name and courtly by nature.' When, after Edwardes' death, he went to a bigger job, his successor was Garrett Todd, who had been stage manager but was in the right succession. Mr. Todd was left a handsome legacy by an old lady or gentleman to whom he had, in his official capacity, shown politeness and attention. He retired on that legacy, a well-to-do man. It is the outstanding example of the politeness and courtesy which was part of the Edwardian Theatre. No such legacies are left—or earned —that way to-day.

Malone, the First Lieutenant, was a tall, handsome Irishman—a countryman of Edwardes himself. His father was an Army officer. He had been trained as a doctor but the stage claimed him. He was a fine lieutenant but his manner was not that of his great Chief's. He could drive, he could abuse, he could bully, and he often did. Emilie Reed, the perfect secretary, was the watchdog of the Guv'nor. A wonderful woman, she knew all the secrets—and they were many—but disclosed none. She was tact, diplomacy, alertness, watchfulness and loyalty personified. Nobody unauthorized got past her.

H. W. Anderson, in the box office, always wore a tall hat. He was never seen without it, on or off duty. He knew all the clientele, their names, rank and title. He handled thousands upon thousands of golden sovereigns in his time. Later, when he left Daly's and the pound notes were in circulation, he wilted before the changed times. The combination of the introduction of the entertainment tax and daylight saving over-came him completely. He gave up. "I've never 'paid in' in daylight before," he said tearfully to his manager. "And I don't understand this tax business." He was never the same again ; indeed, he became an agent. He had an extraordinary mind, for he wrote blood-curdling thrillers in his spare time, about desperadoes of modern highwaymen who used armoured cars and machine-guns. Also he took quantities of medicines and powerful smelling lozenges for some unspecified complaint. But that was after Daly's. The complaint was probably the altered times which he could not face.

Probably the apex of the Daly's regime under Edwardes was reached when, in January 1902, he produced *A Country Girl*. This was the most purely English show of all. Greece, Japan, China, and now Devonshire to set the seal. That first act picturing the lovely village so typical of the loveliest county, the old lodge gates, the mellow red brick, the softness, the Englishness of it all. The music this time was by Lionel Monckton, with some additions by a young man named Paul Rubens. The book was by James T. Tanner, a man who understood his job, and Adrian Ross, a scholarly gentleman whose real name was Ropes—his lyrics were little gems. He did not look the part : he was bearded and had a shock of hair and spectacles, but he had a master hand. His earlier background had been scholastic, but his right environment was the lyrical stage. Lionel Monckton, who replaced Sidney Jones, was another man whose original background was anything but theatrical. Son of a man who had been Town Clerk of the City of London, and was knighted for it, he was public school and Oxford, and had been called to the Bar. Yet as a musical comedy composer he was supreme. He knew all about it. Tall, aquiline and saturnine, with a bitter tone and acid manner, he seldom had a good word to say for other people's compositions—but that may have been because he had also been a music critic. And in his own line he was a genius, whose work was always of the highest quality.

Edwardes had made his standard before he produced *A Country Girl*, and there were people who thought it could not go on at the high level. But this English musical comedy proved that it could, and that it could even improve. The Guv'nor gave it a real Daly's cast—composed of people who were now tried favourites in that theatre. Hayden Coffin (again a naval officer) ; Rutland Barrington, an Englishman who had become an Eastern potentate, a Rajah ; Fred Kaye, an old time squire ; Willie Warde, an ancient yokel ; Gilbert Porteous (who was the villain, so far as anyone could be in musical comedy) ; Akerman May, who played a lord and looked it ; Lilian Eldee opened in the sentimental lead but, alas, she died. She was replaced, and ably replaced, by Olive Morrell ; Gracie Leigh played the 'soubrette'—and during the run the part was taken over by Ethel Irving, later to become a great actress in parts demanding tense grip and dramatic appeal. And the chief comedy role was in the sure and safe hands of Huntley Wright, who played a sailor this time. There was another great importation, Evie Greene, who played 'Nan,' a Devonshire girl, and nobody who saw her will ever forget her. It was one of the best things the British light musical stage —or any other—has ever witnessed. What a show it was, what songs, what concerted numbers, what comedy, what dresses, what dancing—what perfection. We listen with pleasure to the music still, we know 'Yo Ho, Little Girls,' 'Under the Deodar' (sung first by Aileen d'Orme and then by Maggie May), to 'My Own Little Girl,' 'Coo,' 'Chick, Chick, Chick' (the last two were by Paul Rubens). And the last-named was the ideal comedy duet, the story of the romance of two chickens, beautifully sung, acted and danced by Huntley Wright and Gracie Leigh. They had a quarrelling duet as well. And Huntley Wright gave us a masterly burlesque of the rage for the gaily uniformed so-called Hungarian bands. Also, in the second act he got into skirts and was the perfect 'Dame.' Hayden Coffin, manly, handsome and fine-voiced, sang his rousing sea song and his love duets with Olive Morrell so that every woman in the house thrilled. The finale to the first act was almost operatic. It rose to great heights—and it was encored nightly, for it was properly sung by real singers. Willie Warde gave us a real little song of Old England with an accompanying dance to match, and Topsy Sinden danced—really danced with grace and perfection of movement—no jerks, no hip waggling, no pounding of tap shoes on the stage. We liked melody in music and movement then. From Rutland Barrington came the model topical song of all time : 'Peace, Peace,' kept as up-to-date as the last edition of the evening papers—new verses nightly. And he had a clever duet, 'The Rajah of Bhong.' But it was Evie Greene who transcended everything. As the gay, careless, straight-talking and big-hearted Devonshire girl her performance was high comedy. She looked the embodiment of English beauty, as we understood it then—real femininity, not 'boyishness.' And how she sang, how she used her superb voice ! With what complete mastery of intonation, character and understanding she sang her light songs, 'Johnny Came from London Town,' in which she told us that 'You can't get the better of a Devonshire girl'—and we believed her. And in 'Molly the Marchioness,' how we revelled in the rustic maid who had married into the aristocracy, who drank champagne in a tumbler and who, when consulted as to her taste in liqueurs, declared for the lot. Despite a long and weary wait between the acts on the first night, caused by the scenery being only just delivered in the theatre, we did not mind when the beautiful ballroom scene greeted our eyes and all signs of restiveness upstairs were swept away in the cheers which hailed it and the enthusiasm at the end. That night was the first of 729 performances.

Those Edwardes' first nights were the same as the other great theatres from the point of view of names and smartness but yet they had an atmosphere of their own. He took the greatest care about the audiences. He knew exactly who was sitting in the stalls and dress circle ; there every name was scrutinized, but he let the rest of the house take care of itself. Debrett and Burke sprinkled the stalls, but the gayer and more sporting department of it. Indeed, the stalls and circle of Daly's were very like the Enclosure and Paddock at Ascot as regards personnel. For his connection with the Turf was reflected in his audiences. You would always see Lord Lonsdale, you would see the pointed long nose of W. B. Purefoy, Fallon (the celebrated trainer), Major J. D. Edwards, Harry Slowburn (the famous bookmaker), Danny Maher, the jockey (who married a Daly's chorus girl, Dora Fraser), the two Griggs, the Hartigans (one of whom married the Guv'nor's daughter). You would see 'Lucille,' the famous dressmaker, who was Lady Duff Gordon ; Sir Milsom Rees, the great throat specialist : Sir Anderson Critchett, the eye specialist ; Harry Forsyth, famous dentist—those three men looked after everyone in Daly's according to their speciality—Colonel Newnham Davis ('The Dwarf of Blood'), whilst from a box there looked on Alfred de Rothschild. And all around thronged earls, countesses, viscounts, barons, baronets and such smaller fry of wealth and position as could get seats. Edwardes, too, sat in a box—the stage box on the O.P. side. He never watched the play, he watched the audience. And anything which did not keep them sitting forward in their seats came out before the next night. The upper circle at a Daly's first night was something never seen elsewhere. It was amazing. Up there went the wealthy members of the Old Faith who could not get into the more exclusive parts. And they wore their jewels. It was just a blaze of diamonds, a glow of rubies, a glint of emeralds, a lustre of pearls. For sheer solid money it was worth all the rest of the theatre four times over. One lady, who never missed, and who was of ample proportions, was dazzling to look at. Every inch of her considerable anatomy flashed and glittered. It was the Rue de la Paix in concentrated form.

And there they all sat, stalls, boxes, dress and upper circle, all a-glitter and shining, the pit and gallery packed with joyful, enthusiastic, excited people, overjoyed to be there, the whole framed in the dark wood polished like a mirror, the quiet upholstery, the subdued lighting, which went to give Daly's its tone and quality. Their carriages had stretched for a mile, right beyond the confines of Leicester Square. For it was an Edwardes' first night at Daly's—and all London was there. Those first nights were always Saturday nights. Edwardes believed in that. It was a fetish with him. Week-ends were not the social duty they now are, people did not tear about the countryside to get a cocktail. And what week-end would have been worth missing a Daly's *première*?

No Daly's first night audience would disperse until the Guv'nor himself had taken a call. He gave the stars as many as they liked. But he was always diffident of coming forward. So the house would begin to yell, led by the gallery : "We—want Edwardes. We—want—Edwardes," and they would keep it up until the curtain would at last go up on an empty stage, and then, to thunders of applause and deafening cheers, George Edwardes would walk on, between the two chief stars, holding a hand of each. His usually fresh complexion would be pale, his self-confidence would not be apparent, he would appear very, very nervous indeed. Then he would bow to the audience, to each of the stars, shaking their hands the while, and then turning to his audience, he would bow again and the curtain would come down. He very, very seldom made a speech. And he was always genuinely nervous when taking a call. But he did so, and showed his gratitude at the acclamations of the delighted house when they streamed out chattering happily, to spread the news of another George Edwardes' triumph. But that call was for him—quite apart from the players or the play. It was the public's tribute to the man they knew was responsible for it all.

His Press notices ran to columns—always a column per paper, of careful criticism, just as if they had been Shakespeare. Well, of their kind, they were equal to it. Sometimes there was a disagreement as to quality. But if there was a weakness he put it right and people went all the same. His shortest run was *Les Merveilleuses* (196 performances). He had himself to blame—nobody could pronounce it. The next shortest was *Gipsy Love* (229) ; then came *The Count of Luxembourg* (345), *The Cingalee* (363), and *The Little Michus* (397). These represented the nearest thing he had to failures. *The Marriage Market* ran for 423 performances, *The Dollar Princess* 428, and *The Merry Widow* for 778. Ah, *The Merry Widow*. That is the play at Daly's most people remember. - That was the play which gave us the transcendent combination of the grace, the loveliness, the glamour and talent of Lily Elsie, and the charm and delight of Joseph Coyne. That was an evening to engrave on the memory in letters of gold. That was something also which we shall hardly see again in our lifetimes. It was the beginning of his Viennese importations at Daly's. It was a complete change. It introduced us formally to Lehar. It was Romance. And it was fantastic. So much has been written about it, so much is known, that it is useless to gild the lily. But it was an evening which to those who knew was fraught with drama. For it was touch-and-go for Daly's and for George Edwardes.

The Guv'nor's finances were in a bad way. His lavish spending had not kept pace with receipts. His luck was out. Something was happening which had seemingly got the better of his wondrous flair. It was Edwardes's dictum that the public knew what they wanted, and it was also true that he always seemed to know their taste. But runs had been shorter, and takings poorer. Edwardes was in straits. His flair told him that a change was wanted. So instead of China, Japan, Ceylon, Paris, England, we went to Vienna. Instead of Jones, Monckton and Messager, we had Lehar. He believed he was right, he took the chance. It was a gambler's throw, but he was always a gambler. Lehar came over for rehearsals. They dared not let him see Joseph Coyne rehearse, for Joe was no singer. When the secret that Danilo was to be played by a light comedian burst upon Lehar he was beside himself. "But he's a very funny man," they told him. "I have not written funny music," he retorted. Edwardes gave the name part to Lily Elsie. She had been unlucky, too, but the flair of the Guv'nor endured. George Graves was there ; Fred Kaye ; Lennox Pawle ; Robert Evett, the tenor ; W. H. Berry, who had joined Daly's in *Les Merveilleuses*, and was a tower of strength ; Gordon Cleather ; Ralph Roberts (to score in a study of a comic waiter) ; Elizabeth Firth ; Mabel Russell ; Daisie Irving ; Phyllis Le Grand ; and later Gabrielle Ray joined the cast to dance for our delight. And, of course, Lily Elsie and Joseph Coyne—the ideal couple ever.

So bad were things that Edwardes was little short of desperate. His lieutenant, J. A. E. Malone, knew ; all Daly's knew. For the first time they feared for the Guv'nor. Malone never left his side. They watched him, they protected him. And he took his chance. The rest is history. The singing of Evett and Elizabeth Firth, the gaiety of Pawle, Kaye and the rest of them, the inspired fooling of W. H. Berry, the genius of George Graves—for he rose to the greatest heights in *The Widow*—and, above all, the terrific fascination and perfection of Lily Elsie and Joseph Coyne—superb is the only word—they were champagne, they were Tokay—they intoxicated us, and the pleasant 'hangover' became a treasured tradition. Daly's and Edwardes were themselves again. *The Widow* ran for 778 performances, Elsie and Joe were the idols of the day, Graves's gags the talk of the town, Lehar's music on every band, on every piano organ (the broadcasts of those days) and on the screwed-up whistling lips of every lad in London. 'Merry Widow' hats were worn by every woman. The last night was as brilliant as the first. It was perhaps the most complete triumph of them all.

So once again in the Theatre, what seemed the last throw paid for all. It was the real tribute to the greatness of Edwardes, to his flair, his judgment, his genius. It was Daly's all through. It was the crowning glory of his career, this chance he took. And he knew it.

It was, indeed, the acme of the musical shows of the day, those days when we wanted melody, comedy and beauty in our theatre—and when, by the grace of George Edwardes, we got it. No wonder we older folk cherish them, no wonder Daly's set the fashion, no wonder that its girls married into the peerage. For the Edwardesian days of Daly's were the Edwardian days of the Theatre in concrete form. And they both vanished together.

CHAPTER VII

Old Drury

THEATRE ROYAL, DRURY LANE, IS NOT FOR AN AGE BUT FOR ALL TIME— at least so it is to be devoutly hoped. For if ever that building disappears and anything but a playhouse stands upon its site, London will lose one of its treasures. This link with the Restoration was great before the Edwardian days—it remains great to-day. Yet, thanks to Arthur Collins, who was its general manager, its managing director, its producer and its *alter ego* in Edwardian times, Drury Lane was destined to shine brightly in that golden era. It has had its ups and downs—but the days of Collins were glorious.

Drury Lane is especially important to those people who lived in Victorian and Edwardian years because it was nearly always the first theatre they ever entered. Or, even if they went to a local suburban theatre for their first visit, they got their first theatre thrill when they were taken to Drury Lane. For they would go there to see Pantomime in the days when Drury Lane pantomime was an institution. And, to modern minds, no doubt, that word 'institution' is the right one. For the pantomimes were great, massive, tremendous affairs, which ran for hours on end. They also ran from Boxing Day to Easter.

But that was what the Victorian and Edwardian children wanted. They were not confirmed amusement seekers. They did not have weekly, sometimes bi-weekly, visits to the pictures. They were not taken to see plays, they were not allowed to go to the music halls. So it was Christmas and Drury Lane which to them was the high spot of the year. And if it thrilled them then, it left a memory which thrills them still in their middle and old age.

Put yourself in the position of a child of those days. Try to recall what it was like. If you can do so, you will feel the years drop off you and you will be young again. It is the finest tonic in the world.

All good children of those days, if their parents were not people who disapproved of the Theatre, went at least once in their youth to a Drury Lane pantomime. Many of them went every year. Some lucky ones went to Drury Lane and the local pantomime, if any. The proviso of parental disapproval is mentioned because there were many people then who never entered a theatre, even to see Shakespeare. There were many who only went to Shakespeare and nothing else. They did this in a reverential spirit, similar to church-going. Sir Herbert Tree and His Majesty's got their money. Many Victorians and Edwardians saw a play for the first time during the First World War when their boys came home on leave and insisted on going to a show. They found it was not so sinful, not so bad. In fact they rather liked it. They became theatre-goers. That war added tens of thousands to the audiences in theatres, and the war which has just ceased will add scores of thousands more—younger people this time—who had previously only been to a cinema. So does the wheel go round.

But to the young people of the late 'nineties and the early 1900's a visit to the pantomime was their first essay in play-going. And it nearly always brought forth the theatre habit.

Suppose yourself a child in those days. You would have woken up one morning with a curious sense of well-being. You would, as you emerged from the mists of sleep, have a feeling that this was going to be a good day, that something nice was going to happen. Then you would remember. You were going to the pantomime. At once you were excited. At once you clamoured to get up. Scaling the sides of your iron cot or bedstead, which enclosed you like a roofless cage, you would be out of bed and shouting. Your nurse or your mother would come in to superintend your dressing, and your ablutions, with due regard to behind the ears. In reply to your urgent request, you would be assured that this was indeed the day on which you were going to the pantomime, so you must be good, or perhaps you would not go after all. Bad little boys were not let into theatres. Perhaps you believed that—most likely you did not—but the covert threat was sufficient. You kept a hold on yourself, jigging about to let off your spirits. You were then told not to over-excite yourself. You did not see how this was possible. At breakfast you had little appetite, your mind was on the forthcoming treat. You then learned the astonishing fact that little boys who did not eat their breakfasts were not let in to see pantomimes either. You gave this your earnest attention and consideration. Astonishing beings, these people who gave pantomimes. How would they know? But at the back of your mind you knew pantomimes were fairy tales and that fairy tales were magic—perhaps that was it. So you polished off your porridge and you ate your egg—yes, white and all—without demur in case that business of leaving the white of the egg for the prettier and more appetising yellow yolk might bar your entrance as well ; best to take no chances. You asked a few questions about what you were to see, and you got rather evasive answers. The grown-ups were not going to tell you they did not know themselves. But you learnt that Auntie May and Cousin Maud were coming with you. You were not so pleased about this. Cousin Maud was only a girl and you had hoped to show your masculine superiority by lording it over her later. However, it could not be helped. The great thing was to go to the pantomime, anyway. You were told not to run about and tire yourself out. And also told to hold yourself in readiness in an hour's time, to assume your best clothes. For you were going to an afternoon performance, and would have your lunch in London, with Daddy and Uncle James. This was better. For you lived a bit down the line, say fourteen miles or so outside London, right in the country in those days. So there would be a train ride, a bus—and there might even be a hansom cab. One never knew. So, as soon as breakfast was over, you sneaked off to the kitchen, to tell the servants—who knew all about it—of the forthcoming treat. They would enlarge on their own visits to such things. Cook, it appeared, had even been to Drury Lane and was still starry-eyed at the wonders she recounted. Such goings on, she said, nobody would believe. She drew a vivid picture of slaughter, bloodshed and murder, for the pantomime she had seen was *Bluebeard* and she dilated on the horrors. You got another thrill, but nervousness crept in. You did not know if you wanted to see people having their heads cut off, with blood all over the floor, as she gloatingly described. But she told you of the funny men and their antics, and that sounded better. She told you of the wonders of the transformation scene—"Well, there, you wouldn't believe it"— and she aroused your sympathy for the lawless, mischievous Clown, who stole and cheated, knocked down policemen, burned people with a red-hot poker—and got away with it all. That was the stuff. For you, as a child, had a streak of lawlessness in you. The hide of convention had not yet entirely closed around you and you had a fellow feeling for that clown. He broke windows with impunity, he even jumped through them, you heard, and never got hurt. That was something like. You were asking for more, when a voice summoned you to be washed again and to put on your best suit. Well, even a second washing and that best suit could be endured for pantomime. By this time a great excitement consumed you, you were burning inside and prickling all over. The outward and visible sign of this was described as fidgeting and you were told to stop it. But that was beyond you. You were invested with your best suit. It was probably a sailor suit, for we were all in the Navy in the days of our youth. It had a sailor blouse, nice and baggy, with elastic round the waist, your knickerbockers came to the knee and you had black stockings and probably button boots. But you also had a sailor collar of a true salt's design, a black silk handkerchief round your neck like a real sailor, a singlet which had to be tied around you, and probably, if you had not already lost it, a wooden whistle on a white lanyard to go into that breast pocket which bore an emblem of cross anchors. Sometimes you even had cross anchors on your arm, too. Your hair was brushed and parted, you were inspected from all angles and told to go and look at a book until Mother was ready. You went and got the book, but even the most thrilling of your Christmas presents —the latest Henty, a Ballantyne, or a Manville Fenn—failed to hold your attention. For anxiety was consuming you. You might be late. You might miss a few seconds of the wonders—tragedy, indeed. You went and peeped to see how Mother was getting on. You were told to go and sit down. Perhaps you mentioned your fear, and it was scoffed at. Plenty of time, the pantomime was not until two o'clock. Your perception of time did not allow you to space out the interval. But after what seemed years to you, your leisurely mother was ready, and there was a knock at the door. Auntie May and Cousin Maud arrived at last. Now you could at least start, but it seemed not. Auntie May had to see Mother's new hat and dress, and exclaim as she examined it. She had to have her own costume taken stock of and admired in turn. You and Cousin Maud stared at each other. There did not seem much to say, the imminence of the pantomime silenced you. Perhaps you said, in a careless and jocular manner, "What ho for the panto," and Cousin Maud nodded her head. It dawned on you that she was excited, too. She was experiencing just the same feelings as you were. That was better. So you expressed your horror of being late. You found she felt just the same. That was a bond between you and you began to talk of the matters which interested you, reciting your Christmas presents and brushing aside her list of dolls and other stupidities with your tale of swords, guns which fired caps, boxes of soldiers by Britain, Lifeguards which you could take off their horses (to find that a long peg of lead fitting into a hole kept them in place, and that, as becomes true cavalry-men, they were very bandy), or Gordon Highlanders charging in the full panoply of war, bearskins and all, or maybe a regiment of West Indian soldiers. Fine these were. And maybe some Lancers, with lances couched and movable arms.

But these slow grown-ups were ready at last. You were actually getting into your coat—a blue reefer, and assuming the round sailor's hat, the band of which proclaimed you as a member of the crew of H.M.S. *Victory*—and before you knew where you were—after a last moment hold-up because you had no 'hanky'—you were actually going out of the door and down the steps. You took a look at Cousin Maud. She had on her best as well. Rather a large hat, and a frock which by its fullness made her look a bit stout and dumpy, the skirt coming just below the knees. She too had black stockings and button boots, but she had a sash of a bright colour to set her off—her dress was silk, but the main effect of the sash, with its large bow behind, was to make her dumpier still. But you knew she thought she looked nice—and your mother had commented on the excellence of her effect whilst Aunt May had given her sundry pulls and jerks which were presumably aids to the toilet.

Now, you thought, we are off. You got a bit ahead and pulled at your mother's hand to make her get a move on. You noticed Cousin Maud was doing the same. Good for her. She wasn't so bad for a girl. But it appeared there was no hurry. Wasn't there, you thought? The aggravating calm of these grown-ups! As you crossed at the corner, your escort exclaimed at the sudden passing of a high, horse-driven butcher's cart, which dashed by at a spanking twelve miles an hour. You heard, in accents of disgust, that it was a scandal, these reckless butcher boys and the way they drove. No wonder so many people were run over! Your hand was held tighter and it was then observed that you were not wearing your gloves. A breathless search discovered them in the pocket of your reefer coat. Well, that was a relief, otherwise you might have had to go back. But you had to assume them, the greatest degradation known to a boy, because it seemed that boys with dirty hands were not allowed in theatres either. You thought, for a fleeting moment, that theatres gave themselves a few airs, but this passed away in your desire to see the pantomime.

You then found another horror awaiting you. You were not going straight to the station. Mother had to call at some shops first. This was serious. You exchanged agonized glances with Cousin Maud, who, you now observed, was wearing gloves herself and, in her agony of mind, actually biting the fingers' end. You tried this yourself, to see if it was any good. The kid tasted a bit funny but your mastication was observed by your parent and put a stop to promptly. At the butcher's, Mr. Baldwin himself served—a big, whiskered man in his blue and white striped apron with his steel hanging down it, and straw hat on head, although it was mid-winter. He took the order with respect, showed Mother just the shoulder of mutton she wanted and shouted the particulars of other things required to the young lady in the desk, who apparently wrote it all down at lightning speed. Mother asked if he would send the things up soon and he replied, "Now dircctly, Mum," and was horrified at the complaint of the swift and might-be-deadly butcher's cart from which, according to Mother, they had escaped so narrowly. He conducted them from the shop and touched the straw hat with respect. It was the same in the grocer's. Here a pale-faced man (Mr. Baldwin was as ruddy as his own steaks) with a brown pointed beard, and a very white shirt with sleeves turned up to his elbows, was deferential to a degree. He entered the requirements in a book, and kept saying, "And the next thing, please?" There appeared no end to what he could supply, and no end to what he wanted you to buy. Both you and Cousin Maud liked this shop—they were roasting coffee, too, and the smell was delicious. Huge boxes of biscuits, there seemed to be hundreds of varieties, flaunted their succulence, raisins were in huge piles, candied peel abounded, sugar was in snowy mountains, tea in great lead-lined chests, redolent of the mysterious East, jellies in packets, blancmange powders, currants in heaps, so many things to make a boy's mouth water. And in the corner of the shop was the errand boy. He glowered at you and you glowered back. You knew that boy and in your heart you feared him. You and he were sworn enemies. You saw him so often crawling along the road, his big basket slung over his shoulder, intent on a small paper book, held close to his eyes and folded over to make reading whilst walking easier. You knew it was a Penny Dreadful, probably *The Magnet*, and your heart yearned, for you were not allowed to read these books, they were banned. But this boy had them and it established a feeling of superiority. Perhaps that was why you hated him, you did not know. All you knew was that for no rhyme or reason there was enmity between you, never displayed in the presence of elders but real enough when by yourselves. He had the advantage of you— he did not care what he did or how his clothes were spoiled. Also he was older. That was why you took advantage of your own garden, with closed gates, from which to throw stones. But you found that the boy could also throw stones, harder than you—and straighter as well. He muttered when you passed him in the street, accompanied by Mother, dark threats of vengeance. But he yelled them openly at you over your gate, through which he dared not pass to the offensive. "You wait till I get yer alone—I'll sort yer, yer young imp," he shouted, and you knew he lurked in ambush. In the shop, however, he was powerless. So you said in a loud voice to Cousin Maud, "Isn't it spiffing to be going to the Drury Lane pantomime?" And you said it loudly and clearly for him to hear and suffer the pangs of jealousy. And Cousin Maud played up. Your mother told you to "Come along, dear," as escorted by the obsequious grocer she and Auntie May made for the door. You threw the errand boy a glance of defiance, you saw him clench his fist and you saw, to your amazement, Cousin Maud put out her tongue at him. She had sensed the feud. Ripping kid, after all, young Maud. The greengrocer could not do enough to please. Fruits of all kinds were ordered and these also would be sent up 'immediate' with the vegetables. Then at last you moved stationward. Now, again, the fear of lateness returned. But there was the station, and your mother took tickets and paid for them, whilst Auntie May fumbled with her purse and protested. "Two and two halves to Waterloo, second class, please," was what your mother said. She did not take returns. Here was the train and in you got. This second-class carriage was not so sumptuous and luxurious as the first class for which you had hoped, but better than the third class which had hard wooden seats and no cushions. The second class had cushions but lacked those luxurious arm-rests which moved up and down and made the first class so entrancing. You glanced at the roof, interested for a moment in the oil lamp which provided the light at night time, and gazed for a little while at the dark, turgid oil which swayed and lapped like thick dirty water in its glass container, as the train moved. If Daddy had been with you, you would have travelled first class, but women never seemed to want to spend money and do the thing well. Corner seats for you and Maud, and you looked out of the windows as the train sped townward. You played a game of your own, Battles. The smoke of the train, billowing over the meadows and the hedges, was the smoke of a great battle and you were the victorious general leading your troops to the attack. But soon the babble of Maud engrossed your attention, and you were talking and laughing together, but still a little anxious over the time. "Wouldn't it be awful if they had started before we get there?" you ask, and Maud blanches at the thought. "Oh, don't," she pleaded. Here was Waterloo in London. It is a dark, murky day with lots of noise, smoke and mud. But you all climb on to a funny omnibus which takes you over the bridge for a halfpenny each, and gives you a marvellous glimpse of the Thames into the bargain. You know the river, because you live by it, but it is different here. It is London's river, not your own. You get off at the corner of a big street which you hear is The Strand. Simply crowds of people and you would like to watch a dirty man sweeping a crossing for people through the mud of the street—a fascinating occupation, it seems to you. But you walk along holding your mother's hand tightly, past shops all brilliant still with Christmas flavour and mostly lit up. You cross the road with care when a policeman holds up what seems to you a torrent of horse omnibuses—you like the ones with the little Union Jacks— hansom cabs and huge, rumbling waggons and lorries. But here you are, going into a large building with palms and ferns and there are Daddy and Uncle James waiting to give you lunch. Joy, it is Gatti's, where you came last year. Cousin Maud has not been there. You scored heavily, for you told her to watch the big metal covers which protected the huge joints go speeding up to the roof on chains. And when she gazed open-mouthed at this delectable sight, you had a moment of triumph, for you had seen it before. A wonderful lunch, whilst the grown-ups talked of incomprehensible matters. But that urgent thought returned. It must be nearly two o'clock. Oh, crikey, would they never make a move? You and Maud looked at each other with tense, drawn faces. Tragedy loomed. At last you burst out. "Oh, Daddy, don't let's be late." "Plenty of time, old boy," said Daddy, laughing. Uncle James was serious. "Perhaps," said he, "we can't go at all. Perhaps Daddy has lost the tickets." Horror upon horror. Daddy fumbles in his pockets. Oh, if it should be true. But at last he finds them, and you can scarcely breathe with relief. And he says, "Well, these youngsters are anxious. Better be getting along." Oh, bless him. He pays the waiter, taking a golden sovereign out of his sovereign case. And the waiter seems pleased, for he hopes you will enjoy the show and mentions that he has seven like you at home. So out you go, and as if by magic, Daddy has you and Maud, one on each knee, in a hansom, with Mother beside him, and Uncle James and Auntie May follow close behind in another. Down curious streets you go, the horse's hooves ringing, and his bells tinkling, through narrow lanes, very muddy and not too clean, past heaps of refuse of cabbages, and other rubbish, where a strange smell of stale oranges and something more pungent strikes the nostrils, up a short hill and—you are there.

There it is—Drury Lane Theatre, a vast, enormous place, yet for all its immense size, kindly and smiling. It seems to actually welcome you. The hansoms are paid off and Uncle James says, "I always think it a pity the sentries have gone now." You prick up your ears. Soldiers? Where? Daddy explains that up to a couple of years or so ago they always had soldiers outside on guard. But you have no time to miss them, for you join the stream of eager, excited children tumbling out of hansoms, out of broughams (private and hired), out of four-wheelers, and scurrying up on foot. Under the great pillared portico you go, up the steps and in the huge doors. You cross a great hall, with a ceiling so high to small people that it seems out of sight, up one more step, into a sort of circular hall and there—wonder of wonders—is the very tallest and most splendid Christmas tree you have ever seen. It has its band of children worshippers, gazing at the tree, its lights, the presents adorning it, and the large fairy doll which surmounts its almost invisible top which you craned your neck to see. And on each side of the tree stand two men, silent and dignified. They wear scarlet coats with tails, black satin waistcoats, pink silk stockings, black satin knickers, and yes! their heads are powdered. You know, from the picture books, that they are footmen—like those Cinderella's Fairy Godmother created from the lizards. For you the pantomime has already begun. It is all breath-taking, wonderful. Uncle James tells you they wear the Queen's livery and you think how nice of her it is to lend them—but you must get inside—they might be starting. Daddy shows his ticket to another of these magnificent creatures, and dimly aware also of massive statues—one of whom you recognize as Shakespeare from the pictured edition of his plays at home—you are ushered by the footman up a grand staircase with a red carpet, conscious of lights, of groups of statuary and of wonder all around. You go, under conduct of another powdered head, down a long passage. He opens a green baize door, you step into what seems a small room—and there in front of you is the entire vast, mysterious and glorious auditorium of Drury Lane Theatre itself. It's all right, the show has not begun. You are in time. For ever since you came away from that Christmas tree you have been lugging the seemingly indolent and maddeningly calm elders along with you. But now, you are inside . . . "There, you see, plenty of time," says Mother. But not too much, for the orchestra pit is full of the musicians. They are tuning up, almost as good as the show itself, this is. But, thank heaven, they haven't started yet. Before you stretches the magnificent theatre. You are conscious of a sea of faces, all turned the one way, towards that huge curtain which masks the coming marvels. You are dimly conscious of red seats here and there rapidly filling up, of dark red walls, of circles with gold fronts piled one on top of the other, of bright lights and a constellation of stars somewhere in the spaces of the ceiling, which is a painted heaven to you. Somewhere up near this you hear voices shouting, "Programmes, two pence. Book of words, sixpence." It comes down, dim but distinct. If you could have a book of words you could act the pantomime yourself at home—you turn to Daddy. He is dealing with a lady in black with a white apron. And he gives you a book of words each. He gives you a programme each. You clutch yours but Cousin Maud lays hers down. "No, no," she says, "don't tell me, I don't want to know now—I want to see it all happen." You are consumed by curiosity as to what is to come but you cannot let Maud down, so you put your programme down reluctantly. From nowhere a splendid box of chocolates, of a size to match the theatre, appears between you, but at the moment you are too excited even for chocolate—and they taste so much better in places like this, too. Out of that door, only half seen in the orchestra, comes an enormous man, in a morning coat, a bit too tight for him. His nose is in proportion. The orchestra tap with their bows and their feet. The audience gives him its applause. Uncle James says, "Oh, Jimmy Glover's conducting this afternoon." A special treat, kiddies, if you only knew. This large person surveys the house with the air of a Sultan looking at his slaves. He sees some friends in the stalls, yes, he does, and he actually waves to them. They wave back delightedly and immediately become persons of some consequence in their immediate vicinity. The conductor sweeps the house in its entirety with his imperious gaze over his noble nose. Apparently it satisfies him. He taps with his baton. The musicians rise. He faces the audience, who are by now all on their feet. He waves his baton, and out swells the National Anthem, for this is Theatre Royal. When it is over, he seats himself. So does the orchestra. After a few

moments, during which he condescends to speak to the leader, he taps
his baton. The musicians are all at attention. Bows are poised over
violins, flutes and piccolos are at lips, the woodwind is ready, the brass
has its instruments in its mouths, the very harp seems to strain at the
leash. Mr. Glover glances to his left and his right. He raises his baton,
surely a magic wand. It descends and—oh, moment of exquisite bliss—
the pantomime overture crashes forth. You may hear marvellous concerts in your adult days, but nothing transcends that moment.

Was there ever music like this in the whole world? Gay, tinkling,
sparkling, dainty, and then the popular songs of the day, which the
people in the pit and gallery sing softly but gather strength as they go
on. Then snatches of classic—"Music composed, selected and arranged
by James W. Glover," you would see if you looked at the programme.
You are entranced, you are carried away. All you are conscious of is
that wave of sound, that half comprehended playhouse of glory, gold
and red, stately yet friendly—a welcoming host who will supply you
with Fairyland—surely this is Fairyland, where else? Even the faint
but distinct smell of oranges must be right—for it penetrates to your
box—and you feel it is indeed also part of the show. The music crashes
on—it rises to a crescendo. With a scurry of strings, cadenza from harp,
brave assistance from wood-wind, and noble batter of drums and blare
of brass, it finishes. You clap madly with the hundreds of other children.
But wait—oh, wait—the lights go down, the place is dim, the audience
hushes to an almost agonized silence—and then, yes, to the muted and
somewhat sinister strains of the orchestra the mighty curtain flies upwards.
The pantomime has begun.

You find yourself gazing at a scene in which terrific snakes appear
to be wriggling about all over the scenery. Gnomes are at work at
anvils, others dance about, the air is blue and sinister. Dirty work is
evidently toward. A very unpleasant creature, whom your mother
informs you is the Demon Worm, has something to say about someone
called Jack. For it now appears that you are seeing *Jack and the Beanstalk* and that you are looking at the Roots of the Magic Beanstalk, then
being made by the gnome artificers. But the Demon Worm is not going
to have it all his own way, apparently, for his declamatory, boastful
rhyming couplets are interrupted by some dainty, tripping music, a
great white beam of light shines, and a gorgeous lady enters—complete
with magic wand. Yes, it is the Fairy Queen, and her name is Fairy
Queen-Ant. She defies the Demon Worm, he in turn flouts her, but you
are rather inclined to think that she will be able to look after Jack, in
spite of all the Worm can do—and in a glorious mix-up of challenge and
riposte and blaring music, the scene changes to 'Dame Trot's Dairy.'
Here the fun begins.

Never were there such gaily dressed or more beautiful customers as
the village lads and lasses who trip in to buy milk. Never was there
such an outrageous cow as this one—so different to those cumbersome
beasts one hurries by with watchful eye, in the meadows at home, never
was there such an extraordinary fat boy as 'Bobbie,' and surely never
before such a dairy keeper as this Dame Trot. She is a small woman
with a wistful face, who does the most unusual things. She and Bobbie

have drawn excited cheers as soon as they showed themselves. Daddy says, "Ah, there's never been anyone like Dan Leno and Herbert Campbell." It is borne upon you that Dame Trot is this same Dan Leno, of whom you have heard. You have even been allowed to read a comic paper in which he is the central figure and whose strange adventures, together with his family, are the chief topic of the publication. You remember a picture of him standing somewhat forlorn, whilst his family escape through windows and doors, holding his nose in one hand and an egg in the other. But at the moment, he is not Dan Leno to you— he is Dame Trot and nobody else, the very embodiment of the quaint type of womanhood which exists in the world outside, descendants of Dickens' 'Sairey Gamp' and 'Betsy Prig' (though you have not met those great characters yet). Bobbie may very likely be Herbert Campbell, for there never was such an outrageous lad, but Dame Trot, for all the caricature, is clearly recognizable as a type. Even you have seen her, helping with the washing, or in that small village shop where they sell those sweets at eight ounces for the penny and don't disdain farthings- worths—she is real, so she is glorious. You roar at the two of them, but you love Dame Trot.

But where is Jack, the hero ? He is what you want to see. A fanfare from the band, a dashing in of the villagers so that the vast stage is crowded with hundreds of people, a quick, brisk triumphant march— and Jack is here. He is a likely lad with a remarkably well developed chest and legs. He is not like any lad of your acquaintance, with his majestic stride, his masses of golden hair, his gleaming eyes, his silken legs. You hear one of the men behind you say, "Nellie Stewart is stunning as a boy," and you are conscious of a weight upon you. It is caused by your Daddy and your Uncle James leaning forward to see better, with their opera glasses glued to their eyes. You catch a glimpse of your mother glancing with raised eyebrows at your aunt. Nellie Stewart— Jack ? Not to you. This is no man, no woman, no girl, no boy. This is indeed Jack the Giant Killer, the very personification of the hero of a Fairy Tale—having no sex and no earthly counterpart. This is the epic spirit of glorious romance, of magic, of something which is not of this world but belonging to the Realm of the Faëry, a true Hero of an Heroic Age. Later, when you are yourself taking your grandchildren to a Drury Lane pantomime, you will see a figure in this role which might indeed be a boy, which is indeed as boyish, and even more so, than many young males you have noticed. And you know that figure for the Principal Boy. But she is too near the real thing, no matter how well she plays. She is almost of this world, she is not out of, or part of, Fairyland—like the Jack you saw in your youth. You accept Nellie Stewart as your ideal Jack. And that is that.

The pantomime goes on. You go along the 'Road to the Market' where remarkable things occur. You are at the Market—if only such markets could be found round where you live ! You are in agony when you recognize the Demon Worm, who tricks poor Jack into a bag of gold which are really Beans. But you guess that the Fairy is not far off and will see fair play. You hear rumours of the Giant. Then Jack meets a truly delightful creature whose name is 'Princess Pretty 1' and he

BEERBOHM TREE AS
'MARK ANTONY,' BASIL GILL AS
'OCTAVIUS CAESAR,' AND
CONSTANCE COLLIER AS
'CLEOPATRA' IN
'ANTONY AND CLEOPATRA'

EVELYN MILLARD AND
HENRY AINLEY IN
'PAOLA AND FRANCESCA'

ALFRED BISHOP AS 'PROFESSOR GOLIGHTLY,' MARIE TEMPEST AS 'PENELOP[E]'
GRAHAM BROWNE AS 'DR. O'FARRELL,' AND KATE BISHOP
AS 'MRS. GOLIGHTLY' IN 'PENELOPE'

GEORGE ALEXANDER AND JOHN THOROLD IN 'JOHN CHILCOTE, M.P.'

falls in love with her, as he should do, and she in love with him—and how could she help it? But what is this? The note of music changes to menace, the skies grow black, innumerable crowds of people run across the stage, shouting in terror. There is a great clump-clump-clump as of heavy footsteps. Yes, the Giant is approaching. You and Cousin Maud instinctively clutch hands—the suspense is awful. And then he comes, treading down houses like grass before him. Not the whole Giant, he is too big for that, but his gigantic legs, moving with the slow relentlessness of Greek tragedy, straight—oh, horror of horrors—at the Princess, who stands petrified with fear in his path. Then, when you can hardly bear it, down sweeps the largest hand ever seen. The Princess screams, but is borne aloft, out of sight, in that mighty grip, whilst huge and thunderous laughter resounds and the Giant moves on. The broken-hearted King, Rat-Tat-Tat, whom Daddy says is Johnny Danvers, offers the traditional reward and Jack is there to claim it. He will kill the Giant and rescue the Princess. And you shout, cheer and clap in your excitement, but never doubt him.

You are back in Dame Trot's attic. Jack brings back the gold and it is found to consist of beans only, which the outraged Dame throws out of the window. And then—then you are in her Garden. The Fairy Queen-Ant tells Jack she will guard him, and all of a sudden, after she has summoned the Spirit of Spring out of the ground, before your very eyes the Beanstalk begins to grow. Up and up it soars—this is real magic. Amazing birds bearing a distinct resemblance to girls flit through the air. Your mother says they are the Grigolatti Troupe on wires—but you can't see the wires. You *know* it is magic. The Fairy Queen instructs Jack, and he, like the hero he is, starts to climb the Beanstalk. Up and up he goes, despite his Dame-Mother's protests and Bobbie's assistance to her, up and up, right into the clouds, over the 'Roof of the City,' up into 'Harmony Land' where music and song hold glorious sway and those Grigolatti Birds again fly through the air with the greatest of ease. Jack is after the Giant—the hunt is afoot and on a glorious picture, the curtain descends—and the first half is over.

You breathe again and come out of a trance. You see that Maud's eyes are bright and her cheeks pink. You feel your own burning. A glance at the box of chocolates shows that a great many have been eaten. And round the corners of Maud's mouth are suspicious traces. Mother says, "Come here, you must have your faces washed in the interval and all that chocolate off it." So you have helped yourself, too, but you hardly remember. There is talk of tea—but you only want the pantomime to start again. However, outside with Daddy and two glasses of most delicious lemonade greatly refresh you. And on your way back to the box you meet a tall gentleman with shining dark hair, a rather strongly marked nose and kindly smiling eyes He greets your Daddy by name, and your Daddy calls him Arthur. They chat for a moment, but you want to get back to the box. But Daddy says, "This is Mr. Arthur Collins, who made this pantomime, sonny. Aren't you going to say thank you?" You gaze with awe and he actually shakes you by the hand and asks if you are enjoying it. "Oh, yes, it's simply scrumptious, it's corking—it's the most wonderful thing I've seen,"

G

bursts from you. And Mr. Collins laughs and says to Daddy: "The best Notice I've ever had. That's a really sincere one. But take him back, the orchestra's just going to begin."

You bless Mr. Collins for the right sort of grown-up. You are back in the box, Maud and you are in a bond of fellowship now. Again the conductor comes out, but it is not the same man. That large gentleman whom you were told was Mr. Glover appears to have been called away. But what does it matter? The orchestra strikes up and the curtain swishes away, and there are 'The Mountain Tops.' More rows between the Demon Worm and the Fairy Queen, but your money is now on her. How could she and Jack fail? And here is Jack, finding time to sing a song whilst he toils along to meet the Giant and free his Princess. And here also are his Mother and Bobbie, and the King, all being excruciatingly funny. Here are all the rest of the people. They must have all climbed the beanstalk—but Jack went first. And then you find yourself in the Giant's Dining Room. Here everything is of a size to match the Giant, whose name by the way is Blunderboer—for there is a war on with a race of Boers somewhere in Africa, you know. Now you see what he looks like, but still you don't see him all. He is seated at his table, and his face is awful, his mouth cavernous. Slaves bear in gigantic dishes. The lid being removed, a human life-sized rabbit is revealed to view. The Giant opens his mouth, the rabbit bows and leaps into it. The mouth closes with a snap. Heavens, your eyes are starting out of your head! More slaves bring in huge bottles of champagne. The corks pop out and fly through the air, and attached to each is a lovely girl. On comes Dame Trot, in comes Bobbie, in comes the King, and glorious foolery takes place. But here is the Princess—on the table and in tears. The Dame and the rest of them have been seized by the slaves. Oh, don't say the Giant is going to eat them all? He is, his mouth opens— but at last, at last, here is Jack. He hurls defiance, he frees everyone. They rush away but he himself escorts his Princess whilst thunder rolls and lightning flashes. For the moment they are safe. You see them 'On the Road Home' and it leads to the Dame's Garden again. They have all escaped down the Beanstalk, but the Giant is coming down, too. Jack seizes his magic sword which the kindly Fairy has provided. He hacks at the Beanstalk's vast girth. You hear the Giant coming nearer and nearer. In the very nick of time the stalk is severed. There is a noise of twenty avalanches and everything is dark, for the Giant is tumbling down—down—obscuring the very sun by his size.

The lights go up again. For the first time you see the whole Giant. He lies there, dead and helpless, occupying the entire stage, big as it is. Everyone cheers and by now your hands are sore with clapping.

Everyone climbs over him. Jack delivers an oration from his chest, clasping the Princess to his ample bosom. The King bestows a blessing and even you realize that there is every likelihood of his marrying into the family by wedding Dame Trot.

Then a thoughtful soul opens the pockets of the Giant's tunic, and out of them, oh, crowning glory, comes the entire British Army in khaki (a novel sight then)—horse, foot and artillery—even nurses, whilst Jack waves a Union Jack and the whole crowded theatre goes mad with delight.

You are quite speechless. But you are hurried to the wedding breakfast. There is apparently not time to eat it, for all the characters come down, one by one and two by two, to get their meed of applause. You applaud them all, even the Demon Worm. You hurt your hands for Dame Trot and Bobbie, but when, last of all, Jack and his Princess enter, you shout as loudly as you can as well. For the Princess is a gleaming white bride and Jack is in black, shining armour, with a light blue cloak and his golden head surmounted by a jewelled helmet. They speak. They hope you have enjoyed the show. They don't speak as ordinary people but in verse. . You feel it could not be otherwise. Have you enjoyed it ? Oh, crumbs ! You stamp, you clap, you yell your approval, and Maud's shrill voice joins your own. Even the grown-ups behind you are clapping loudly, too. But it is not over. Before your very eyes the scene dissolves and Fairyland takes its place. Strange things happen, mists seem to rise, oyster shells roll on with girls for pearls, red and blue fire lights the sides of the stage and crowds and crowds of glorious people throng it. It takes shape into something symbolic, so the grown-ups say, of 'Fin de Siècle'—a phrase you are constantly hearing—it is the end of the 1800's, the beginning of the 1900's. But to you it is just the magic of Pantomime.

And before you have hardly taken everything in, the band strikes up a lively air and to a shout of "Here we are again," on bound the Clown, the Pantaloon, the Columbine and the Harlequin. Round and round they dash, in 'Ring-a-Ring-a-Roses,' the Clown smacks the Pantaloon's face, the Pantaloon returns the compliment, round and round they go again—and, hey presto, you are in Leicester Square. But what a strange Leicester Square. The Clown steals everything in sight. He bonnets policemen, he shares the swag with his old father—to whom he refers as "Father, you old fool"—by a process known to himself—which although he says "There's one for you, and one for me," he gets the lion's share. And every time the Pantaloon protests, his face is smacked. Across the stage dance Harlequin and Columbine. Sometimes the Harlequin smacks the Clown with his lath sword, to the Clown's great bewilderment, sometimes he shakes it between the legs of the Clown, to his even greater amazement. And every time the Pantaloon gets his face smacked. For the Harlequin's black mask is down. He is invisible. But if the Clown does not share fairly with the Pantaloon, he is generous to girls and boys, for he has stolen a huge Christmas Cracker which bears the name Tom Smith. This convinces you it is real and you are as yet unlearned in the sweet uses of advertisement. He and the Pantaloon pull it. It explodes and they both fall over. But out of it comes a Cupid, who gives the Clown a very big basket indeed, containing crackers much larger than any you ever saw at home. The Clown is going to throw them to the audience. Wild yells of excitement rend the air, a forest of tiny hands shoot up. Oh, will he see you in your box ? What a frightful thing if he missed you. But he does not. He comes to the side of the stage and grins. Up hurtles a cracker and you catch it. Up flies another and lands on Maud's lap. What a grand chap the Clown is. And whilst the excitement is at its height the scene changes and you are in a strange place which your Uncle James says is a Turkish Bath. Well, if that is a

Turkish bath, the sooner you go there the better. It is an improvement on your bathroom at home. The wildest things happen, towel-clad people are tripped by the Clown, burned by his red hot poker, everyone falls down scores of times, the policeman who comes to restore order is routed by Joey the Clown's poker. And the Clown and the Pantaloon blow him up until his size is enormous ! And then there is whitewash, whitewash in floods, everyone is smothered in it, and down comes the curtain on the most glorious mess you have ever seen—and, oh dear, oh dear, the pantomime is over !

Clutching your cracker, you can hardly speak. Cousin Maud refuses to move ! "I want to see it all over again," she clamours. For the moment you have wild hopes—but the next thing you know is that you are in a hansom cab again, chattering gaily, laughing, excited to the roots of your being. And you are at Waterloo and in the train. Daddy is in charge now and you are in a first-class carriage—sitting back in a state of bliss. You don't want to talk, you want to remember. You hear vaguely your elders discussing what they have seen. You hear praise for Dan Leno, for Herbert Campbell, for Johnny Danvers ; you hear of the sweetness of Mabel Nelson as Principal Girl, you hear the menfolk ecstatic about Nellie Stewart, whom Daddy says is, according to his friend, Mr. Collins, the best principal boy the Lane has had. You hear Mother say she doesn't know how she dares wear those tights, and Auntie May remark that, of course, she's an actress so it's different. You are sure it is. It ought to be. There is talk, too, of the wonderful scenery of Bruce Smith, McCleery, Emden, Harford and the rest, the ballets of Coppee, of John D'Auban and Ernest D'Auban and the costumes of Comelli. You agree when they praise Whimsical Walker as the clown. You are still clutching your cracker, and have felt something hard and promising inside. Then the men read their papers, a pink *Globe*, a green *Westminster Gazette*, a white *St. James's*, and there is a *Star*, a *Pall Mall* and *Evening Standard* and an *Echo* lying about. You look at Maud. She is very quiet and a little green. You feel a bit funny yourself. Perhaps it is the chocolates, perhaps the lemonade. Mother thinks it is all these things—and the pantomime. But before anything can happen, here is your station and, oh, delightful, here are two broughams, one for your family and one for Uncle James, Auntie May and Cousin Maud. "Kiss Maud good night," says Mother. And you do it without self-consciousness and indeed with some pleasure—for there is now a definite bond between you. You have seen your first Drury Lane pantomime together. . . .

For those who ordered their carriages at eleven, and went to Drury Lane in the autumn, there were dramas to see. Always terrific excitement, always big thrills, always big acting. Avalanches swept away riders, crimes were committed, Academy pictures were slashed, divers fought under the sea. Places familiar to everyone, Boulter's Lock, the House of Commons, the Military Tournament showed in their full glory. Trains were smashed, ships were wrecked. The autumn drama drew London, from King Edward himself, the fountain of it all, downwards. And the carriages bore well-pleased people through the flickering London gaslight along the wet roads where the very mud gleamed, back home to their mansions, or to one of the new hotels to supper. And the general impression was that Arthur Collins had excelled himself again. For Old Drury in the Edwardian days had a genius in command. In the person of Arthur Collins, it had a man who was a giant amongst giants, a master of pantomime, a wizard of the drama. A man who knew exactly what that grand old playhouse wanted, and filled it with glory, who made it glitter like the golden sovereign which was the standard of the time.

Drury Lane has had many masters, it is a storehouse of memories, but it is always vital and alive, always moving with the times. Although it contains the ages, it keeps its youth. It is a friendly, welcoming place, and it knows those who love it and wish it well. And to those who understand it, it gives great rewards. It did so to Arthur Collins, who was its moving spirit right through the Edwardian days and whose memory there will never fade. Drury Lane Theatre will see to that. But perhaps he will be best remembered by Edwardians for those great moments in their lives which he gave them when they saw their first Panto at Old Drury. For Arthur Collins himself had the heart of a child—he never quite grew up inside—that was his great secret and the secret of his greatness.

CHAPTER VIII

The Gaiety and the Girls

IF DALY'S WAS ONE LENS OF THE OPERA GLASS THROUGH WHICH YOU surveyed the musical stage of George Edwardes, the Gaiety was the other. Daly's and the Gaiety were his twins. They were alike inasmuch as they both provided musical comedy, they were alike inasmuch as they were controlled by his genius, but there was a considerable difference in texture. It was the shimmer of Gaiety silk against the lustre of Daly's velvet.

The shows at the Gaiety were lighter, more carefree, less operatic and, as its name implied, gayer, as well.

Edwardes did not found Daly's (although he built it) but he brought it fame and success after Augustin Daly had opened it. He did not found the Gaiety, nor did he build it, for that honour belongs to John Hollingshead. But when he took over the Gaiety, he transformed it as he did Daly's and made its greatness and glory. Hollingshead had lit the 'sacred lamp of burlesque,' Edwardes made that lamp into a Roman candle of musical comedy, for that form of entertainment which owes so much to him, made the Gaiety its headquarters. And it may be said to have started with the transfer there of *In Town*.

He had gone to the Gaiety in partnership with Hollingshead and when that great man retired, he took sole control. Still light opera such as *Dorothy* and burlesques held sway, still that Gaiety combination of Nellie Farren and Fred Leslie made history, but Edwardes's flair was sensing something different. He knew that in all things theatrical there is constant change of public taste. He knew that Opera Bouffe had been laid out by the Gilbert and Sullivan operas, and he knew that burlesque had almost run its course. That change came sooner than expected, owing to the death of Fred Leslie and the serious illness of Nellie Farren. But Edwardes was seldom caught napping. He had, at the Prince of Wales's Theatre, which he also controlled, an entertainment called *In Town*. It was not burlesque, it was not revue, it was almost—but not quite—musical comedy. He brought it to the Gaiety. It succeeded and it was the seed from which he was to cultivate that typical English stage form known as Musical Comedy. Whilst working out his ideas he staged other shows at the Gaiety, another burlesque called *Don Juan*, then Réjane played a season of *Madame Sans Gêne* and his last burlesque, in 1894, *Little Jack Sheppard*.

Musical comedy was ready. It made its bow in the person of a Girl, the first of those famous Gaiety 'Girls' linked always with the name of George Edwardes—and it was *The Shop Girl*. How this first Gaiety 'Girl' was welcomed ! Indeed she ran for two years. She brought a composer named Ivan Caryll (whose real name was Tilkins), she brought old favourites and new, many of them to form a stock company at the Gaiety for many years—Arthur Williams, Seymour Hicks, George Grossmith Junior, Robert Nainby, Edmund Payne, Ada Reeve. The book was by H. J. W. Dam. There were lyrics by Adrian Ross, a Cambridge professor, and additional numbers by Lionel Monckton, whose name was to be so closely associated with the Gaiety in the near future. *The Shop Girl* was followed by *My Girl* (1896), *The Circus Girl* (1896), *The Runaway Girl* (1898), and then a Gaiety Boy, *The Messenger Boy* in 1900. And after *The Messenger Boy* came *The Toreador* in 1901. That was to be the last show at the old Gaiety—afterwards they were all to move a few yards down the Strand, but that was the only difference.

It is, however, necessary to remember nowadays that there have been two Gaiety Theatres, and it says much for the strength of the Gaiety tradition that it survived the change. For there is an atmosphere about certain theatres which make a subtle change in most things when a breakaway is made. The players, the management, the authors and composers may be the same, but something has been left behind in the old home. It is, of course, the spirit of creation which has surrounded the enterprise at its birth. But that did not happen at the Gaiety. For it was the spirit of George Edwardes which was the motive force. He could create atmosphere for himself. As stated, Daly's was different to the Gaiety, and although he staged shows at the Prince of Wales's, the Apollo and elsewhere, they were again different in texture and in feeling, although the mixture was much the same. Yet all were in the main successful. This he achieved by keeping a team spirit in a theatre and getting the public attached to it. You went to see old and tried friends. It was his substitute for the lack of being an actor-manager himself; he substituted a team for his own acting, and he achieved the same result. That team spirit is the surest card in the Theatre, yet it is so seldom played to-day.

The old Gaiety stood in the Strand, as does the Gaiety which succeeded it (which is now an empty shell). It stood on what is now the island site between Aldwych and Wellington Street, and its surroundings were different from to-day. It was a small house, but a delightful one. Hollingshead had built it on the site of the old 'Strand Musick Hall' and its creation is a romance in itself, a tale of risk, adventure and ultimate success.

When Edwardes joined him, the Gaiety at once began to take new shape. Hollingshead had believed in, and had practically created, the Chorus. But he favoured leg-show and scanty, not too carefully created or thought-out attire. Edwardes glorified the Chorus and introduced glamour. When his reign of musical comedy started, the tights of the chorus gave place to the feminine allure of skirts and multitudinous petticoats which foamed around the slim, lovely ankles of his girls. Then when, on one or two occasions in the show, they showed their legs, the effect was electrical—on the male members of the audience, at least. He knew that expectation and anticipation are things of value in the theatre. He did not disclose his secrets lavishly, he believed in the peep which whetted the appetite. And he was right. For Edwardes exploited femininity and the charm of women. He dressed them with perfection of taste, and thus attracted not only the men, to gaze at the girls, but the women, to gaze at their frocks. It was one of his most successful double events.

That succession of 'Girl' productions had made the Gaiety Girl one of the sights of London. She was the typical girl of her period, she was the yardstick of comparison in the eyes of all young men. She was something that had no rival, no equal. The girls of Daly's were equally lovely, equally talented, and married almost as freely into the Peerage. But there was something about a Gaiety Girl, some magic, some allure, some mysterious glamour which no theatrical corps of girls achieved before or since. Even Mr. Cochran's Young Ladies never reached the same romantic level. The Gaiety was the centre of gaiety in London, its girls were the centre of the Gaiety. There was a sense of rapture about the whole thing, a sense of youth and devil-may-care which has no counterpart to-day. A Gaiety Girl was a Gaiety Girl, and that was that. And it made no difference if she was of the old or the new Gaiety—whilst George Edwardes was in command.

The stage door of the old Gaiety had a glamour of its own. A little time ago it was shown in a film, and old-timers who knew it gazed in bewilderment, for this large, imposing entrance, with pillars and a flight of steps was not the stage door of their youth. They rubbed their eyes in amazement. The stage door they knew was a small, obscure little place, with a sudden step down, and inside was old Tierney, bearded and the possessor of a deep and somewhat surly voice—a watchful Cerberus, but at the gateway of Olympus and not Hades. He knew everyone, he knew all the people who could come in and those who could not. He had a strange habit of repeating himself. "You 'aven't got an appointment— I say you 'aven't got an appointment," he would growl at a determined aspirant for such a thing. But he was to be placated if his unerring sense told him that the person with whom he parleyed was not up to mischief and might indeed have some reason for the call. It was this method of appeasement and the accompanying pecuniary compliment which enabled him to build a whole road of good-sized houses in a select suburb, a road which still bears his name. That alone is witness to the magic which the Gaiety exerted over its devotees. And having grasped the sovereign in his hand (or such lesser amount as had been given him) he would say, "I can't promise anything, I say I can't promise anything, but I'll see what I can do, I say I'll see what I can do." And, if he set his mind to it, there was little he could not do. For he was the keeper of the secrets, the repository of romance, he knew all that was going on, and was as silent as a mouse. No wonder he reaped a reward. The stage door at the Gaiety was a golden job in a golden time.

Right opposite the stage door, in Wellington Street, were the offices of George Edwardes, which he used as headquarters until he had his suite built at Daly's, which he then made his office. At no time did he have his offices in the Gaiety itself. Daly's was his headquarters for years.

The Toreador, the last of the shows at the old Gaiety, was absolutely typical of the Edwardian era. Also, it made considerable history, for it saw the birth of a new star, who was to be the personification of the Gaiety Theatre and a George Edwardes show for years to come. True to tradition, she too married into the peerage, which she still adorns, and 'adorns' is absolutely the right word.

The Toreador was produced on 17th June 1901. It was the Edwardian era in miniature. The first night was electric, for the Gaiety playgoers knew they would never see a first night again at this renowned house. They gazed at the curtain which had become so familiar to them, the painted act-drop (not 'tabs') which showed the white-clad figure of a girl, her long skirt held above her knees and caught across her left arm, her low-cut bodice with the crimson rose in the middle, her pierrot's ruffle and big white bow, and the white tricorne hat on her golden hair. There she stood, this painted emblem of the Spirit of the lamp of burlesque, parting golden curtains with her hands, covered in their elbow-length white gloves, against a crimson background, her right foot in its dainty, silk, high-heeled shoe just about to descend from a step, upon which lay three old-fashioned posy bouquets. How well they knew that curtain, those Gaiety-goers, how often had they sat and watched it, waiting for the joys it was to display to them. And to-night, it would descend and fall on a Gaiety first night for the last time. Not that there was any depression about—there was not ; there was only the excited anticipation of another Gaiety show and the knowledge that the Gaiety and its girls was to move on into more commodious premises a mere stone's-throw away. It was only the older brigade which had a momentary feeling of sorrow, such as one experiences when leaving a house which has been one's home for a long time.

But there, on the programme, was an array of stars, all well-loved favourites. There was Marie Studholme, that gracious beauty with the beaming smile, one of the leading queens of the postcard craze, there was Ethel Sydney, charming and clever, Florence Lloyd, Fred Wright Junior, Arthur Hatherton, Lionel Mackinder, George Grossmith Junior, Robert Nainby, Topsy Sinden and all the Gaiety small part and chorus favourites. There was also Claire Romaine, who was to play 'Mrs. Malton Hoppings' and had come out of the chorus a little earlier on, whilst *In Town* was being played. Edmund Payne, suddenly taken ill, had no understudy. An eager, smiling, cheeky girl in the chorus volunteered. "You cannot do it. You cannot look like a boy," said the scornful stage manager. But she put on Teddie Payne's wig and clothes, she ran through his lines—and she played that night. Now she had a principal part, and when she left for pantomime at Christmas (for she had developed into a grand Principal Boy), Connie Ediss returned to the Gaiety to play for the rest of the run.

And thereby hangs a tale.

It was a brilliant cast and a brilliant occasion. There was a new name on the programme. 'Cora . . . a Professional Bridesmaid . . . Miss Gertie Millar.' The Gaiety-goers wondered how she would make out. She soon showed them. This slender girl, whose slightness gave her an appearance of extra height, with the swan-like neck, and the expansive smile, showing gleaming teeth, proved that she belonged to the Gaiety. She played a small part, and she had two songs—both of which swept the house into enthusiasm. She sang of 'Cora, Cora, Captivating Cora, Just a little Bridesmaid that is all ; With a smile-ah, Walking down the aisle-ah, Captivating Cora Makes the Bride Look Small.' Not a wonderful lyric, maybe, but a tune from the master-hand of Lionel Monckton, who was to be her husband. And she showed us that she could dance as well and as daintily as we then desired. Also, you could hear every word—every syllable. And then, she warned us—addressing us as 'little boys'—to 'Take Care Now, Keep off the grass, Keep off the Grass, Such misconduct I'll not pardon, Play at your ease, but if you please, Keep Off the grass in the Garden.' It sounds all very simple now, but the music of Monckton, the atmosphere of the Gaiety, and the charm, personality and talent of Gertie Millar herself made us surrender at once. It was unconditional surrender to a new favourite. A star, and a great one, was born that night, which was to prove a major planet and light up the nights of London for years with its silver radiance. Lots happened that night. But Gertie Millar's success was the high spot.

There was George Grossmith who then, his father being alive, always had the suffix 'junior' to his name. No Edwardian ever thought of him otherwise when he dropped it. For to the young men of his period, Grossmith was the guiding light. A very clever man indeed, his stage art was nevertheless limited. He was supreme in two types. The rather inane, stupid young man about town of the period, with much more money than sense, but always a gentleman and always wonderfully dressed. And the light-hearted, wicked, daredevil, gay Lothario, the *bon viveur*, the stealer of hearts who roamed from girl to girl, dallying with all, but serious with none—the very envy of most of the men who watched him, and the embodiment of all they would have liked to have done, given the opportunity, courage and the money. He showed this side of his art in *The Spring Chicken*, in *The Girls of Gottenberg* and other plays. It was in *The Spring Chicken* that he gave us a perfect picture of man's roving fancy. He played 'Maître Babori'—a thinly veiled portrait of a famous French advocate much in the news (you see how near real revue Gaiety shows were in their emergence from burlesque), a man of great probity and steadiness in the bad weather, but——

When the autumn leaves are falling
I can hear my conscience calling
Duty waits for me
Down are all the bars between us

For the present, farewell Venus
Wine and revelry :
I abandon Jane's caresses
Kitty's eyes and Maudie's tresses
Hold me in no thrall
Though in wintertime I urge
Each melody's a perfect dirge
In Spring I adore them all.

CHORUS :
I'm fond of any blonde
If any blonde be fond of me
I'll let a sweet brunette
Come walking in my company
I'll smile a little while
On any shade of maid you bring
I'll kiss that one or this
I'm not capricious in the Spring.

That was the real Gaiety spirit and the spirit of George Grossmith who typified the Gaiety—male side. No saxophone wailed, no muted trumpets moaned funereal notes, no crooners gurgled as if drowning—instead the bows danced over the strings and the notes fell like silver bells. Grossmith was said to be a snob. He was certainly the spoilt boy of society. But perhaps he always felt oppressed by the fact that his family had produced one of the best books in our language, *The Diary of a Nobody*. He was determined not to be a nobody, but a Somebody. He succeeded.

He was a tall, thin man, with no claims to good looks. He did not sing very well, but, better than singing, he knew how to put over a song. He was not a very good dancer—true, he was light on his feet and gay, he used his elbows a good deal, but we did not want the intricate dancing demanded to-day. We wanted to see young George Grossmith as the 'Young Man of the Period'—the very fellow we should all have liked to be, the very spirit of the West End of London, in either of his phases. For he was essentially West End, as is his counterpart of to-day, Jack Buchanan. But Jack sings and dances better. He knew all about musical comedy, his judgment seldom erred. He could write a good 'book,' he could sing a good song, he could play a part and do a dance. His judgment of female beauty was superb, and in his person the male side of musical comedy reached its zenith. The Gaiety would have been unthinkable without him. And indeed, when he did leave, the glory faded. For he was the backbone of it all, so far as the stage went.

In *The Toreador* he was 'Sir Archibald Slackitt, Bart.' He made his entrance into the Biarritz scene which opened the play wearing a straw boater, a white double fold linen collar, a white overcoat with a velvet collar, a white suit, with the trousers turned up (unusual then), dark socks and brown shoes. He carried a large travelling bag, a huge brown paper parcel and a travelling rug, and he enquired of the lady he was escorting—"Have you seen the Cathedral, or will you have an ice ?" Always the gentleman, you observe. Later he donned a Panama and he very nearly made that headgear popular with the young bloods of the day. But not quite. It remained to be worn by elderly gentlemen only. He informed us that he was

> "Archie, Archie, of the Upper Ten
> The Idol of the ladies and the envy of the men
> Doesn't care a single jot
> If the girl be dark or fair or what
> For they all look beautiful to Archie."

Believe me, we believed him. And then he told us

> "Everybody's awfully good to me, don't you know
> I'm just about as spoilt as I can be, don't you know
> One day I introduced her to a friend of mine called Brown
> Well, he actually looked after her whilst I was out of town
> It was so unselfish of him, for he's married, too, is Brown
> Everybody's awfully good to me."

You observe the name 'Slackitt'? Still a link in the Edwardian days with the old dramatic form which described its characters by their names. You remember 'Squire Broadacres' and the like? And that 'Don't you know' was our English equivalent of the American 'Get me?'

It was tradition at the Gaiety that Grossmith and Teddy Payne had a duet. In *The Toreador* they sang one called 'The East End and the West.' Edmund Payne represented the plebeian and Grossmith the patrician end of the town. We yelled our approval. And Payne and the soubrette always had a duet too. On that occasion the girl was clever Florence Lloyd and the duet was called, 'You Wouldn't Get On With a Man Like That.' Both of these items were always topical, much more topical and witty than anything you will find in modern revue. There was dainty Ethel Sydney, disguised as a boy in a knickerbocker cycling suit, to sing 'The Language of Flowers,' there was clever, sprightly Lionel Mackinder as the other young man, who could also sing, act and dance. He was not so sartorially perfect as Grossmith. He also wore a boater—we all did. But he had a double fold linen collar (soft ones were still unheard of) with a striped bow tie, a light suit with a double breasted waistcoat (very smart then) and he, too, had his trousers turned up. You see they were abroad. The rules of Piccadilly were relaxed. There was handsome Queenie Leighton, to flirt with Edmund Payne and generally make trouble, there was bustling, busy Fred Wright Junior, who sang to us 'When I Marry Amelia,' as 'Pettifer,' a dealer in wild animals. What, you may ask, was such a person as that doing there? Well, a 'Tiger' had been advertised for, and he took it literally. What they wanted was a 'tiger' for a carriage, that small man or boy who in full livery, blue or black coat with its silver buttons, belt round the waist, white buckskin breeches, tall cockaded hat and shiny top boots with their turned over buff tops, sat on the box beside the footman with his arms tightly folded, elbows sticking out (most unnatural and uncomfortable) to leap up and down, open carriage doors, be handy with the rugs and generally make a show. There was, of course, as stated, sweet Marie Studholme, serene and smiling in her charm, there was Harry Grattan, as the Governor of Villaya (with song), Robert Nainby as a Spanish conspirator (with bombs), tall Herbert Clayton as the Toreador (afterwards to be a great musical comedy manager himself), Florence Ward and Olive May to dance for us, and at the beginning there was Claire Romaine as 'Mrs. Malton Hoppings.' She had a song called 'Maud, Maud, Maud. It stopped the show, this tale of 'The Girl Who

Had Studied Abroad.' It was music she had studied but the neighbours did not like it. 'They threw brickbats at her, But that did not matter, to Maud, Maud, Maud.' It was encored over and over again. But back stage there was trouble. It was an interpolated number and such things did not meet with approval. Lionel Monckton did not mind a number or two by Paul Rubens, or Ivan Caryll, and they returned the compliment, but not from others. You see in Edwardes' musical comedies the songs emerged from the stories, as in light opera. So there was a demand for 'Maud' to be removed. Against his better judgment, Edwardes gave way. This reduced Claire Romaine to tears and sent her husband, Edgar Romaine, on the war path. The decision had been taken after curtain fall on the triumphant first night. Early next morning Edgar Romaine was round at the stage door. He wanted to see Mr. Edwardes. Tierney said he was over in the offices. So over went Master Edgar. By determined bribery and persistence, he got to the door of Edwardes' office. He knocked. A sleepy, drawling voice said "Come in," and in he strode. The Guv'nor was sitting at his desk, reading the Press notices and eating a large bunch of enormous black grapes. "What d'ye want, my boy," he queried. "I'm Edgar Romaine, Claire Romaine's husband," began Edgar, "and I want to know . . ." "Sit down, my boy," said Edwardes. "You look hot. Now what is it all about?" Edgar Romaine said his piece, eloquently and at length. He pointed out the success of the song and the success of his wife in singing it. It was unfair to cut it out, he said. Edwardes listened to it all. "I know, I know," he said placatingly, "but the others don't like it." So Edgar returned to the charge. With his wife's wrongs thick upon her, he put up impassioned pleas, he raved, he ranted, he appealed, he demanded. At length Edwardes got up and approached him. Pushing the largest of the large grapes in Romaine's mouth he said, "Shut up, shut up. This grape's in your mouth and the song's in the show. Go and tell Claire, there's a good boy." And so it was. Afterwards Connie Ediss, that stout but delightful comedienne, sang the song with equal success. She was part of the Gaiety tradition, too, this clever burlesque artiste who smoked cigars, and a wonderful foil to Edmund Payne. How she could play a scene. How she could sing a song ! With what abandon she told us of the delights of a popular seaside resort, in a later play, when she asked 'Put me on the Pier at Brighton,' and how droll she was about the delights of the Durbar. And what a glory she looked in blue tights in *The New Aladdin*.

There remains Edmund Payne, the most successful low comedian of his day. Nature had conspired to make Teddy a funny man. He had a funny face, he had a funny voice with the oddest lisp, he had a funny walk and the smallest feet imaginable. Whether he was a gardener, as in *The Orchid*, a tiger as in *The Toreador*, a 'simple country gentleman on his wedding trip' in *The Girls of Gottenberg*, a Yorkshire brass bandsman, as in *Our Miss Gibbs*, a lazy man connected with a soap works as in *The Sunshine Girl*, or an English tripper in Paris as in *The Spring Chicken*, it mattered little to us. He was the fun of the Gaiety, it was his perfect setting and he its supreme exponent. He enjoyed himself hugely, and we joined in. His spirits were infectious, his grin a joy, his wink a wonder. His artistry was beyond compare. To see him with Grossmith, a perfect contrast, in their scenes and duets—to see him in difficulties, and being a comedian he was always in difficulties, to see him play scenes with Gertie Millar, or battling with and outwitting the heavyweight Connie Ediss when caught ogling the girls, was enough to make our nights gay. And they were gay nights in Edwardian times. Off stage he was curious in many ways. He was a very careful man with his money ; he would ask you in Gow's to have a drink and always say as a prelude, "Mine's a bitter." He rode to and from the theatre on a tricycle. It was healthy exercise and saved fares. When given his part in a new show, he weighed it carefully in his palm. If it felt heavy, he was wreathed in smiles ; if it felt light, he augured the worst for the show. His comedy was always 'inside the picture.' He never stepped outside the framework of the story. For although the critics of those days scoffed at the story of a Gaiety show, these were gripping and ingenious when compared with the 'musicals' of to-day. And there was wit in them, too, and no 'dirt' of any kind. Payne did not need to be vulgar, even as vulgarity was understood then. But there is not his equal to-day.

That was the team which meant 'Gaiety' to us in every sense. And behind it were the girls—the Gaiety Girls. What adorable creatures they were. There were the dancers, who were a bit smaller and livelier, and there were the show girls. These got big salaries, for they 'drew money into the house.' Young men took stalls and boxes for every night of the run, just to gaze upon them—and meet them later. Some of those girls got £15 per week, against the two pounds of the ordinary chorus, and they were cheap at the price. They travelled in hansom cabs, they dressed expensively—people who were nasty said beyond their purses ; they wore ropes of pearls and their fingers flashed with rings. Brooches adorned them, bracelets dangled and gleamed on their wrists, lovely furs wrapped them in the cold weather. But there was a cut about every Gaiety Girl which marked her as something apart. Her successors (there are no Gaiety Girls now) all dress alike, a hard-working, keen set of young ladies from the suburbs, who travel up by bus or tube and scurry home at nights. They have to keep fit, for they do things in the show undreamed of by the Gaiety Girls, who mostly had to look and be lovely and graceful—and sing. The chorus girl of to-day seldom sups at Romanos or Rules and is seldom, if ever, driven home by a wildly excited young man in evening dress and tails. More often than not she goes home to her husband and children. And good luck to her, for she is a skilled and trained artiste and is just as pretty as were her forebears. But she lacks their individuality, their remoteness, their aura of being of another world. No young sprig of nobility, no young man about town, spends the day with whirling head because she has promised to sup with him. She has none of the frou-frou of skirts, the swirl of petticoats, the allure of a slim ankle shown for a second beneath a foam of white lace. More often than not she wears trousers.

So the charm of the femininity of those Gaiety Girls will never, one thinks, be known again by the generations to follow the Edwardians. It is a memory for the older to cherish, something which, when conjured up, brings back the joy of those wonderful times when nights were times of pleasure and we could go to the Gaiety.

The Toreador succeeded wildly and ran until 1903, when the old Gaiety closed for the last time. But the end was wonderful. For George Edwardes staged a show called *The Linkman*, which was a revue of the Gaiety's history cleverly written by George Grossmith. All the old stars who were still living and who could get there turned up. Sir Henry Irving himself spoke from its stage—as he had played there when a young man. The wonderful history of the place came to life once more and its newest star, Gertie Millar, was linked with those who had gone before her.

Amidst indescribable scenes the last curtain fell, and we left the Gaiety for the last time. That home of brightness—and it was quite in keeping that it had been the first theatre to have electric lights outside it, in 1878—became a Pandora's box of memories ; but the memories did not die. They betook themselves to a new and handsome theatre almost next door, standing on a corner, imposing, and yet not over-powering—a new Gaiety worthy of the tradition, if some few of the old hands poked fun at it. The stage door was no longer a dingy gateway to romance, but a large and airy opening on a main road, Aldwych, boldly facing the Waldorf Hotel, then new and very smart indeed. All could see the Gaiety Girls go in and out. But it made no difference. The young men were there, for the stage door Johnnie was still with us. At the entrance, in charge of the secrets, sat Jupp, the new Cerberus. A different type of man to old Tierney. He had been a soldier with service in India, he had been a policeman with service in London, but he was the stage door keeper who was typical of his class. Dark, swarthy, and heavily moustached, with sweeping hair, in his somewhat pouched but keen eyes there was a twinkle. His manners were good, if hearty, he had tact and diplomacy and a nice sense of the fitness of things. He knew just how much deference to show, just when to unbend, just when to be severe. He could get rid of an unwelcome suitor, he could send happily away the young man whose appointment with a forgetful fair one had clashed with a wealthier admirer, he knew all the secrets and all the romance. And he knew the Gaiety bar next door. He must have taken thousands of pounds, but he left no street named after him. When he died, he was no longer at the Gaiety, but at the Duke of York's. The golden days had gone and had left him nothing tangible at all. But in his day he was one of the best known men in London.

The Gaiety addicts were not long homeless, London was not long without its beloved Gaiety Girls, its idolized stock company of stars and regulars. For Edwardes had his new theatre open on 26th October 1903 (the old one had closed in the February) and that opening night was one of the smartest and most exciting occasions a theatre has ever known. Everyone wanted to be there and everyone who was anyone was there. The pittites and gallery boys and girls waited all day in heavy rain. From errand boys and shop girls (had the Gaiety not glorified them ?) to earls and countesses, butcher boys to barons, dust-men to dukes—there they were ready to welcome back the Gaiety again, in its new home. And more than that, King Edward VII and Queen Alexandra graced the proceedings from the Royal Box. Royalty at a première was something entirely new ; but then, this was the new Gaiety ! And the Gaiety-goers in the cheaper parts who had stood since five a.m. (hundreds having failed to get inside) never thought of their dampness and their approaching colds. No, if they were hoarse, it was with cheering. That was what the Gaiety meant to the Edwardians.

They liked the new house. There, on the act drop, stood the Gaiety Girl, not quite so flamboyant as her predecessor at the old place, for instead of white, she was tastefully dressed in revealing black, through which her limbs shimmered. But she held aloft the Sacred Lamp still, and, owing to the progress of electric lighting, that lamp actually glowed of itself. So she stood until the end, until just before the Second Great War, when London lost both its gaiety and its Gaiety.

But those days were undreamed of in 1903. What would the show be like ? *The Toreador* had broken the succession of Girls, and this time the name was floral. It was *The Orchid*. The programme had all the old names on it, but there was one new one. Well, the stars were born at the Gaiety. Perhaps the theatre's rebirth would see the birth of a new star as well. It did.

There was Gertie Millar, a leading lady now, and justly so. There was Marie Studholme, there was Connie Ediss, there was Lionel Mackinder, Fred Wright, Robert Nainby, Arthur Hatherton (made up to exactly resemble Joe Chamberlain, orchid, eyeglass, sharp nose and all), there was Hilda Jacobsen, Olive May, Kitty Mason, and all the rest. And there was 'The Hon. Guy Scrymgeour' in the elegant person of George Grossmith (in brown morning coat and topper), and a quaint little gardener named Meakin, who was Edmund Payne. It was all for our delight. But the new name on the programme was attached to the character of 'Thisbe,' described as 'The Minister's Private Secretary,' and the new name proclaimed itself to be Gabrielle Ray.ʳ These were before the days of the publicity agent and we knew nothing about her. It was said that she had been one of the girls with the Guv'nor's touring companies, which were the glasshouses where the stars were raised. The Minister, by the way, was Arthur Hatherton, a Gaiety regular, who was 'The Minister of Commerce.' No such rank in the Cabinet, of course, but what did we care ? He told us that he was pushful, pushful, oh, so very pushful, and that he pursued the pathway of a pushful perseverance. As he also informed us that his fortune was based on a new kind of screw which fastened by the way you pushed it in, we had no doubt in spotting his prototype. If we had, his make-up proclaimed it. For these were the days when Joe Chamberlain was beginning the cry of 'Tariff Reform,' when you either worshipped Joe or reviled him. But we were also agog to see this pushful Minister's Private Secretary. And then, she burst upon us. She came into our sight, a demure figure in a Quaker grey gown, with a white lace collar and an accordion pleated skirt. A grey confection of a picture hat rested on her glorious golden head, and her face, which was prettier than any we had ever seen on a chocolate box, had large and sparkling blue eyes. In a tiny voice she told us

> "I am the Minister's Private Secretary
> Always exceedingly circumspect and wary
> If he should order iced champagne
> Surely nobody can complain
> Of the Minister's charming private secretary."

And then—she danced. Danced? It was not dancing. It was a piece of silvery thistledown floating in a sunbeam. She did not touch the stage with her dainty feet, she was blown by the breeze, hither and thither. She was grace, she was allure, she was another Gaiety incarnation. And then she kicked. Up went her leg, up went her little shoe far above that golden head, without any visible effort, just as the wind might blow a spray of apple blossom or honeysuckle. And her kick knocked us for six, we acclaimed with all our power. There was a new star in the new Gaiety. Seldom has anyone fresh so completely danced into prominence. In the space of a few days her face was to be everywhere, to gaze at us from magazines, from photographers, from the innumerable picture postcards which we bought so eagerly, stuck in our albums and sent to our friends. Young men and girls competed to see who could get the most postcards of Gabrielle Ray—and it was a breathless hunt— for they poured forth daily, or so it seemed.

Payne and Grossmith sang us their duet. They were Unemployed Workmen. The unemployed were then a joke. We considered them the unemployables. These were prosperous days and there was work for all (or so we believed). And certain it is that the unemployed were few. But the Gaiety was no place for seriousness, nor did Payne and Grossmith take this seriously.

> "When will justice be done to England?
> When will they allow us to earn our own bread
>   It ain't much enjoyment
>   To ask for employment
> And only get work instead."

they chanted whilst we cheered.

Gertie Millar showed us now that she was truly great. Her dancing, her singing—and her acting—were of the highest class. Here was a real star emerged from the small professional bridesmaid part of *The Toreador*. Here was an actress who could sing the delightful songs her composer-husband, Lionel Monckton, was to write for her down the years. Seldom has there been a more delightful combination than this. In *The Orchid* she gave us a bit of character—with Fred Wright she sang 'Liza Ann,' the story of a Yorkshire mill girl, who was working up at Brigg's Mill. It was a little gem and we treasured it. Connie Ediss was on hand to sing to us about fancy dress and of the difficulty of getting her breath with a waist like Queen Elizabeth. Edmund Payne was to get involved in a duel with the clever Robert Nainby, this time an irascible French nobleman, and to attend that duel as a Crusader with an enormous double-handed sword. But in the second act Gabrielle Ray danced to us again. She wore a wine-coloured ballet dress. Later on, in the second edition, she wore pink pyjamas. Oh, the thrill. Women did not wear pyjamas then, many men were still true to nightshirts, but Gabs wore the simplest and daintiest pink silk pyjamas, and looked so appealing as she sang :

> "I'm a Pink Pyjama Girl, all pink and rosy
> I'm a lovely little lady to adore
> If you're a pink pyjama girlie you're all righty
> And you'll never wear a nighty any more."

We could not have agreed with her more.

George Grossmith, dressed as Beau Brummell, for the second act was a fancy dress ball, obliged with another interpolated number. This was called 'Bedelia' and was a raging success. It was the thin end of the wedge. Outside numbers, even foreign numbers, were now beginning to get into musical comedy. The last link which bound it to light opera was snapping. Soon numbers of composers and scores of authors would be needed to make a musical show, instead of the clever James T. Tanner for the book, the lyrics by Adrian Ross, and the music by Monckton or Ivan Caryll, with a number or two by Paul Rubens. But not whilst George Edwardes held sway. And not in *The Orchid*. The new girl was a success, the old team was a success, the new Gaiety was a success, and the spirit of the Gaiety went on.

How it went on! We had *The Spring Chicken*, we had *The New Aladdin*, which introduced another star in the melancholy art of Alfred Lester, who was a policeman lost in the London idealized by Aladdin's lamp. Lily Elsie led in this play but left, and Gertie Millar returned, so all was well. The time of Lily Elsie's triumph was not yet. Her crowning glory was reserved for Daly's and *The Merry Widow*. So Gertie, welcomed back, and Edmund Payne sang to us, both as Pearly Kings, of the glories of Covent Garden. There was *The Girls of Gottenberg*, with Grossmith as a German cavalry officer whose name was Otto—

> "The girls all call me Otto
> For they know that my heart never closes
> If things are getting hotto
> Stand a lunch to all the lotto
> Is the motto
> Of Otto
> Of Roses."

Gertie Millar took the girls to Berlin because it was on the Spree. And although Robert Blatchford in the *Weekly Dispatch*, Northcliffe in the *Mail*, and Lord Roberts from the platform told us of the German menace steadily growing in the background, we preferred the Germany as shown us at the Gaiety. *The Spring Chicken* had glorified the Entente Cordiale, that bit of super-Edwardian world politics, France was our friend, Germany would not dare. We did not believe in war. We were English. We were equal to any five foreigners—besides we could go with Gertie to Berlin which was on the Spree—and for hundreds of nights we went.

Havana broke new ground. The old Gaiety lot went to America, to show the Yanks what musical comedy meant. So to the Gaiety went *Havana* with a new team. Evie Greene, Leonard Mackay, Alfred Lester (who had been there before), W. H. Berry—and a score by Leslie Stuart. It was magnificent, but it was not the Gaiety.

So back came the old crowd over the Atlantic and the Gaiety was herself again with a grand show, one of her very best—*Our Miss Gibbs*.

Gertie Millar was Mary Gibbs, a shop girl; Robert Hale (who had been there in *Gottenberg*) was 'Slithers,' a crook; Grossmith was again the rather brainless young man about town who wanted notoriety, and who succeeded in stealing the Ascot Gold Cup (which really had been stolen, for the Gaiety was often as topical as Drury Lane drama). Teddy

H

Payne was a man from Yorkshire—a member of a prize-winning brass band in which he played the trombone. Gertie was from Yorkshire, too, and told us "They never do that in Yorkshire." There was also lovely Jean Aylwyn. And the second act was at our beloved White City, whose size and magnificence had dwarfed our equally beloved Earl's Court. It was, of course, necessary for Teddie Payne to be mistaken for Dorando, the Marathon Race winner. And Gertie Millar sang us her best song, 'Moonstruck.' Dressed in a loose pierrot costume, with the Gaiety Girls around her, she charmed us as she had never charmed us before. The thing was memorable. And *Our Miss Gibbs* was a triumph. Indeed, it was the very apex of Edwardesian Gaiety. It was never the same again.

Let us look at some Gaiety details. Take those songs of Grossmith. He had startled London in *The Toreador* with a Cakewalk, a novelty then which we thought most amusing, if a little gauche and unsophisticated, as befitting that distant and strange country called America. We did not speak American. We had never seen a talkie. Many had never seen a moving picture. He gave us 'Bedelia,' which we liked. He drew our generous applause when he sang us 'Waltz Me Once Round Again, Willie.' But he got the bird—like all the other great Edwardian players. He got it when he sang 'Yip-I-Addy-I-Ay.' The Gaiety-goers did not like it. It was too wild, too much abandoned. It was un-English, it was not the sort of thing they expected. So they booed him. But Grossmith, who was, in this song, before his time, was tenacious. He held on. He kept the song in. And he made us like it. It became the rage. It showed his judgment and the judgment of the great man who stood behind him. For Grossmith was a great man of musical comedy. His taste in female beauty has been mentioned. It showed itself when he brought over Gaby Deslys who, in *The New Aladdin*, played 'The Charm of Paris.' She could not do much then, her singing was not too good, her dancing was not too strong, but how lovely she was—and she did indeed radiate the charm of Paris from her pretty face, her china blue eyes, her lovely legs and figure, which she displayed in a Folies Bergère dress, a bathing costume and gym attire when for no reason at all except that it showed her off, she gave a display of ju-jitsu with a little Jap. Grossmith was to score heavily at the Gaiety much later on, when Edwardes had died, and when Grossmith (himself) and Laurillard were to revive Gaiety glory with *To-night's the Night* and bring out another new star in the person of Leslie Henson. In that show Grossmith sang 'Murders,' a clever number of a new type, and he has never done anything better.

But *Our Miss Gibbs* saw the end of the Edwardian Gaiety. After that the marvellous team split up. Gertie Millar went first. Grossmith, Payne and Connie Ediss were there in *The Sunshine Girl*, but it wasn't quite the same thing. Nor were any of the successors. Phyllis Dare was a delightful leading lady, but times were changing. It was the end of an epoch, if we had only known. Gertie Millar was to triumph at Daly's and at the Adelphi, where in one show Edmund Payne played his last part—but the Gaiety of Edwardes and Edward VII was no more. Indeed, one show which was presented there in Edwardes' absence upset the true Gaiety-goers so much that they called for Malone and told him they would report him to the Guv'nor. And he knew he deserved it. For it was awful. It was called *Adele*, but it is best to draw a veil. The end of George Edwardes did indeed mean the end of the Gaiety as we had known it.

But what a place it was. It had magic. It had glamour such as nowadays is not to be found. Its stage door callers were Debrett and Burke, and the landed gentry with a large smattering of 'Who's Who.' It was a piece of enchanted ground in the old, the age-old Strand. It was the eastern bulwark of Theatreland but still it was the centre of stage romance. The girls from its old and new stage door enriched the peerage. Connie Gilchrist became a legend. Rosie Boote became a Marchioness. In hansoms, in broughams, in carriages, the gilded youth came there. Its chorus girls knew the delight of a bouquet from which tinkled a valuable bracelet. They drank champagne in Maiden Lane and in the restaurant run by the Roman. They penetrated the Savoy Grill and the Carlton. They added beauty to the Thames at Maidenhead—they subdued the invincible Brigade of Guards. They were Girls—they were the essence of that mysterious feminity.

Those summer nights in the 1900's seemed longer and warmer than the nights of to-day. The sun got low, the streets were full, the lights glittered here and there. And to the stage door of the Gaiety came the girls. They moved with majesty, or they tripped with grace. They were conscious that they were a race apart. There might be—indeed, there were—other girls going through other stage doors, but these were of no account, for they did not belong to the Gaiety. To get a smile from one sent a young man's temperature bounding. To be said good-bye to with the promise that she wouldn't be long after the curtain came down and then off to supper—that said to a young man in his white tie, tails and tall hat and stick, put him amongst the elect. He went into the stalls and sat and adored. Or he went into the Gaiety Bar, where Rhoda and Gloria knew him, and had a drink to celebrate his good fortune. There he would meet and talk to some of the male members of the company. He might see Charlie Brown, the very image of young Grossmith, a clever performer himself and an old Carthusian, or Dodson, the moustached stage-manager. He might see little Joe Grande, a regular small part player, who had a magnificent tenor voice but far too few inches for a good part. He would certainly have the privilege of buying a drink for Jupp. Or it might be the caller at the stage door was an Eastern potentate, a fabulously rich Rajah. For the Gaiety was as great an attraction to them as a candle is to a moth. And Jupp knew just how to deal with them.

That stage door, that whole theatre, was something which enshrined its time. There is little Gaiety now. But then, we knew no thought of to-morrow. We had lived for years of peace. We played our games and did our work, and we went to the Gaiety. In the early days of motors you were sure to see one at the Gaiety stage door, and the Girl whose boy had one dressed accordingly, in a long cloak and muffled up her head in yards of chiffon. For motoring was fast and dangerous and not too reliable. But it was very smart. And a Gaiety Girl was always smart

You did not bother much what the show was—you just went to the Gaiety. In its stalls sat smart women and smart men. Many of the men were bronzed. They were just back from overseas exile—and the Gaiety was one of their first calls. In the upper circle, pit and gallery sat the people of London, that workaday London, who got a glimpse of another world by going to the Gaiety, who knew all about it and its inhabitants and who vied with each other who saw the show the greatest number of times. Its staff were personalities, its quality without question. Some of the humbler of its audience, those who had no carriages to come at eleven, found its location inconvenient. There were no tubes then. But when the curtain fell, they would risk their last trains to run round to the stage door, to hover for a few precious moments, all eyes and excitement. And if they were rewarded by the sight of a Gaiety Girl coming out, gracious, charming, adorable and lovely, meeting and smiling at her gallant escort, being helped into a hansom and disappearing fairy-like into the purple dark of a summer night in London—in the 1900's—when the world was stable and we were young, well, even a long walk home had its points ; for one could think, and dream of the Gaiety—and of the next time you would go there. For in those days there was a next time ; it was not only a possibility, but a certainty, for those were the days of continuity. What a good world it was, when the Gaiety filled the Strand with joy, and its girls gilded it with beauty.

CHAPTER IX

The Street of Actors

FAR MORE THAN ANY OTHER STREET OR PLACE IN LONDON, EXCEPT Leicester Square, the Strand, in Edwardian times, was pre-eminently the Street of Actors. It held many theatres, and a great music hall. In streets near by were many more, and in Maiden Lane, Bedford Street and other tributaries were the agents' offices. Part of the Strand was called the Actors' Mile, and even in the busiest time of the day in that busy, bustling thoroughfare you could almost smell the greasepaint.

Drury Lane was round the corner, so was the 'Old Mo,' or the Middlesex Music Hall. There were music halls just over the bridge—Waterloo Bridge—and it was the hub of the entertainment world, was the Strand. It was essentially a man's street, and it nearly always has been. It was no shopping centre, and such late Victorian or early Edwardian ladies as you might meet there were either escorted by the menfolk from lunch at Gatti's, staying at the Hotel Cecil or Savoy, or taking their children to buy toys at the Lowther Arcade, that children's Paradise of Toyland, now swept away, its entrance covered by Coutts' Bank. That bank had always been a Strand bank, too, for its original home was the site of the Little Theatre, in John Street, destroyed by the blitz. Or if the ladies did not fall into any of these categories, then they were shop assistants out on business, possibly some of the rapidly growing army of typists, or most likely of all, actresses or music hall performers.

The main crowd in the Strand was composed of men, straw-hatted in summer, top-hatted or bowler-hatted in winter—and amongst them the clean-shaven actors stood out, for most men then, if not actors or barristers, wore hair on their upper lip. Yet it was in the Strand that one of the moustached actor-managers—Sir Charles Hawtrey—shaved off his moustache to perform in a costume play at the Vaudeville, called *Mr. George*. But it was no use. Hawtrey in knee-breeches and buckles, paying courtly attentions to sweet Billie Burke? Hawtrey not telling lies on the stage? Hawtrey without a moustache? Perish the thought! *Mr. George* ran for a bare two months. Hawtrey got back into his ordinary clothes, grew his moustache, and his outraged public forgave him. That was in 1907, at the height of the Edwardian era. We did not want any monkey tricks from our actor-managers, thank you. We wanted them as we knew them. And they, like sensible men, obeyed. Yet Hawtrey looked very well in his powder and buckles and played very well, too. But it was no good.

The Strand was a man's street. Its main dramatic fare was manly, too. There was the Gaiety, the young man's Mecca. There was the Vaudeville, where Hawtrey played, or where Seymour Hicks and his delightful wife gave musical comedy, and where Gibson Girls attracted the males ; there was the Adelphi, with its melodramas and later its musical shows ; there was the Tivoli—a very male music hall. There was the Savoy, which after its great Gilbert and Sullivan period, had no fixed policy, but revived the operas from time to time—appealing equally to both sexes—and there was Terry's Theatre. So women thronged the Strand on matinee days—the matinee started at the Gaiety—and also in the evenings—but seldom alone—to go to the shows. But for the main part of the day it was male. Did not Vesta Tilley, herself the supreme male impersonator, sing of it as the Land of the Midnight Son? And how right she was. The Strand has altered a great deal since Edwardian days. Gone is Lowther Arcade, the old shops which formed the bottle-neck, gone is Terry's Theatre itself. The outsides of the Vaudeville and the Adelphi are altered (the insides, too, for that matter), the Tivoli is there in name only, showing films instead of the real British artistry of the music hall. Gow's, that old eating-house with its Dickensian pews, its ancient atmosphere and its first-class food, has left the Strand and occupies modern premises in St. Martin's Lane. Its white-painted front is a landmark which we miss. Whilst it was there, the old atmosphere could be recaptured. Once inside, the years dropped away. You went straight in its narrow door, and there was a small bar. Through this was the coffee room, where the best fish, the finest oysters, the most luscious steaks and chops, the richest steak, kidney and lark puddings or pies were yours to revel in. You sat where your forefathers had sat, you were served by waiters who knew you and what you wanted, who were friends, not alien servitors. They exchanged news with you, gave you messages from your friends and looked after you with personal attention. This was the real Strand, the real male Strand, even more than Romano's, its near neighbour, and as much as Simpson's opposite. That was very English—is still very English—but so much vaster and grander, so much less friendly than Gow's. Gow's was the Strand of Bohemia—for the Strand was High Street Bohemia. Simpson's was magnificent, remains magnificent—but had not quite the same touch. In its later days, whilst the food remained at the same high standard, whilst the carvers performed feats of dexterity at your side off their noble joints on their trolleys (one excludes the years of war), it is not so very masculine in atmosphere or clientele as Gow's remained persistently to the end. There was always a flavour of Dickens, of port wine, of hearty appetites, of foaming tankards at Gow's. One could always conjure up the giants of the old Gaiety, Drury Lane, the Lyceum, and the Strand Theatres, of the variety stars from the Tivoli, of Phil May, whose spiritual home was the Strand, and all the cream of Edwardian Bohemia, for Gow's, Rule's, and Romano's had them all.

Long past the Edwardian era its survivors gathered there. One man especially, in a suit of clothes which would have been quite in keeping on a coach and four, or a smart dogcart, gave it an air. As befitted him, he had the gout, he often moved painfully and slowly aided by a stick. But he never abated his taste and his appetite for Gow's best, whether the gout was with him or not. No dieting for him ! He was of an age which knew it not. No, steak pudding, oysters, beer in a tankard, under-done steak, slices of salmon, and to top off with, two glasses of port. One wonders where he is to-day, now that Gow's has moved away. Right up to the beginning of the late war his presence brought Victorian and Edwardian days to life in Gow's in the Strand. You could only see his like in those streets off Piccadilly in the afternoon or just before lunch, when the real old diehards of the days of the golden sovereign took the air after a visit to, or en route for, their clubs. But he—this Gow's customer —preferred the Strand. No doubt he had in his day cheered Charlie Whittle when he invited us to 'Let's all go down the Strand.' No doubt he had approved Vesta Tilley's 'The Midnight Son.' No doubt he had waited at the Gaiety stage door, had applauded Bill Terriss and delighted in Seymour Hicks and Terriss's lovely daughter. He was the embodiment of the Strand of the Edwardian and Victorian days—and he was really the right person in the right place in Gow's.

Many other things have gone from the Strand, which for so many years was faithfully portrayed on the magazine cover of that periodical named after it. The hansoms have gone, the horse buses have gone, that shop on the corner of Southampton Street which sold theatrical photographs and coloured views of Switzerland and other foreign parts, in glorious juxtaposition, has made way for an outfitter's with chromium plating. So much has altered—yet still something remains. The Strand is too old a thoroughfare to change all at once. Even though the Hotel Cecil has given place to a vast modern building devoted to oil, there are still some shops which retain the old air. There are still some public houses which have not altered. Though Shorts is to a large extent modernized, Yates's Wine Lodge remains, and an old oyster shop just as it was when the Edwardians were young, and before their time, too. There is still a Roman bath off the Strand, to remind us that the Strand was an ancient roadway then. And there is 43 Strand, that famous public house, just as it used to be, when the actors used it, the music hall stars used it, and when—in those days, be it understood—you might also find a 'lady of the town' or two, who plied her old trade in that quarter.

You will find the customers changed to-day, but not the fare or the liquor, or the surroundings. You can still step back from fifty to seventy years when you enter.

There was also the famous perfumier's, Rimmel's, which called itself 'The Scenter of the Strand,' and lived up to it. You could buy 'Etoile du Nord,' Romanoff, Ihlang-Ihlang, Vanda, Henna, Cuir de Russie for 2s. 6d. per bottle. Or his Toilet Vinegar, said to be 'highly refreshing and salubrious,' for 1s. ; his lime juice and glycerine for the hair was 1s. 6d., whilst Velvetine, 'a refined, imperceptible toilet powder,' was 1s. 6d. This firm sold a variety of novelties for Christmas as well, all highly scented, and what is more, when they advertised in theatre programmes, which they often did, they supplied a scent which was applied in some way to the paper and retained its pungency for many years.

And, of course, the Bodega is still in Bedford Street, where you really could, in the old days, sometimes meet the 'laddie' type of actor—so much written up but so seldom seen—who could punish the free cheese and accept a drink as his perfect right. But there are not many actors in the Bodega now. Once there were plenty. And on one occasion an actor in his cups got overlooked at closing time. When he awoke, he found he was locked in. He hammered on the door to attract attention. He was finally heard by the policeman on the beat. Not much could be done, for it would be necessary to send for the manager, who had the keys, and he lived at a considerable distance. So the actor decided to make a night of it. He was surrounded by good liquor. He partook. He asked the policeman outside the door to join him. The policeman told him not to be stupid, how could he get a drink with the door locked ? But the prisoner of the Bodega, being an actor, had an alert mind. He told the constable to wait. He got a straw (such as we drank lemon squash through) from a glass on the counter, he filled a glass with whisky (there was plenty behind the bar). He put the straw through the letter box, the policeman knelt down and applied suction. So well did it work that in the small hours, when dawn sent its pale light over the Strand and Bedford Street, an inspector found his constable lying flat on the pavement, deep in the spell of Bacchus, so deep that he could not be awakened, even by the rough means applied. He was carted off, to recover at Bow Street, whilst entrance was effected in respect of the Bodega (the inspector being mystified as to how the policeman had got into such a state). Inside the door lay the actor, in a similar condition, whilst good liquor and plenty of straws lay around. That sort of thing could not happen to-day—but whisky was 3d. a 'go' then—and plenty of it. Also it was stronger. But these two had not stopped at Scotch. They had sampled every bottle within reach.

Actor-managers abounded in the Strand, as was natural. In the early days of the Edwardian era, John Hare—Sir John Hare—was at the old Globe. This theatre vanished in 1902. It was a very unfortunate place, and nobody had much luck there. Hare had as much as anyone. He ran it, as he ran everything, with great distinction. It was not his fault that the Globe was known as one of 'The Ricketty Twins'—the other being the Opera Comique, a jerry-built, insecure and altogether undesirable playhouse. Hare was a great actor-manager and managed to get some of his own personal aura into the place. His presentatio.ns included *The Gay Lord Quex,* that fine play of Pinero's, in 1899, which was probably the Globe's greatest success. What a play it was, and how beautifully he did it. To-day it would not raise an eyebrow, but then, it was very daring—with women smoking cigarettes and gentlemen visiting their bedrooms. Everyone went to see it. He gave it a magnificent cast, with himself as 'The Marquess of Quex,' Gilbert Hare as 'Sir Chichester Frayne,' Charles Cherry as 'Captain Eastling,' Frank Gilmore as 'Valma' the palmist, Miss Fortescue as 'The Duchess of Strood,' Fanny Coleman as the 'Countess of Owbridge,' Mabel Terry-Lewis as 'Muriel Eden,' and the one and only Irene Vanbrugh as 'Sophie Fullgarney,' the Bond Street beauty specialist, in whose emporium the play opened. Her performance was something to see and remember, it did much to put her in the front rank. The ease and polish of John Hare was delightful. His decisive style, his command, his diction, his complete understanding of the business of the stage is something we lack to-day. He had done so much for the drama. He had been one of the team with the Bancrofts who had revolutionized the stage. With the Kendals he had changed the luck of St. James's. His knighthood was well deserved. Off stage, but for the imaginative eyes and mobile face, he might have been a family lawyer, in whose deed boxes the secrets of old families and estates grew sere and yellow. But he was an actor to whom the British stage owes much. He did not know the meaning of 'second rate.' There were 'No Fees' at the Globe, there was an excellent orchestra under the direction of Haydn Waud, and gentlemen were earnestly requested not to light cigarettes in any part of the theatre except the smoking room. No need to appeal to the ladies. His manager was C. T. H. Helmsley, to whom all complaints and enquiries were to be addressed. And seats might be booked by letter, telegram or telephone—the number was Gerrard 2614. To-day it would be Temple Bar, for the Globe stood in Newcastle Street, now swept away by improvements, which gave us Bush House but took away much old London. But so few were telephones then that Gerrard covered the whole of the West End.

Hare also gave us, at the Globe, *A Bachelor's Romance,* which he produced on Saturday, 8th January 1898. He had Frederick Kerr, Gilbert Hare, Frank Gillmore, Charles Cherry, James Leigh, May Harvey, Mona K. Oram, Susie Vaughan and Nellie Thorne with him in the cast. The stage manager was E. Vivian Reynolds, who was to be so long with Alexander at the St. James's. The theatre had been newly decorated and heated, and there was a new act drop by W. Harford.

In the same year John L. Shine had a season, and presented *The Three Musketeers.* This was the Henry Hamilton version. There was an outbreak of musketeers that year, for Tree did a version, too, at His Majesty's.[1] But great as he was, Tree was not the right 'D'Artagnan.' On the other hand, at the Globe, Lewis Waller was the ideal. There could never be, and there never has been, a better Gascon musketeer than he. Here was the dash, the swagger, the gallantry, the speed and the romance. Here was an actor who might have been created for the part. In the long cast at the Globe besides Lewis Waller, the names that stand out are John Beauchamp as 'Richelieu,' Vincent Sternroyd as

Buckingham,' Arthur Wontner as 'de Rochefort,' Bassett Roe as 'Athos,' Charles Goodheart as 'Porthos,' Gerald Gurney as 'Aramis,' a small boy playing a page who is now Leon M. Lion, an actor-manager himself, Kate Rorke as 'Anne of Austria,' a very pretty and clever girl as 'Gabrielle' who is and was Eva Moore, and the name of Florence West as 'Miladi.' Florence West was Mrs. Lewis Waller. Between them, they stole the show. Never was there a better 'D'Artagnan' or a better 'Miladi.' A man to-day approaching sixty sat as a boy at that theatre and saw that production, open-mouthed and spellbound. He had seen it also at the Garrick, before its transfer to the Globe and that time he saw Robert Loraine play 'D'Artagnan.' It made not much difference to him, but he was of the opinion that the one at the Globe was the best. He remembers every detail to this day. He could tell you what the costumes were like, he could tell you all about it. He was carried away by the recital of the famous dash to save the diamonds and the final triumphant shout of D'Artagnan at the end that he had saved the Queen. He was in agony of excitement in the bedroom scene between D'Artagnan and 'Miladi,' with its desperate struggle and D'Artagnan's dash through the door, leaving 'Miladi,' breathless but vengeful, hacking at the slammed portal with her gleaming dagger. For weeks afterwards he was 'D'Artagnan,' with a long cape of his mother's for the cloak, a real sword by his side, an old sombrero hat decorated with a feather—the hat was too large for him, but what mattered that?—and he could, even to-day, whistle you the incidental music, especially that which accompanied the entrance of the Musketeers. For this was real romantic melodrama, with music 'themes' for all performers and plenty of background music as well, to swell and die away as occasion demanded and make everything said and done exciting and colourful. It was composed by Frederick Rosse.

That 'D'Artagnan' of Lewis Waller was a high water mark of Edwardian acting. It was the real thing. Here was an actor with a glorious voice, a terrific personality, who knew his job, who could wear his costumes as if they were his habitual clothes. He never appeared to be wearing stage clothes, he never once seemed an actor in a 'period' play. Whether he was a noble Roman (and his 'Brutus' was the noblest Roman of them all), whether he was 'Faulconbridge,' the armoured hero in *King John*, or 'Henry V' himself, whether he was a dashing brigadier in Napoleon's time, a silken, white-wigged gentleman of the eighteenth century, or as in this case, a brave cadet of Gascony under Louis XIII, that is what Lewis Waller was. He had the authentic ring, the authentic atmosphere. His clothes were part of him, as everyday wear. It was only when he appeared in modern dress that he did not always convince. In costume, there has never been such a romantic figure, such a real hero as he. Of the later players, Ainley came nearest, but he never possessed the verve, the speed, the breathless sweep of Waller. No wonder Waller was the beau ideal of the ladies. He played 'D'Artagnan' just as one had pictured this hero in one's imagination. He made the most incredible things seem credible, because he did them. He was not afraid of anything, and he let himself go so that the audience swayed before him like a field of corn before the wind. He had them in the palm of his hand, they were his slaves. He was larger than life, as all real actors should be, for that is the mission of the stage. And he acted—he did not mutter, he did not lurk about upstage to turn his back, or 'throw lines away.' He aimed those lines straight at you, you never saw him throw them. He ran through the emotions, his love-making swept every woman in the house off her feet. In his hands, a sword was better handled than the modern actor handles his inevitable cigarette.

One of the greatest 'Henry the Fifths' of all time, he was certainly the greatest 'D'Artagnan.' To-day, his acting and that of his brilliant wife would be called Ham. All one knows is that it made one yell with enthusiasm, and that its memory to-day shines bright and clear in every detail after half a century of crowded life. One would imagine it must have been good acting that could effect such a thing. It remains whilst the modern, quiet, restrained under-statement of to-day is dimmed after a few weeks. But Waller's acting was as sunshine compared to a cloudy day—and one remembers the sunshine.

The Opera Comique, which closed in 1899, does not really concern us. It got its death blow when Gilbert and Sullivan moved to the Savoy. But across the road, a little higher up, was a theatre which is now vanished, although its name graces a newer playhouse. That was the Strand, an old theatre, a small theatre. And in early Edwardian days this little playhouse, the Strand, was making history.

Although an actor-manager was not in command, it was run by a man who had been an actor and had become a manager, so it was the next best thing. His name was Frank Curzon (born Deeley). He had been on the stage, he had even been with Benson, but he had taken up management. He knew all about it. He had his ups and downs, but the period at the Strand was one of the 'ups.' It was his wise habit to associate himself with an actor-manager or manageress, and present plays with them, he controlling the business side and they the stage side. He had done so with Charles Hawtrey, at the old Avenue (now the Playhouse) and it had worked out well. It was to do so many times again. But at the Strand he had no great star with him, and things had not been too good.

He got hold of a musical comedy which was doing good business in the country and he brought it to the Strand in 1901. It was called *A Chinese Honeymoon* and it made his fortune and that of several other people. Curzon had been hard pressed when he got hold of it. But after it had run for over 1,000 performances he was in easy street. So was its author, George Dance. This strange man of the Theatre laid the foundation of his vast fortune by that play. He was a great figure of the Edwardian Theatre, behind the scenes in Town, but striding the provinces like a colossal Napoleon when it came to touring companies. For so far as musical comedies went, he *was* the provincial theatre. Later he added Drury Lane dramas and the famous *Kismet* to his attractions. The profits were terrific, for Dance was a man of business —theatre business. He knew the value of those pence which bred the pounds.

When *A Chinese Honeymoon* was produced, this son of Nottingham, who had started by writing music hall songs (and good ones), had already several successes to his credit. He had, notably, *The Nautch Girl* (one of the best libretti ever written), he had *Ma Mie Rosette*, *The Lady Slavey*, *The Gay Parisienne*—all big successes—and several more. But it was *A Chinese Honeymoon* which made him really famous and gave him the power he afterwards wielded.

This very successful play was in many ways a model musical show. It had a good story. Dance saw to that. It had situations which were amusing, it was well told, it had a love story which was interesting and not too intrusive, it had good lines, and it had a rich set of characters. For Dance knew his job. It was all well made, and the mixture was in just the right proportion. It did not take half a dozen script writers to pool a lack of ideas and then build up the old gags. It was a perfect piece of cabinet-makers, and it had a part which was specially built for a great little droll who had already scored in a George Dance show, and whose name was Louie Freear. She was a tiny little woman, almost a dwarf. She had a funny face and a funny nose. She had a funny walk, a funny voice—everything about her was funny. But she did not rely on her grotesque appearance for her success—that was merely a lucky adjunct. She had great talent. Indeed, she had been with Ben Greet in Shakespeare and she had, just before the production of *A Chinese Honeymoon*, played 'Puck' in *A Midsummer Night's Dream* at His Majesty's for Sir Herbert Tree. She had been lucky for George Dance (and he knew how to fit her) in *The Gay Parisienne*, in which she had made an immense success, and her singing of 'Sister Mary Jane's Top Note' was a furore. Those who only remember her in *A Chinese Honeymoon* will be astonished that her career included Shakespeare (she played 'Mopsa' in *A Winter's Tale* as well as 'Puck' in *The Dream*, and many other parts), a nigger minstrel troupe and the music halls. That was the sort of artiste the Edwardian Theatre boasted. *A Chinese Honeymoon* was her biggest success. As 'Fifi' she was unforgettable, and her songs, 'The Twiddley Bits' and 'Martha Spanks the Grand Piano,' were sung and whistled by all the town and played on all the organs. It is a curious thing, but the Dance songs which she sang with so much success were all about music and musicians. There was the 'Top Note' to start with. 'Martha Spanks the Grand Piano' told of a musical family, of which Louie was the conductor, and she diverted us nobly when she showed us how she did it. 'The Twiddley Bits' concerned her passion for an instrumentalist—he was either a cornet player or a flautist—and was evidently something of a virtuoso, for she told us her headlong fall was :

> "All through those twiddley bits he used to play
> When all alone with me
> Bobbing around
> Whenever he found
> An opportunity
> All through those twiddley bits he used to play
> They fairly gave me fits
> The deed was done and my heart was won
> By his dear little twiddley bits."

She also informed us that she wanted to be a 'Lidy' and peroxide her hair.

Dance wrote all the words and Howard Talbot all the music—there was only one interpolated number called 'Egypt,' which was sung by

Lily Elsie—yes, Lily Elsie—who played 'Soo-Soo,' the Emperor of China's niece. Her lover, 'Tom Hatherton,' was played by J. Farren Soutar, a charming and well graced actor still with us and fresh in the mind. The 'Emperor' was Picton Roxborough, the tallest actor on the stage. The honeymoon couple were 'Mr. and Mrs. Pineapple' in the persons of Arthur Williams, the richest comedian who ever raised a laugh (not in money but in art) and Marie Dainton, whose song, 'The A La Girl', was another big hit, giving her powers of mimicry scope when she pictured for us the typical girls of each nation :

"Oh the A La Girl
Is a knowing girl
With lots of A La talk
And when she walks
Down Regent Street
She does an A La walk."

We adored that sort of thing. It was packed full of good things, it was well dressed and mounted and beautifully played and it became an institution. It laid the sure foundation of the fortune which was to enable Frank Curzon to win the Derby with 'Call Boy' and the foundation of the fortune which made George Dance the great power he was to become. For Dance always had ready money, and lots of it. This enabled him to get what was practically a stranglehold where he wanted it. He was behind the scenes of many a West End show, but it was in the provinces that he believed. His command of money got him all the successes, the failures he left to others. Also he ran theatre bars. He disliked drink, he disliked his staff to 'have one,' but he sold it to others. Under the trading name of Westby and Co. he ran the bars of all the most successful theatres in town, a most profitable concern. He disliked the idea of anyone (save those directly concerned) knowing that he did this. But as he trusted nobody, he signed all the cheques himself and was always surprised and aggravated when people knew that he was Westby's. He would accuse his staff of 'yapping,' or as we say now, 'spilling the beans,' whereas he had done so himself with his own hands. Let a management with whom he had no working arrangement produce a success. The next morning an emissary of Dance's was round there, with a very big roll of 'fivers' which he would rustle alluringly. It never failed. There was not too much ready cash in the Theatre then (there is not a great deal more to-day) and the sight of that £500 or £1,000, theirs for the asking, never failed to work. He got the theatre bars in the same way. £1,000 on account of rent, after a bad flop or two, was a tempting bait.

He did all this and ran twenty-four touring companies all at the same time, with a staff of two men and three girls, one of whom worked the telephone. Miracles of work and organization were performed, with him always impeding progress, for he firmly believed that was the way to get the best out of people. He had a fierce nature and a fiercer style, his eyes were fiery—not bloodshot, but literally fiery. They were of a browny-red and they shot sparks. If you want to know what it was like to bear the brunt of George Dance's gaze, go and look into the eyes of a tiger in the Zoo just before feeding time. He economized in the small things ; if the weekly account of a wardrobe mistress of one of his companies exceeded 15s. the heavens fell. Yet he would spend £5,000 with no likelihood of getting it back—at the moment. It was just ground bait and sooner or later he knew it would come home, with double force. He was, in many respects, a great man. He hated people who talked or chattered. He would not have a fair-haired person near him—yet his general manager for years, T. C. Wray, was anything but dark. If an applicant faced him who was inclined to be blond, he would shout, "My God, the wrong colour—get him out," and the unfortunate man, whatever his qualifications, was hustled from the presence. He was a man with a big brain, he was a thinker. He compelled fear, but he compelled admiration. And when he chose, he was given to acts of unexpected and princely generosity. Although in his greatest days his offices were in Leicester Square, he was of the Strand. His great success was made there, at the theatre which bore that thoroughfare's name, and every day he lunched at Romano's in the Strand, where he talked to other theatrical people, and after lunch over a crème de menthe would hatch out his great schemes. He had the poorest opinion of actors and of the Theatre as a business. He had the poorest opinion of theatrical art. His object was to make money, and he did. He would often stagger his staff with the seemingly meaningless tasks he gave them, yet he always had a reason which time alone showed. He had a great affection for his native city of Nottingham (his real name, by the way, was George Cabon) and always kept an account at the Nottingham and Notts Bank, for which the then London County and Westminster Bank were London agents and where his daily credit was 'unlimited'—an amazing thing. His private account he kept at the Bank of England—for whose dignified methods he had the heartiest contempt. But to work for him was an experience and from his office came the best of the men of the succeeding generation. For he knew all about it—and all of them treasure his recollection in their hearts—despite all the trouble they went through, his memory is revered. Nor should it be forgotten that his princely gift put the Old Vic on its feet. He died—Sir George Dance.

Terry's Theatre in the Strand has now vanished. Woolworth's establishment covers its site. It was not a very successful theatre—it gave Victorian London a great success in *Sweet Lavender*—a personal triumph for its founder, Edward Terry, too. In Edwardian days it was failing. Its actor-manager had gone. But in those years there was a curious man in the Theatre called W. H. C. Nation. He was a staunch Devonian and very rich. He was a relation of the Vanbrugh family. And he loved the Theatre. In the summer months—or rather in August and early September—when the West End was dead, he would take a theatre and give a London season. Few theatres were open in August then. Business languished directly Goodwood was over and did not come to life until mid-September when the early darkness (no Daylight Saving then) and the chillier evenings made people look for indoor entertainment. During that late summer period most theatres carried a bill outside which said, 'Closed in preparation for the Autumn Season. Details will be announced shortly.' That was the time when Mr. William Hamilton Codrington Nation came to town. He was educated at Eton and Oriel College, Oxford ; but the Theatre claimed him. He had been at Sadler's Wells, at Astley's. He had run magazines, he wrote plays (which he produced himself with his own money), he lectured on the Drama, he was prominent in theatrical charitable work ; indeed, he was a vice-president of the Royal General Theatrical Fund. But he did not make any money out of the Theatre. It is, indeed, doubtful if he ever wished to. He had the satisfaction of seeing his own plays performed and his own songs sung—great satisfaction to him, if to nobody else. He also gave work to actors and actresses at a time when they would otherwise have been idle. So he was a philanthropist, anyway.

On one occasion, in 1906, he took Terry's Theatre. He risked a bit then, for he opened in October, instead of the summer, with the full blast of the ordinary theatres against him. How he succeeded will be shown.

W. H. C. Nation was a curious man, who did things in a curious way. Outside the theatre, where photographs of the actors and the show were usually displayed, he hung old faded photographs which interested him. You would see a photo of some cows in a field, and under it would be the caption 'Cows in a field near Tavistock, owned by W. H. C. Nation.' Then there would be a photo of some houses, described as 'Houses in Tavistock, owned by W. H. C. Nation.' Of what value he considered these, nobody knew. He presented old, un-heard-of plays and some written by himself. There was usually a triple bill. But in each play he interpolated one or two songs written and composed by himself. He did not care whether the public liked them or not ; he did. He would sit in an armchair in the wings, with a stick or umbrella in his hands, and the carpenter was instructed to fix an iron plate upon which he would hammer with his stick by way of applause. He encored every song, sometimes more than once, irrespective of applause (if any) from the audience (also if any). For on the occasion of his season at Terry's Theatre a young man in the profession thought he would go and sample Mr. Nation's wares. He did not present his card, which would have insured him a courteous reception from Mr. Friend, who stood in the capacity his name implied to Mr. Nation, and was also his manager ; he elected to pay. But he did not think he would risk more than a shilling. So, ascending the gallery stairs, he paid the shilling at the gallery pay-box, which was a little way up, received his metal check, and went on up the stairs. He was stopped by a shout. He turned and found that the gallery money-taker had come out of the box and was calling him back, with the shilling in his hand. He went back and asked what was wrong. The money-taker looked him straight in the face. "Sir," he said, "I can't take this." "What's the matter with it ?" demanded the young man. "It's a good shilling, isn't it ?" "Oh, yes, sir," came the reply, "the bob's all right, only—" and then in a burst of confidence, "I can't take it, guv'nor. You see, there's nobody up there at all. You are the only one who has paid anything. Go on, take it back, and go in just the same. I don't like to take your money." But the young man refused. He went in, having paid, and sat in solitary state all by himself in the gallery and had the pleasure of seeing the show and hearing Mr. Nation's numerous hammered encores. He sur-veyed the almost empty house, and from the look of the few seated there he formed the conclusion that the gross takings that night were represented by his shilling.

Terry's went over to pictures and vanished, but a good musical show, *My Lady Molly*, was one of its swan songs.

At two of the famous Strand theatres, the Adelphi and the Vaudeville, you might see the good Strand name of Gatti emblazoned. These brothers of fine standing and reputation, both as caterers and theatre proprietors, were pillars of the Strand. There was the Adelaide Galleries —Gatti's, where you got excellent food and service. And their theatre interests still endure, and still their name is as good as the Bank of England's. Charming people to deal with, they were men of business who understood the Theatre and made it their business, too.

At the Adelphi you are on historic ground. But at the very beginning of the Edwardian period a cloud passed over it, when William Terriss —Breezy Bill—was foully murdered by a madman as he was entering the private door, which he always used—with a vast audience waiting to greet him. His death—mourned by the whole country—closed the chapter of Adelphi Drama, which had started before him, but which he had raised to a high pinnacle of fame. The story of Terriss's death is well known. But there are some curious features which may be fresh to many, dealing with the strange premonition of his sudden and dreadful end. The Sunday before his death he told his family about a man who had died suddenly of heart disease and gave them a wonderful and realistic presentation of how the man expired, acting it so skilfully that he frightened them all. Then he said, "A splendid death to die ; no lingering illness, no bedside agonies, no doctors, no cries, no moans or tears, heartrending to all ; but peace, perfect peace." In a few days a similar death was to come to him from an assassin's knife. But even something more strange had occurred a few days before. His wife had read the 'notices' of a play called *Charlotte Corday* and told him she thought the part of 'Marat' would be an admirable one for him. But he revolted at the idea and shuddered. "Ah, no. Horrible," he said. "I could not bear that scene with the knife ; to be stabbed like that seems terrible." Yet in the shortest space of time that was to be his end. And there is yet another curious happening. It was told in a contemporary newspaper. In the early hours of the morning of 16th December 1897 (the night Terriss was killed), his understudy—a Mr. Lane—dreamed that he saw Terriss lying unconscious on the stairs leading to his dressing-room. He dreamed that the great actor was surrounded by a crowd of people, including Miss Millward, the leading lady, other members of the cast, and one of the footmen, whose duty it was to attend to the curtain, was helping, too. A few hours later he saw the actual scene in reality, with the people grouped exactly as he had witnessed in his dream. There was no hallucination about it, for so vivid had been the dream that Mr. Lane had mentioned it to several people during the day, a fact to which they all bore testimony. Terriss was appearing in *Secret Service*, an exciting melodrama.

The Adelphi was rebuilt in 1900 and reopened in 1901 as the New Century Theatre, but nobody liked the new name. It was a foolish idea to alter so famous a name, and Tom B. Davis, a well-known manager of the time, made a bad mistake over this. The title was changed again to the Adelphi. For a long while it had no settled policy, although many notable people played there in Edwardian days. And there was one play which did, to some extent, bring back the old melodramatic atmosphere. This was called *The House of Temperley*, and was a free adaptation of Conan Doyle's fine story, *Rodney Stone*. It was a very exciting show, dealing with Regency days, the prize ring and the Peninsular War—to say nothing of the clubs of the time and the gambling which took place. There was a marvellous representation of Tom Cribb's Parlour, with its fighting men and its Corinthians, in which a fight took place between a brutal prizefighter and a young man who was something of an aspirant to Championship honours. Following the story of Rodney Stone, he was backed for pounds, shilling and pence by 'Sir Charles Temperley'— played by that handsome actor of grace, Ben Webster. The young man was kidnapped and his place taken in the Championship contest by a young and amateur scion of the House of Temperley. This full-sized fight, on the Downs, with its ring, its ringkeepers armed with whips, its referee in the person of 'Gentleman Jackson' (played by Stanley Turnbull), its swaying, cheering, yelling, bloodthirsty crowd, was a masterpiece. So much did it catch the fancy of the town that sportsmen would drop in to the Adelphi just to see it, night after night. This play was also notable for one of the best 'doubles' the stage has ever seen. This feat was performed by A. S. Homewood, who was the drunken, brutish, foul-mouthed, bloodthirsty 'Joe Birks' of the Tom Cribb's parlour scene, who also did some fine boxing in the course of the action and got knocked out, and then appeared as 'The Duke of Broadacres,' a grand, courtly and polished nobleman of the period, whose duty it was to expel the villain, 'Sir John Hawker,' portrayed by that sterling actor, Charles Rock, from his club. These two utterly different parts were so wonderfully played that nobody could have believed the same man did it. It was a complete difference in style, appearance and approach. Charles Maude played the amateur 'pug' who fought the big fight, a good actor and a handsome young man with a fine figure, who also knew how to use his fists.

Another drama followed this, in 1910, and again it was a Conan Doyle story, *The Speckled Band*. In this a snake slid down a bellrope to kill the sleeping occupant of a bed, and all London shivered. And in it that fine actor, Lyn Harding, rose to great heights as the villainous 'Dr. Grimesby Rylott.'

And then George Edwardes took over. His name had appeared on Adelphi bills before, in the unusual role of author—or part-author—of one of its best Terriss melodramas, *One of the Best*, which he wrote in collaboration with Seymour Hicks. But now he was to start a new page of his own, and the Adelphi's—glory.

Musical comedy reigned, and Gertie Millar came along from the Gaiety to entrance us with *The Quaker Girl*, commencing on 5th November 1910. The Adelphi's gain was the Gaiety's loss. It was never the same without Gertie. But *The Quaker Girl* enchanted us all. She and Joe Coyne—Gertie as 'Prudence,' a Quaker maiden, and he as 'Tony Chute,' an American—provided the Edwardians with a memory which will never fade and which is written in letters of gold in theatrical archives.

The Gattis also had—and have—the Vaudeville. There all sorts of things happened. In association with them, Charles Hawtrey presented many plays, the best of which was *Jack Straw*, by the then omnipresent Somerset Maugham, who had plays running at five or six theatres at once. Hawtrey gave revivals of *Mr. Ponderbury's Past* and of an extraordinary piece of nonsense called *The Cuckoo*, in which a cannibal king had supper and ate cigars, and Holman Clark made a wonderful character of a dishonest butler—who insisted on his dishonesty.

But before then history had been made by an actor and his wife who can still charm us at any time they wish. To-day they are Sir Seymour and Lady Hicks—then they were just plain Seymour Hicks and Ellaline Terriss—although the word plain could be applied to neither. For Ellaline was every playgoer's sweetheart and Hicks the ideal representative of the man about town. To-day he is almost the last man who can give the real suggestion of those golden days. He has kept abreast of the times, he is the youngest man of his age in the world, but there is always the aura of sovereigns, of coach and four meetings, of broughams, of tall hats, gold-mounted sticks, and good wine about him. He is one of the great wits of his time and the sorrow is that he never had a Boswell to take it all down and pass to posterity those lightning flashes of Seymour's alert mind. That wit is as keen and nimble to-day. Seymour, too, could start fashions, and did so. On one occasion he gave evidence in some law suit, and it was observed that he wore a pink shirt and black silk tie. Within a week, every smart young man in London was wearing the same. Hicks could have been the David Garrick of his generation, but he loved to have a lark. He knew and he understood the attraction of musical shows, and his wife was supreme in them. During the time they were at the Vaudeville they did some splendid productions. And they also gave us *Quality Street*. *The Belle of Mayfair*, *The Catch of the Season*, both true Edwardian musical shows, produced in the early years of the century, almost challenged the Gaiety's supremacy. In *The Catch of the Season* Seymour Hicks presented us with living examples of the Gibson Girls—those creations of American womanhood drawn with such mastery by Charles Dana Gibson. Camille Clifford was the very embodiment of this majestically curved femininity. But London had its own girls, also situated in the Strand. They were the Gaiety Girls. Both began with a G, and London rather preferred the home sample.

What versatility Hicks showed at the Vaudeville—a true sample of the Edwardian actor's power and resource. For he presented that great portrait of 'Scrooge' there as well, and two very lovely children's plays, *Bluebell in Fairyland* and *Alice in Wonderland*. Ella was the daintiest 'Alice' imaginable. She had stepped out of Tenniel. And the Hicks' time at the Vaudeville in the Strand gave us one of the great popular songs. Ellaline Terriss sang it in *Bluebell in Fairyland*. Soon everybody sang it, everybody whistled it, everybody played it. It was on all the organs, and in the repertoire of every band. It is even heard to-day, this ballad so typical of its time. Its name is 'The Honeysuckle and the Bee'—and it came from The Strand, so far as this country is concerned.

He gave us two new stars, too, both at the Vaudeville, the two Dares—Zena and Phyllis. Both had started in pantomime, both got their

I

big chances at the Vaudeville with Hicks. Phyllis as 'Mab' in *Bluebell* and Zena in *The Catch of the Season*—written for Ella, who, however, fell ill. So during that time the Vaudeville ran the Gaiety close in the picture postcard stakes, for in Ellaline Terriss and the Sisters Dare it had three great favourites, whose smiling pictures sold like wildfire. And Seymour himself was well in the van of the men.

Afterwards the Hickses went to the Aldwych, in association with Charles Frohman, to give us other musical delights, including the sight of Seymour Hicks as a Gay Gordon.

The skill and resource of this remarkable man is still unappreciated. He could—and did—do it all. He wrote dramas, comedies, musical comedies—he produced, he sang, he danced, and he acted. He even had a theatre named after him. The cleverest young men of the day have nothing on him. He was not looked upon as a marvel, as something to wonder at, for it was expected of him in those days. It was a time of achievement, a time of giants, and he was a giant amongst them.

That Aldwych Theatre arose in 1905, and with another new theatre, then called the Waldorf, flanked the new Waldorf Hotel. The theatre of that name was to undergo some vicissitudes before, at last, it took the name of the Strand Theatre, for the old playhouse which, by the way, called itself the Royal Strand, was closed and pulled down to make a Tube Station.

There were other delectable spots in the Strand. There was the Tivoli Music Hall, where you found the real music hall atmosphere and where you got twenty-four star turns per night for your money. You had your drinks—whisky at threepence a time, beer at twopence, popular cigarettes at twopence-halfpenny or threepence for ten, and everything else in proportion, you sat in your seat or you stood by the bar, and you saw the pageant of British Music Hall go by. It was a man's place. You smoked pipes if you wanted to, or your cigar (you could get a smokable cigar for threepence, too), and you roared out the choruses. You were free and easy, you hailed your friends, you told stories, you laughed loudly and long. The world was gay, you had not a care, and the glorious bonhomie of music hall surrounded you. Odd things happened there sometimes. A Japanese wrestler topped the bill—Yokio Tani, who introduced ju-jitsu. Tani issued challenges. One night a famous wrestler was to oppose him, but did not put in an appearance. Rather than that the Tiv. public should be disappointed, a substitute was found. A tall, stalwart man with a beaming smile and happy expression tried conclusions with the Jap. He put up a good show, but Tani was too expert. But, just to show the resources of the Tivoli, the man who filled the bill was one of their own 'linkmen.' He got tremendous applause. And he is still a linkman to-day—still upright, still alert, and still smiling happily and brightly. His name is Albert Key, and he is linkman at the Phœnix Theatre. He is more than a linkman—he is a direct link with Edwardian London and the dear old Tiv. When the show at this hall was over, the Strand was full of men, all in the happiest of moods, and the adjacent pubs were filled to overflowing. Some would go over to Yates's Wine Lodge, which still retains its old flavour. But Yates, its founder, died a millionaire. He was a Strand character. Port was his great speciality.

On his birthday he gave his customers a treat. His special ninepenny port was sold for sixpence. He did not lose by the reduction. He made more money than ever by his customers' desire to make the most of the bargain and to drink the health of kind Mr. Yates.

Some might pop into Romano's for supper. There they would see theatreland eating and drinking. They would also most likely see that artist who—best of everyone—caught the spirit of London, of Cockneys and the Strand—Phil May. There he was, looking something like an ostler, with his clipped hair, his fringe, and his rather lank, clean-shaven face, with either a straw or a cigar in his mouth. And you were almost certain to see Arthur Collins, King of Drury Lane, seated at his own table, where he had very likely been since lunch-time, talking, talking, talking to a circle of friends. In conversation he rivalled the famous poetic brook.

You could have seen the last of Irving at the Lyceum, and you could, in Edwardian days, have seen pantomimes run by Smith and Carpenter, or dramas staged by the same combination management. Also you could have seen Shakespeare too, with Matheson Lang as 'Hamlet.' Or romantic drama, with that same fine actor as 'The Proud Prince.' If it was Hall Caine you fancied, he was just off the Strand too, at the Lyceum, again with Lang, either as 'John Storm' in *The Christian*, or as 'Pete.' If your taste ran to real full-blooded melodrama, again Smith and Carpenter would oblige you. One of these shows, *The Prince and the Beggar Maid*, was a terrific success, with handsome, romantic Norman Partreidge in the lead, and also in *Her Midnight Wedding*. And there was another real 'cut and thruster' in *The Fighting Chance*, written by an actor called Edward Ferris, which had a true transpontine smack. When the hero was accused of cheating at cards and the facts looked all against him, his friend said, "Damn the evidence, I know him to be innocent." How we cheered. We were amused at the sight of the British army marching to war, seen through a window, apparently an endless procession of men. But the constant reappearance of a tall and very round-shouldered officer caused us to believe that this mighty fighting force consisted of a few supers marching round and round in a circle. But we forgave all that when we watched deeds of defiance and daring in a Himalayan hill-fort, and when the second hero had his eyes put out by the wily and cruel Pathans, and appeared before us bloodstained and blind. We knew it would all come right, and sure enough it did, for, his villainy unmasked, Eric Mayne, the Lyceum 'bad man' par excellence, shot himself before our very eyes. Virtue—and the Flag—triumphed.

There remains the Savoy, whose story and whose operas everyone knows. They belong to the Victorian times, but the Edwardians saw delightful revivals with Walter Passmore, and later with that neat and finished comedian, Charles Workman, whom many liked best of all.

The Strand is changed. But still the tide of life beats along it, still Nelson's Column is glimpsed by wayfarers westward, and if its St. Clement's is blitzed, its spirit and its walls still stand erect. And still, despite its crowd of women workers, the Strand remains a man's street, and still the Edwardian spirit lingers and can be found by those who know it when they see it. For the Strand is immortal—like the city of which it forms a part. It is not for Edwardian but for all time.

CHAPTER X

Charles Frohman

EVER SINCE THERE HAS BEEN AN AMERICAN STAGE, THERE HAS BEEN THE closest theatrical interchange between it and the stage of our country. Its sons and daughters have come here, many to triumph, a few to fail, and some to remain for the rest of their lives. And the same is true of many British actors and actresses as regards the U.S.A. They have gone to the States on a visit, and they have remained there permanently. We have, on the other hand, many American stars whom we have forgotten are not of our own land, so much have they become part of our lives.

But of all the great American men of the Theatre, perhaps none loved London, and was in turn by London beloved, as was Charles Frohman, the American who 'presented.' England, by the side of the most English river in the world, our own Thames, holds his memory in a cenotaph in Marlow churchyard, a place he loved. He met his death in an English ship off our shores, a victim of German brutality. But his real spirit lives in the Theatre.

Charles Frohman, who made such a mark on the British Theatre, was on his way to London to settle a lawsuit arising out of a theatre dispute when a torpedo from a German U-boat sent the magnificent *Lusitania* to the bottom.

Charles Frohman, who was to achieve so much, was the son of a German peasant, one Henry Frohman, who left his own country for the freedom America offered in making a fortune. There he met his old sweetheart, whose parents had also crossed the Atlantic, and they married. Henry Frohman loved the Theatre and all things connected with it. He never made a fortune, but he found love and happiness. The spark of greatness in him was passed on to his third son, Charles, in whom it glowed and kindled and finally burst into flame.

Born in Ohio, he was a real American. The blood might have been German, but the air of America aerated it with American ideas. Charles Frohman was typical of his country, in energy, in ideas, in outlook, and in drive. But enough of the European remained to make him love London when he came to that city, to conquer it by his artistic productions, his idealism, and, above all things, by his affection, compelling charm, and his great honesty.

He had, as a small boy, the ready smile and the great charm which inspired so much devotion. There was not a lot of money in the Frohman *ménage*, but Charles satisfied his urge for the Theatre by his own ingenuity. It was his calling and he always knew it. He saw his first play by selling souvenirs of it, he walked on as a page, he got in by free passes. Step by step the Theatre claimed him, grade by grade he mounted, until he knew every one of the multifarious jobs which go to make up the profession— and knew them inside out because he had done them all. He was never at a loss, that quick, alert mind surmounted a thousand difficulties which would have nonplussed a lesser man. Back stage, box office, 'advance,' acting itself, he knew it all!

He made his first visit to England in 1880. He was then advance manager, and assistant manager, too, for Haverly's Minstrels—a great American minstrel troupe for which he had done wonderful work. They came to town and they created a sensation. Their highly coloured posters—the work of Frohman—struck a new note.

They performed at Her Majesty's Theatre—then an opera house—in the Haymarket—black-faced minstrels trod the boards where diva had warbled, 'darkie's' ditties took the place of arias—and London loved it. But young Charles Frohman flew at high game, indeed the Highest. He wanted a Royal Visit. And he got it. The Prince of Wales (King Edward VII) came to see the show, with the Princess (to be Queen Alexandra), the Duke of Clarence, and as many of the rest of the Royal children as were old enough to stay up at night. And young Frohman received them himself, adorned in evening dress, which he hated—for Bill Foote, the real manager, took fright at the last moment. Haverly's Minstrels were a huge success. Most of it was due to that small, smiling, dark, round figure, who looked just like one of those little 'Billikin' mascots. After a triumphant visit they went home. But Big Bill Foote, the Mastodon Minstrels manager, had surrendered to England, and having purchased an hotel, settled down near London. Charles succeeded to the post, his highest yet. England had made it possible. Thus early did it enter into his life.

He never looked back. He did, however, look for new fields to conquer, and he found them in the Theatre. In face, again, of incredible difficulties, he won, and eventually he assaulted New York. And he conquered it. He began to get the best around him. He began to make the stars. He made a constellation of them, the greatest of their time. He said once, that all you had to do was to put up a name in big electric lights and the imagination of the public did the rest. But he knew that the metal must be right or the star could not be forged.

Three things brought about his final conquest of London. A star, dramatist, and himself. The star was a woman—Maude Adams ; the dramatist was a little Scotsman, named J. M. Barrie—the rest was the Frohman brain, charm and integrity.

Barrie was a rising dramatist. *Walker London* and *A Professor's Love Story* had arisen to point the way to future greatness. Barrie's book, *The Little Minister*, for which he had not obtained American copyright, had been pirated. Frohman, who had seen the American production of *The Professor's Love Story*, cabled to Barrie to dramatize *The Little Minister* himself. Barrie did not want to do it. But Frohman, who never took No for an answer, sent cable after cable. So Barrie went off to see what it was all about. He told Frohman that his difficulty was to find an actress in America who could play 'Lady Babbie.' Frohman said he would do some thinking, and artfully sent Barrie down into the Empire Theatre, which he was controlling, to see *Rosemary*, an English play which he was 'presenting.' At the end of the show, as he had expected, an excited Barrie rushed back, saying he had found the girl for 'Babbie.' It was Maude Adams, who was playing lead in *Rosemary*. That was what Frohman had hoped for. Barrie came home and wrote the play. Over here Winifred Emery played 'Babbie' and Cyril Maude played 'The

Little Minister.' Over there Maude Adams stepped into real stardom in the role. Robert Edeson played the title part. After that Frohman did all of Barrie's plays in America. A combination had formed which was to give great plays, great acting and great productions to the stage of two hemispheres.

The rest of this story must now centre in London, the London of the Edwardian days. Frohman opened London offices, in Henrietta Street, by the Strand. This was of great importance, it is now realized, for he was the first American manager to do so. Others had paid visits, had come over with plays. One—Augustin Daly—had even opened a theatre named after him, but none of them had stayed. Frohman established himself in a modest way. He engaged W. Lestocq as his London manager. He told Lestocq that he was coming in to produce plays quite humbly by the back door, but that he would get to the front door and Lestocq would go with him. And it did happen that way. Frohman always knew.

He did not open with a flourish of trumpets, he did not make a big individual splash. His astute mind told him to learn the ropes, to feel his way, to avoid mistakes through ignorance of tastes, methods and manners. He knew that American ways were not English ways. But he liked English ways and he loved London. He associated himself with the Gattis, who were, like him, upright honourable men of their world. He started at the Adelphi with *The Lost Paradise*. It failed. Frohman was not downcast. It only spurred him on. In Gattis' other theatre, the Vaudeville, he joined up with the great George Edwardes. The result was *A Night Out !* That play gave Londoners a night out for a long time ; it was a raging success. It joined the hands of two giants of the Theatre—Edwardes and Frohman. It started Frohman's dual control of New York and London, for by his dual interest he got control of the English play exportation to the States, then very considerable. Through Frohman the Edwardes' shows went to America. And he imported the best American plays here. And it is significant that in all the dealings he had then and afterwards with the Gattis no contract ever existed between them. Neither needed it. Both had their word as bond.

Frohman sold out his rights in *A Night Out*—Seymour Hicks' championship of the play had much to do with its production in the first place. He carried the cheque around in his pocket so long that it was just a dirty crumpled piece of paper when Lestocq got it from him and paid it in. It was typical of his regard for money.

In 1897—Diamond Jubilee Year and the year which started Edwardian London, Frohman came again to the Adelphi, where he had tasted defeat. He brought over *Secret Service* and with it he brought an American actor, William Gillette. *Secret Service* was produced at the Adelphi. William Terriss—most flamboyant of actors—was the hero ; Gillette, most restrained of actors, was the villain. They shared the honours, Gillette being at once taken to the hearts of the British public for showing them something good—and something new. It was during the run of this play that poor Terriss was murdered. It was about Gillette's success in this play that Frohman laid down a dictum which showed his grasp of theatre knowledge. For, commenting on Gillette's modesty and reserve, he said that nothing kills the proper growth of an actor's art, or his usefulness, as the idea that social enjoyment makes for public success, and that because he is a social lion it is no longer necessary for him to take pains. That is worth repeating, for it is apt to be forgotten to-day. Gillette's success in the Strand made him a star in America, a joke which Frohman enjoyed hugely.

But Frohman was established in London. Now he wished to take root. He was associated with the Gattis and with George Edwardes ; he had shows running at the Adelphi, the Garrick and the Vaudeville. But he wanted his own shop window.

He fancied the Duke of York's Theatre, in St. Martin's Lane. This had been built and was owned by Violet Melnotte, one of theatreland's most curious characters. She had been an actress ; she had married Frank Wyatt, an actor. He was a descendant of the beautiful Misses Gunning. Violet Melnotte made them at once her own ancestresses and would boast about them, expecting (and often receiving) compliments about the good looks being hereditary. Their son was called Frank Gunning Wyatt. Although she lived to be over eighty, Violet Melnotte —known to her staff as 'Madam'—was always the epitome of Victorianism so far as dress and appearance went. In her the so-called Naughty Nineties lived on. Snow-white hair, a 'fine' figure, piercing eyes heavily made-up, a pale face (made paler by cosmetic), elbow gloves, large hats or saucy bonnets, gleaming with jewels and lustrous with pearls, she was an awe-inspiring figure. Her head, however, moved with the times, and although she always protested she was being swindled, she usually got the best of the bargain. She could be a thunderstorm and a summer breeze in successive moments, and nobody ever made up their minds which was the worst. She always quarrelled with her tenants and associates, but when she forgot the fight, she expected the antagonist to do the same. To the few people she trusted and to whom she was well known, she was a delightful companion and could be generous, but she regarded most people as foes. Much of her trouble was loneliness.

Charles Frohman, however, took a nineteen-years' lease of her theatre from 1897, and she never quarrelled with him. Nobody could have done so.

He made the Duke of York's Theatre his London home. He was as proud of it as of his New York home, the Empire Theatre. Indeed, on the walls of the Empire he emblazoned his London address. His work there made the Duke of York's the most distinguished theatre in London. It became a home of art, of real drama and comedy, a nursery for stars, and a place from which future actor-managers emerged to carry on. He had everything of the best. His own office was, in reality, the Royal Retiring Room, a long, low, underground room beneath and behind the Royal Box. The room was all in red, a colour he loved, and there he would sit, cross-legged like a little Buddha (whom he much resembled), do his business, work with his staff and entertain his friends. The room was famous. Years after his death, it became famous again. For a manager of the Duke of York's made it his reception room and informal club. Decorated then in stippled blue, with cherry red upholstery, beautiful old furniture and Waterford glass, it became the Mecca of

Bohemian London. An opponent called it 'The Poison Parlour.' Its habitués welcomed the name and always used it. For many years everyone who was anyone in Fleet Street, literature, stage, films, sport, the Law—even the Ring and the Police Force—could be found there nightly. Its founder always attributed the delightful atmosphere of that room to the spirit of Charles Frohman, its greatest inhabitant. And how Frohman would have enjoyed those evenings.

Frohman surrounded himself with personalities. His manager was Lestocq. A first lieutenant and publicity director was Chester Fox—a most notable man who drifted out of Insurance into the Theatre. Fox was tall, thin, with a clear-cut face decorated with a 'Captain Cuttle beard.' His hair and colouring suggested the animal from whom he got his name. At night he always wore full evening dress, with an opera hat tilted on one side, white gloves, a long black cane with a golden knob and tassel, and an opera cloak lined with red. You could not miss him— and he took care that you should not. He was nicknamed 'The Flying Fox,' for, as Frohman's emissary, he would appear in provincial towns, in the great cities of the Continent and in America, with the speed of the uninvented aeroplane. And he knew his business backward. As house-manager, Frohman had James W. Mathews. He was another great character. He ran that theatre with an air. He had an air himself. In the vestibule, in place of ashtrays fastened on the walls, stood four small but immaculate page boys, each bearing the maximum amount of bright buttons on their diminutive persons, their small heads decorated with little round caps set rakishly askew. They stood in the four corners, each holding a large ashtray in their cupped hands. But primarily they were Mathews' slaves. Let him appear *en route* to going out to dinner. Those boys jumped into activity. The first brought his coat, and helped him into it, the second handed him his glossy silk hat, giving it a final rub to make it shine the brighter, the third handed him his white or bright wash-leather gloves, and the fourth offered his walking-stick. And by this time Boy Number One had a lighted match ready to apply to Mr. Mathews' cigar. When that important ceremony was over, they dashed to the centre door, and two on each side, stiff as ramrods, they held it open whilst he sallied forth, saluting smartly as he passed them by. Then, they closed the doors and returned to their posts. Mr. Mathews' going out to dinner was one of the sights of London. He was a real manager and he lived in the theatre—actually lived in it. For the suite of offices above he turned into a flat. The large one he slept in and had a bath installed, which is still there. The smaller central room was his living-room, and the one at the end of the corridor he equipped as a kitchen. In later years Violet Melnotte had all her meals cooked there too. For although she slept at the Piccadilly Hotel, she lived her days and nights in the Duke of York's—when not at the Metropole Hotel, Brighton. And even when there, some sort of telepathic system or spy service worked very efficiently, for one day a chimney pot from the theatre roof crashed into St. Martin's Lane, narrowly missing some passers-by. Within five minutes Madam was on the phone to know how it had happened.

But Frohman had as his producer-in-chief the best man of his day—

Dion Boucicault, a very genius at his work and a fine actor into the bargain. He, more than anyone else, helped Frohman to make the glory that lit the Duke of York's in Edwardian days, and his wife, our revered and beloved Irene Vanbrugh, was the theatre's great leading lady.

Frohman opened with *The Adventure of Lady Ursula*, by Anthony Hope, then in the height of his fame. It was a lavish and beautiful production, and even the most captious critics admitted that every detail was right—down to the last button. That was the Frohman way—and the Boucicault way. That was on the 11th October 1898, and the play was a big success. Lovely Evelyn Millard played the title role and looked bewitching in her eighteenth century male attire—for it was a patch and powder play.

Frohman started off with the right foot. It was the beginning of a golden era. Play followed play, star followed star, newcomers stepped into stardom, or got their feet on the ladder. Great dramatists were only too eager to let him have plays and he was only too eager to produce them. There is nothing like it to-day. They were not all successes, of course, Frohman had his full share of failures. But they were all done with the meticulous care and first-class casting and mounting upon which he always insisted and which Boucicault knew so well how to give.

One can take a few landmarks and deal with them, the whole story would require a book, a book which must one day be written. For it is really the history of the stage of the time. In 1901 Frohman had, in London alone, interests in five theatres and five plays—the Aldwych, the Shaftesbury, the Vaudeville, the Criterion and the Duke of York's, and his London plays were *Sherlock Holmes*, *Are You a Mason*, *Bluebell in Fairyland* (with the Hickses), *The Twin Sister* and *The Girl from Maxim's*. *Sherlock Holmes* was at the Duke of York's, and in it, playing the part of a small but saucy boy, was a lad called Charles Chaplin.

One of Frohman's failures was *The Christian*, by Hall Caine. A friend expressed sorrow. But Frohman replied : "Forget it. Don't let's revive the past. Let's get busy, and pulverise the future." That was exactly Charles Frohman. Another failure, though not at the Duke of York's, was *Nelly Neil*, in 1907. In that Edna May said farewell to the stage she so greatly adorned. It was a lovely production and Frohman thought it a lovely play. He had lavished money on it. But its only appeal was the fact that it was farewell to Edna May, who had decided to retire and marry. She had a tremendous farewell, and incidentally she refused to play in *The Merry Widow*, and alter her matrimonial plans.

Frohman had to take off *Nelly Neil*. He put up the usual fortnight's notice. Lestocq said it seemed a shame. "Shut up, or I'll change my mind," said Frohman. "If you don't I shall run it another month, and if I don't keep myself in hand sometimes, sentiment will ruin me."

But Edna May had been with him at the Duke of York's, too, in *The Girl from Up There*, in 1901. And along that alley which leads to the stage door had walked a young, tall, American light comedian, to appear with her, and make his English début. His name was Joseph Coyne. He was with her, too, in *Nelly Neil*. He did not refuse the invitation to appear in *The Merry Widow*, as all the world knows. And he stayed in England and died here—regarded as one of ourselves.

But the highlights of the many wonders at the Duke of York's in Frohman's time came from his bosom friend, J. M. Barrie—Frohman described them himself as "the two shyest men in the world."

Those highlights are *Peter Pan*, *The Admirable Crichton*, and *What Every Woman Knows*. It is safe to call them classics. They represent, with Pinero, and Henry Arthur Jones, the best of the Edwardian Theatre, with Galsworthy and Maugham joined at the end. The great Shaw is a thing apart—he is for no particular time, like Shakespeare. But Barrie, Pinero, Maugham and Galsworthy were all associated with Frohman at the Duke of York's. Barrie was pre-eminently the Frohman British dramatist.

The Admirable Crichton was a Barrie masterpiece. It is often revived. But its first cast and its first production were so perfectly chosen and carried out that it was one of the great events of the Edwardian theatre. Its novelty, its satire, its wit, its drama burst upon the public on 4th November 1902, and it ran for 328 performances. Most playgoers have seen it at revivals. But the story of the butler who proved the only capable man when his employers were wrecked on a desert island, who became their uncrowned king and was about to marry the peer's eldest daughter, who adored his mastery, when the relief ship arrived, took them back to civilization, and paired off the butler with the tweenymaid, who worshipped him from afar, caught everybody's fancy. And the butler, a man of tact, retired from the service of the family, to become landlord of a pub with the unusual but highly suitable name of 'The Case is Altered.' Frohman gave Barrie a cast worthy of him and Boucicault staged it with genius. What a cast it was. H. B. Irving as 'Crichton,' probably his finest performance, Irene Vanbrugh as 'Lady Mary Lasenby' (also one of her finest performances), Sybil Carlisle and Muriel Beaumont as her two sisters, Henry Kemble was 'The Earl of Loam'—and Kemble (nicknamed 'The Beetle') was a terrific personality ; Pattie Browne was a delightful Tweeny, Clarence Blakiston was 'Rev. John Treherne,' the cricket-mad clergyman so kindly provided by Barrie so that the conventions might be safe for the shipwrecked party, Fanny Coleman was 'Lady Brocklehurst,' and last, but by no means least, Gerald du Maurier played 'The Hon. Ernest Woolley,' the empty-headed young man about town given to making bad epigrams. H. B. Irving, perfect butler of the first act, a man without a vestige of humanity showing,—the perfect, efficient automaton, struck the note which Barrie wished to play, the key in which the play was set, when, at the party given by the Earl (who believed himself a democrat) to his servants, he informed Lady Mary, but only in response to her cross-examination, that he disapproved of such things as this. "There must always be a master and servant in all civilized communities, my lady, for it is natural, and whatever is natural, is right." Barrie proceeded to debunk the sham democracy of the aristocrats of his time by wrecking them on a desert island, showing them all to be hopelessly inefficient (though the cricket enthusiast of a clergyman showed a desire to be helpful) and then putting the former butler in complete and utter control. He became dictator, king, they became his servants. He knew how to do everything—hence the title—they had to learn and he taught them without the gloves on. And in due course, his one-time fancy of a servant shifted from the lovable, common little tweeny-maid, to the former proud and haughty beauty, his master's daughter, 'Lady Mary,' now breeched in deerskins, and showing an aptitude with the bow and arrow. Woolley and his epigrams—and laziness—he disposed of by frequently immersing the honourable head in a bucket.

But love grew between the butler and the titled fair—and in a most poignant and beautifully played scene, he told her of it. She responded —one will never cease to hear Irving recite, "I was a King in Babylon. You were a Christian slave," and her trembling reply of, "It might have been." It was a love scene played by two consummate artists, a difficult scene which in lesser hands might have been border line—but in theirs it swept the audience away. And then the scene when, his choice acclaimed by all, the clergyman ready for the ceremony, and a wild feast and dance is at his height—a ship is sighted. All go mad—except Crichton. To them it means release, a return to their own society, civilization and status. To Crichton it means servitude—to Lady Mary it means—what? The loss of the man she loves—the loss of the paramount position she would hold on the island? Or to be Lady Mary once more, in the position in town and country to which, as testified in the Catechism, it had pleased God to call her? Crichton has set his own downfall. In his preparations for an emergency he has fixed up a signal which no passing ship could ignore. There is anxiety on the heels of joy. Will the ship see them—or will it pass on its way? If Crichton does not pull the lever which will bring it to their aid—it will not come to them. To Bill Crichton the temptation is terrible. For a wild second Lady Mary has the mind to prevent him. But training exerts itself, the old tradition of the perfect servant tells—"Bill Crichton's got to play the game," he declares—and make the signal which means so much to everyone. And, as the bonfires blaze on the heights and the cheers of the rest report the answering signals of the ship, Lady Mary turns to him. She uses the name they know him by on the island. "Guv," she whispers. Crichton's arms go out, his gay robe of parrots' feathers, the signal of his mastership, falls from him, his head falls, his shoulders droop, and his hands clasp and wash themselves in invisible soap, the outward sign of servitude, as he answers, "My Lady."

After one of the finest middle acts ever written, the first nighters at the Duke of York's feared for the last act. There was no need. It was one of the perfect last acts of all time, ruthless in its satire, keen in observation and penetration, yet with a background of real sentiment. A triumph for all concerned.

Old playgoers will never forget the beautiful graduation of character expressed by H. B. Irving, the gradual growth of mastery over servility in the early island scenes the emergence of the man from the machine. Nor will they forget Irene Vanbrugh's perfect handling of the big love scene, nor her expression of modest, self-conscious triumph when she had accepted 'Crichton,' sat at table with him alone, and heard him say to her sister, "Serve your mistress first, girl." It was one of those moments which skilled playing can make immortal.

The Admirable Crichton firmly established Gerald du Maurier in the public favour. *Raffles* at the Comedy came after. His association with

Frohman at the Duke of York's, however, was the corner stone of his brilliant career. And of H. B. Irving's performances there, one must remember *Letty*, the Pinero play.

Perhaps the best remembered of all Frohman's wonderful work at the Duke of York's is *Peter Pan*. Barrie gave him this script in a rather shame-faced fashion, saying he did not think it commercial. For it was a dream child of his. Frohman read it. It entranced him. He could talk of nothing else, he would even act scenes from it to his friends. It became an obsession. Yet the production presented great difficulties at the Duke of York's, as its form was entirely new. But there was Dion Boucicault to handle it. It was originally called *The Great White Father*, but Barrie soon altered that and called it after its hero. It was all the same to Frohman, whose enthusiasm bubbled and whose money flowed like water to make this thing a success. Yet, when the night of its first production came, 27th December 1904, Frohman was not at the Duke of York's to see it. Business had called him to America. He was not to see the beautiful thing which Barrie, he and Boucicault had created take its first steps and make its first impact on a London audience. He was at his house in White Plains, with his friend, Paul M. Potter. A system of messages had been organized. Lestocq was to cable from London to Frohman's secretary in New York, who was in turn to telephone to Frohman. A snowstorm raged as Frohman waited—and waited. The storm interfered with the telephones. Frohman waited on tenterhooks. He acted the whole play to Potter during that period of suspense, interspersed with exclamations of, "Will it never come?" And then—the telephone rang. It was Potter who answered it, whilst Frohman stood breathless. "What's the verdict?" he gasped to the listening man. The message from Lestocq was, 'Peter Pan all right. Looks like a big success.' Frohman was in the seventh heaven.

It was under-statement from Lestocq, who was always on the careful side. *Peter Pan* was more than all right. And many people think that the 'Peter Pan' of that night, Nina Boucicault, was the best of them all. But then, of course, first impressions go for so much in the Theatre. The cast bristled with stars, of to-day and to-morrow—but *Peter Pan* is history, so why labour it?

But one of the players of tiny parts plays such a large part in the story of Frohman and the Duke of York's that she must be mentioned. She is Pauline Chase, one of the daintiest and loveliest things which ever crossed a stage. Frohman believed in her and thought much of her. She rose from small parts to stardom because of that belief. He, Barrie and Pauline Chase were great friends. She had been a small part girl in *The Girl from Up There*, she had been a pink pyjama girl in *Liberty Belles* in New York, she had had a tiny part in *The School Girl* at the Prince of Wales's, she had a tiny part in *Peter Pan*. But the eyes of two great men were on her, the eyes of the man who had written *Peter Pan* and the man who had put it on the stage. Neither of these two had ever grown up, that was their bond of friendship and that was the secret of Frohman's greatness. Neither ever lost their enthusiasm because in their hearts they retained their youth. Men such as this do much in the Theatre, because, to them, there is always to-morrow, there is always an exciting freshness, the freshness of creation. They never get tired or stale. *Peter Pan* eventually went on tour with Cissie Loftus as 'Peter.' Pauline Chase played one of the twins and understudied Cissie Loftus. At Liverpool Miss Loftus was ill and Pauline had to play. She got a wire from Frohman : 'Barrie and I are coming down to see you act. If we like you well enough to play Peter I will send you back a sheet of paper with a cross mark on it after the play.' That wire was enough to scare pretty Pauline Chase right on to her toes. But mark the genius of Frohman, as expressed in the method by which he would show his satisfaction. No going round and uttering words of praise—that is for the grown-ups who don't know any better. No, a piece of paper marked with a cross ! Something so definite, so delightful—something which, if received, to keep and treasure forever. She played 'Peter,' the two creators watched. Then they hurried off to catch their train, whilst in her dressing room, Pauline stood, breathless, scared, hopeful and wondering. There was a tap on the door. Her heart stood still. An attendant handed her a piece of paper. She undid it with trembling hands—and there was the black cross. Pauline Chase was to become 'Peter Pan.' And she was a delightful, fascinating 'Peter Pan' for many seasons.

Friendship was to grow between the players of that little paper game. Barrie wrote a little play especially for her which Frohman did at the Duke of York's, which was played in conjunction with *Peter Pan*. It was called *Pantaloon*. It was the figures of the harlequinade seen through the eyes of Barrie and it was wholly delightful. So was Pauline Chase, she was the incarnation of Columbine. One remembers yet her appeal with Harlequin for permission to marry. 'Pantaloon' asked how much money they had and shook his head when he found it just a few shillings. "I had a pound and a piano case when I married," he told them. Du Maurier was 'Pantaloon.'

Pauline Chase lived near Marlow-on-Thames, which Frohman came to love. In the porch of her cottage he would smoke his long, black cigars, and indulge in his only exercise, a game of croquet with Barrie, or with Captain Scott, the hero of the Antarctic. And all the time he read plays.

Frohman was a manager who actually read plays himself. One of Pauline Chase's friendly duties for Frohman was to cut his finger nails. She was abroad. He sent her a cable—'Nails.' She replied, 'I am afraid you will have to bite them.' Frohman cabled back, 'I have.' That is what things were like for people who worked for Frohman. He loved Marlow and once said that the sight of its church made him want to die and stay there. A memorial to him is in the churchyard. And in that same little haven of peace lie the bones of Richardson, the great English showman, who took the drama the length and breadth of the kingdom in his great booth, and who numbered Edmund Kean in his company. The two men would have been great friends. Frohman loved everything about Marlow and was a great customer in its antique shops. He chuckled over this and said that when he bought things the proprietors always told him if they were real or not, because they were friends of his. Also the local barber always shaved him for a penny, because he also was a friend.

Another great Frohman triumph at the Duke of York's was *What Every Woman Knows*—again by Barrie. This play has also become a classic.

First produced on 3rd September 1908, it was a sensation and it has remained one. Here Du Maurier showed us the real star quality and his great power of acting in true colours. His 'John Shand,' the poor working Scot who rose to such great heights, was a masterpiece. The first act was an amazing piece of work, and the members of the Wylie family were just superb. Sydney Valentine, Henry Vibart, Edmund Gwenn and Hilda Trevelyan formed this clan, and were the perfect Scottish family. Yet none of them were Scots. Hilda Trevelyan was a Frohman star—her 'Wendy' in *Peter Pan* was perfection, so was her 'Maggie' in *What Every Woman Knows*. Those who saw this play will recall that memorable interview between the family and John Shand, and the pact made, and also the breathless excitement of the election scene with Edmund Gwenn the epitome of Scottish excitement—than which nothing is more feverish. A landmark in theatre history, the whole thing, and one of Frohman's great nights.

But it must not be thought by the younger generations that Frohman had no failures. He had a great many. Indeed one season he lost so much money that Sir John Hare did a memorable thing. Frohman was the most retiring of men. He never took a call, he was never in the limelight, though nobody knew better than he how to shine it on others. But there was a dearth of limelight for anyone that particular season, and Frohman, who put failures resolutely behind him, found they had accumulated in a great pile. That was when Sir John Hare, great gentle-man of the Theatre, took action. He got together his most distinguished colleagues of the profession. He said to them : "Frohman has done big things. He loses his money like a gentleman. Let us make him feel that he is not just an American, but one of us." That was the way the Edwardian Theatre behaved itself. So they arranged, in true British style, a dinner in his honour at the Garrick Club. Frohman was then the only American theatrical manager who had been made a member of that exclusive valhalla. But the idea of the dinner frightened the life out of him. He said he did not like that sort of thing, and besides, he could not make a speech. Pinero, who was on the committee, reassured him by saying that he would not have to. But still he tried every artifice he could to dodge the dinner, but the cream of the English stage was relentless. He capitulated by making a condition that all he would have to say was, "Thank you." It was agreed.

The dinner was held, with Hare in the chair. They gave him a silver cigarette box on which were facsimile autographs of Pinero, Wyndham, Hare, Tree, Barrie, Sutro, Maude, H. B. Irving, Laurence Irving, Louis N. Parker, Anthony Hope, A. E. W. Mason, Seymour Hicks, Robert Marshall, W. Comyns Carr, Weedon Grossmith, Gerald du Maurier, Eric Lewis, Dion Boucicault, A. E. Matthews, Arthur Bourchier, Cosmo Hamilton, Allan Aynesworth, R. C. Carton, Sam Sothern and C. Aubrey Smith—in other words all the best of the Edwardian Theatre itself. And Frohman just managed to say, "Thank you," but never lost his feeling of gratitude.

Frohman knew, too, what it was to get the bird, and in the Duke of York's at that. He had it more than once, but a very virulent occasion was the first night of Pinero's *Mind the Paint Girl* in 1912. This play was a curious affair. Rumours had leaked out that it was to be an exposé of back stage secrets of musical comedy, of the Gaiety and Daly's and of the great George Edwardes. The public did not like the idea. Although always ready to lend an ear to theatrical scandals, their idolatry of Edwardes made the thing seem repugnant to them, and they could not understand it either. Frohman and Edwardes were friends, colleagues, they worked together. What was this all about? Marie Lohr, then a new star, in the very flower of her lovely youth, played the heroine. It was further put about that Edwardes himself would be represented on the stage. e The title came from a song which Marie Lohr was to sing, in her character of leading lady of musical comedy.

The first night saw the theatre packed from ceiling to floor and with an atmosphere of electricity. George Edwardes himself was there, silver-haired, fresh-complexioned and smiling, with his lieutenants, Arthur Cohen, and big, handsome J. A. E. Malone, as bodyguards. In the vestibule members of the audience assured him of their confidence in him. He thanked them and smiled. The curtain went up on a tense house. The play proceeded, and in due course, the actor who was to represent Edwardes made his appearance and his exit. He was not made up to resemble the 'Guv'nor,' only the sleepy, drawling voice showed any like-ness, for John Tresahar, who played the part, had dark hair and wore a dark beard. As the play went on, one thing became clear. There was no scandal at all, only a bad play about a subject which was so unimpor-tant as to seem ridiculous. The booing started during the last act. Vainly did Marie Lohr and Allan Aynesworth, now disguised in a beard as well, struggle against it. It was no good at all, and Frohman or no Frohman, Pinero or no Pinero, the public would have nothing of it and signified the same in the usual way, only rather more lustily. They did not like the *Mind the Paint Girl*, and they were right. It was in this play that the undercurrent of suggested salacity which marred the later works of that great dramatist showed itself clearly. It became more apparent in *Preserving Mr. Panmure* at another theatre, it had been present in *The Wife Without a Smile*. It was not worthy of the author of *The Second Mrs. Tanqueray*, *His House in Order* and *Trelawney of the Wells*. And the public would not have it.

Frohman encouraged dramatists. He often inspired their ideas for plays. He told Somerset Maugham he wanted a play from him. "Why not re-write *The Taming of the Shrew* with a new background?" said Frohman. "All right," agreed Maugham, and wrote *The Land of Promise*, a vast success with Irene Vanbrugh and Godfrey Tearle. The background was Canada. Perhaps, however, Frohman's greatest feat at the Duke of York's was his Repertory Theatre there. The idea was not new. Vedrenne and Barker had tried it at the Court, and Shaw had been the upshot. But there never seemed money in it. That did not worry Frohman. It was enough that Barrie suggested it. "I'll do it," said 'C. F.' as he was always affectionately called. He had, however, his own ideas on the subject and this was his manifesto.

'Repertory companies are usually associated in the public mind with the revival of old masterpieces, but if you want to know the character of my repertory project at the Duke of York's, I should describe it as the production of new plays by living authors. Whatever it accomplishes, it will represent the combined resources of actor and playwright working with each other, a combination that seems to me to represent the most necessary foundation of any theatrical success.'

He engaged Granville Barker as his producer for this scheme, he had brilliant scenic designers such as Norman Wilkinson to work for him, and the result was something to remember, something of which our Theatre can be proud, and which was one of the extreme peaks of distinction in the Edwardian Theatre.

For that is what it brought forth. *Justice*, by Galsworthy; *Misalliance*, by Shaw; *Old Friends* and *The Twelve Pound Look*, by Barrie; *The Sentimentalists*, by Meredith; *The Madras House*, by Granville Barker; *Chains*, by Elizabeth Baker; *Prunella* (revived), by Laurence Housman and Granville Barker; *Helena's Path*, by Cosmo Gordon Lennox and Anthony Hope, and a revival of *Trelawney of the Wells*, by Pinero.

Each play was treated as a new production, there was no second-hand scenery, no makeshift, no old clothes, no careless casting. The production of *Justice* alone was prodigious. Barrie's *Twelve Pound Look* was found in a drawer in his desk. It became a classic.

This repertory season ran from February 1910 until May of the same year. Then, when the audience came out of the Duke of York's after seeing *Prunella*, one May night when the rich folks were getting into their eleven o'clock carriages and the cheaper parts were pouring out talking excitedly, down St. Martin's Lane came the newsboys, bearing placards and shouting their news. King Edward VII was dead. A pall fell and that heaviness made it impossible to continue with the great repertory season. For an epoch—a short but a wonderful one—was closing—the Edwardian days—with their continuous wonders—were over. The death of the Peacemaker sent the country into mourning. If the blow was not so stunning as the death of the old Queen, still it was bad enough. There seemed a chill, menacing breath everywhere—a signal of a change in the world. Only four years later that change was to come. Victorian stability had lasted with Edward, and been lit by gayer times—what would happen now? Keen, experienced ears heard the faint, far-off rumble of guns; those behind the scenes wrinkled their brows. The Georgian days were come again. A new King, whom we did not know very well, was in the throne of his father. We remembered, however, his speech when at the Mansion House he trumpeted, "Wake up England." And we took heart. Events later proved us right. For the Edwardian method and manner went on for four years more—and then the German Emperor—Kaiser Bill—changed the world forever. But the great Frohman Repertory passed with the Edwardian days and the man who gave them their name.

All the plays had been wonderful. *Trelawney of the Wells* was memorable, especially the acting of Irene Vanbrugh, Dion Boucicault, Sydney Valentine, Gerald Lawrence, and Edmund Gwenn. It was a superb Edwardian memory, that revival.

That night, too, was to have much to do with the fate of Charles Frohman. He was then at the top of the world. He had vast interests. He had moved his headquarters from the Duke of York's to the Aldwych,

SIR H. B. TREE AS 'CARDINAL WOLSEY,' A. BOURCHIER AS 'KING HENRY VIII,' VIOLET VANBRUGH AS 'QUEEN CATHERINE' IN 'KING HENRY VIII'

GERTRUDE ELLIOT AS 'CLEOPATRA' AND FORBES ROBERTSON AS 'CAESAR'

CHARLES FROHMAN

RUTLAND
BARRINGTON

GEORGE
EDWARDE

FRANK CURZON

GEORGE DANCE

where there was more room. Later he was to go to a suite in Waterloc Place, in Trafalgar House, thus inhabiting premises named after two great victories and suitable for one who had conquered the British Theatre. For that is exactly what he did. He lived at the Savoy, and with him everywhere went the photographs of his stars with which he loved to surround himself. Once when he had the Globe Theatre, he got stuck in the small lift which led to the offices. His staff worked like beavers to get him out, but he was in there suspended between two floors with a brick wall within two inches of his nose for two hours. When they got him up they expected fireworks. But Frohman was all smiles. "Quietest morning I've had for years. A nice little holiday," was his comment. That was the sort of man he was.

But of all the theatres he ran, two were his best beloved—the Empire in New York and the Duke of York's in London. Both were milestones in his march of achievement. So much did he like the Duke of York's that he would sit through some of his plays there over twenty times, just for the pleasure of being in that theatre. And he made it a theatre, a real theatre. All round the walls hung pictures of his stars, American and British, you were never allowed to forget you were at a playhouse to see a play. For Frohman understood the value of this. With him, a theatre was a playhouse—not a bar where a play was being performed.

Endless tales are told of him. Once a new checktaker would not let him in. "I'm Frohman," said 'C. F.' "Can't help it, sir, you haven't got a ticket," replied the man. Frohman said, "You are quite right." He went to the box office, astounded the box office manager by buying a stall, and presented it cheerfully to the man—and went in. Jimmy Mathews said he would discharge the over-zealous checktaker. "Certainly not," said Frohman, "he was doing his duty. If he *had* let me in, *then* you should have discharged him." Once, when he had a bad knee, he telephoned the theatre to keep him a box. The thoughtful Mathews had some extra steps made to make it easier for him. Frohman thanked him. But a few days later, when he was better, he phoned to say he was coming again. "I am better now," he said, "don't trouble to build a theatre for me." His staff adored him, for his justice and fairness. A new young man who helped in the publicity side had been told by Frohman to send a story out to the Press. He did so. Not one line appeared. He was heartbroken. He wrote to Frohman and apologized. The next time they met Frohman said, "Why did you write me that letter?" The young man explained that he was horrified that no word had appeared in print. "But you sent it out, didn't you?" asked Frohman. "Certainly, sir," replied the apologist. "Then I don't see why you need trouble. You did your job. You are not running the papers," said Frohman, with one of his wonderful smiles. Needless to say that young man adored him.

The last production of this great figure was a curious one. It was a revue. But it was a revue by J. M. Barrie, written and built especially for another astounding personality, Gaby Deslys. There was also a Barrie one-act play, *The New World*. And very suitably the place of production was his beloved Duke of York's. This double bill was presented on 22nd March 1915. It was a failure. Frohman therefore began his London career with a failure and ended with one. But what

K

glory lay between—those years from 1892 until 1915 were indeed star decked. He had revivified the drama, he had ventured greatly, he had failed greatly, but he had succeeded very greatly indeed. He was one of the pillars of the Edwardian Theatre, he was one of its brightest lights, this little American of German origin, whom few people outside his own profession knew, but whom to know was to love and respect. His word was his bond, and his life was the Theatre's.

Yet he was to come to a tragic end. Rheumatism racked him ; he feared for the future of the Theatre. He did not see in his mind what was to follow. War had come, standards were falling. But still he kept on. He got much pleasure out of one tune—'Alexander's Ragtime Band.' Yet a note of fate crept in. He pulled out his little red notebook to make an entry. He stared. "Queer," he said, "the book is full. There is no more room." And this was on the eve of his departure for England. He had one of his very few lawsuits to settle. He wanted to see the Thames and Marlow again. He wanted to produce more plays. His friends warned him of the danger of U-boats. "I'm going, all the same," said 'C. F.' He sailed on the *Lusitania* on 1st May 1915 from New York. His friend Potter saw him off. "Aren't you afraid of U-boats, C. F. ?" he asked. "I'm only afraid of I.O.U.s," smiled Frohman.

But a U-boat got him on the afternoon of 7th May, off the Irish coast. When the impact came he was on the upper deck. He was perfectly unruffled, and went on smoking his cigar. An English friend brought him a lifebelt and insisted on his wearing it. "You have not one yourself," said Frohman, in protest. "If you must die, it is only once," replied the Englishman, who was a soldier. The boat lurched, the end was near. Frohman's famous smile was on his face. "Why fear death ? It is the most beautiful adventure in life," he said, paraphrasing the famous line from *Peter Pan*, which was undoubtedly in his mind—and then the end came. . . . But not the end of Charles Frohman. He left a memory behind which is an impetus and inspiration to every man of the Theatre who knows it.

He lived greatly for his work, his work was great, he himself was great in a great time—and when his own time came—he died greatly, too. However much glory may come to the Theatre in days to come, it will have to be very bright and shining indeed if it is to eclipse those days when, in London, Paris and New York, you knew you were to receive something very worth while, when you read on the posters, or outside the theatre, 'Charles Frohman presents . . .'

CHAPTER XI

The Sportsman Manager

THE THEATRE IS A WORLD OF CONTRASTS. IT IS NOT ONLY COMPOSED OF people who think merely of the stage, of the footlights, of the size of their name on the bills, of box office returns, and of personal glory. Sometimes a being creeps in whose rightful place seems the countryside, who would look more at home in the stubble, shooting partridges, in the October woods performing a right and left at rocketing pheasants, mounted and in 'pink' at a Meet, or standing in the Enclosure on a great racecourse. Indeed figures such as that frequently come into the Theatre. But they usually leave it again pretty quickly, and go back to their country pursuits, poorer in pocket, if richer in memories. But sometimes there comes a man who brings off 'the double event,' and such a one was Frank Curzon, actor, manager and sportsman. As an actor he did not make much of a mark, as a manager he was in the very first flight, leading the field with the pick of them, and as a sportsman he won the Derby. You cannot do much more than that. We have met him before, at the old Royal Strand Theatre, where, with *A Chinese Honeymoon*, he gambled and won, as becomes a sportsman. Indeed, he controlled several theatres at the same time, but his true home was the Prince of Wales's, in Coventry Street.

Frank Curzon looked a gentleman of the countryside. He was burly, he was strong, he had an appearance of fresh air, and that shiny cleanliness which comes from dealing with horses. He rode to hounds, until his increasing weight stopped him (but he was never really fat), he was never far away when the kill was made. He was a fine shot, he fished, there was no sport he did not love and at which he was not expert. He looked the English sportsman of his period, he dressed like one and he smoked fine cigars. Had you sat opposite to him in a railway train, you would have sensed a squire, and you would have been right. Only the keenest observer might have deduced from his clean-shaven face and his alert eyes that he was something else as well. But it is doubtful if you would have put him down as belonging to the Theatre.

But belong to the Theatre he did and in a wholesale way. For early in the Edwardian days, in 1903, he controlled the Avenue, the Camden, the Coronet, Prince of Wales's, Comedy, Criterion, Wyndham's and the Strand theatres. Other people had driven teams like this before, and had come a cropper. But Curzon gradually shed certain of the interests until he retained only the Prince of Wales's and Wyndham's, and he made history at both.

He was born at Wavertree, and its nearness to the Grand National course may have been the origin of his love for horses, racing, and the steeplechase of the Theatre. His real name was Deeley, and his father's business was oil. Frank went into oil, but left it for the Theatre. The name of Curzon he took from Curzon Park, his birthplace. His brother, Mallaby-Deeley, was also a character and a financial wizard. He made history by a line of 'gents' suitings' and by building the Piccadilly Hotel. Frank made his history in the playhouse.

He became an actor at Yarmouth, he toured in *Our Boys*, *Two Roses*, and other plays. He was for a time with Frank Benson. He got to London and there he became an actor-manager with a play called *Tom, Dick and Harry*. But he gave up acting and stuck to management, having a very wise policy from which, save when he staged musical plays, he never departed. He joined hands with theatreless actor-managers, men like Charles Hawtrey, women like Marie Tempest. He provided the theatre, they the plays and they worked together, sharing things. So he was really an actor's actor-manager all the time. And he made it pay.

At the Prince of Wales's he was for some time associated jointly with

George Edwardes and Charles Frohman in some lovely and adorable musical plays of the Edwardian days. Some call for special mention.

In 1902 London had a treat. It was a musical play called *The School Girl*. It had a cast such as you could not assemble to-day. It had the twin charms of smiling Marie Studholme and beautiful Edna May, both at the top of their careers. It had a young man making his first real London mark by playing an old man, and what a mark he made ! His name was George Graves. It had another young man who in this production played an elderly noodle (but a gentleman always) whose name was G. P. Huntley. It had a fine, robust comedian, with a laughter-compelling face and an unctuous smile, Jimmy Blakeley. It had Violet Cameron, who had been the toast of the town, as a 'Mother Superior.' It had clever men, it had pretty girls, and lilting music by a magician whose name was Leslie Stuart, it had a brisk player of French parts called Marianne Caldwell, and an actor called Gilbert Porteous. It had a promising young *jeune première* in J. Edward Fraser, and lots of other good things, as we shall see. Its first scene was a lovely convent garden, from which the two school girls, well-grown lassies (Marie Studholme and Edna May) escaped to see the great world. Its second scene was the Open Stock Exchange, Paris, where everyone arrived, and its last scene was an artist's studio in Paris (which underwent a transformation for a party) which everyone attended. Real musical comedy, you will observe. It had some delightful songs, too.

James Blakeley had one which is redolent of its time and may cause a whiff of nostalgia, for it went like this :

"She had read Marie Corelli and emphatically swore
That she'd never wed a man who'd ever kissed a girl before
But her maiden Aunt said to her
'You've an awful task in view
But if you doubt my word, my dear
I'll tell you what to do.
CHORUS :
Go looking for a needle in a haystack
The chances of your finding one are small
But if you do, why, don't forget to say so
And come and tell your Auntie first of all.' "

It went on for several verses, but Auntie finally solved the problem by sitting on a haystack and finding the needle herself. It was, of course, a case of the needle finding Auntie, after all, the song informed us.

Marie Studholme told us that she knew 'The length that a girl may go to.' We would have gone far for her. Edna May's songs were a bit more serious, as became her delicate, wistful beauty. Blakeley made us chuckle, as always, as 'Tubby Bedford.' George Graves made us laugh immoderately—a feat he has accomplished with amazing ease and artistry ever since—as 'General Marchmont.' J. Edward Fraser discoursed in song on the general excellence of an English girl. And Violet Cameron, as the Mother Superior, can hardly have been surprised when her pupils ran away, for she sang to them of how in the days of her youth she had longed for a lover, but 'nobody came at all.' The girls all took the hint and decided to get busy on their own account. But in the person of G. P. Huntley we have the light comedian of the Edwardian days in his prime. For this consummate actor represented a type which passed away when the machine age arrived. He was of the spacious days, when sovereigns were gold and plentiful, when there was plenty of time, and when men of his type did not have to work for their living. He was always the young—or old—man about town, always gallant, always ready to help, never in the possession of any brains, but always most unmistakably the chivalrous gentleman. He was the type which was variously described as a 'toff,' a 'swell,' a 'masher,' a 'dude' (much later the type became a 'knut' but a 'knut' was never quite the same). He was inevitably of the West End, the Burlington Arcade, Piccadilly, and the best clubs. He was also of the country house. But toil or business of any kind was utterly foreign to him. He took an admiring interest in it when he encountered it in others—especially of the fair sex. He was always beautifully dressed, and he was never in a hurry. He spoke in a manner then known as 'Lah-di-dah.' And he usually had a monocle. In those days, this character did actually exist, it was not merely a creation of the stage. But on the stage its supreme exponent was G. P. Huntley. His men were of a different kind to those of George Grossmith. They probably went to the same school, and belonged to the same club. It was probable that they were related by marriage, or might even have been cousins. But the Huntley type was much more ponderous, much slower in the uptake, much more easily surprised and had a much more limited knowledge and vision than the Grossmith variety. Had they had to take up a profession they would have been professional soldiers, never getting above the rank of major, and then only after a devastating war, but the Grossmith variety probably dabbled on the Stock Exchange.

G. P. Huntley has no successor. For a while that clever comedian, George Clarke, gave us a music hall counterpart, but it was not quite the same thing. It had not the full flavour, the same rich vintage, the same scent of matured cigar. It was much brisker, because Clarke, who was not an Edwardian actor, would break into a wonderful dance, whereas Huntley never did that. His sort of man never got beyond the polka and was not very good at that. As became a gentleman—for he was a gentleman on and off the stage, who worked for George Edwardes and Frank Curzon, both racing enthusiasts, G. P. Huntley ran racehorses, too. But although often 'placed' they seldom won. After a long run of 'seconds' a friend commiserated with him. "Ah, dear old chap, my horses are well trained," said the comedian, "they are gentlemen, you know, they know their manners. They always say, 'After you.' "

Huntley was a 'creator.' Although he was nearly always the same, there was always something new. He excelled in little thumbnail sketches which formed part of the show. In *Three Little Maids*, which opened at the Apollo, but went to the Prince of Wales's, he gave us what was the first of a long and never-ending line of golf burlesques. Since then we have had glorious examples from Harry Tate, Syd Field, and many others. But Huntley was different to them. Smooth, unruffled, urbane, he brought to the game of golf a fixed determination that it should be played like billiards, the only game he knew. He was the despair of his 'caddie,' a little man called George Carroll, for his complete misunderstanding of anything at all, but he had his own ideas, and most diverting they were. When, in a wild attempt at a drive, he detached a vast 'divot' he turned to Carroll and said in a rather worried tone, "I say, I'm afraid I've torn the cloth." In *Lady Madcap*, another gay Prince of Wales's show, the plot demanded his being disguised as a butler. This gave him great delight. A slow but beaming smile broke out on his stolid, blunt countenance. "I'd love to buttle," he chuckled. It was, he thought, something he knew about. But his attempts at buttling were side-splitting, and in this show he gave us one of those wonderful little monologues of his, which were always about ordinary things but which he made supreme. On being handed the keys of the mansion, he examined them one by one, he commented on each, deducing its uses and its character from its appearance. He endowed each one of them with real life. It was a *tour-de-force*.

It was in *The School Girl* that he gave us one of his old men studies. He was delighted when some fresh young Parisienne asked him the way up the stairs, and was tremendously courtly about it—but 'was on to it' all the same.

In the chorus, with a few lines, was a dainty little piece of blonde femininity who was Pauline Chase, and playing another small part was one of the prettiest and most charming girls who have ever walked the stage. She went to great heights, and even now she is a film star, still retaining her beauty and her charm. But that night when *The School Girl* was produced, this auburn-haired, plump girl stepped forward, sang a song called 'My Little Canoe'—and stopped the show. Her name was—and is—Billie Burke. She was to become a great Frohman star. He trained her as a father might a daughter. Once, much later on, when he was one day out from New York *en route* for London, she married Flo Ziegfeld, the great showman. There had been no suspicion of this, it came like a bombshell. His staff knew they must acquaint Frohman, who was in mid-ocean. They did not know how he would take it. It was Charles Dillingham who sent the cable—which said simply, 'Billie Burke married Flo Ziegfeld this morning.' They waited anxiously for the answer. It came. 'Another Ziegfeld folly,' cabled Frohman.

In *Three Little Maids* was another great Prince of Wales's artist—who was also in *Lady Madcap*. This was a Frenchman, handsome in the Gallic way, dark, with a white forelock, and possessed of a tenor voice of good quality and great charm of manner. He sang songs then considered a little *risqué*, but he sang them with such an air of delicacy that there was no offence, only a pleasurable thrill and a sense of being in Paris. To-day they would not raise an eyebrow or a blush. Here is an example :

> "I like you in velvet
> I love you in plush,
> In satin you're just like
> Your own lovely blush
> You're charming in silk, or a plain woollen shawl
> But you're simply delightful
> In—anything—at all."

The naughtiness lay in the artful pause before the word 'anything.' The wicked Edwardian mind did the rest. Maurice Farkoa, for that was his name, was extremely popular, especially with the ladies, for his love-making was of the insinuating French manner.

Others at the Prince of Wales's then were Madge Crichton, Delia Mason, and Hilda Moody—who in *Three Little Maids* had a good song called 'She Was the Miller's Daughter'—another piece of Edwardian naughtiness. Zena Dare made a success there, too, in *Lady Madcap*, in which G. P. Huntley not only 'buttled' but was a trooper in the Yeomanry with most amusing results. The Prince of Wales's was a great place.

Curzon was, amongst other things, a man who loved a joke. In the box office was William Blakeley, brother to Jimmy Blakeley, the comedian. Willie was a great character but he had a testy, irritable temper, which is not the best qualification for a box office man. His temper suffered very severely when telephones grew popular. He never liked them, he always suspected them. He was annoyed when one rang, and he vented his anger on the unfortunate soul who was ringing up. He broke more telephones than anyone else in the world, for when business was good—and it was nearly always good at the Prince of Wales's, and the phones rang merrily, he would get beside himself with rage, and throw the instruments against the wall, causing much carnage and slaughter for the National Telephone Company to repair. Much of his dislike and suffering in respect of the telephone was brought about by Frank Curzon himself. Curzon loved a practical joke, and loved to annoy Blakeley. So, in an assumed voice, he would ring up, and ask hundreds of questions. He would enquire about stalls ; if two were offered in the third row, he would say, "Haven't you two further back ?" Then, when the sixth row was offered, he would ask : "That's rather far, haven't you something nearer ?" He would take Blakeley all over the stalls plan, rejecting everything, and then tackle the dress circle. Unable to be satisfied there, the upper circle would be visited. Then, still in his assumed voice, he would ask about the boxes, and when nothing would suit, would ask about the pit, and on being told that it was unreserved, would give at length his views of theatre managers and their foolishness. By this time Blakeley was raving mad, but Curzon was always quick to say that he was a friend of Mr. Curzon's, and would be coming round to see him—so Blakeley was never sure. Then they would tackle the stalls again, and at long last, agreement would almost be reached about a couple. Then Curzon would say, "Well, they are not for me, so I'll have to ask my friend and ring you again. Oh, and could you tell me the right time ?" Smash would go the instrument, Blakeley could stand no more. With a broken phone, he was safe for a bit. He never knew for years that Curzon was his unknown horror. If he had found out, nobody knows what would have happened, for Blakeley adored his Guv'nor.

This curious man once took up golf. He went to the links with a very full and complete set of clubs. He got a caddie. For a while things went fairly well, and Blakeley, having beginner's luck, was pleased with himself. But the reaction set in and bunker after bunker claimed him. His natural hasty temper got frayed. Just as he was addressing the ball, just as he had raised the club for a good hard swipe, a nearby sheep baa-ed loudly. Blakeley foozled the shot completely. Silently he picked up his clubs, and placed them all in the bag, his lips tightly set. Then with a mighty heave, he flung the lot into an adjacent pond, and walked all the way home. But he felt much better. In later life he lived in a world of clichés, a world of his own, where only the past was real. Somebody wanted seats for a date in March. "Oh, March," he would chuckle, "the windy month." Or he would say, glancing at the paper, "The runners for the Lincoln are out. When I see that I know Spring is coming." It appeared he would not have been aware otherwise. He had one great joke. He hugged it to the end. In the year 1910 *The Chocolate Soldier* was staged at the Lyric Theatre. A poster was used in connection with this, which showed a fierce and wonderfully arrayed and whiskered Balkan warrior, of bloodthirsty aspect, pointing into space. As the accusing finger was dead in the middle of the poster, when you looked at it, it was always pointing at you. And underneath was the slogan, '*You* have not seen *The Chocolate Soldier*.' Blakeley used to gaze upon it entranced. To him it was the acme of wit, the height of humorous ingenuity. And for thirty years afterwards, if he saw you coming down the street, he would level a forefinger at you, say, "You have not seen *The Chocolate Soldier*," and roar with laughter. The fact that the same idea, with a picture of Lord Kitchener, had much to do with forming that soldier's army in the First World War, entirely escaped him. He always mourned the passing of the days of Curzon at the Prince of Wales's. He ended his career at the Shaftesbury (now a wreck through bombing) and still lived in the memory of happier days. But he had the satisfaction of backing 'Call Boy' when his beloved but leg-pulling old Guv'nor won the Derby.

Those musical comedy days at the Prince of Wales's leave happy memories. *Three Little Maids* was full of good things. Edna May had been in it, but was succeeded by Madge Crichton, who had a Paul Rubens song salled 'Sal,' and another called 'Men.' It was a Paul Rubens show. Huntley was 'Lord Cheyne,' first in panama hat, high white stiff collar, white shirt with stiff cuffs, Norfolk jacket, white riding breeches and leather gaiters and brown boots. Then when the action shifted to town, a glossy silk hat, a single linen collar of considerable height, with an Ascot tie, a white vest slip (if you know what that was), a light waistcoat, a tightly-buttoned frock coat, tight spongebag trousers, and patent boots with light cloth uppers, and of course, a walking stick—and an orchid in his buttonhole. It was 1902, and motoring was beginning to become noticeable. So there was a motoring sextette, with the three men in caps similar to those worn by bus drivers to-day, but bigger, dark goggles and long fawn coats. Nobody would have dreamed of jumping into a car and driving off in those days, unsuitably attired. Motoring then was more a sport than a means of transport—it was as uncertain as sport, too, as regards the finish. The women were dressed in large and long dust coats as well, and thus attired they sang :

"You pull a lever or press a knob
And the wheels begin to hum
You notice a kind of a sort of a throb
And you smell petroleum
The wind and dust in your faces will blow
But you'll have to sit tight and smile
And soon you'll arrive where you wanted to go
If you don't come to grief meanwhile."

That was how motoring was regarded in the year of grace—and security —1902. Only just over forty years ago. Huntley, Farkoa and J. L. Mackay were the three men.

The first act of *Three Little Maids* took place in the beautiful garden of a country vicarage. Something, nobody perhaps remembers what, took place, and the Vicar lost his money, for in the second act the three little maids of the vicarage were running a very charming Dutch Tea Room in wicked London, and doing pretty well, by the look of things. Probably they were more businesslike than their priestly father, who was presumably ruined, and this labour was forced upon them. But their three swains, who had known them in the vicarage days, became customers at the tea shop, and as there were three of them, and three of the little maids—little maids always seem to run in triplicate, like Government forms—what more natural than a general and musical pairing off so that the curtain could come down and those carriages be there at eleven? It was all very simple and straightforward but those musical shows, like the Edwardes' productions at Daly's and the Gaiety, gave us tunes which we remember—and words too—after the lapse of nearly half a century. Whereas some from shows seen only a few months ago have not registered at all. Was it because they were better, or because youth is more impressionable? A bit of both, very likely. But one thing is sure. Those tunes were all individual. Whereas to-day they are all in the same manner and get jumbled up, by their continual plugging, thus leaving no clear imprint on the mind.

What Monckton was to the Gaiety and Daly's, Paul Rubens was to the Prince of Wales's. That was his spiritual home. He lived just around the corner, in the Haymarket. He wrote what he called 'jingles and tunes,' instead of words and music, but those 'jingles' still jingle and those 'tunes' still live in the memory.

Lady Madcap was his, too, with book by Colonel Newnham-Davis, the *Pink'Un's* 'Dwarf of Blood.' Adrienne Augarde, a little piece of Dresden china, was the original 'Lady Madcap,' whose name was 'Lady Betty.' She was succeeded by Zena Dare, and for a time Madge Crichton played it, too. Herbert Sparling, Fred Emney, Paul Arthur, Delia Mason, J. Edward Fraser, little George Carroll, Maurice Farkoa and G. P. Huntley were all in the cast—again it was almost the P.O.W. stock company.

It was all about a young lady of title who would give parties. To-day she would have given them without her parents being either consulted or giving a hoot. But Edwardian fathers were not like that. This one confined his daughter to her room, and she escaped with much daring and a great deal of fluttering of petticoats down a ladder in a most un-Edwardian ladylike way. The local yeomanry attended the party *en masse* (and in uniform). G. P. Huntley was a trooper, and not at all soldierly. The Colonel was Leedham Bantock, who sang a catchy song against a background of lovely girls in lovely graceful long frocks, about a beetle who loved a boot and got badly crushed for its pains. And two young men in small parts, singing and dancing, were Spencer Trevor and Dennis Eadie (the latter to become a great actor-manager). The ladies practised archery in picture hats, long gloves and longer skirts, but managed to do considerable execution amongst the male members of the audience. All ended happily, needless to say.

Many people considered, until one which is now a classic appeared, that *Sergeant Brue* was the best of the Prince of Wales's musical plays. It certainly was a gem, and it had a plot which lifted it right out of the ordinary rut. It had a cast to match that plot, too, for it contained Willie Edouin, J. Farren Soutar (a delightful *jeune première*), Arthur Williams as 'Cookie Scrubbs' (an ex-criminal), Zena Dare and many other stars. Arthur Williams was one of the finest comedians who ever cracked a gag. He was more than a comedian, he was a very great character actor, with a Dickensian flavour and a rich understanding of comic acting. His 'Lurcher' in the light opera *Dorothy* was a classic and it was equalled by his 'Scrubbs' in *Sergeant Brue*.

But when Curzon was on his own, after the Edwardes-Frohman combination had left him, some great plays were to be seen also. He ran his theatre perfectly ; it was then, as now, beautifully placed and had a great passing public, a great portion of which stopped and came in. But he got his own personality into it. He was a showman as well as a sportsman. Once, when plagued, as were his brother actor-managers, by the matinée hat nuisance, he turned a lady out who was wearing one of huge dimensions. There was a lawsuit and much space in the papers. But brother managers whispered that it was all fixed up (we did not know the word 'stunt' then, our English was English). It certainly did not solve the hat problem, but it was a first-class advertisement.

In the year 1907 Curzon touched his musical high spot. This he shared with Paul Rubens and with his own wife, Isobel Jay. For that year saw the production of *Miss Hook of Holland*. This was surely one of the most delightful musical shows ever staged or ever to be staged. It is young and lively to-day. It stands out in an age which likes moans of the jungle and swamp, as an example of what light music was really meant to be—melody, freshness and sparkle. Here was Holland on the stage : canals, tulips, dykes, old houses, stiff headdresses and stiffer petticoats, baggy, patched breeches, sabots and all complete. Perhaps it was the memory of that Dutch interior in *Three Little Maids* which first gave the idea—perhaps it was just pure inspiration. But Edwardian London all went to Holland at the Prince of Wales's. It went there for four hundred and sixty-two performances. *Miss Hook of Holland* was memorable. It was absolutely of its time but inside its framework, a perfect musical comedy, which lives on. It had the advantage of the finest cast that the astute Frank Curzon could get together. Its leading lady was Isobel Jay, in private life Mrs. Frank Curzon. What grace she had, what true womanly beauty—and what a voice ! It was beyond ordinary musical comedy, even above light opera ; it could have held its own at Covent Garden. Yet she never overpowered the other singers, so well did she understand her art. And she could not only sing, she could act as well. Gracie Leigh, that delightful comedienne, swept through the show with glory. Her singing of 'A Little Pink Pettie for Peter,' in which she displayed one petticoat after another, until she referred to the 'one which she hadn't got on.' There was Pope Stamper, a handsome young actor then, as the juvenile lead. And there was

George Barrett, nephew of the great Wilson Barrett. He had made a hit at Wyndham's in a musical comedy called *The Girl Behind the Counter*, but as 'Simon Slinks' in *Hook* he made an abiding name. It was a performance worthy of any actor, it was a real character study. He was to follow it up with a grand piece of comedy and dramatic acting as 'Tom Lambert,' the trainer, in *The Whip* at Drury Lane, his real high spot. Alas, he met his end there when, many years after, he was rehearsing for *Glamorous Night* at that theatre.   Wounds in the First World War had affected him, and he committed suicide in a railway train. But in those happy days of *Miss Hook of Holland* nobody dreamed of war. George Barrett can have had no premonition of what it was to do with him, as he made us roar with delight at the artfulness of the lazy 'Slinks.' The sort of soldiers we liked then were the type that Pope Stamper presented in that very play—a gallant bandmaster, who sang about 'The Soldiers of the Netherland' in smart colourful uniform.

Miss Hook of Holland was a triumph also for G. P. Huntley.   He was 'Mr. Hook,' an elderly manufacturer of a liqueur called 'Cream of the Skies,' whom he made into a masterly piece of characterization, right in the picture and atmosphere, whilst still remaining our beloved G. P.

Miss Hook of Holland was Paul Rubens' masterpiece, all done by himself. At that time he was living even nearer to the Prince of Wales's than the Haymarket, where he afterwards moved. His flat, now pulled down, was in sight of the stage door of the theatre where his works were presented. And his songs in that show, 'Cream of the Sky,' 'Flyaway Kite,' 'Sleepy Canal,' 'Little Pink Pettie' and many others, give us as much pleasure now as then. What melodies he wrote. One of his best ballads—'I Love the Moon'—came to him whilst he was out dining. He made some rough notes on his shirt cuff (stiff starched linen, of course) and then forgot all about it. A little later he remembered. But where was the shirt? Gone to the laundry. Alas—what tragedy—that song might never be written, for although Rubens remembered making the note, he did not remember what it was about. His valet went post haste to the laundry, and the shirt was retrieved, notes and all, at the very brink of the wash-tub. And thus 'I Love the Moon' came to triumph over the soap suds and charm us to-day.

Paul Rubens died all too young—he had weak lungs, and he left a gap in the ranks of our light composers which nobody has yet filled with the same grace. And he was as charming and pleasant—and harmonious as his music.

That stage door of the Prince of Wales's, which Rubens could see from his windows, lay down a little court, through an archway. It was a dark, romantic-looking little alley, like one in an Eastern city. Its chief inhabitant was a very well-known street bookmaker, who did an enormous trade and had scores of 'runners,' and who, rumour said, was never caught by the police.   This may be apocryphal, for everyone knew him. And perhaps the police, with that tact which so distinguishes them, looked the other way. For he was a jolly, good-natured chap, as honest as the day, and paid out with the very greatest regularity. Another inhabitant was an engineer who had his workshop there. His name was Reece, and if you wanted anything difficult in the way of engineering done for a show, it was to him you went. He was a genius who shared the alley with the bookmaker and the stars of Frank Curzon.

And beside that alley was a shooting gallery which must have been the original of the one which Dickens featured in *Bleak House*, as being kept by 'Mr. George.' All the young men about town, and many of the stars, would practise shooting there and some marvellous 'cards' resulted. If the Guv'nor considered them good enough, he got you to sign them, and displayed them in the window. The sight of one of those targets with the 'bull' shot away and your name attached filled you with great pride. It has vanished now, and although the alley remains, it is no longer the romantic place it was in Edwardian days, for the stage door through which such a cavalcade of stars entered was moved, when the theatre was recently rebuilt, to the open day of Whitcomb Street. The old door through which all the famous of Victorian and Edwardian days passed into the Prince of Wales's—and every great one except Irving and a small handful played there—has gone for ever, like the times in which they lived.

Curzon did other successful musical plays. There was *The King of Cadonia*, the book of which was written by Frederick Lonsdale, before he became the society dramatist of later days. It was an early—a very early—Lonsdale, but a very good one. For Lonsdale from the Channel Isles knew how to write a musical play book. He was just a beginner in 1908 when *The King of Cadonia* was produced, and even in 1914, in that amazingly valuable and infallible publication, *Who's Who in the Theatre*, he had only four plays to his name, two of them musical, and both at the Prince of Wales's, which theatre he gave modestly as his address.

Isobel Jay was again leading lady and again perfect. George Barrett was 'Bran,' and Daly's own comedian, Huntley Wright, deserting that house for a while, was the 'Duke of Alasia.' But there was another sensation in *The King of Cadonia*. He played the King, and, of course, disguised himself as a subject, so as to test his people and win the heart of his ladylove for himself alone. He had already been on the stage for some years. He had been with Alexander at the St. James's, he had toured, he had played in town, he had made a success in America, but it was Frank Curzon who gave him his fame. He cast this splendid figure of a man, handsome of face and bearing, fine-voiced and majestic, to play the lead in *The King of Cadonia*. And on the opening night he was a sensation. Every inch a king, every inch a man, every inch a singer and actor, he caused the biggest flutter amongst feminine hearts since the début of Henry Ainley six years before. Overnight he became a matinée idol. The Press acclaimed, the public raved. The female portion went mad. Such things do not happen now, when the young women waste their sighs on a shadow on a screen, imprinted across the Atlantic.

This was no shadow, this was real masculine flesh and blood. This was the Lewis Waller of the musical stage. This was the dream of the maiden's heart—this was a man. Crowds of women of all ages went to performance after performance of *The King of Cadonia*. Crowds more stood at the stage door to watch him arrive and leave. And a very faithful little crowd stood outside that stage door—their means not permitting frequent visits to the show, to see him pass a window on the staircase, on his way to and from the stage. His name is Bertram Wallis, and he is still handsome, upright and brave, the very epitome of what we considered a man in Edwardian days.

His success in *The King of Cadonia* was epoch-making. What a magnificent couple he and Isobel Jay made—the ideal couple of the musical stage of all time, standing abreast of Lily Elsie and Joseph Coyne. Wallis was also to appear with Lily Elsie in *The Count of Luxembourg*, and audiences swooned with delight.

The King of Cadonia was a success, as was *Dear Little Denmark* in a lesser degree, and *The Balkan Princess*, the last a gay, fizzing, champagnelike show. All three were at the Prince of Wales's, all three were Frank Curzon's, and the music of all three was by Paul Rubens, who composed all the music, wrote every word of *Dear Little Denmark*, and nearly every word of *Hook of Holland* and part of the lyrics for *The Balkan Princess*, the rest being by Lonsdale and Curzon himself, which applied also to the 'book.' That was a famous Prince of Wales's trio, and a famous Prince of Wales's stock company. For they made their following for their own theatre, and kept it. You got the Prince of Wales's habit, as you got the Daly's and Gaiety habit. That was the Edwardian policy, and like the honest policy it was, it paid.

Wallis and Isobel Jay were together in all those three shows. Jimmy Blakeley was back again, too. He had been to America, and on his return took over 'Bran' in *King of Cadonia* from George Barrett, who went elsewhere—to the Lane, to be exact. Blakeley was in both *Dear Little Denmark* and *The Balkan Princess*. He was one of the great Prince of Wales's comedians. In *The Balkan Princess* also was Charles Brown, from the Gaiety, giving an excellent performance. Charles Brown remains typical of the Edwardian age, and it was his ease and polish which in after years, in America, got him a fine position in a great firm of wine merchants He knew about wine, too. And he knew, or thought he knew, how to make gin. For in Prohibition days in the States he made some at home, and blew out all the windows whilst so doing because the potent brew exploded, but still enough remained to practically lay out the company on the last night of their tour at a curtain fall celebration. A man of many parts—but every one of them English. He had a penthouse in New York, and with immense labour and trouble he constructed an English garden to surround it on the skyscraper roof where it stood, bringing all the earth from the country and carting the bulk of it up himself. A charming and gay companion and friend, he never forsook the days of the sovereign and the manners of Piccadilly, even in the Middle West. Also in *The Balkan Princess* was a young and rapidly rising comedian called Lauri de Frece, a brother of Sir Walter de Frece (Vesta Tilley's husband and great music hall magnate). He played 'Blatz' and made a great hit. His red hair, his sad expression and his perfect understanding of comedy pointed the way to great things. He died too young. Nor must another member of that cast be forgotten —Mabel Sealby, one of the daintiest of soubrettes and clever dancer, had already gained fame but she was wonderful in that play. She is just as sweet and pretty to-day, in retirement as a happy wife, as she was then. We Edwardians do not forget her or our gratitude for the pleasure she gave us. She went on from that show, in 1910, which was her first important London success, to please us at the Gaiety and elsewhere, and to shine in straight plays as well as musical comedy. She could do it all.

Curzon did musical plays at other theatres, too ; there was, amongst many more, *The White Chrysanthemum* at the Criterion, and how he got a musical comedy, chorus and all, on to that tiny stage was one of his secrets. He had presented them at Wyndham's also. His straight plays at the Prince of Wales's were often brilliant. They were presented jointly with actor-managers and manageresses. One recalls some typical Hawtrey plays—*Inconstant George*, in which the usually light-hearted and lying Charles played a scene of great tenderness with perfect skill, and one of the characters wore a harem skirt, the first approach by women (exclusive of bloomers for cycling) to wearing the trousers. They were considered daring, and shocking, these very veiled Turkish trousers, but they never became popular. There was *Dear Old Charlie* and the row it caused with the gods over the fact that it had originally been refused a licence by the Censor but was granted one by its author, brilliant Charles Brookfield, when he assumed that onerous post. There was, too, *The Uninvited Guest*, in which O. B. Clarence, who still graces our stage, shared the honours. At the end of this play there was the usual speech by Hawtrey and a hearty call for "Author." The play had been adapted from the French by J. N. Raphael, a famous journalist who was, amongst many other things, 'Percival' of *The Referee*, that journal pre-eminent in sport and drama, to which we looked forward so eagerly every Sunday. Raphael was its Paris correspondent and wrote a sparkling column entitled 'Gossip from the Gay City,' with all the inside Parisian news. There is nothing so good to-day.

He had adapted this play from the French, and as the French author was there the two of them elected to take a call. They did not time it well, for Hawtrey had not finished. But they strode on, one immediately behind the other, in perfect step, just like a couple of simultaneous dancers. The Frenchman was in front, short, fat, round, bald, with a nose shining red with excitement in a pale face, half hidden in one of those square-cut beards you never see out of France, above which his bald pate gleamed like a dome of snow. Immediately behind, and touching him, came the tall, thin Raphael, towering over him, pale of face, too, in the footlights' glare, but clean-shaven and very aquiline. He wore immaculate English evening dress, whilst that of his Parisian colleague was of the kind which, in France, had seen hard wear at weddings and funerals, and which shone like his scalp. They marched on, halted, and, one behind the other, faced the audience, who yelled with laughter. Hawtrey, who had his back to them, looked surprised. He turned, caught sight of the couple looking just like a music hall act about to begin, turned to the audience, and exploded with laughter himself. The applause became frantic, and the only solemn people in the whole house were the two authors, who probably never knew what all the laughter was about and took it as their just due.

Marie Tempest was another regular Prince of Wales's visitor. She did much fine work there by just being Marie Tempest, supreme mistress of charm—and of stage technique. The tragedy of this magnificent actress was that she never had a great part. She was always condemned by her adoring public to do the same things, to be in cup and saucer comedies in which she was gay, tempting, played with the men like an angler plays with a hooked fish, cried daintily into her tiny handkerchief and got her man in the end. Such plays as *At the Barn*, *Art and Opportunity* and others in her Prince of Wales's days were nice little successes but starved her of what she could really have done. Just as the Edwardian public sent Hawtrey—another of their people—to Coventry when he shaved off his moustache, so they insisted on Marie Tempest being just the Marie Tempest they liked to see. It was not until the end of her long and brilliant career, in *Dear Octopus*, that she was allowed to show what tenderness, what pathos, she could have plumbed—had she been permitted. She was an old woman then, but her art was as fresh as in the 'nineties and she was undoubted Queen of the Stage. Yet back at the beginning of the Edwardian era, at that very same theatre, she had commenced as an actress-manageress, with a most distinguished production of *English Nell*, in which she made the most roguish and bewitching 'Nell Gwynne' imaginable, with a lovely production and incidental music. Yet who remembers it to-day? That amazing and beloved couple, Fred Terry and Julia Neilson, opened *Sweet Nell of Old Drury* at the Haymarket almost immediately afterwards, and ran away with it—it was their stand-by for years. That is the figure of 'Nell' we remember—not the Marie Tempest one.

Marie followed her 'Nell' with another of the Old Drury hierarchy, 'Peg Woffington,' and topped this with 'Becky Sharp.' Fewer still remember those, maybe. But they were fine. Perhaps the best part she ever had was 'Polly' in *Caste* when revived at the Haymarket. The best, that is, until *Dear Octopus* came along.

Charles Hawtrey, easy-going soul, was remarkably careless—shall we say?—over money matters, and often had anxious Monday mornings, chasing the wherewithal to meet cheques issued over the week-ends. In this dilemma his friend and colleague, Frank Curzon, was always the rescuing angel, if they were associated at the time or not. Indeed, Hawtrey developed a technique. Another pal of his, Lyston Lyle, a first-class actor and of dominating and distinguished appearance, whom Hawtrey always had in his plays when there was anything like a part, was another of the financially careless. Perhaps it was a bond between them. Both knew that they had only to ask the long-suffering and generous Frank Curzon to receive help, within reason, but both had finer feelings. So they took it in turns—sometimes in frequent turns— to appeal for each other. Hawtrey would call round at the Prince of Wales's, chat about this and that and then say, "Poor old Lyston, it's terrible. He's had the most frightfully hard luck"—and then, out it would come—with Curzon to the rescue. A week or so afterwards Lyston Lyle would drop in to see his friend Frank. After a little chat and a couple of stories, maybe, out would go a heartrending appeal for dear old Charlie, with the inevitable result. When in funds, both would pay

up and would help anyone in need—and had Frank been in need, these
two gallants would have robbed the Bank of England. They were both
men of education and social standing, they were both gentlemen, they
were both good actors—but neither ever understood the value of money.
Frank had plenty, so like two children in search of an uncle famous for
his pockets full of sweets, both went to him. Curzon did not mind.

He had a watchdog, a general manager, a blunt, astute and kind-
hearted Lancastrian named T. B. Vaughan. Tommy to most people,
he knew all there was to know about the theatre business and his advice
and guidance were invaluable. Curzon was not good at saying "No,"
but Vaughan could and did say it for him. He made few mistakes in
personal values, he had an unerring eye for a player or a play and a
great discernment as regards public taste and fancy. He was Curzon's
friend as well as manager, and he was a very honest man indeed. He
spoke the truth and expected it from others. He did not flatter but he
pointed out irrefutable facts, and everyone trusted him and went to him
for help. They always got it—and the best of it. As staff, Curzon only
had two more people to run his big and complex business, one man and
one woman. The man was Jack Houston, a very neat, tiny, lovable
fellow, with a perky bird-like air, a fresh complexion and bright eye, a
beaming smile and an absolutely infallible mastery of figures. The
other was Gertrude Butler, Curzon's trusted secretary. In the days
when we were not so sure about the equality of women, Gertrude
Butler was conceded by all the brains of a man—and so she had—and
so she still has. Brisk, quick-moving, rapid and accurate in work and
judgment, she knew all about it. She knew the grain from the chaff,
the useful from the useless—she still does. She carried out the duties of
secretary—and the duties of a theatrical manager's secretary are mani-
fold and onerous to a degree. Gertrude Butler was the ideal. She knew
all the secrets, and kept them, she knew when to speak and when to
hold her tongue. She could judge a man or a woman at a glance. She
is one of the people whom nobody ever sees behind the scenes, but who
helps the wheels to go round easily and smoothly—a real treasure.
When Curzon had Wyndham's for some time, his brother-in-law, Herbert
Jay, was his manager there. And that was the firm—except for the
Sergeant in the enquiry office, an old soldier who had served in China
during the Boxer Rising and who had in that campaign formed a low
opinion of the Dowager Empress. Thereafter, if he wished to express
the worst possible of anyone, male or female, he would describe him or
her as a "perfect Dow-wagger," which was his method of pronouncing
that rank.

The Prince of Wales's in Curzon's day was a very different theatre
to the modern, shiny, alert playhouse which bears its name now. It
was by comparison very quiet in decoration, a little dingy with the
passing years, a place of winding corridors and unexpected corners and
rooms, with a curious kink in its gallery where the seats resembled those
tiers on which plants are arranged at flower shows. But it had an atmosphere, a charm and a touch of friendliness all at the same time. It made
you feel at home, it held the fragrance of success about it. There was,
somewhere in its intricacies, a room where a gentleman of great splendour

MARIE STUDHOLME

EVIE GREENE AS 'CONSUELO' IN
'HAVANA'

CYRIL MAUDE

EDNA MAY

GEORGE GROSSMITH, JUNR., AS 'PRINCE OTTO' IN 'THE GIRLS OF GOTTENBERG'

H. G. PELISSIER AS 'MEPHISTOPHE IN 'FAUST'

MAUD ALLAN AS 'SALOME'

GERTIE MILLAR

sat in state. He was a tall, a very imposing man, with a considerable presence and the very air which Dickens draped about those immortal 'Tite Barnacles.' He had something to do with the lease, he was some sort of trustee, and for some time he controlled the bars, cloakrooms and programmes. Strangely enough, this amazingly Victorian English figure inhabited a room entirely without windows and which was to all intents and purposes the interior of a Chinese pagoda. The whole thing was Chinese. Silken draperies and screens draped the walls, lacquer gleaming, porcelain glowing, and a vast umbrella covering the entire ceiling, from which was suspended a Chinese lantern, in which an electric light was securely hidden. To interview this gentleman, having come into that room unsuspectingly from the brightness of Edwardian Coventry Street, was a bit breath-taking, not to say unnerving. And after the interview, which he conducted with the greatest pomp, as of an ambassador receiving a defeated enemy come to beg for terms, and during which he looked straight through you, you never had a very clear idea of what was the upshot, which was probably his entire plan. You were glad to get out into the fresh air, to stand for a while under the glass verandah of the Prince of Wales's from which hung baskets gay with flowers, to get your breath and try to recollect what had passed within. That sort of thing was not at all unusual in the Edwardian Theatre but you could not find it to-day.

But the theatre itself reflected the real, solid humanity of Frank Curzon. It was a home, it had the atmosphere of an English home and this man was the host. He brought the breath of the fields, the coverts, the grouse-moor. He did not subscribe entirely to town attire at a time when we were most meticulous. Let the summer be very hot, and Frank Curzon would stroll to his theatre from his London home clad in a loose suit of bright fawn Shantung silk and a panama hat, what time other mortals in his business sweated in tall hats and morning coats.

But he knew his theatre as he knew his countryside. His eye missed nothing. He and his delightful wife made that theatre worth while ; indeed, under Curzon it was always worth while. For he was one of the men who understood, who had been right through the mill. He knew that he was a trusted host who must never let his guests, the public, down ; and it was very, very seldom that he did. So on summer nights in the season, on frosty nights when the stars over Eros twinkled brightly and coldly, and even on nights of fog such as we don't see now, we came out of the Prince of Wales's and got into those carriages at eleven, with a tune on our lips, or a laugh in our hearts—for we had been entertained by Frank Curzon, the actor-manager-squire.

CHAPTER XII

His Name Endures in Stone

THERE HAVE BEEN SOME ACTORS WHO FILLED THEATRES BY THEIR ART, SOME who made certain theatres famous by their association with them, and some who not only did both of these things but built theatres themselves

L

which they endowed with their personality. The last category is limited. For, in living memory, only two have succeeded in doing so, Sir Herbert Tree and Sir Charles Wyndham. And here the palm must go to Wyndham, for he made the Criterion famous, although he did not build it, and he filled it for many years. But he did build two other theatres, the New Theatre, and the one in which he endures himself, by name and title—Wyndham's Theatre. There is his name perpetuated in stone, and his is the only actor's name which now shines over the portico which he himself built. For the Garrick Theatre was not built by Garrick, and, indeed, was not there at all until 1889, one hundred and ten years after the Great Little David had passed away. Augustin Daly gave his name to Daly's—where is Daly's now? Edward Terry gave his name to a theatre in the Strand, which is gone without a trace, nor does any sign of Toole's Theatre linger. Astley's went the way of all things long ago, and although the Globe, in Shaftesbury Avenue, opened as the Hicks (named after the volatile Seymour), it soon changed its title. An American, F. C. Whitney, boldly placarded his cognomen outside what was then the Waldorf, but for a very short time, and that playhouse became The Strand—and prospered.

That vast building which began as the London Opera House, built by Oscar Hammerstein, now bears the name of the man who bought it —Stoll, the music hall magnate, but it is not wholly a theatre ; it has been cinema, music hall, opera house, what you will, as well. Seldom has it been a theatre in the true sense of the word.

An American actress of considerable avoirdupois, who became a film star, once re-christened the Aldwych after herself, but the new name was scarcely up before it was down again. There is still Collins's Music Hall, in Islington, named after its performer-founder, and there is, of course, Sadler's Wells Theatre ; but although there was a Sadler and he did have wells, that title really comes from the Spa which he opened, for he never built the theatre—the nearest he got to it was a wooden erection with a platform, which was known as 'The Musick House.'

Sir Herbert Tree built His Majesty's and made it in his time the most famous theatre in the world, but never gave it his name. But Sir Charles Wyndham built that theatre which still bears his name, and also in his own way made it famous. And to-day it stands, a reminder of a very great man for all to see.

For Sir Charles Wyndham was one of the very greatest Edwardian managers, whose fame was not only of that epoch, but went well back into the days of Victoria. It seems incredible now that he was also a qualified doctor and that, as an army surgeon, he served in the American Civil War on the losing side, that of the Confederates. That was as long ago as 1862. It is difficult to imagine Wyndham being on the losing side in anything. He went to America to enlist, so as to escape from the stage. He was in action at many of the great engagements of that war, and saw plenty of hard service. But nobody can escape their destiny, and the Theatre was his. So although he had served with the South, as soon as the war was over he was appearing in New York, the capital of the Yankee Federals. He did not make at that time much of a success—and maybe it was because he had fought with the South. So he came home, for Wyndham was a native of Liverpool, where he was born in 1837.

He had come to the Criterion with his play *Brighton* in 1875, on 27th December of that year, and was already a full-fledged actor-manager, to help over a bad patch, and on 15th April 1876 he took over the management of that theatre, which he was to retain until his death. So, despite his building of the New and Wyndham's, it is the little Criterion with which his name is most associated. It was a very long association, for Wyndham died in 1919, at the venerable age of eighty-one. And of those years, forty-three had been spent in direct control of the 'Cri.' For some years before his end, his control was nominal only, but the theatre was always in the forefront of his thoughts, and although in his later years his memory was hazy, it was never so hazy but that he would often drive to the Criterion to see how things were going on. Few men or women have been in control of a theatre for so long and so splendidly.

But although he was a fixed star at the Criterion, he was an astute man who knew that a star was all the better for enlarging its orbit. He knew that people in distant—not too distant—towns could not come and see him, so he determined to go to them, and still remain at the Criterion. He did this by means of the 'Flying Matinée' which he invented. Suburban playgoers saw him, people in towns which could be reached in time to allow him to be back by the evening saw him. It was a great idea and a great success. Of course, he did not fly. The aeroplane was not invented. He went by train. But it was regarded as very go-ahead and very energetic. And it was. It also caused his staff many headaches, but they got through somehow and the idea spread to other actor-managers as a whole.

When the Edwardian era dawned, Wyndham was still in his prime—and that word meant something where Wyndham was concerned. Born in the year of Queen Victoria's coronation, he had become famous in her day, and then, when she became a recluse after the Diamond Jubilee, and the Edwardian days really commenced, Wyndham was an institution in London, practically one of the 'sights.' And he was then sixty.

But you cannot reckon years in connection with a man like that. They meant nothing to him or his art, save that both he and the art had mellowed. For Wyndham's acting was mellow, full of the glowing tints of the sunset, no glare, no shouting, no noise, nor rushing about—just mellowness. His work, like himself at that time, was like a gentle, charming September day. The trees were still in full leaf, there was colour everywhere, there was the robust richness of the garnered harvest and all the delicate charm of an autumn afternoon. His voice had the same quality. He had mannerisms, of course—all good actors have—but his voice was like a caress. Everything about him spoke of distinction, and he conveyed that to his plays, his parts, his company and his theatres. It still remains in his triumvirate of playhouses, for Wyndham was a triumvirate in himself. He made the Criterion a leading theatre, giving it a decided policy, and when he built the New and Wyndham's he managed, by some great gift, to have that same personality and distinctiveness put into their very bricks and mortar. It is still there, you can still feel it and be aware of it. And his success still abides, for those three are amongst the most consistently successful theatres in town.

Wyndham himself is the subject for a new book, which would of necessity be a history of the lighter drama of his age. But here we are concerned only with that phase of the Edwardian time, and it was one of his finest. At the very threshold of that time, his colleagues of the Theatre gave a great performance in his honour at the Lyceum. It began there in the afternoon and it overlapped into the Criterion in the evening. It was on 1st May 1896, to celebrate his twentieth year of Criterion management. The performances raised £2,452 6s. 4d., all of which he gave to the Actors' Benevolent Fund.

He had already produced those great masterpieces of classical comedy in which he shone so brightly, also those farces in which he was so adept, he had already begun the later series of his Arthur Jones comedies and his other productions which made him memorable. And he was on the verge of opening his new theatre which was called by his name. And he had also made that play of Robertson's, *David Garrick*, which Sothern had first played, his very own, something with which he was to be always connected. He loved playing 'David Garrick.' He did not look the least bit like little David, but what did we care? Here was a great actor portraying another great actor in the most artistic manner possible. As a play it meant nothing, it was just a piece of carpenter's work ; but the character of 'Garrick,' from the actor's point of view, was a perfect piece of craftsmanship, beautifully turned and finished and capable of the greatest polish. And nobody could apply such polish in such a polished manner as Sir Charles Wyndham. There is a story about him in connection with this play which is worth repeating. Wyndham adored to sit under the portrait of Garrick in the Garrick Club. He was seated there one afternoon prior to going to the Criterion to perform as 'David Garrick,' when Charles Brookfield entered the room. Brookfield was one of the greatest wits who ever blessed the Theatre. He came over to Wyndham, stared at him, then at the portrait of Garrick, then at Wyndham again, and said, almost as if to himself : "It's most extraordinary, I think you grow more like Garrick every afternoon." Wyndham was delighted, and his deep voice spoke his thanks. "My dear fellow," he said, all smiles, "do you really think I grow more like David Garrick every afternoon?" "Yes," retorted Brookfield, "I do. And less like him every evening." Upon which he made his exit.

There was not room for Wyndham to have his offices in the Criterion, so he had an adjacent suite fitted out like a yacht and from there he controlled it. Like all the other defamed and infamous scoundrels of actor-managers, he made many stars, for his companies were always of the best. His eye for talent was unerring. Men like Cyril Maude, to become great as well, have set down their gratitude in print. And Maude tells a poignant story of him. He told Maude, once, that his prayer was, "O Lord, keep my memory green." He asked Maude if he understood what it meant. Maude said he presumed it meant that Wyndham hoped he would not be forgotten. "No, no," replied the great actor, "it means, O Lord, keep me young in my ideas." In one sense, that prayer was not granted, for in his last few years Wyndham's memory failed.

And there is another delightful Maude story which concerns Wyndham. It was during a rehearsal for the wonderful gala performance of *Money* at Drury Lane, when the German Kaiser came over to unveil the statue of Queen Victoria outside Buckingham Palace, in 1911—a ceremony done in the sacred name of Peace which the Kaiser was, so soon and so disastrously, to break. But the gala performance was a great affair and all the stars, including Sir Charles Wyndham, were in it. Maude and Irene Vanbrugh were at the rehearsals and Wyndham always brought along a little dog which became a general nuisance, barked at everyone and got persistently in the way. Sir Herbert Tree, Irene Vanbrugh and Cyril Maude were standing together. Maude, as a joke, asked them if they knew that the wretched little animal had been trained by Lady Wyndham to bite Sir Charles's ankles if he seemed disposed to talk too long to any charming lady. They both laughed at this absurdity, and Irene Vanbrugh, with mischief in her eyes and an innocent expression, gazed up at Sir Herbert's face and said, "Tell me, Sir Herbert, has Lady Tree ever trained a little dog to watch over your goings-on?" At once Tree became aloof and mysterious. His expression became rapt and faraway, as always when a joke was toward. "Once, dear lady, once"—he whispered—"but . . . it died from want of sleep."

Now that Lady Wyndham was the other half of Sir Charles Wyndham. Her name was Mary Moore. She had joined him at the Criterion as a girl, and she had risen with him. She owed much to him, and he owed much to her. No wonder that they were eventually to marry and make a life partnership of that great stage partnership. For she was his ideal leading lady in every respect, his perfect foil. They were flint and steel of the stage and when they played together—as they practically always did, especially at the 'Cri'—the most lovely flames of acting were kindled.

Her fame grew with his at the Criterion. When she came there she was a very lovely young girl, and her charm endured all of her days. She took enormous pains, she would cry at rehearsals if she thought she had not done as well as she should, or had not reproduced the full power within her. And always, like Wyndham, she was most thoughtful for and kind to the other members of the Criterion—and to her end she loved Youth.

These two together gave some of the most beautiful contemporary acting of comedy which the stage has seen. It was that fine thing, a perfect stage combination, which is the very bedrock of the Theatre. Dramatists wrote for them, they knew how to fit them. Wyndham would have been, in these days, regarded as a fine 'producer,' but he did not know the word in the sense it has to-day. It was part of the job with him, this giving coherence and completeness to the play in hand. And he put the finishing polish on so many stars of later days. The Criterion was an academy for comedy.

In 1896 Wyndham presented a play by Louis N. Parker which had the fragrance of its own name, *Rosemary*. In it, he and Mary Moore gave unforgettable performances. It was a delightful piece of nostalgia, of runaway couples ; of a senior man taking charge and staving off a romantic disaster, to be left much later alone with his memories. There was a scene on a village green, where the eloping couple's carriage came to grief, and they took refuge with the Squire, and that Squire, handsome and very English, was Charles Wyndham, as 'Sir Jasper Thorndyke.' He became everyone's friend—Wyndham's invariable role. He placated the angry and pursuing parents, he made things well for the young couple. And he fell in love with the eloping bride, 'Dorothy Cruickshank,' who was Mary Moore. But, as was so often the case with Wyndham, 'he never spoke his love.' Being some years senior to the young lady, he adopted the usual method then of believing that, so far as she was concerned, he had one foot in the grave. The age of forty then was as advanced as seventy to-day. But they all got to a room in London to watch a great event. It may have been Queen Victoria's Coronation. It is a long time to recall the details of a play seen fifty years ago. One remembers the hush which fell when an onlooker said, "The Queen is passing," and the loud roar of cheers from off stage. Also there were stilt-walkers who peeped through the window, to the horror of the ladies, until dismissed by small silver from the men. But Dorothy gave Sir Jasper some rosemary from her bouquet. Years passed, and Sir Jasper was in the same room, and again a great procession was passing by. Again a stilt-walker peered in at the window, but this time he had a black face and a banjo. Again Sir Jasper gave him money, and his thoughts stirred. In an old desk or drawer which he opened he found that sprig of rosemary given him years before by the young and blooming girl whom he had loved and whom he had lost through his own nobility of character. And Wyndham played that scene in his own manner. It may sound trite and sentimental to-day but in Wyndham's hands it had poignancy, humanity and the sharp sad tang of the sprig of rosemary itself. When he opened the New Theatre in 1903, he did so with a revival of that play, and a plaque chronicles the fact in the theatre vestibule. But those who saw that marvellous couple in that play need no rosemary for remembrance.

At the Criterion, in Edwardian days, he gave us *The Liars*, a masterpiece for Henry Arthur Jones, Mary Moore and himself. He was again the great man, the *raisonneur*, with the big speech in the penultimate act, so well written and so magnificently delivered, which would put all right for everyone in the last act. This was Wyndham's high spot always. He knew all about long speeches, and he could deliver them with an art which is lost to-day. That deep voice, a little hoarse at times, could rumble to the depths, could compel tears, could be as soft and delicate as velvet in cajolery, in persuasion, could strike, compel and command, and could take on a lightness of tone and touch which drew immediate laughter. His timing, his gestures, his stance, his movements were alike perfection. For he was a total actor in the sense of the total war we have since lived through. All of him acted at once and together, producing perfect symmetry of character and effect. He could make love—manly love— there was nothing of the ardent young 'juvenile' about him. No, this was the man of mature years, who knew his world and knew women. Those who heard him will never forget the homage and meaning in his voice when, helping a lady on with her sable coat, he murmured, "How furs become you." It was the entire tribute of admiring man to delighted woman. Or his approving smile when came the riposte, "I'll tell you a secret, they become every woman." But still he conveyed the under-standing that the lady he spoke to contained all the charms of woman-hood in her single person.

At Wyndham's Theatre, in another Arthur Jones's play, *Mrs. Dane's Defence*, he played 'Sir Daniel Carteret,' and he showed us another side to his talent. There, as a lawyer, a great cross-examiner, he tore to pieces the soul of the woman who had captured the heart of his ward, the boy who was the son of the woman he had loved and lost—for Wyndham had, in his professional capacity, a whole graveyard of lost loves. In fact, one sometimes speculated on the mentality of the women who had preferred the other fellow to this handsome, gentle, persuasive man of honour and distinction and wondered if perhaps it had not been his own fault, if he had not been too retiring, a shade too noble, a shade too gentlemanly.

But in *Mrs. Dane's Defence* he showed us the whip-lash. He fought to save his lad, the lad he considered as his son. The fascinating 'Mrs. Dane,' the woman with a murky past, did all she knew. In a scene which rose from a storm in a teacup to a tornado, which embraced every phase of feeling and the whole gamut of emotion, Sir Daniel was adamant, fierce, unrelenting. One by one he tore her lies from her, one by one he demolished her lines of defence, until at last, his fine voice using every art that was in it, his accusing finger straight at her face, he said in icy, deadly tones full of vibrant passion, "You—are Felicia Hindmarsh." And she collapsed. She was beaten, she confessed, she told her story. And his nobility of character helped her, now that his boy was safe. Those who saw Wyndham and Lena Ashwell in this scene saw the finest of Edwardian acting—and Edwardian acting was very fine indeed.

Having opened Wyndham's with his own name thereon, naturally Wyndham stayed there for some time. He had another fine part in *Mrs. Gorringe's Necklace*. Mary Moore was with him in both of these plays. In *Mrs. Dane's Defence* she played 'Lady Eastney,' a cultured, polished woman of the world, witty and observant and in love with 'Sir Daniel,' the typical role of that time which she always graced—and you knew that at the end these two would come together, in spite of her frequent refusals of his tactful and delicate proposals. In *Mrs. Gorringe's Necklace* she played 'Mrs. Gorringe,' showing another side to her talent. For when it came to playing pretty, feather-brained women, who exerted their femininity like tyrants over the then submissive, if nominally master animal, Man, well, then Mary Moore was something to see. Her chat-tering, foolish, scatter-brained 'Mrs. Gorringe,' the loss of whose necklace aroused such a to-do and a tumult, was a masterpiece. And she exploited the art of crying as the most powerful weapon in woman's armoury in *The Tyranny of Tears*. Had she not been Mary Moore, one would have longed to shake her. But as she was Mary Moore, one simply adored.

There was one of the plays, it might have been *The Liars*, it might have been *The Case of Rebellious Susan* (the plays are not to hand for reference), in which she had a daring and illicit dinner with an admirer at a Thames-side hotel. Here she had expected 'Sauce Tartare' with the fish and it was not forthcoming. How she went on about this, how she nagged in the most genteel and ladylike manner, how she came back to the subject, how she mentioned her liking, indeed her passion, for this delectable sauce, was as delicious as the sauce itself. It was a little thing, but she made it memorable. She could take a trifle light as air and invest it with a world of meaning. She was a perfect comedy actress whose like we have not to-day.

This theatre-building actor-manager had opened Wyndham's in 1899 with his other *pièce-de-resistance, David Garrick*. And the opening performance brought in £4,000, which he gave to the Soldiers' and Sailors' Families Mission, for the Boer War was on. Wyndham, Prince of the Stage, did things in a princely manner.

He was, however, back at the Criterion in 1907, when he produced a play which has become memorable. This was called *The Mollusc*. It was by Hubert Henry Davies, and it saw the footlights on 15th October 1907. It was a sensation, for it contained only four characters. This was a novelty indeed. News got out and it was looked forward to with eager curiosity. Its title was intriguing to a degree. What did it mean? We were soon to find out. For it was a masterly play, played by masterly hands. The 'Mollusc' was our beloved Mary Moore. 'A mollusc,' explained the dramatist, 'was a thing which although endowed with plenty of life and power, remained stationary and compelled those around it to do its work, bear its burdens, feed it, clothe it and be its slaves, even if they were unaware of the fact.' And indeed, for nearly every moment of those three acts, Mary Moore remained stationary on a sofa whilst the other three characters revolved around her. But what characters they were. They were Sir Charles Wyndham, Sam Sothern, and Elaine Inescourt, playing her first really big new part in London. The battle of wits, the sparkling dialogue, so beautifully spoken, the clever plot, the weaving and unravelling of it, the perfect playing, made the whole thing a *tour de force*. It was, of course, Wyndham who finally beat the Mollusc, he was the man with the oyster knife—but Mary Moore was perhaps the victor by and large. *The Mollusc* ran for well over three hundred performances, and every playgoer worthy of the name went to the little underground Criterion to see it. And they saw the perfection of comedy acting by four people (one of them new but wholly successful—trust Wyndham for that), and they saw what a comedy of the Edwardian days was really like. Sam Sothern, the fourth in this comedy quartette, was a perfect actor of 'ineffective' men, gentlemen without force of character, who drifted with the tide, amiable creatures with the best manners and intentions, but totally unable to impress themselves upon anything or anybody, and like wax in the hands of a woman, be she their wife or somebody else's. In this line he excelled and has left no real successor. He was himself the third son of the great E. A. Sothern, who had created 'Lord Dundreary' and indeed that 'David Garrick' which Wyndham carried on. Sothern played many parts with Wyndham, and always to perfection. All London went to the Criterion for *The Mollusc*. Indeed, all London playgoers nearly always went to the Criterion when Wyndham and Mary Moore were there. It is still a curious, subterranean place, indeed that same Charles Brookfield of whom mention has been made once said of a woman who was a great Criterion fan, that she had one foot in the grave and the other in the Criterion Theatre. But the Criterion was no grave of ambitions, of delayed hopes or of elusive success. It was, perhaps, an Aladdin's Cave crammed with jewels of plays and acting. Playgoers flocked there. For it stands in the very centre of the world, in Piccadilly Circus. And when Wyndham ruled there, Piccadilly Circus meant something. Eros presided over a whirlpool of humanity, of jostling crowds speaking every tongue, wearing every kind of dress, from every rank and station of life. In the earlier days the horse buses clattered by, dropping their humbler playgoers, who ran round to Jermyn Street, to line up for the Criterion's very small pit. It was an unobtrusive entrance, difficult to distinguish from a nearby exit door and another leading to the Criterion Restaurant, but we Wyndhamites knew it all right. It was joyfully near to the stage door, down which the stars proceeded by a corkscrew iron staircase. The carriages did not come there, they dropped their loads of well-dressed men in white waistcoats, their swishing silks and satins of womanhood, befurred and bejewelled, in Piccadilly Circus itself. And you went into the front door, with its tiny vestibule, its small box office, its Doulton tiling, downstairs and along corridors, with misleading mirrors at the end, until you found yourself in the drawing-room of its auditorium, small, select, bright, atmospheric and very intimate indeed. It was the perfect home for plays like *The Mollusc*. It was the perfect home for Charles Wyndham and Mary Moore, though they could fill any theatre, as they frequently proved. But they were 'at home' at the Criterion, and so were you. You felt their friendliness, you felt that you were their guests. You could have leaned forward and shaken hands with them. And if there were some pillars—and there were, even in the very front row of the circle—well, nobody minded in the least. The Edwardian playgoer put up with things like that. He was not the pampered darling of the cinema age, who expects, and gets, the luxury of a millionaire's home on Riverside Drive for ninepence. He was just an Englishman, who lived at home, and who had, in his own house, quite a few inconveniences to put up with. So the little matter of a pillar in front of him, though it may have annoyed, seldom drove him to any lengths of disapproval. He—or she—was content to be there, in the company of such great people, to see such amusing plays so beautifully acted. If he got a crick in the neck, it was in a good cause and always he enjoyed himself.

But Wyndham was not responsible for those pillars. They were there before him. But when he built his own two theatres, Wyndham's and the New, he built them as models of what theatres should be. They are both just the right size for what is required of them. They both have comfort, line of sight and convenience—and what is more, atmosphere. The smiles and delight, the satisfaction and the applause which Wyndham and Mary Moore caused still remain to make them happy places. And backstage, too, you find things as they should be. Plenty of stage room, plenty of space, workshops in the right positions—all set for the business of the drama. They are Edwardian theatres, and that means a great deal. In many new theatres the last thing considered is the stage, which is the heart, soul, and being of the place. Indeed, at one of them this trifle was entirely omitted from the architect's plans, and an additional piece of ground had to be secured at great expense, to make a most inconvenient and limited structure for the progress of the very thing for which the theatre was erected. Not so with Wyndham ! And furthermore, his seating was always in the right proportions. He was never led away by success to think that he could fill a whole floorful of stalls as a general rule. It is very seldom that happens, and usually during great world wars. At other and more normal times the seats thus ambitiously installed have to be 'jobbed' at reduced prices, and that way confusion and complaints lie, for whatever theatrical managers of to-day imagine, a certain portion of the general public, no longer their guests but just their 'customers,' possess memories. And it is an awkward thing to persuade a man—and even more awkward to persuade a woman—that the value of the seat for which they paid five shillings a few weeks ago has now risen to sixteen. Actor-managers avoided this, though they, too, were guilty of the movable pit, which ebbed and flowed with the tide of success. Only one theatre remains—and always has remained—perfectly true to its printed plan and that is Theatre Royal Drury Lane, which naturally stands alone in its nobility in every respect.

Charles Wyndham, as became him and his times, was an Edwardian Knight. He received the accolade from King Edward VII in 1902, on the occasion of the monarch's Coronation. And it must have afforded as much satisfaction to the King as it did to Wyndham and the play-going public, for never was a knighthood better deserved.

The young generation of to-day who did not know Wyndham missed a great deal. They missed a man who was a great actor, a great manager, a great producer and a great gentleman. They missed a man who cast distinction on everything around him. He was the finest light comedian of his day, in the very best sense of that term. He was capable of much more than he did, but he had to please his public, the great family of the Edwardian public, and in that he always succeeded. He had his failures, but they are lost beneath the mountain of his successes. He was tall and he was handsome. His broad brow, with its beautiful and shining hair so perfectly cared for, his distinctive voice, his presence, his smiling eyes, his dignity, marked him out for what he was in any company, any crowd. He always dressed the part, he was always perfectly groomed, perfectly immaculate. If you saw him in the street, it was an event, as he passed by. He seemed unaware of his surroundings as he walked, his eyes gazing into the future from under the brim of his grey tall hat, which matched his grey morning coat. His stick was often under his arm, his hands behind him. And even when his memory failed him, his courtesy did not. If he came to see a play with his devoted wife, he never left the theatre without asking to see the manager and tendering his thanks and appreciation for the show he had seen. Often it had made little impression, for that hazy mind had been hovering elsewhere. But he joined his thanks with those of his dear wife, Mary Moore, as courteous as he was ; he gave his wholly charming smile and he passed on, a great figure of a great time. He left a blank when he finally vanished in death. It was a shock felt by all. But that prayer of his was answered all the same, and that play of his came true. His memory is fresh and green amongst the living Edwardians, and as unmistakably scented as that of his delightful play *Rosemary*—which stands for remembrance. Besides which there is still the Criterion, with his monogram on the walls, there is still the New, and there is still Wyndham's Theatre to carry on his eternal success.

For the tradition goes on, the family still reigns at those playhouses. There is Howard Wyndham, Sir Charles's son, with the charm of his father and the Edwardian courtliness of manner, and there is Bronson Albery, son of Mary Moore, with his mother's shrewdness which was so valuable, knowledge of the theatre and uprightness of purpose—and a lot of her charm as well, to run those theatres. They are no blood relations, they are both the children of their respective parent's first marriages—but there is the bond of that great marriage of art and companionship and theatre consciousness—to make them a brotherhood of the theatre. And the success goes on.

There were other plays at the Criterion when Wyndham was not there. Many of them were in the right Criterion vein, too. There was a farce called *Mr. Preedy and the Countess*, in which Weedon Grossmith as 'Mr. Preedy' (and looking exactly like it) was wildly funny, and there was Miss Compton as 'The Countess of Rushmore' (and looking exactly like it, too). These two were often associated and always with joy. She had been 'Lady Huntworth' in *Lady Huntworth's Experiment* and he had played her blackguardly drunken husband. That was a little out of his usual line for he excelled either as a harassed little man in the greatest trouble or as a real, bounding vulgarian. In either type he was inimitable. Miss Compton was the daughter of Henry Compton, so of real theatrical stock. And she married R. C. Carton, a fine dramatist, who wrote parts for her which she played magnificently. She had a curious incisive style, and was a past mistress of 'timing.' She could get a laugh, she could hold a scene, and she could be charming. She was always distinguished and ranks highly in the Edwardian portrait gallery of the Theatre—for she was typical of it.

In *Mr. Preedy and the Countess* they were both at their best and much joy ensued. Then there was, in 1911, another farce called *Baby Mine*. This was an affair of younger stars. It was also a wildly comic business which has often been revived. But its chief delight, on its original production, was Iris Hoey, then in the first full flush of beauty and individuality. For she had her share of the individuality which was a note of the time and she retains it to-day. Her very walk shows it.

In *Baby Mine*, as a mother in search of a baby, she gave a sparkling performance. The baby was the misunderstanding on which the farce was founded—for all farces must have that foundation. Iris Hoey had London at her dainty feet, where it remains. Whether in pink silk nightgown and adorable cap, or in a blue and white striped dress, as vivid as herself, she was the essence of allure. There was a young man in that show who scored a very big success as the bewildered young husband. His name was Donald Calthrop. He had theatrical ancestry and parentage, he had youth, good looks, and ability. Indeed he had great ability. Here, we said, is a young man with a future. True, he did go a long way, but like so many of his profession he threw away his chances in the end. And his end was in many respects a tragic one. He had known poverty and starvation before it came. Yet, right up to his last curtain, when he got the chance, he was a grand actor and would steal a show or a film from other stars.

Both those farces were typical of their time, both of them slick, clever, well thought out, witty and well written. Dramatists then did not rely on casual absurdity for laughter—they created it in serious form and always had as a basis a credible situation, which is the true basis of farce, the hardest thing in the Theatre to write, play, or judge beforehand.

To that theatre named after Wyndham came that other great Edwardian, Frank Curzon. There he did plays which were excellent. And there he put a man who was also to become a great actor-manager and also a knight. And who was, incidentally, to start a new school of acting of which he alone was a real master, which looked so easy and was so hard. He was Gerald Du Maurier.

Son of the great George Du Maurier, the artist, he was a born creator himself. He started much, he rose to heights, he was an idol of the crowd, but he never got to the greatest height which was within his reach. He typed himself very severely. He allowed tricks and mannerisms to get the upper hand. But whilst he was at Wyndham's in the days of Curzon, in Edwardian days, he was fine and the man of promise. For he required a controlling hand, as do so many geniuses, and he was undoubtedly in the genius class. He had been educated at Harrow. He never forgot it, why should he? But he did not allow others to forget it either and that was something of a pity. He had been one of Sir Herbert Tree's young men and had therefore learnt his trade in the best possible school. He went into comedy roles later and showed us that charm which was his great asset, of which he had much and to spare. He was never a handsome man, he was thin, cadaverous, and a bit sad in expression. But he could exploit that charm and charm a bird off a bough. That was much better than good looks, for the charm lasts and good looks do not. He was groomed into stardom by Charles Frohman and his performances under that mighty master at the Duke of York's were without blemish. When he played 'Raffles' at the Comedy Theatre, he performed another miracle. He made the villain of the piece the hero of the play. For 'Raffles,' in whatever light you regard him, was a thorough-paced blackguard, or, as we Edwardians would have said, a perfect cad. There was nothing to recommend him except that he was a daring and successful thief. Yet Du Maurier made us love him. He burst the old idea of virtue being triumphant and glorified a mean, sneaking, selfish robber—who robbed his friends, his hosts, and everyone with no compunction—into a greater hero than any of the white-souled, long-suffering, brave young heroes of melodrama had ever been. We just fell down and worshipped this piece of immorality. We cheered when he outwitted the law, we thrilled with pride when a virtuous, innocent girl told him that she knew all and still loved him, and we even took the pursuing but baffled detective to our hearts when, at the end of the play, he exclaimed : "He's got away. I'm glad. He's bully." It was really a terrible state of things, when you come to work it out. But it was all due to the great acting and terrific charm of one young man—Gerald Du Maurier. If he had not created 'Raffles,' villains might still have been villains, heroes might still have been heroes, and white would never have become black. Also scores of other plays and hundreds of films would never have been written. But then, you see, he did play 'Raffles.' And thank God for the memory.

He and Curzon became associated as the management of Wyndham's Theatre in 1910, and opened with an unpretentious but charming play called *Nobody's Daughter*. The new actor-manager and his play were welcomed. It was a well-played trifle, enough to whet our appetites for what was to come. In it with Du Maurier were Marsh Allen, Rosalie Toller and that fine actor, Sydney Valentine. The next venture was not so successful. It was called *Mr. Jervis* and was a Jacobite play. That has never been a lucky theatrical subject. Actually, Gerald was very good indeed, but the play, in the phrase of those days, 'failed to attract.' But the next one, *Passers By*, was different. That was a truly Edwardian comedy and it pleased. We then had *The Perplexed Husband* and we found that Wyndham's was becoming the home of English comedy as well as the Haymarket. For Gerald Du Maurier was getting a stamp of quality on everything, and he was impressing himself upon us. And behind him was the sure, guiding hand of T. B. Vaughan and behind that again of Frank Curzon. Even before then he had made history at Wyndham's by producing a play of his soldier-brother—called *An Englishman's Home* —which, in 1909, did much to thicken the ranks of the recently formed Territorial Army, which had succeeded the old Volunteers. That play showed us Du Maurier the producer, and his managerial career was to show us and prove to us that he was the best producer of his day.

We had *The Dust of Egypt*, *Jelf's*, originally called *The Kangaroo*, in which he played a banker who was regarded as a bit of a bounder—and then *Doormats*, a play of considerable charm. In March 1913 he and Curzon presented a revival of *Diplomacy*, which was to become a landmark. For it was the best revival of this great play we have ever had. It must have rivalled the original production by the Bancrofts. The famous scene between the three men, played by Norman Forbes as 'Baron Stein,' Arthur Wontner as 'Count Orloff,' and Du Maurier as 'Henry Beauclerk,' was something to remember. Owen Nares was 'Julian' and gave a beautiful performance, proving to those who looked upon him as just a very handsome young man that he was capable of drama and grip. Gladys Cooper, at the height of her beauty, was the ideal 'Dora.' Their great scene together lingers with gratitude. Ellis Jeffreys was 'Countess Zicka' and must surely have been the greatest exponent of that role. What an actress she was, what an air she had, with what distinction she wore her clothes and carried herself, what poise, what *savoir faire* ! She was Edwardian mature womanhood in its perfection. They do not breed women like her to-day. She was of the type of which our revered Queen Mary stands at the head. And how Ellis Jeffreys could play a scene, how she could speak a line ! With the surest aim she hit the bullseye every time, and, if she so desired, that line hit the back of the theatre with a plonk. She threw nothing away, she aimed it truly. Lady Tree, who had now become a great character actress, gave a wholly enchanting performance as 'Lady Henry Fairfax,' and A. E. Matthews (still as young to-day as he was then, and the living example to any youthful actor as a model) was 'Algy Fairfax,' consumed with a burning desire to know where 'Henry Beauclerk' got his boots. He, by the way, was succeeded during the run by Donald Calthrop, good but never so good as the ever youthful 'Matty.' That man's art is prodigious. The cast was rounded off by Annie Schletter as Dora's mother. That revival covered Wyndham's and everyone connected with it with glory. It was at the very end of the Edwardian days—and the very next year was to come that war which altered the whole world. Edward himself had passed on, George V sat on the throne in 1913, but still the Edwardian days held in the Theatre. And Gerald Du Maurier was the last of the Edwardian actor-managers. During those times he gave us much to be thankful for, besides his own performances. One remembers with pleasure old Alfred Bishop in *Doormats* when he played 'Uncle Rufus.' He had been made a Governor of somewhere and it had been announced in *The Times*— he was very proud of this but was always reduced to collapse and chagrin because he could not find anyone else who had seen it in print. "It *was* in the daily papers," he kept telling them wistfully. And in the same play he was delightfully handled by his wife, played by Nina Boucicault, when there was trouble at breakfast over his inability to make up his mind what to have and his hungering after the only remaining portion of kedgeree, which she had taken for herself. It was a scene of pure, human comedy, played by two consummate artists. What a beautiful actor Alfred Bishop was ; he adorned every part. And how lovely was Nina Boucicault, who had been the first 'Peter Pan.' Du Maurier was to go on at Wyndham's for years. Eventually the first glory was to depart, when Vaughan and Curzon were no more, but that is no part of this story.

What is part of it is the fact that Du Maurier, besides being a fine actor, and magnificent producer and a great actor-manager, was also a revolutionary. He was to start a new style of acting, just as Garrick, and later Bancroft, had done before him. He was to mark an epoch, the passing of a style and the substitution of a new method.

Whether he did this with reason aforethought, or whether it was just his own method which he could not—and very wisely did not—avoid, we shall never know. He founded the school of natural acting which holds to-day. He made it untheatrical. When he started the days of ranting had gone, and there was very little of what they are pleased to-day to call 'Ham' acting. But still the actors knew that you must be a bit larger than life in the theatre, still they knew it was necessary to have highlights and that you must force the point home, unobtrusively, of course, but still force it. Now Gerald Du Maurier knew all this, too, and did it. But he did it in his own way, by using that art which conceals art. And so well did he conceal it, alas, that those who should have known it failed to do so.

On the stage, apparently, Gerald Du Maurier exploited his own personality. He was 'Gerald.' He moved swiftly and with a curious effect of being blown along ; when he crossed the stage, his shoulders seemed to go before his feet, as if compelled by a wind. He would always get to a chair and hold on to the back of it. He had not a voice of great range, but he used it expertly, shooting out the sentences, in speedy jerks, to make up for the lack of the deeper notes. He always had a cigarette case handy—and tapped a cigarette (you remember those 'Sullivan's' in *Raffles*?). He spoke quietly and naturally, he played up stage, behind furniture and he turned his back on the audience. He was not being himself at all, in reality. He was seeming to be himself. He was throwing into vivid relief, by means of his acting, those characteristics which the audience liked and expected of him. He knew all the tricks and did them like a superb conjuror. None of these things are derogatory to his power as an actor, for he was a very fine actor indeed. But his 'naturalness' was acting, and that is where the not-very-observant young actors who watched him went wrong. They saw this easy, effective performance of this consummate artist as just a man being himself. It seemed to them that there was nothing in this acting. You just had to go on and be yourself. It did not matter what you did, so long as it was your way, it did not matter if you were heard or not—so long as you were natural. That was, they said, how Gerald did it, and look at Gerald. Yes, but to really look at Gerald was just what they never did. They never troubled to find out what he was doing, what he was up to. They never saw the actor underneath the man, the first of the really 'naturalistic' actors (although Hawtrey had done it in another way), who was not natural in their sense at all. The trouble caused was that nearly a generation was wasted by lazy, slipshod young men being natural instead of acting naturally and of writing down as old-fashioned those who tried to correct them in their fault. It has got its roots still in the earth, when the idea of 'throwing away' a line is carelessly talked of—not only by players, but by producers who should know better. For you don't throw the line away at all. You only pretend to do so, thereby giving it the prominence it requires in relation to its perspective. Heaven knows there are few enough lines in plays to-day, after economic authors have been cut by enthusiastic producers, whose chief idea, very often, is to further hew down the few branches which remain to deck the dramatist's little tree.

One cannot believe that it was Gerald's fault ; of course it was not. But he was responsible for it, nevertheless, even if indirectly. But the Edwardians, who understood plays and play-going a good deal better than the playgoers of to-day, welcomed Gerald Du Maurier and recognized his talent. His first nights were glorious affairs, with lots of cars—carriages were fewer then—lots of smart people, lots of enthusiastic pittites, adoring upper circle-ites, and hysterically vocal and highly excited galleryites, ready to assure him that he was 'wonderful,' even if it got a laugh.

And at the end he would come before the curtain with a curious swing, and he would clutch at his heart—a very favourite movement of his. He would look all round at the cheering audience from those deep eyes under their rather cavernous brows, and his gaunt face would seem rather drawn. Then he would begin to speak—and one would listen to a curtain speech of the very best kind, delivered as if each word came straight from the inspiration of the moment. For spontaneity was a great gift of his—part of his excellent acting. And then came the smile which lit the face like a floodlight, and then the bow and disappearance, whilst into Charing Cross Road poured the Edwardians, into their cars and carriages, into the adjacent Tube, chattering of Gerald and the company and of how Wyndham's, that theatre with a smile, that theatre of success, had got another success coming to it.

Gerald was one of the first actor-managers who did not form something of a stock company. That may have been because he was the last of the age. He had no regular leading lady, even in successive plays, he had no regular actor who so frequently appeared with him as to almost form one of those Edwardian theatrical combinations. He was one of the few actor-managers who was a lone wolf always, who hunted on his own and stood very much alone. It was perhaps enough. For it was Gerald his audience wanted to see, and he was the last of a great time and race which is only now perhaps coming into being again.

But he belongs to the greatness of the Edwardians, and he is a noble figure in a noble company—associated as he was with one of the greatest managers, in a theatre built by Sir Charles Wyndham himself. He added to that great man's achievement and he gave further atmosphere of success and tradition to that house which still bears, alone in the West End, the name of the actor who made it.

CHAPTER XIII

From the Palace to the 'Pav'

IT WAS DURING THE EDWARDIAN ERA THAT SHAFTESBURY AVENUE BECAME London's street of theatres. Up to then the Strand was the centre of theatreland. And, indeed, Shaftesbury Avenue, when the Edwardian days dawned, had only two theatres standing actually in it, the Lyric, built in 1888, and the Shaftesbury, built in the same year, whilst the Palace, not actually facing into the Avenue, but into Cambridge Circus, went up in 1891. The London Pavilion, abutting on the Avenue, faces Piccadilly Circus, and was a music hall anyway. So theatre history in the Avenue is new and has its roots in Edward's time. For during that time up went the Apollo, in 1901, the Globe in 1906, and the Queen's in 1907. At the extreme northern end of the Avenue, the Prince's arose in 1911, almost at the end of the era.

Shaftesbury Avenue was a different place in those days. It was—for a main thoroughfare—very new and shiny. It had an air of gaiety and brightness, and no definite category. It was a mixture of flats, jewellers', dress-shops, pubs and theatres, mingled with offices mixed in for luck. But it housed the old Eccentric Club, before that gay mixture of the stage, bohemia and the racecourse moved into the more select quarter of St. James's. In Edwardian days the Avenue had more pubs than it has now. There was the 'Prince Rupert,' on the corner of that thoroughfare, which perpetuates that noble cavalier leader of cavalry charges and forlorn hopes. The 'Prince Rupert' did a big trade with the actors, and was a very cheery place indeed, with a predominance of crystal in its decorations. Upstairs there was a curious bar, more like a club lounge than a public drinking place, which was called 'Fitz's Bar,' and was run by Aubrey Fitzgerald, a well-known actor himself. This place was one of London's minor night-life sights, for the habitués were the remnants of the young men who, in the days of Oscar Wilde, had sported the Green Carnation. Both pub and bar have vanished to make room for a shop. And on the corner of Great Windmill Street and the Avenue was 'The Avenue Buffet,' now a bank. This was a great place for professionals to lunch at, and also to have snacks. In its later days it was controlled by a man called Moss Vernon, who had started as a costumier, made a lot of money and who had some very good racehorses. You got good food at the Avenue. On one occasion, during some hectic dress rehearsals, R. C. McCleery, the scenic artist, went there with a friend. Both were in a hurry. The friend got there first and ordered Irish stew with apple pudding to follow. McCleery soon arrived. He was a curious character, who took his work very seriously, and who was always talking in a tone of nasal, grumbling, sad complaint—not that he was a dismal soul, quite the reverse. It was just his manner. Nobody could paint trees like he could. He asked what his pal was having. He decided on the same. "Here, miss," he said to the waitress. "Bring me some Irish stew and apple pudding, and as I'm in a hurry, bring 'em both together on the same plate. They all go down the same way in the end. May as well do so in the beginning." He got this strange mixture, and ate it with every sign of enjoyment, going back to his rehearsal like a giant refreshed.

The Palace, which was of Shaftesbury Avenue but not in it, had, in the days of Edward, achieved its true destiny. It was a place apart. Under Charles Morton it had ceased to be an unsuccessful Opera House, and had become a great house of Variety. That veteran with the golden touch transformed its fortunes, as he had done at so many places. He it was who made it great. For the Palace was not a theatre, and it was not a music hall. It was exactly as it described itself—'A Theatre of Varieties.' The difference was subtle but distinct. Variety held the stage, but there was no trace of the roaring choruses, the noisy bonhomie of the ordinary music hall. Here white shirts and silk dresses filled the boxes, the stalls,. and the dress circle. Here the carriages set down, and 'took up' at eleven. But although women, with their escorts of course, occupied many of the seats, it preserved a masculine atmosphere, as befitted a theatre of varieties. The air was blue with the smoke of good cigars. Champagne and whisky were the drinks in the bars—it even had a cigar bar at the back of the stalls, where good cigars were sold—for the Palace patrons knew a cigar and did not want inferior brands. There was, under the staircase leading from the stalls to the lounge, a bar where champagne was the drink supplied, to the exclusion of all else. And the real, regular Palace patrons liked a Rover Ticket, which cost five shillings, but which took you wherever you wanted to go, but did not entitle you to a seat. As most of the habitués dropped into the building as they dropped into their club, would watch a special act or so, and then have recourse to the bar, seats did not bother them. They stood along that passage at the back of the stalls, either leaning against the golden rail at the back, or the partition which terminated the seats. Here you could see all the men about town, all the people who mattered in Edwardian bohemia. Some went every night. You would always meet Louis Bauer there. He was a man who 'managed' artists, not an agent, he would inform you. He was a tall, imposing-looking man, with a slight foreign accent, who inevitably wore a tall hat, a morning coat, adorned with a large buttonhole, and who carried a malacca cane. It had to be several degrees below freezing

M

with thick snow on the ground before he wore an overcoat, and when he did it was a very heavy ulster. He would go from the Palace to the Empire and back again. That was his evening. That was, for him, all that London contained. And he would drink champagne. If you were a particular friend of his, he would ask you to meet him at the Motor Club—at the corner of Whitcomb and Coventry Street—at eleven a.m. There he would regale you with a pint of the best champagne, and dry biscuits. An astute man of business, who made several stars, that was what life meant to him. He asked no more. His only preoccupation outside of that was a collection of model owls, of which he had hundreds. This probably arose because he was a member of the Eccentric Club. He was a great figure around his own little corner in Edwardian days, and the Palace and the Empire were his spiritual homes.

Then there was Frank Otter. Here was a man of some standing, who had married into the Theatre. To see Frank far away from a bottle of 'fizz' was to see a wonder. His genial face was the colour of a ripe Victoria plum. He had a curious voice, with slurring tones, but very characteristic. Nothing disturbed him. A bottle of champagne, a pal or two, and the worst of the blitz, even an atomic bomb, would not have made Frank Otter turn a hair. For those things, especially in that little understairs Palace bar, formed his world. On one occasion in that sanctum where casual strangers were not at all welcome, he was chatting with some friends, when a little, pushing outsider butted in. Frank gazed at him in silent wonder but ignored his remarks and went on with the conversation. The man butted in again. Frank spoke to him. "Excuse me, sir," he said, "this may be a public bar—I believe it is. But this is a private conversation, as between gentlemen (he stressed this word with just the slightest emphasis), so kindly keep your conversation to yourself, if you don't mind." The man was silent, and Frank's group went on with their talk. But the chatty stranger could not resist it, he was listening. Once more Frank regarded him with pained surprise. "Are you a foreigner?" he asked. (He had a pretty hearty contempt for such things, in the good old Edwardian way.) The butter-in denied it indignantly. "Then you haven't that excuse. Now listen, there's a good chap. I don't know you, I don't want to know you. I'm speaking to my friends. So shut up, please, and don't butt in. Otherwise I'll get angry." Silenced again, the stupid man could not tear himself away. He went on listening. Something which was said got him going. Ducking under the arm of one of the group, he took the centre of the floor. Otter, in the most matter-of-fact manner, seized his bottle of champagne off the bar and without even looking at him, or interrupting his speech, rapped the man over the head with it, who fell down, absolutely stunned. Frank then resumed the conversation where it had been so rudely interrupted as if nothing had happened, and the attendants removed the importunate man who had so rudely transgressed the Palace social law. That was the sort of thing which happened at the Palace. All done in the most gentlemanly-like manner.

Sometimes gentlemen got a little tipsy at the Palace, and in that condition they were not wanted. There was, at the back of the stalls, what was known as 'the drunks' door.' This was an exit leading to the street, which only opened outwards. It was covered with curtains. If a drunk got a little obstreperous, one of the efficient Palace attendants— and they were all most tactful attendants, too—would edge the recalcitrant man to this door, and when he reached it, give him the slightest push, and he found himself out in the street, to his intense astonishment. Nor did he ever get in again.

D'Oyly Carte built the Palace, but Charles Morton gave it a soul. That grand old man died in 1904 and he was succeeded by Alfred Butt, who had left a big store to give Morton a hand in the accountancy side, which wasn't the Father of Music Halls' strongest point. Butt was a magician with figures, and the atmosphere got hold of him. He succeeded Morton as general manager and managing director, and he added even more glory to the Palace. It became the smartest of the smart. It was run magnificently. And Butt soon showed that he was as expert a showman as he was an accountant. He gave us variety in the Variety Theatre. There was always something new, something sensational. Not gaudily or highly-coloured sensation, but real novelty. When he introduced Maud Allan to the Palace, it was a first-class sensation. Here was barefoot—barelegged—dancing, to classical music. Some held it to be mere sensationalism, some said it was a delicate new art form. The arguments filled the Palace, for everyone went to see. But it was Maud Allan's dance as 'Salome' which was the real *tour-de-force* of her offering. In most exotically scanty oriental attire, to the sensuous waltz tune of Archibald Joyce, she depicted Salome dancing, with the head of John the Baptist, before Herod. This caused a real storm. Even those who were—or professed to be—shocked went along to see. She was the rage of London, and we felt the Victorian days were gone indeed. Butt followed this up with more barelegged dancing— even barer legs, and aristocratic legs at that, for they belonged to Lady Constance Stewart Richardson. It was all art, of course, and classic art at that. If she did not cause so much uproar as Maud Allan, it was because she had no 'prop' head of a prophet to stir up public opinion. But she did cause something, for King Edward VII was annoyed that a member of such a family should thus appear in a place of public resort, even though it was the Palace ! In those days there was still an aristocracy, there was still class distinction. To-day nobody would care twopence about a titled dancer, they are used to them. All they would require would be for her to dance well. She did that.

Another of Butt's captures was Margaret Cooper, a very distinguished-looking artist of great refinement, who sang very charming songs at the piano very well. She was first-rate. She swept languidly on to the stage, surveyed her audience with some hauteur, vouchsafed them the slightest movement of her upper lip by way of a smile, removed her long gloves very leisurely and put them on the piano. Removed her handsome and expensive furs very leisurely, and put them on the piano. Removed her many and flashing rings very leisurely—and put them on the piano. Then she sat down at the piano herself—and she charmed us all. There was a dispute between Miss Cooper and Alfred Butt which occasioned speeches and the ringing up and down of the curtain, but Butt won. He usually did.

The greatest of all novelties which Alfred Butt gave us—to earn our eternal gratitude—was Anna Pavlova. In one night she revolutionized our ideas of dancing. In one night she conquered London. She is a cherished legend to-day, a beloved one. Butt's finest epitaph would be that he gave us Anna Pavlova. No man could desire more. There was another sensation, too, when she slapped the face of her dancing partner when he dropped her. She did this in full view of the audience—and England rang with the news.

This partner was Michael Mordkin. He was a magnificent-looking man and a good enough dancer, but he was not in the Pavlova class. But then, who was ? The applause and the cheers which greeted their dancing went to his head. He thought he earned as much of it as she. So he got troublesome, he got a swollen head. He complained of everything, of the way in which he was billed, of his dressing-room—he ran the whole gamut of theatrical temperament. On that eventful night, he may have dropped her on purpose, or he may not. Anyway, it was he who got slapped and Anna who got the sympathy. Even when, after the curtain was lowered, he rushed on to the stage to 'say his piece' they blacked out on him and turned on the 'Bioscope,' with the orchestra going full blast, and all the audience saw was his excited figure bobbing about until he retired, hurt in every sense. But as he was in the habit of wearing a top hat, frock coat and brown boots, he got little sympathy from the Edwardians and he did not appear again. But who would have been cross with Pavlova in London ?

Speaking about the orchestra brings in Herman Finck, who wielded the baton at the Palace for thirty years. He was the incarnation of the place ; his orchestra was one of the best in the land and was not just part of the show, but an asset to it. When it played in the interval, the interval seemed too short. Finck made history at the Palace in many ways. His tune, 'In the Shadows,' to which the delectable Palace Girls (always one of the turns, and studiously copied to-day) did a skipping-rope dance, was so much in the vein of the period that it went all over the world, even to China. For Finck was not only a fine conductor but a first-class composer. Though to-day he is in the shadows himself, that tune to which he gave the name still lives in the sun of popularity. He gave us also 'Melodious Memories'—a potpourri of popular airs, ranging from classics and grand opera to music hall songs, and thereby started a fashion in musical 'switches.' The audience of the Palace, even those of the Rovers, deserted the bars to listen to it and try and name the melodies before he switched to the next. It was a masterpiece. He was as much at home conducting for performing animals as he was for Pavlova or Maud Allan, or a symphony orchestra. Once he caught the wheel which had come off a trick cyclist's machine as it was dashing straight at him and the audience, and returned it to the frightened man who had lost it, without missing a beat. For you could not flurry Herman in that respect. In addition to all this, Finck was one of the wittiest men in London. He was of middle height, inclined to stoutness, dark, with luxuriant dark hair parted in the middle, full in the face, and had a dark moustache and a beaky nose. He was never at a loss for a joke. And his jokes always had point. As when he received a wire from a well-known borrower which read, 'Send five pounds immediate.' Finck's reply was, 'Send ten pounds urgent.' He was not troubled again. Herman Finck was a man-about-town, a musician, a wit and a good friend. He himself liked being a man-about-town best.

But he was to play that 'Melodious Memories' of his on a very important occasion, no less than the first (and only) Royal Command performance that has ever been given by the Variety profession.

For Music Hall was at its very zenith. It deserved Royal recognition which it had never achieved. King Edward had often commanded its stars to appear before him privately at Sandringham and elsewhere, but never had Royalty, in state, graced a variety show. King George V did this gracious thing, and Music Hall thrilled with pride. The Palace —where more suitable ?—was chosen as the venue, and the performance took place on 1st July 1912. This event had nearly been given outside London, for Sir Edward Moss, the boss of Moss Empires, in whom the arrangements were vested, decided to hold it at the Empire, Edinburgh, whilst the Court was in Scotland. But that place was burned down and London got the chance. There was incredible difficulty over the selection of the artists, and a revolution was threatened with all the proposed 'rejects' in a bill at a rival house called 'The Popular Demand Performance.' But by dint of hard work and diplomacy, things were smoothed out. Those who could not give a solo turn, by reason of time, all appeared in a scene, staged as a finale, called 'Variety's Garden Party' and joined in singing the National Anthem, led by Harry Claff in his shining armour as 'The White Knight.'

The Palace was transformed into a bower of lovely blooms, things were done in the most lavish manner. Indeed, Their Majesties were almost buried in flowers. The King and Queen brought the Grand Duchess George of Russia and Princess Victoria with them. The whole theatre cheered them, and it was one of those occasions which will never come again. For London in those days could do things well, and this was one of the occasions when no pains or expense were spared. Austerity was undreamed of, and every attempt was made, and made successfully, to make this as a great occasion. Although the place glittered and blazed, the same cannot be said of the behaviour of the audience. Nearly everyone was overcome, 'acts' included. Things had been timed to the fraction of a second, everyone was on edge. Also points had to be watched, for nothing the slightest bit vulgar must creep in to shock the Royal ears. So most of the performers were not really at ease. The audience, largely composed of music hall folks and their supporters, were simply bursting with pride, dressed in their best, and on their best behaviour. They were determined to show the world that they knew how to behave as well as the smartest West End playgoer who ordered carriages at eleven. To them, also, the Royal Box and the behaviour of its occupants was of more interest than the traffic on the stage. The consequence was an audience which, after its burst of loyal enthusiasm to welcome the King and Queen, sat frigid and rather reserved, indulging in only polite applause, for fear of seeming ostentatious and free-and-easy. Yet the whole thing was electrical and unforgettable.

But there was one incident which marked the times as could nothing else. When Vesta Tilley took the stage, dressed, as always, as a man—and beautifully tailored, too—the Royal ladies averted their eyes, and studied their programmes. A woman in trousers was shocking ! It was not the thing upon which Royalty could gaze. As we used to say—"not in these trousers." Yet that Queen was our own Mary, who now chats with land girls, factory workers, all dressed in male attire, without the slightest qualm and with every appearance of pleasure. Far, far away are those Edwardian and early Georgian days now. The two wars have made a gap of centuries.

Alfred Butt the showman sandwiched the novelties at the Palace with regular favourites. One of the greatest of these—in every sense of the word—was Barclay Gammon. A very big man in evening dress, he sat at a piano and sang to us, and the Palace could never have enough of him. He was there, with very slight absences, for years.

There were many Palace personalities besides Blake, its ferocious stage door keeper, who has become a theatrical legend. Blake had many 'hates,' women and education being the greatest of them. Telephone girls were anathema. He carried on an eternal feud also with the succession of call boys, for whom he laid in wait, ambushed, harassed, but seldom caught. He thought little of the lovely chorus girls whom he saw daily. They, you see, were women. But one night a chorus girl did something he had never succeeded in doing. She was revenged on the call boy. This young lady was in the habit of looking on the wine when red, and its effect on her was an access of regal dignity. She did not like the call boy of that time. Once she arrived with the bearing and mien of an archduchess. Her companion knew she was 'tight,' but one girl protects another in the theatre. The call boy knew she was 'tight' and told her so. When she was in her dressing-room, preparing for the opening of the show, his insult penetrated to her bemused brain. She swore revenge. Although without one particle of clothing upon her, she went right down the stairs to the stage door. Completely nude, she caught the call boy, aghast with wonder, and she bashed his head three times, very resoundingly, against the iron door leading to the stage. Then, satisfied, she proceeded back to her room, her dignity in no way abated but slightly humanized by a contented smile on her placid face. Even Blake did not interfere. The manager was sent for but he had a sense of humour. He reproved and 'suspended' the unclothed lady for a week. She never did it again. That never happens in the Theatre to-day—and perhaps it is a pity.

Blake took a holiday once a year. Arrayed in a complete set of new clothes, even down to socks and vest and pants, new hat, new gloves, he would get on a bus on the Sunday morning, and ride to its destination. From there he would proceed outwards for a week by whatever transport was available, turning on the following Sunday and arriving back on the following Sunday night, ready to report as usual on the Monday. North, east, south, west, he went on these mysterious journeys and would never say where he had been or discuss them. It was a curious but perhaps a satisfying form of vacation of which he never tired.

Arthur Wimperis, a great wit and a man who loved country life, wrote many songs and sketches—and in later days, revues—for the

Palace. And there, too, you would see Comelli, the great costume designer ; Tom Reynolds, the producer—a truly delightful man with sometimes a hot Irish temper but a fund of humour and a heart of gold. He would quarrel with you, and if you knew him you would do nothing about it. For one day the phone would ring and Tom would take up the conversation where it had left off and you knew it was all right. Tom did grand work at the Palace, and still remains his humorous, witty self.

When revue came to the Palace in 1914, Finck gave us another memorable song, called 'Gilbert the Filbert,' which popularized the word Knut. It was the swan-song of Edwardianism, if we had only known, for the war came and Basil Hallam, the perfect knut, who sang the song, died on active service. In that same revue, *The Passing Show*, Butt gave us Elsie Janis—and her mother—as remarkable a couple as ever existed. Elsie was one of the greatest stars of all time, but she appeared only when our world was changing and her story is not for here.

And once as a stop-gap, Butt engaged a little concert party which shone so brightly that in a London plunged in a real peasoup fog of the old-fashioned variety, they packed the Palace. For they were 'The Follies.' And their great leader, Pelissier, was to crack a great gag in the auditorium one afternoon some time later. For a film had been made of Sir Herbert Tree's great production of *Henry the Eighth* and a trial show was given at the Palace (where Sir Herbert had appeared on one occasion). The profession were invited and attended in strength, Pelissier amongst them. The film began to unwind its majestic self on the screen. It was, of course, a silent picture—no talkies then. All the great members of His Majesty's company stalked in shadow on the screen. Then Sir Herbert himself, as Cardinal Wolsey, swept on majestically. You saw his eyes move, you saw his gestures, you saw his mouth opening and shutting, but the music of Shakespeare was not there. But it was Harry Pelissier's great chance. "Speak up," he shouted—and there was a burst of Homeric laughter.

If there has been a long stop at the Palace, it is because it was so much the Edwardian place of amusement of the lighter kind, so typical of its day, so much a mixture of wealth and modest means, each getting plenty of fun, for no great disbursement. It was not to be found elsewhere, this particular brand of evening's enjoyment, yet it was truly Edwardian in its richness, its flavour, its air of complete security. It was the other end of the same pole which balanced the local music halls, then in great number, and midway hung the Oxford, the Tivoli and the London Pavilion. The London Hippodrome was still a bit of a hybrid. It had begun as a circus, it had altered its policy—and like the Palace, when the Edwardian days were over, it was to change again. But the Palace, with its innumerable window boxes aglow with flowers, its terracotta and its red, its gleaming glass verandah beneath which stepped the people from their carriages, their cars, and beneath which entered the bohemians and the men-about-town, was a bright spot of those days.

Opposite the side of the Palace was the Shaftesbury. Alas that one should say 'was,' but a bomb put the Shaftesbury the Edwardians knew into the past tense. It was never an actor-manager's theatre for long. People came and went, some succeeded, more failed. *The Belle of New*

York set a milestone of success. An American importation this, which taught us all something, even the great George Edwardes himself. But for the Edwardians the great man of the Shaftesbury was Robert Court-neidge. This master of musical comedy was a Scot, born in Glasgow, but Shaftesbury Avenue was his stamping ground. He had been an actor, he had played all sorts of parts, and he became a producing manager. He made a kind of showman's progress up Shaftesbury Avenue, beginning at the Lyric, at the Piccadilly end, in 1903 with *The Duchess of Dantzig*, in which he was associated with George Edwardes and in which Evie Greene was so magnificent. Then he did another musical play, *The Blue Moon*, there in 1905. He moved next door, to the Apollo, in 1906 and presented *The Dairymaids*. Here he sprang a new comedian on the town, Dan Rolyat (Taylor spelt backwards), who was not only a laugh-maker but a fine dancer and tumbler. Remaining at the Apollo, he enriched our musical stage with *Tom Jones*, a grand light opera, in 1907. He revived *The Dairymaids* at the Queen's in 1908 and then, having only missed out the Globe, he took over the Shaftesbury Theatre in 1909. There, at a theatre not famed for its good fortune, he proceeded to produce one of the very best musical comedies of the time when musical comedy was at its best, for he showed us *The Arcadians*. This was a slightly different musical show to any we had seen. It had something of a plot—more than the average even for those days. It was in three acts. It had a moment of near-drama. And it had that great foundation of the theatre—contrast. Its book was by Mark Ambient, who had written straight plays, and A. M. Thompson, its music by Lionel Monckton and Howard Talbot. No better team could have been selected. It had a cast which glittered. Florence Smithson, who had a marvellous soprano voice; Phyllis Dare, at her very best; Ada Blanche, a great robust comedienne; Dan Rolyat, Courtneidge's own comedian; Nelson Keys, then a rising actor; Harry Welchman, who had taken his first big chance under Courtneidge at the Lyric in *Tom Jones* where he understudied Hayden Coffin, who let him play and make a success; George Elton, a splendid character actor; the producer's own daughter Cicely, making her first important appearance; Akerman May, an imposing, handsome figure of a man with a real Edwardian moustache, who played the villain; and Alfred Lester, as a jockey who was always miserable. Much of the play was so unusual that the company had their doubts. They admitted the book and the music, and the beauty of the scenery but would London take to Arcadia? For the first scene was in Arcadia, with lovely maidens in classical attire, a comedian in ditto, 'Father Time' —who admitted that Arcadia remained Arcadia because he had forgotten it—and a Well of Truth. For the comedian told a lie and was banished. So he went, Arcadian costume and all, to London—or if not to London, to London in the country—to the enclosure at Ascot. Those two scenes deserve hanging on the line in the Royal Academy of Theatre memories. Anything more like Arcadia had never been seen, and the Ascot scene showed all the glories of that delectable place, which was never more glorious than in Edward's days. In the third act we got back to a smart London restaurant, to clear up the plot, which had stood up manfully all through the play. The second act ended with a very exciting race, taking place apparently in the audience, which the players watched from the stage, with growing excitement, and ours grew with them as they described what was happening and at last the winning horse, ridden by Rolyat the Arcadian, galloped on the stage. Beauty succeeded beauty. Florence Smithson's top notes rose crystal clear beyond the roof to the very moon of London town. The final curtain fell on an audience stunned and hushed. Courtneidge, who had gone back stage, rushed on amongst his company, who stood tense and apprehensive. They thought they had failed. Then it came, a crashing roar of cheers and applause. Arcadia stayed at the Shaftesbury for over two years. Its music dances on, too well known and loved to need reference. This was a show—when comes such another? For he never did anything as good again. *The Mousme*, which followed, was Japanese and had an earthquake, but we preferred Arcadia. *Oh, Oh, Delphine, Princess Caprice*, were just pretty good musical comedies, as were a few others. But perhaps it is too much to expect any man to transcend *The Arcadians*. Such things happen to a man only once—unless he is a George Edwardes, and Courtneidge, excellent as he was, was not quite that. He had not the same background, he had not the same able team of helpers. So much more honour to him for doing what he did. His memory endures and is honoured. Incidentally he was a Pantomine King, too, and his pantomimes were kingly in all respects. And George Edwardes could not do that. Courtneidge's name and fame are kept green by his remarkable daughter Cicely, a great star and a consummate artiste of to-day.

There was one other picturesque happening at the Shaftesbury, which is worthy of note. There were many good productions, but we cannot deal with them all. But a company of Sicilian actors, led by Giovanni Grasso, went there in 1908 and made a real sensation. Nothing like their elemental force and fury had ever been seen. These people were of the soil, their passions were of the sub-tropical sun. Of reserve they knew nothing. They murdered, they slew, they buried their teeth in each others' necks, they strangled, they suffered and they made love mightily and with abandon. Grasso was feted. He certainly was terrific. His English confrères expressed their admiration by giving him a complimentary dinner one Sunday evening at the Green Room Club, with Sir Herbert Tree in the chair. Grasso, accompanied by an interpreter, was all bows and smiles. Tree made a speech of eulogy. Grasso, his eyes rolling, his hands flying in the rapidity of his gestures, made a reply in a veritable torrent of Sicilian, which the interpreter, struggling in the spate, did his best to render. Then, having paused dramatically, Grasso rushed round the table, embracing and kissing each English actor, ending up with the astonished and amused Sir Herbert. Then with a few shouted words, he dashed from the room. "Where has he gone?" was demanded of the interpreter. "Signor Grasso say he must go to the Shaftesbury Theatre," said that man. "I expect he's forgotten to kiss the fireman," was Sir Herbert's pithy comment.

At the Queen's, Shaftesbury Avenue's youngest theatre at that time, there is not a great deal to say of Edwardian days. H. B. Irving did a season there, but no actor-manager came along to make it his home. For a while it did well with Tango Teas, for the craze was at its height, and for half a crown you got tea, watched and could dance a Tango yourself—if you felt capable of such an exotic thing. *Potash and Perlmutter* put it on the road to success—those two Hebrew partners which London delighted in. But by then the Edwardian time was almost over.

What is now the Globe opened as The Hicks Theatre and gave us that unforgettable memory—*A Waltz Dream*. Frohman opened the theatre but its name was soon changed to the Globe. Plays came and went and then a peripatetic actor-manager came along with his clever wife, and stayed there for a bit. But it was also near the end of the real era. Oscar Asche and Lily Brayton, back from a world tour, revived *Kismet*. Then they did a queer kind of play, all about Zulus, called *Mameena*. Then came the war. But there had been other successes at the Globe. There was that farce which so many thought very naughty, and which further popularized a phrase which we had borrowed from America, perhaps the first scout of the invading squadrons—called *The Glad Eye*. This show was considered saucy and ran for over 400 performances. It was written by Jose G. Levy, a young man then active in the theatre, who spoke fluent French and adapted French plays (this was one) and wore a monocle. It was presented by Louis B. Meyer, who had edited *Black and White*, then a weekly 'glossy' publication for which he had also worked as an artist. The theatre attracted him and he did very well out of it, but journalism never lost its grip for he was also Art Editor and managing director of *London Opinion*. The link between Fleet Street and the Theatre has always been a close one. Meyer took *The Glad Eye* from the Globe to the Strand, of which theatre he took command and he was also interested in the Garrick. In *The Glad Eye* that fine [actor, E. (Teddy) Dagnall, gave a lovely performance. He was one of those actors who could play anything from pantomime to Shakespeare and play it with distinction ; we had a lot of them in the Edwardian days. Ethel Dane was 'Kiki.'

There was another play at the Globe which was notable. Lewis Waller entered into an agreement with Charles Frohman to do plays there. What could have been better ? Waller opened with *Bardelys the Magnificent*—not one of his best, and on 18th April 1911 he produced and played in *A Butterfly on the Wheel*. This was one of the plays in which he wore modern clothes, for it was a modern divorce play. It was written by E. G. Hemmerde and Francis Neilson. That magnificent actress, Madge Titheradge, was Waller's leading lady, the butterfly who was broken on the wheel of the Divorce Court. Other principals were Sam Sothern and Norman McKinnel. The great scene was the one in the Court, where McKinnel as 'Sir Robert Fyffe,' a merciless cross-examining K.C., put them all on the rack and flayed the unfortunate heroine alive. It is noteworthy that when Waller toured this play, he doubled this part with his original one—for he escaped cross-examination. A man like Waller could not be humbled. McKinnel's watchful, smiling persistence and Madge Titheradge's agonized attempts at evasion made excellent society drama. The Court scene was authentic, for E. G. Hemmerde is a prominent and clever K.C. himself, and is now Recorder of Liverpool. He is an astounding man, who has also been an M.P.

and who shone, in his younger days, not only at the Law and politics, but in cricket and golf and who won the Diamond Sculls at Henley. He was a determined dramatist, but not a very successful one, for this particular play was his only real success, but he retains his love for the Theatre together with his distinction and his good looks—and his extraordinarily acute legal brain. People of celebrity enjoyed going on in that Court scene as spectators.

Sam Sothern played one of those men which he represented so well. One can hear him now repeating the phrase which was to form part of the defence—"We all got into the wrong train." He said it over and over again, in different tones, and each time it seemed more incredible—and he knew it himself.

The Globe had another great Court scene—French this time—in *Madame X*, with super-acting by Lena Ashwell and Arthur Wontner.

The Globe is a successful theatre, and although the story is not long it is a good one.

At the Apollo some lovely things happened in Edwardian days, not the least being Messager's delightful *Veronique*. With Ruth Vincent, gracious, pretty and silver-voiced, and Laurence Rea as her partner, they sang us high into happiness with 'The Swing Song.' That show was just the thing for us ; it was merry, tuneful, colourful, romantic, and melodious—just like the days in which we lived.

Charles Hawtrey was an actor-manager who came to the Apollo, and gave us *General John Regan*, that delicious play by George A. Birmingham (Canon Hannay) which made us laugh all the time and which also gave Hawtrey a part to which he did full justice. And there was Leonard Boyne, a superb actor, to play 'Doyle,' the innkeeper. What a rich performance that was and how inherent of the Irish soil. Nobody will forget his instructions to the little servant girl—whose chief remark was 'I might'—"If there are no chops in the house—and there are not—away to the butchers and get some"—or the sly, unctuous persuasiveness with which he got the committee to buy the statue of the alleged 'General John Regan.' "It's a nephew of my own," he told them, who had carved it for a grave and had it left on his hands. He had his way and that statue was duly unveiled by a very English and very confused representative from Dublin Castle who came from the Viceroy to make trouble, but who was so blarneyed and bewildered that he not only unveiled the statue to the non-existent general, but removed his hat when the band played 'The Wearing of the Green' instead of 'God Save the King.' This was played by A. Vane-Tempest, who was unrivalled in that kind of part. So he should have been, for he was the son of Lord Adolphus Vane-Tempest and his wife, formerly Lady Susan Pelham-Clinton, a daughter of the 5th Duke of Newcastle, and had been educated at Harrow and Balliol, Oxford. The Stage had married into the aristocracy and now the aristocracy was invading the stage—a sort of Edwardian lease-lend.' Henry Wenman, a fine actor, played the American who caused all the trouble.

But for most of us the best Edwardian memory at the Apollo is 'The Follies'—the Follies and their great—in every sense—chief, H. G. Pelissier. To the outward eye 'The Follies' were a concert party, just a bunch of pierrots whom you might find on the sands, the esplanade or the bandstand. For that is how they dressed, right up to the end. Though they took West End theatres, mostly the Apollo, and packed them for months on end, they still appeared as pierrots. It was the grandeur of simplicity indeed. For they were more than that, much more. They were the wittiest, the brightest, the most up-to-date show in the country—perhaps in the world. They were real revue, in its best sense. Every one of them was an expert, every one of them was versatile, yet every one of them had his or her speciality. They were as perfect a team as ever graced the stage. They could be uproarious, they could be witty, they could be pathetic, they could be harmonious. And they were always bang up-to-date. The Follies were a happy family, who thought only of their show— they were the spokes of the wheel, and Harry Pelissier was the hub, that great solid hub of absolute genius. They all practically lived in his house out Finchley way, they all knew all about each other, and they all worked together with the most perfect rhythm and clockwork. But if the ensemble was like clockwork, there was no monotony. For each would step forward and do his or her turn like a supreme artist. Morris Harvey, in his days with them, was the best mimic of his time. Dan Everard sang spoof patriotic or music hall type songs like the star he was. Douglas Maclaren was the light comedian, Lewis Sydney was the one more or less morose member, who was the foil, the necessary foil, to the rest. But what a comedian he was and what a master of burlesque. Muriel George had a gift of comedy which she still shows us and a soprano voice which was pure joy. Ethel Allandale, Gwennie Mars—(who will ever forget her startled cry of "Coo, I've eat a maggit," when as a charlady in the gallery of their music hall burlesque, she refreshed herself with an apple)—they were all stars. That Music Hall item of theirs showed them in their true colours, for one moment they were actually on the stage, giving superb distortions of music hall acts, and the next minute, their 'turn' ended, they were in the 'gods' which formed part of the set, guying the performance in quite different style. One recalls Morris Harvey, as the Dickens impersonator, having a rough time of it from the gentry 'up aloft.' He announced "The Grandfather from the Old Curiosity Shop" and started to moan "Where's Little Nell," to be informed in strident tones, "She's gorn to the 'Ippodrome." Then switching to Fagin he demanded "Vere's liddle Oliver?" to be greeted with cries of "Gorn to Look for Little Nell." Their potted versions of popular successes, marvellously done, were gems of satirical observation, for not only the plays but the players were perfectly caricatured—even if you had not seen the show they so treated, it was wildly funny in itself. And then they would give moments of real beauty with little song cycles, always based on something homely—like 'Beverages.' Their very property man was a star—his name was 'Ben' and they often used him in the show. Their manager was a 'character.' His name was Willie Albert. He wore the most extraordinary hats, of which he had scores, he had always a beaming smile, a pair of twinkling if blinking eyes, a blandness and a cheerful imperturbability which defeated everyone. If you were a friend whom he had not seen for some time, his face would light up, his smile stretch from ear to ear. He would throw wide his arms and exclaim, "My dear old boy. How delightful. This calls for a semi-reunion." A 'semi-reunion' took the form of considerable liquid refreshment. One wondered what a full reunion would have been like. But apparently it never got beyond the 'semi' stage.

But the greatness of 'the Follies' lay in their creator and master mind, Harry Pelissier. That word genius is often misused, but is the only one which can be applied to Pelissier. For he towered over everything around him. He was tall, he was of vast girth, he was big in every sense of the word. He was the perfect compère—his commentaries were ripples of mirth and laughter, sly, malicious, and wonderfully witty. His audience command was a thing to wonder at. His mastery of the piano was equalled by his mastery of music, for he could have been a famous composer, had he taken the trouble to exert himself that way. As it was his setting of 'Awake' is immortal. And he even burlesqued that in a scene called 'The Voice Trial,' where every applicant sang this song—thinking to please him. He was the hub of it all, from him the whole thing radiated—the words, the ideas, the music. Unlike another 'concert party' which came later and was the only thing within sight of 'the Follies,' he and his troupe had 'busked,' had worked in the open—all over the place and even at Earl's Court Exhibition. And via the Palace they got control of the hearts of London's West End and all the component parts which go to make the West End theatre audiences. Nothing like it has happened before or since. Other parties arose, played their little season and departed. But 'the Follies' went on. 'The Co-Optimists' were formed specially for West End performance, and were stars in their own right when they appeared in their pierrot clothes. 'The Follies' were strolling troupers whom their own sterling worth and the genius of Harry Pelissier brought from the sands to the stage—and which kept them there as long as he lived. When he died, it was all over. The sun had set, the soul had gone. They struggled on, a good troupe, an excellent troupe—but it was 'Hamlet' without the Prince.

To say that H. G. Pelissier was 'the Follies' is to cast no slight on the rest of them. And they would have been the first to admit it. Thanks for their memory. They made a gay life gayer, they gave us evenings of delight, and just after eleven, on the way home, the people in the carriages and the people on the buses were still laughing at what they had seen and heard at the Apollo when 'the Follies' were there.

But the man who created the Apollo Theatre deserves a memory. His name was Henry Lowenfeld. He opened the Apollo in 1901 with *The Belle of Bohemia*. He was already a well-known figure in theatreland. He was of the ancient Faith and probably of mid-European extraction. That he shared with the great Charles Frohman. Now, with Frohman you never wanted a contract. That was another link between them but there was a difference. Frohman's word was his bond so no contract was necessary, he did not desire it, nor did you. But with Lowenfeld it was another story. He always wanted you to have a contract. For having once entered into one, his keen business instinct was alive to get the better of you. If you said you would take his word and required no written bond, you got the squarest of square deals, but he was a little disappointed for he was in his seventh heaven in business deals. He would always beat you and still keep within the bond. There was a dancer, not an important dancer, who signed an agreement with him in which it was stipulated that she was to appear in solo dances or, if she appeared with others, it was never to be more than a quartette. Rehearsals began and she sought out Lowenfeld in a raging fury. "What is this?" she demanded. "You have broken your contract." "Now let's be careful what we say," warned Lowenfeld, "who says I break contracts? Never!" "But you have," insisted the irate dancer, "my agreement says that I dance solo or as part of a quartette, never more. And here I am with a troupe of sixteen on the stage all at the same time." "Now, now, now," said Lowenfeld, "see how little you understand contracts. That is all right. There are you and three others, that's a quartette, isn't it? Very well then. On the stage at the same time are three other quartettes. You have nothing to do with them. They have nothing to do with you. They perform the same dance, the same steps. But you stick to your own quartette, you don't mix with them, and they don't mix with you. That's all in your contract. Just you and a quartette. Don't bother your pretty head with the rest. The contract's all right." She gave up. Lowenfeld was one of those men who could never resist telling everyone how to run their business, and ideas he gave them turned out to their great advantage. And he knew his own business backwards.

Next door to the Apollo, at the Lyric, theatre history goes back farther than the Edwardian years. Right on the eve of those days, however, in 1896, it housed a very great actor-manager indeed, in Wilson Barrett, who gave London and the whole country a thrill with *The Sign of the Cross*. He remained there some time but he never did anything greater than that play. His history was Victorian. He was a terrific actor, with a terrific torso and terrific power. But in Edwardian days a glittering memory belongs to the Lyric of a musical comedy which has become a classic. This was *Florodora*. It was running when Queen Victoria died, it ran on under Edward. It made fame and fortune for many. Its music, which is in our national repertoire, was some of the best that master of melody, Leslie Stuart, ever gave us. Its sextette, 'Tell Me, Pretty Maiden,' is immortal. This was originally a duet but little Sydney Ellison, the producer, made it into a sextette after a battle with the composer. It is one of the most typical things of its time, this charming number, with its pretty girls, with their long skirts and their parasols, and their top-hatted and frock-coated admirers, declaring their emotion 'on bended knee.' Evie Greene, the superb, was 'Dolores.' Willie Edouin was 'Tweedlepunch' and Ada Reeve played 'Lady Holyrood.' What an artist she was, and is. Her song, 'Tact,' was beautifully delivered; she was the essence of pointed charm and she knew how to put things over. It was a triumph for her, that song. Indeed it was a triumph for everybody. The book—and what a good book—was written by Owen Hall, who was a character in himself. He was a brilliant writer, with many musical comedy books to his credit and his real name was James Davis. He was originally a solicitor, but the law was too slow for him and the Theatre far more exciting. So he went to the Theatre. A great character and a great bohemian, he had no idea about money and was always in debt. So he took the name of Owen Hall, because he said he was indeed owing all to everyone, and he was one of the first men to turn himself into a limited company. But there was nothing limited about his ability and his wit. The man who presented *Florodora*, that perfect example of early Edwardianism, to London was Tom B. Davis, who ran the Lyric. He it was who gave London Evie Greene in the first place, and at the Lyric, in a show called *L'Amour Mouille*, and he it was who gave the first commission to Leslie Stuart for a musical score, for that same *Florodora*. Stuart was already famous for his wonderful songs which Eugene Stratton sang on the halls, songs which we all know to-day. Davis was a quiet, dark, astute man, with very pink cheeks, and he gave London some grand shows, both at the Lyric and when he moved to the Apollo next door. He made one mistake. He took the Adelphi and tried to alter its name to the New Century Theatre. The public would have none of it, so he put the old name back. Then all was well.

The Lyric was a great home for peripatetic actor-managers. Forbes Robertson, that actor of genius and grace, did some splendid work there. He produced a play of tender charm by Madeline Lucette Ryley called *Mice and Men*. As Mark Embury, eighteenth century student and philoso-pher, he not only looked the personification of charm and dignity, but he was. This unworldly scholar tried to train a little orphan girl, beauti-fully played by his own lovely wife, Gertrude Elliott, up into the ideal wife. But young love, in the form of a gallant captain and the handsome person of Ben Webster, upset his ideas. 'Mark Embury' bowed to the inevitable, and his scene with the sobbing girl when he explained his understanding and hid his own deep wound, was as great a piece of work as you could wish to see. Forbes Robertson also did Kipling at the Lyric in the stage version of *The Light That Failed*, playing 'Dick Heldar,' the war correspondent who went blind. We saw him first in one of those odd little desert dust-ups which we called 'war.' Here he took off his eye bandages too soon. Later he was an artist who had painted a lovely picture and he loved his 'Maisie' with whom he had grown up. But his model, Nina Boucicault, had other views and, goaded by jealousy, slashed his great picture to ribbons. Dick's blindness returned. Nobody who saw it will forget the tragedy of that blind figure, feeling his way about his studio and fingering that destroyed masterpiece, the last thing he was ever to paint. Nor the inward radiance which glowed through his ascetic and beautiful face as he found happiness in 'Maisie's' arms. And 'Maisie' was his wife, Gertrude Elliott.

Forbes Robertson, justly knighted, was one of the greatest actors of his time. His voice was like a silver bell and he conveyed beauty to everything he touched. He was the greatest 'Hamlet' of his time, perhaps the greatest we shall ever see. And later on when he was to portray the Christ idea in Jerome K. Jerome's play, *The Passing of the Third Floor Back*, he transcended anything the stage of that, or any other era, has shown us, for saintly humanity. It is good to know that it brought him fortune.

Lewis Waller did gallant things in Edwardian days at the Lyric. He revived *The Rivals*, he revived his *Henry Vth*—it has never been better played. The fine, imposing, handsome figure of Lily Hanbury as

'Chorus,' his own perfect embodiment of the gallant King, this was Shakespeare. His speech at Harfleur, his 'Honour' speech ringing like a peal of trumpets, his humble prayer before battle, his 'Upon the King'— this was Shakespearean acting as it should be. How the soldiers gathered first in ones and twos and then in shouting, maddened crowds to hear him speak "We few, we happy few." Ah, there were giants in the land then. And then he also gave us `The White Man`. In this his fans loved him. He began as a British officer in mess dress. Then, in trouble, he betook himself to the Wild and Woolly West and ran a ranch. There were cowboys, there were redskins, everything the heart could desire. There was a 'bad man'—a two gun villain, called 'Cash Hawkins'—who got Waller on the point of his two guns, in the position in which all true heroes of melodrama should find themselves. A shot rang out, 'Cash Hawkins' fell dead, still gripping his guns. An Indian girl, befriended by Waller and in love with him, saved his life (no hero ever saved his own, it was not heroic). Later came Herbert Sleath, a good actor, for whose sake Waller had sacrificed himself (for heroes are always innocent but can never prove it) to make restitution and recall Waller to England, home and regiment (for he had 'sent in his papers'). But Waller remained with his Indian girl—and the little papoose, a true English gentleman to the end. No wonder his host of female fans swooned with admiration. He was the first actor to have a fan club. The girls called themselves the 'Keen on Wallers' and wore badges—but the initials brought them to derision, to their own dismay and Waller's joy. For he loathed it all.

The Girl in the Taxi was a great Lyric musical show of later Edwardian days and gave us a star who has twinkled ever since. Her name is Yvonne Arnaud, and she got that part by sheer persistence. That persistence was conveyed to the public who exhibited it at the box office and were slaves at her dainty feet and delightful gurgle. And there was a manager at the Lyric, called Tom Pitt. He had gone there with The Sign of the Cross and the world had stopped for him with that play. Years afterwards, nearly thirty years, when complaints were made to him about some furniture in the dressing rooms, he grunted, "Rubbish. It was all right in The Sign of the Cross so it's all right now." But in respect of The Girl in the Taxi he had an alarming experience which could not happen now. It was Monday morning and he had to bank Saturday's takings and the advance booking, a very considerable sum of money. And nearly all in gold, a small proportion being in silver and five pound notes. Pitt would never carry the money in a bag, he was afraid of being robbed. He put, as usual, the sovereigns in a canvas bag and stowed it in a pocket in his ulster, he put the notes and silver in another pocket with the 'paying-in' book, and sallied forth to the Capital and Counties Bank, in Swallow Street, where of course he was well-known. He put the money and the book over the counter. The cashier counted it. "Where's the gold, Mr. Pitt?" he asked. "Sorry!" said Pitt and plunged his hand in the deep pocket. It was not there. He went cold. "Must have left it in the safe," he muttered and sped back to the theatre. But the safe was empty. Pitt was in a panic. A further search in the pocket revealed no gold but—a large and gaping hole. Pitt was now beside himself. He rushed to Vine Street police station, where, like every West End

SEYMOUR HICKS AND
ELLALINE TERRISS IN
'THE FLY-BY-NIGHT'

IRENE VANBRUGH AS
'MARISE CHELFORD,' AND
LILIAN BRAITHWAITE AS
'ISABEL LEYTON' IN
'THE THIEF'

CAMILLE CLIFFORD

PAULINE CHASE IN 'PETER PAN'

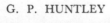

G. P. HUNTLEY

LEWIS WALLER IN 'THE WHITE M[...]'

manager, he was known as well. The Chief Inspector was sorry but he was busy. Would Mr. Pitt wait? Pitt fumed and fretted. It was a big loss, some hundreds of pounds. The chance was slender but he must report to the police. Still he waited and at last anxiety got the better of him. He pushed into the inspector's room. There sat the inspector at a table, and there stood an impatient, angry gentleman, dressed in full Edwardian rig and complaining of being kept waiting, for he was on his way to a wedding reception at Princes' restaurant in Piccadilly. "I say, you know," he said, "I object to this." "Sorry, sir," said the inspector, "you must wait until I've counted it all." And believe it or not, what the inspector was counting was heaps of golden sovereigns— Pitt's golden sovereigns, which that Edwardian gentleman had kicked, in their bag, in the gutter, where they had fallen from Pitt's pocket, had heard their musical ring, and had brought them, as they were, round to the police station. Now he was cross because his act of honesty was delaying him. There was a scene of thanks and gratitude, of relief and delight—and Pitt got his lost gold. Always afterwards he used a leather bag and the escort of 'Nobby Clark,' the ex-soldier linkman, who is still a West End linkman. But that was what life was like in Edwardian days between the Palace and the Pav.

CHAPTER XIV

A Rich Edwardian Tapestry

IN THE YEAR 1904, WITH EDWARDIAN DAYS IN THE PRIME, TWO MEN STARTED embroidering a bright new golden thread on the theatrical tapestry. Their work was new, arresting, it shone brightly amongst the more ordinary tints of tradition. For they were being modern. They were John E. Vedrenne, manager, and Harley Granville Barker, actor. Their loom was the Royal Court Theatre, Sloane Square, and their main thread was a dramatist named George Bernard Shaw. There were minor threads like Euripides, John Galsworthy, St. John Rankin and Elizabeth Robins, but the motif was Shaw. This was indeed a daring venture into the conventional theatre of a conventional time. But they knew that an epoch was ending and a change was coming and they opened the door to it at the Court. They were regarded as adventurous, which they were. They were regarded as high brow moderns, which, in a sense, they were also. They were regarded as entirely uncommercial and doomed to failure, and this they most definitely were not. Regarded as pioneer work, and as an artistic achievement, their tenure of the Court was a thing of glory. They were the new Edwardians and all credit to them.

When they took the Court it was under a bit of a cloud. It had had some fine periods and some depressed ones. They came at the end of a depression. It was a little far west, it needed some super-attraction to get those eleven o'clock carriages there with regularity. Since the days of Hare, of Arthur Cecil and John Clayton and Mrs. John Wood, it had not had it. People were apt to go to its box office and demand

N

tickets for trains, under the impression it was the Metropolitan station next door. Vedrenne and Barker changed all that.

With a gesture to the past in producing *Hippolytus*, *Troades* and *Electra*, they made it the home of the new dramatists and of the new play form. This, in the Theatre which is so conservative, is always dangerous. But so superbly did they do it that they compelled—and got—attention.

John E. Vedrenne was a curious man. He had first entered commerce, and had indeed been a Vice-Consul. But show business pulled at him. He became a concert agent, then he became a business manager in the Theatre, first for other people and then for himself. Above all things he was a business manager, and he combined his business ability with a supreme gift for 'casting.' He had managed successfully for Benson, for Forbes Robertson, for Nat Goodwin, for J. H. Leigh, and had thereby learned all a man can learn of an unlearnable business. Crystallizing his knowledge and his flair, he and Granville Barker took the Court. It was a magnificent combination.

For Vedrenne was very acute. His sharp pointed nose, which dominated his dark face, was a keynote. He worked to schedules, he was alarmingly punctual. He made appointments at odd times. "Come round and see me at 12.31 sharp to the minute," he would say—and mean it. If you arrived at 12.32 his distress was painful to see. You were late, and you had thrown out his schedule. One man arrived a minute and a half late, having been held up by Vedrenne's own manager on the stairs. Vedrenne was not only furious, he was heartbroken. His morning was ruined. So busy was he that he was lunching in the office. There were a dozen oysters temptingly displayed on his large desk. But the terrible loss of time caused by his visitor's shocking unpunctuality, he declared, made his lunch impossible. No time, no time. The oysters were swept away, and the visitor was so embarrassed by his dreadful behaviour that he agreed at all Vedrenne snapped out.

But mostly Vedrenne's method was that of the open hand, open heart and complete confidence. He would almost weep when terms were being discussed. You gathered from what he said that he had no margin of profit and that the demand you had made would make all the difference to him between solvency and bankruptcy. He would take you into his confidence—he would, in his own phrase, 'lay his cards on the table.' He would speak gently and pityingly of risks, of the terrible gamble of a production, of the mutability of human affairs, and his strange voice carried a covert hint of tears. He would offer you—if you were an actor—what was known as 'summer terms'—salaries taken at a time when most theatres were closed. But he would stress the fairness. He would declare he would not bind you, he would not stand in the way. As soon as a better offer came along—if any—you could have your release and take that salary which you now began to regard yourself as extortionate. Far be it from him to hold you up, to prevent you getting what he knew was your real worth, but which he, a poor man taking such risks, could not afford. You took his terms and very seldom did you leave that play before the end of the run. Those cards on the table were mostly trumps.

He had another method too. He had an unerring eye for young talent. He would give these people, these young aspirants, a contract for a long term, at a very moderate but slowly rising salary. They then belonged to him. During his day there was a perfect eruption on programmes of plays produced by other managers of players who appeared 'By permission of J. E. Vedrenne.' He made a bargain and he took his profit on that sub-letting. Nor was it unfair, for he made those people under contract to him into stars with good salaries, and when they left him, they were worth far more than they would have been had they relied on their own efforts. Many thought it hard at the time, but in maturer years they understood they had profited as well. For although a hard business man, Vedrenne was a fair and very honest manager, who did a very great deal for the Theatre and for those who work in it. He annoyed many but he achieved much.

Harley Granville Barker was a stage genius, a man of much distinction —which distinction endures to-day. He had a standard from which he never departed and his standard was Alpine in its elevation. Yet he always reached it.

They drew all London to Sloane Square. Those perfectly played productions of *John Bull's Other Island*, *You Never Can Tell*, *Man and Superman*, *Candida*, *Major Barbara*, and *The Doctor's Dilemma*, made this country aware that a major dramatist and a great one had come amongst them, that a new play form and a new thought form had arrived. People criticized, argued, disliked, objected, raved, enthused, gloried—but they went to the Court every time. Shaw took his true place as a result of Vedrenne and Barker. A new thing had begun to join the other marvels which were daily crowding on the Edwardians—this new century was bringing new things with a vengeance and the new thing it brought to the Theatre was Bernard Shaw—per Vedrenne and Barker. John Galsworthy's magnificent play, *The Silver Box*, caused a sensation. St. John Hankin's *The Return of the Prodigal* was a promise which never matured. And Elizabeth Robins' *Votes for Women* was a challenge which was eventually fulfilled.

Nor did they stop at this. Plays by John Masefield, Gilbert Murray, Laurence Housman (the lovely little phantasy of *Prunella*), Maurice Hewlett, whose *Forest Lovers* had brought mediæval romance to literature, who gave them *Pan and the Young Shepherd* and *The Youngest of the Angels* (things of real beauty but decidedly not commercial), and Maurice Baring. This was a new field with a vengeance.

The acting was beyond compare. The company included Granville Barker himself, Norman McKinnel, Dennis Eadie (his musical comedy days behind him and a partnership with Vedrenne in the not far distant future), Lewis Casson (now justly Sir Lewis), Edmund Gwenn, that delightful actor, Nigel Playfair, Dorothy Minto (as 'Prunella' and the twin in *You Never Can Tell* to touch the heights), Louis Calvert, Evelyn Weeden, Sarah Brooke, A. E. Matthews and Lillah McCarthy. And now and again came planets from the great firmament of stardom, to shine awhile at the Court amongst its band of brave pioneers. For Ellen Terry herself created the lead in *Captain Brassbound's Conversion* there, and Mrs. Patrick Campbell played 'Hedda Gabler'—to give Ibsen a look in.

Lillah McCarthy created 'Ann Whitefield' in *Man and Superman* and was a sensation.

Distant from Piccadilly, theatrically speaking, the Court might have been, but those who loved the Theatre (and Edwardians did love the Theatre) made the pilgrimage over and over again and were amply rewarded. That Vedrenne-Barker partnership at the Court was indeed a golden patch in the Edwardian tapestry.

Later, they moved into the charmed circle and went to the Savoy. There installed in 1907, they did *The Devil's Disciple*, Matheson Lang was 'Dick Dudgeon' and the part has never been better played, and Granville Barker was a perfect 'General Burgoyne.' But the partnership was ending. Vedrenne migrated to the Queen's, where *The Devil's Disciple* was transferred (they did other revivals of their Court repertory at the Savoy), and Vedrenne remained at the Queen's for a while.

For the moment let us follow Barker. He had married Lillah McCarthy. At the now departed Imperial, he produced his own play, *Waste*, for which the Censor had refused a licence at first ; he was associated with the great Frohman repertory movement at the Duke of York's. He appeared at the Palace in 1911, in a series of 'Anatol' sketches—the clever Schnitzler dialogues. Then in 1911 he began to make Theatre history. For he produced Shaw's *Fanny's First Play* at the Little Theatre, for his wife, and jointly they took over the Kingsway, which Lena Ashwell had put on the map after it had been a derelict for a long time. Here *Fanny's First Play* drew London as no play of Shaw's had done before. In 1912, Barker and Lillah McCarthy went back to the Savoy. Greatly daring, they staged Shakespeare. *The Winter's Tale* done in the most lovely manner and played superbly by Lillah McCarthy failed them. They staged *Twelfth Night*. This poem in a Garden ran for over a hundred performances. It was done in a most arresting manner, full of colour, full of novelty and with costumes by Norman Wilkinson which set London talking. They had a magnificent cast. Henry Ainley was 'Malvolio,' and surprised all playgoers with a great performance in the part. Henry, the character actor, had now supplanted Henry the romantic. Arthur Wontner was 'Orsino' ; Hayden Coffin, his Daly's days behind him, as 'Feste' took to Shakespeare like the actor he was. Dennis Neilson-Terry (quite a beginner then and alas that he died so young) was 'Sebastian' and Evelyn Millard the lovely was 'Olivia.' And as 'Viola' Lillah McCarthy gave one of the most beautiful performances of the late Edwardian days. There were more plays—and good plays—by Barker in *The Voysey Inheritance* and *The Madras House*, there was *The Marrying of Anne Leete*, it was almost the Court come back again. But you cannot do a thing twice in succession in the Theatre, and this wonderful season came to an end.

Vedrenne meanwhile had opened the Queen's Theatre with a play called *The Sugar Bowl*, but unlike flies, the public were not attracted. He did other plays there, but in 1911 he took the Royalty Theatre in Dean Street, a place with a long, if patched history, and once again the magic worked. Once more he was associated with an actor, with Dennis Eadie, that young man who had been in musical comedy at the Prince of Wales's, with Vedrenne and Barker at the Court, with Charles Frohman at the Duke of York's and now became actor-manager with his old leader. They did well. It was again a good combination. They gave good plays. They found new talent. In *Milestones* they produced something memorable. A young actor named Nares made his first real hit, a young actress from musical comedy, Gladys Cooper, stepped into stardom, and many names also famous to-day were in that cast. Some have achieved Hollywood stardom like Lionel Atwell, some have passed on. The abiding memories, however, of that memorable play, truly a milestone of the Theatre, were Dennis Eadie, Mary Jerrold (still as brilliant as ever but nearly always since that play condemned to play mothers), and Haidie Wright, as perfect a performance as ever seen on any stage. What an actress, what an art ! Many were the troubles over *Milestones*, many a fight did Edward Knoblock, the author (with Arnold Bennett) have with Vedrenne, with Eadie and with Frank Vernon, who 'produced' it. As rehearsals progressed, Vedrenne got more and more sad. He was never a cheerful man, but when he thought a flop was toward, his mien was that of an undertaker. He prophesied woe, and was much disgruntled when Knoblock insisted, and Vernon supported him, that the final picture of the two old people sitting in their chairs should have only firelight upon it. Vedrenne believed there should be a blaze of light at the end. He left rehearsal in disgust and told Knoblock he was ruining the play. But Knoblock—that clever, charming and witty man of the Theatre—won, as he usually did. When the first night triumph came, Vedrenne was full of smiles—and, for him, triumphant. "What did I tell you ?" he demanded. Knoblock himself had tried out the play in his own manner. He invited Norman McKinnel, reported to be 'tough,' to see the dress rehearsal and he watched the effect. He saw tears in McKinnel's eyes. He knew it was all right. Edward Knoblock, recently passed on, was a man of great knowledge about the Theatre and about plays. He was the best play 'carpenter' of his time, perhaps of all time. He read plays for Lena Ashwell when she took the Kingsway, he found her winners. He could make a badly constructed play into a finished article with some deft touches. His great triumph, apart from *Milestones*, was *Kismet*—the most rejected play of its time. In *My Lady's Dress* he gave Eadie, Vedrenne and Gladys Cooper a big success. A delightful companion, a man of culture, loyalty and great wit, he is missed by his friends. He felt that his world had changed towards the end—indeed it had—and he clung to those who knew the Edwardian days and times. And his last, maybe his best play, still awaits production. But he never lost his sense of humour. Poor Dennis Eadie passed away far too soon. He was a first-class actor and a link between the older and the newer schools. Handsome and distinguished, he graced the stage and he helped it. He could ill be spared.

Mention has been made of Lena Ashwell and the Kingsway. She was actress-manageress there and brought prosperity to the little theatre off the map. But before she went there she was already a great actress. Indeed, she was one of the greatest actresses of her days. Essentially a lady, she adorned any play in which she appeared. Her interest in her profession is still of the keenest although she acts no more. But she left a portrait gallery of memories. Her 'Mrs. Dane,' her 'Madame X,' her

'Leah Kleschna,' her 'Yo-San' in *The Darling of the Gods*, are only a few of her fine creations. She was easily one of the very best Edwardian actresses.

There was a very beautiful theatre in Edwardian London, which had been made even more beautiful by a Victorian and Edwardian beauty, Mrs. Langtry. There are no sensational beauties like that now, whom people mob in the streets. Rumours attached themselves to her name and made her even more glamorous. She was Edwardian to a degree. The theatre was the Imperial—a gorgeous place like a Greek Temple. It has gone from Westminster—transported stone by stone to the East of London, where it still stands, or did recently, as a cinema. Also for memories of Lily Langtry and of Lewis Waller, who played there many times. Waller took it over in 1903, opening it with a play with which he had saved another theatre, as we shall shortly see. At the Imperial he did Shakespeare, he did romantic drama, he did *Miss Elizabeth's Prisoner* and he did Conan Doyle's *Brigadier Gerard*. He was dashing, he was all that Lewis Waller should be—and always was—but there was a hoodoo on that fine playhouse. Nobody knew why. Perhaps Westminster in those days did not approve of theatres. Yet it had a music hall, the Standard, now the Victoria Palace, and now it has a Westminster Theatre (not the first of that name). But the Imperial was very near the Houses of Parliament and evidently the atmosphere was wrong. Maybe the members resented the actors and wanted all the limelight—and histrionics—for themselves. But one of the very greatest actors, Thomas Betterton, had been born in Tothill Street, just around the corner.

That play with which Waller opened his management of the Imperial had done fine work before he took it there. And in a theatre nearer the centre of things, in Panton Street, which is The Comedy. A dear little place, it still retains its old atmosphere, although that perfect green baize curtain, with its gleaming golden coat of arms, so absolutely and purely of the playhouse, has now gone. But otherwise it is much the same as when Arthur Chudleigh, manager for a long time, reconstructed it. Chudleigh, a son of Devon whose name was really Lillies, took great pride in his reconstruction. He would take all his friends to see the work going on. The vestibule, with its light oak, and its box office with its gleaming grille—then very modern—were his especial joy. "Makes me want to go and book seats myself," he would chuckle.

Chudleigh was a character such as we have not to-day. He was endowed with a remarkable sense of humour, a resilience against knock-down blows—and he had many—which was astounding, and a deafness which, when he liked, was impenetrable. But he always heard what was not intended for his ear. His love of and enthusiasm for the Theatre was only equalled by his adoration of racing. He had forsaken medicine for the stage. He had been an actor, and had played at Drury Lane. He had run the Court Theatre with Mrs. John Wood. And whilst there had made history by booing one of the productions, which he did not like, from the back of the gallery. A man who will do that as a manager is worthy of attention. He was often in financial distress, but he always emerged smiling and cheerful, having somehow or another got the better of his difficulties. The Comedy had also had many bad patches to set off against its purple ones—it had its fair share of these. But on one occasion things were very bad indeed, and looked desperate. But rescue arrived. It came in the most complete and appropriate form, in the person of the great romantic hero of the stage, Lewis Waller. This was before Chudleigh went there but that does not matter. The Comedy was in distress and along came the perfect knight to slay the dragon and set it free. He came in the person of a Frenchman, did Lewis Waller, a certain 'Monsieur Beaucaire.' He came to Bath (on the stage of the Comedy) in the great days of Beau Nash, a most perfect setting for the art of Waller. But he came incognito and was reputed to be a barber. At Bath, however, he was a sensation. He was idolized by the ladies, he was hated by most of the men. He wore his satin clothes as they should be worn, the white wig set off the handsome features, there was a sword, more often out of its scabbard than in it, at his side. There was a lady in distress, the beautiful 'Lady Mary Carlisle.' They met, she dropped a red rose—need we say more? Red roses and romance cannot be kept apart. There was a bullying duellist, 'Captain Badger,' who was set on by the 'Duke of Winterset,' in love with Lady Mary and especially her large fortune, to destroy this impertinent French interloper, who whilst seeming a gentleman, was no more than the French Ambassador's hairdresser. He was all right for men to meet, and to gamble with— Winterset, a desperate and unlucky gambler, had done both. But when it came to lifting his eyes to such a one as Lady Mary, his own ducal prey, then perish the thought and perish the barber. Winterset did not choose to soil his own noble hands, let alone his noble blade, with a barber's blood. It was a job for Badger, the professional duellist. All this became known to 'Major Molyneux'—played by young Mr. Frank Dyall—and he and his French friend were on their guard. Badger tried to pick a quarrel with the urbane, polite Frenchman, who didn't take offence. "Try him with a sneer at the women," hissed Winterset. Badger makes remarks about the French ladies. There is a sharp, resounding crack as his face is smitten. And the Frenchman further established himself in all the Bath ladies' esteem, and in the gratitude of many of its men, by neatly running Badger through the body when they met to fight it out. Winterset is foiled—the natural state of a villain. What makes it doubly hard for him is the fact that he himself has sponsored 'Beaucaire' in Bath. He has been forced to do so, for he has gambled with Beaucaire— believed to be the barber—and he has attempted to cheat. He has been discovered and Beaucaire has made him introduce him to the pump room as the 'Marquis de Chateaurien' as a price of his silence. Rather than fight, Winterset had to consent. But now the dirty upstart must be squashed. Beaucaire had friends besides the gallant Captain Molyneux, not too faithful friends, for they were gambling, rake-helly gallants of the eighteenth century, a Mr. Rakell, a Lord Townbrake and a Mr. Bicksett. But Winterset is powerful, if cowardly. Broken in pocket, with only the chance of Lady Mary's money to save his face, here is this accursed Frenchman cutting him out and laying out his most expert bully. Winterset sets a gang on him. Now, as a true villain he should have known that you cannot kill a hero. So Beaucaire beats the gang but gets wounded—and thus becomes more interesting than ever in the eyes of the fair. Lady Mary scorns the Duke, as who would not when the rival was that perfect master of love-making, Lewis Waller? So the Duke plays his last card. He tells Lady Mary that Beaucaire is not the Marquis de Chateaurien, as he has declared himself to be, but just a man who has been expelled from France and is hiding in disguise. Lady Mary scorns him ; he insists. She will believe it only if Beaucaire himself will acknowledge that he is not a Marquis, but is indeed the man Beaucaire, who came amongst them as a fugitive. With Winterset, she sees Beaucaire, who has just beaten off the Duke's gang and is sorely wounded. Is he, she asks, that same Beaucaire? He acknowledges it, and falls fainting from loss of blood into the arms of his faithful Molyneux, whilst Lady Mary walks proudly, if broken-heartedly, away. But in romantic plays there is always the *Deus ex machina*, and he comes in the person of the French Ambassador. Strange to say he is looking for Beaucaire, which sets Bath a-twitter. What now? Further scandals? Arrests? No, a King's pardon, for Beaucaire has indeed been expelled from France. But for a crime which would endear him to every woman, for he has refused to marry the woman whom the King has chosen for him, because he does not love her. And why has the King butted in on this matter? Because Beaucaire, the *soi-disant* barber, the alleged Marquis de Chateaurien is—none other than the Duke of Orleans. The Duke of Winterset is beaten, the red rose, Lady Mary and Beaucaire triumph—and the audience went mad. They went mad for 430 performances on end at the Comedy in 1902—and did so whenever Waller revived it. To the sophisticates of to-day it may sound very naïve, but then they cannot see and hear Lewis Waller, in his prime and his best part, acting as only he could. For this was the part with which his name will be most remembered, alongside 'Henry V.' There is poetic justice in that. For Henry V was an Englishman who beat the French and Beaucaire was a Frenchman who beat the English. In reality it was a quick-moving, charming, exciting romantic play, full of action, full of love-making, with plenty of comedy, good lines and situations, and the sheen of the period over it all. If the young people of to-day saw its equivalent on the screen they would love it. They have cheered many worse. It was well played. Grace Lane was charming and lovely as Lady Mary, the bullying Badger was S. B. Brereton, Thomas Kingston was the dandy of Bath come to life as Mr. Rakell, and the delineator of the faithful Molyneux we know now as Franklyn Dyall, a pillar of our stage. Edward Ferris was a handsome Winterset, a well graced villain. There were Charles Goodheart, Harvey Long, Charles Allan, and many more. But Lewis Waller was Monsieur Beaucaire and Monsieur Beaucaire, for all of us, was Lewis Waller. And the Comedy Theatre basked in prosperity.

Under Chudleigh, other actor-managers were there too, John Hare to play in *Marionettes* in which that delightful actress, Marie Lohr, made a hit, as she did at the same theatre in *Smith*, by Somerset Maugham. Marie Tempest was there in *Mrs. Dot* and *Penelope*, both by Maugham— it was a Maugham house for some time. For that great playwright had swung into fame in Edwardian times through a play called *Lady Frederick*. It had been well refused before it saw the light at the Court, and made an instantaneous success owing to the brilliant acting of Ethel Irving

and fine support from C. M. Lowne. It practically toured the West
End, going to several theatres, because it would not stop running, and
managers who had turned it down in script form, now opened their doors
to it and raked in the shekels they had failed to see. The scene where
Ethel Irving completed her toilet in the presence of C. M. Lowne, she
as 'Lady Frederick' and he as 'Paradine Fouldes,' was considered daring
but delightful. Ethel Irving was another great Edwardian who came out
of musical comedy at Daly's.

That rejected play which succeeded found a counterpart in the Charing
Cross Road, at the Garrick Theatre. The Garrick had several actor-
managers in its time, but we are chiefly concerned with two of them (the two
most burly and brawny the stage has seen), for the others have crossed our
path before. These two men were Arthur Bourchier and Oscar Asche.

Both these big men, for Bourchier was big and Asche enormous, had
their wives as leading ladies and those wives were no small part of the
success they achieved. In Bourchier's case the lady was Violet Vanbrugh,
in Asche's case, Lily Brayton.

Arthur Bourchier was the senior. He was at the Garrick a very long
time. He was a good but not a great actor. He was son of a Captain
in the 8th Hussars, he was educated at Eton and Christ Church, Oxford,
and he was a member of White's, the Beefsteak and the Garrick Clubs.
So his background was unimpeachable. The stage claimed him at
Oxford where he was instrumental in founding the O.U.D.S., that great
dramatic society. In his long reign at the Garrick, which began in 1900
and lasted for years, he never had an outstanding, memorable success,
although most of his productions had comfortable runs. The nearest
he had to a sensation were *The Walls of Jericho* and *Samson*. In both of
those he appeared in his favourite type of character, a strong man with
contempt for Society, whose designs on his wife he defeated, either by
wile or by personal violence. His own best acting was done when working
for others, such as his truly memorable 'Henry VIII' for Tree at His
Majesty's, his 'Bottom' in *The Dream* at the same theatre, and many light
comedy parts before them. For whatever he thought himself, he was a
fine light comedian. Big, burly, with a large rugged face, a sudden smile,
a good, deep, and sometimes rumbling voice, he seldom gave a poor
performance even if he seldom gave an inspired one. But his wife,
Violet Vanbrugh, that was different. She was indeed a gracious lady
and a fine and versatile actress. She played the part of a lady of easy
virtue in *Find the Woman* with as much effect as she played the ill-fated
'Katherine of Aragon' at His Majesty's—and she was the best of them
all in this. She was a very good 'Lady Macbeth,' and she also could
play a comedy part. If she had not quite the same glow of genius as her
sister Irene, one of the outstanding Edwardians, she was in the very
front rank and had parts in which she was unequalled. And she had
her full share of Vanbrugh charm, as became a great lady of that name.

Bourchier came and went at the Garrick, letting the theatre. Oscar
Asche and Lily Brayton, two of the old Tree school, had gone into
management and done well. Back from a foreign tour, a manuscript
reached them of a play which was dog-eared with refusal. Tree had
turned it down, even when his own play adviser, the cultured and clever

Frederick Whelen, who also acted as his secretary, arranged a reading. So did scores of others.

Edward Knoblock, who had written it, had no more luck with it in America. One manager did say that he had read it and realized that it was an Arabian Night, but that was as far as it got. Knoblock was almost in despair. A play of his, *The Faun,* was produced by Martin-Harvey at the Prince of Wales's. It did not succeed very well, but Harvey was very good in it and liked it. And, as is usual on the stage, when you get one thing going the others follow—right on this Asche bought the play, *Kismet.* The burly Oscar with the lovely Lily was back from Australia with plenty of money, the Garrick Theatre, and a failure therein. He wanted something to follow and he wanted it quickly. Knoblock was away. His agent rang his sister, who went to the cupboard where he kept his manuscripts and picked out a copy of *Kismet.* Now there were two versions of *Kismet,* one as originally written and the other carefully compiled by Knoblock and embodying all the alterations the various managers who had turned it down had suggested as improvements. His sister unwittingly sent the original version to Asche. He got it on a Saturday, he read it on Sunday, he bought it on Monday. It was indeed Kismet—for Knoblock.

Asche and Brayton went to work like demons on the production. They got Percy Anderson to do the costumes, Christopher Wilson to write the music, and they ran out an apron stage so as to have something going on all the time whilst the many changes of scene were being made. This added greatly to the success of *Kismet,* for Asche produced it superbly. Nobody had much sleep during that time. The company was too large for the theatre—so big was the crowd ; the stage too small for the large effects visualized. But Asche overcame it all. News got out that there was nudity in the show. Excitement reigned. At last, after never-ceasing work, it opened on 19th April 1911. It was a vivid first night. The splendour of the Orient came to Charing Cross Road, the Bazaar scene with its ever-changing crowds, its noise, its colour, brought the audience to its feet with cheers. The naked lady went into the bath with an accompanying gasp of excitement. Asche was the ideal 'Hajj,' the beggar to whom so much happened. His cry of "Alms, for the love of Allah, alms !" became the catchword of the town. Lily Brayton was the ideal 'Marsinah.' Its barbaric spectacle and riotous colour, its savagery, its originality—its sweep carried it to vast and overwhelming success. The scenery by Joseph Harker alone was a delightful masterpiece, and walking on in the Bazaar scene as a Chinaman was a young scion of the house of Harker, destined to be a great star in after years and answering to the name of Gordon. *Kismet* was kismet to him too.

At curtain fall Knoblock, trembling with excitement and gratitude, rushed back stage to thank and congratulate Asche. He found the actor still in costume and make-up fast asleep in his chair in his dressing-room, just as he had left the stage. He was completely worn out. Asche had always a flair for the East, and followed *Kismet* later with his own version of *The Forty Thieves,* which under the name of *Chu Chin Chow* made a stage record. But its origin lay in *Kismet.* The Asches did other things at the Garrick, and did them well, but *Kismet* eclipsed all. It went all over the world with them. Guitry failed in it in Paris. But on tour, under the ægis of the great George Dance, it made fabulous sums, even though some North Country audiences desired to know when this fellow Kismet was going to appear. Dance toured it like a circus with crowds of coloured men who paraded the town, great ballyhoo and huge tanks for the bathing scene. The first touring 'Hajj' was Arthur Holmes-Gore, that fine actor killed in the first World War, but the second was the massive, bull-like and stentorian Hubert Carter, who was magnificent and as tireless as enthusiastic. He it was who drank ox-blood every night to make him fierce, and who nearly did drown the stage manager in the bath for blacking out on him too early. That great actor, Sam Livesey, was another touring 'Kismet' and needless to say a fine one. Many people made their first appearances on tour in *Kismet*, Billie Carlton and Dennis Wyndham amongst them. *Kismet* was the rage, 'Kismet charms,' 'Kismet' jewellery sold like wildfire. There was life and excitement in the Edwardian Theatre.

But there is a story of Bourchier at the Garrick which is too good to miss. He had a dresser who was, to all appearances, the perfect servant, the ideal valet. He knew when to speak, when to be silent. He knew when a word of encouragement, on a first night, would cheer the anxious manager, he knew when to be tactfully without ideas. He was always there, always waiting on every exit of the actor-manager. But there came a first night when he seemed strange and aloof, and unusually silent. The play was not going too well. When Bourchier asked a question or two, the answer was very guarded. But at the end, the dresser was not there. For the first time in history he was absent. Bourchier was very annoyed and sent to find him. He was discovered busily discussing the play, which had 'got the bird' from the gods, with several galleryites in Charing Cross Road. He was brought to the presence. "Where have you been?" demanded Bourchier. "In the gallery," came the surprising response. Bourchier was dumbfounded. "In the gallery!" he gasped. "Yes, sir," said the dresser, "and I was one of them that boo-ed." Bourchier nearly collapsed. "You—boo-ed me?" he said, scarcely believing his ears. "How dare you?" The dresser drew himself up. "Sir," he said, "I am a member of the Gallery First Nighters. Every first night, when you go on, I go up to the gallery. I know the play, so I know how long I have before you come off. I have never missed once. But on this occasion my feelings got the better of me. I knew it was a bad play. I knew it was unworthy of you. So I joined in the general condemnation. And I waited behind to tell my friends that I agreed with them. Sack me if you like. In this room I am your servant. In the gallery I am a member of the public and can do and say what I like. That I yield to no man. Sir, I await your judgment." He was not sacked, for Bourchier saw the funny side.

Great actors, great actresses, great playwrights, great designers, jostle each other in the Edwardian tapestry. Most of the actor-managers were content to either remain in town at their own homes or go from one theatre to another, but some preferred to take the drama to the country as well. And when the Edwardian days died, these folk came to town more rarely. And they were some of our best.

Julia Neilson and Fred Terry, perhaps the best stage couple of that time—and where is their equal to-day ?—never had their own theatre. They shared themselves between town and tour. They kept alive the spirit of romantic drama, of cloak and sword, of great acting. *Sweet Nell of Old Drury*, *The Scarlet Pimpernel*—they need no other memories than those, the best of all the plays they did. *The Scarlet Pimpernel* is as immortal as the memory of Nell Gwynne. In that latter play, what did it matter if history was wrong, if the Nell of Julia was utterly unlike the Nell of Lewknor Lane ? It was the Nell we liked, it was the Julia we lay down our hearts to. And Fred Terry—what an actor that was ! What a man he was too. How he moved, how he spoke, what mastery of his difficult art he possessed. He could have—he should have—led the stage. But he preferred to keep the flag flying in the provinces, to see that the playgoers of the great cities were not starved of the best. And he and Julia gave it to them. What a handsome, regal-looking couple they were, and how regal she still is. Phyllis carries it on, this tradition—a mixture of her mother's grace and beauty, her father's art and charm.

And Sir John Martin-Harvey, who has so recently passed away. Here was the chief exponent of the Irving school, a man who was an actor first, last and all the time. He never forgot his calling. He had a curious, elusive charm and beauty about him, a watching, observant look, as became a creator, a refinement of character, a kind of delightful, retiring dignity. A long, and a distinguished career is now identified almost entirely with one play which he made so completely his own— *The Only Way*. That this version of *The Tale of Two Cities* took liberties with Dickens we cared not. All we asked was that Martin-Harvey— who became Sir John—should be the 'Sidney Carton' of our dreams, and that we should hear him say, "It is a far—far—better thing that I do." That was indeed partly true. But he was to show us acting of the true heroic school when he played *Oedipus* at Covent Garden in 1912. Here was the greatest piece of tragic acting since the days of Edmund Kean, savage in its stark horror of relentlessness, heart-moving in its sorrow and grief. It was truly great and it glitters like a jewel. It is almost a pity that *The Only Way* was such a success, so popular. Sir John Martin-Harvey might have risen to undreamed-of heights. But the public, whose obedient servant he was, demanded—and got *The Only Way*. It was the only way for him and wisely he and his devoted wife took it.

The Kendals lasted right into Victorian times. Still they toured, still they filled the theatre. Mrs. Kendal seemed ageless ; he was still the nice, respectable gentleman. And still they trained and launched the stars from the most respectable and moral stage training ground ever known.

Sir Frank Benson and Sir Ben Greet had not then achieved their knighthoods but they kept the name of Shakespeare in the bills and they sent the stars to the West End, finished products and knowing their business. Of the Old Bensonians there was—and is—an army. Two names gleam in the forefront, Henry Ainley and Matheson Lang. Both came from Benson, both rose to greatness in Edwardian times— the one is dead, the other an invalid. Ainley's start was more spectacular, he rose like a rocket in the golden halo of his handsomeness and talent, his marvellous voice. Lang was more steady, more painstaking, more sedate. He took it more slowly but more surely. He never swerved as did erratic, delightful Ainley. Step by step he mounted. He played Shakespeare at His Majesty's—*Hamlet*, and melodrama at the Lyceum, and did it all with the same ease, the same finish, the same sure command. Then an actor-manager himself, he went steadily to the very top. A great man and a great actor.

Robert Loraine was another great Edwardian, who outlasted that golden era. Here was a fine actor too, a little hard at times, but with a swing, a flourish, and a finish which few could beat, and a man who was as much at home in the air, on the battlefield as on the stage—utterly without fear. Melodrama still flourished then, and we loved it. We had it at the Lyceum after the Adelphi had changed its policy, under the banner of Smith and Carpenter. There Lang played in dramas by Hall Caine, and others. There Walter Howard gave us really good ones too, if a little far-fetched, whilst such actors as Norman Partreidge and Eric Mayne fought it out as hero and villain respectively. Edward Ferris, the handsome actor who had played 'Winterset' in *Beaucaire*, wrote good Lyceum drama called *The Fighting Chance*. The Edwardian actors were often playwrights too. Many young stars then are the big stars now. There is Dame Lilian Braithwaite, honoured by her title so well deserved, still as lovely and gracious as ever, and now a very great actress indeed. There is Marie Lohr, who became an actress-manageress and is one of the most accomplished actresses we have, as charming and attractive as she was in her teens at His Majesty's and the Haymarket. There is Mrs. Patrick Campbell, and Constance Collier, both of that epoch. There is Dame Irene Vanbrugh to delight us still. Eva Moore, Ethel Irving, Godfrey Tearle—a splendid fellow and splendid actor—Mrs. Langtry—people like Mrs. Brown Potter, all of the Edwardian times when young, and all of fame and memory—some still as active and good as ever, some retired, some passed away. C. Aubrey Smith, a leading man of the Edwardian days, has made a new career on the screen but remains a true Edwardian Englishman, whatever America can do, and is now a knight.

But think of some of the other people, not complete stars, but leading actors and actresses, whose line *The Stage* of its time would have described as 'leading business.' Kenneth Douglas, the best of light comedians, a typical Edwardian actor; William Haviland, a powerful actor whose death scene in *The Pretenders* was magnificent; J. Fisher White, so magnificent in *Strife*, and his opposite number there, Norman McKinnel; James Hearn, the clergyman-father in *Don*, and scores of other parts; Eric Lewis, the ideal man-about-town, and his big, fat, comedy namesake Fred; Horace Hodges, the villain in *The Scarlet Pimpernel*; C. W. Somerset, another superb villain of the stage; Louis Calvert, excellent in anything; Fred Kerr, a fine actor, and Holman Clark, who had a line and a charm of his own, who oozed benevolence and who was also a fine producer; A. E. George, robust and most reliable and sincere; these amongst a host mentioned and not mentioned in this chronicle were the backbone of the Edwardian Theatre and the peers of any of the supporting actors—always the strong card of the English stage—of all time. For general excellence, hard to equal to-day, if equalled they could be. And the women. Agnes Thomas and Henrietta

Watson, the two ideal middle-aged part players—difficult to choose between them; Annie Hughes, a comedienne of sparkle; Lottie Venne, a whole picture gallery of delight in herself; Sydney Fairbrother, a genius of character parts—Miriam Clements, Marie Illington, and sweet Marion Terry, what memories their mere names evoke; Charlotte Granville, Frances Ivor, and a host more. It is impossible to chronicle them all. What of H. V. Esmond, a fine actor and the author of so many successful plays? If they were sentimental, if the leading men of forty behaved as octogenarians, well, we were all sentimental and it was the fashion of the times. And handsome, fine-voiced Basil Gill? And E. S. Willard? And a step further back, but still there in Edward's time, Lionel Brough, that great comedian, Frank Cooper, J. D. Beveridge (a really grand actor), A. E. Robson, William Mollison, Alfred Bucklaw, James Fernandez, Herman Vezin, Henry Neville and a host of other giants. And, in a class by himself, Laurence Irving of tragic memory. For there were giants in those days—giants of the stage whose talent, whose personality, whose ability, was the background, nay, more than the background, the complement of the actor-managers, whose friends and confrères they were, whose triumphs they shared, and whose defeats they suffered. They were part of a time when the stage mattered, when the drama was of interest, when the Theatre still had charm and mystery and allure. When the magic word 'actor' or 'actress' thrilled the lay folk and when 'a peep behind the scenes'—so ardently desired—was so seldom vouchsafed. For in those days the players were in a world apart, wisely keeping themselves very much to themselves, knowing that mystery attracts and familiarity repels.

And these priests and priestesses of the Edwardian Theatre were the stars of to-day and the horizon's glow of dawn in their own day—a day when a visit to the theatre was worth while, when we went with pleasure and remembered with joy, when neon signs did not dim the street-lights, when we did not need a great glitter, for we made our own nights gay with our own enjoyment and *joie de vivre*—whether we bussed it, trammed it, hansom'ed it, trained it, walked it home, or had our carriages at eleven.

CHAPTER XV

When the Edwardian Dusk Fell. . . .

WHEN DUSK FELL IN EDWARDIAN EVENINGS, IF YOU DID NOT WANT TO go to a theatre, there were plenty of other things to do. When the lamps began to glitter and the electric light standards, where there were any, gleamed like big opals on high, not too steadily, and with a good deal of hiss and splutter on account of the carbons—you had your pick of a night life which was rich. If it was winter time, there were scores of things to tempt you to spend those few—those very few shillings—which would give you a golden time. It was not an Edwardian habit to get bored, life was flowing strongly, and the multiplicity of machine-made aids to amusement did not exist. You made your own fun with other creatures of flesh and blood, and so remained human, congenial, and bonhomous.

In the summer you had an additional choice, for in the earlier period there was Earl's Court, and in the later, the White City, two things which London lacks to-day—an out-of-doors garden in which to spend its summer night, lit with lamps, music, and laughter, in the English fashion which had endured since Tudor days, but which the first World War broke down.

It all depended on your age, your sex, your taste and your pocket how you spent your evening. If you were young and your parents were taking you out (at any time except Christmas), or if you had a respectable relation from the country or a maiden aunt, there was a choice for you as well. You could go, up to 1903, to the Egyptian Hall, or up to 1904, to the St. James's Hall. In the former you got mystery, in the latter you got Minstrels.

The Egyptian Hall stood in Piccadilly, its site now covered by Egyptian House, almost opposite the Burlington Arcade. It was a somewhat gloomy-looking place, with Egyptian figures and design, a little like a desert tomb. But inside it held delights beyond compare for youngsters and simple folk of the time. It had been built as a natural history museum, but became a place of entertainment, its first triumph being the appearance there of General Tom Thumb, the amazing dwarf sponsored by Barnum. That was in Victorian—and early Victorian days. In the Edwardian period it was known as 'England's Home of Mystery'— and it was. For Maskelyne, the great illusionist, held sway, first in partnership with Cooke, and afterwards with David Devant, who had been part of the show. It has no counterpart to-day at all, for the St. George's Hall, where the younger generation of Maskelyne carried on the family magic, never quite had the same air of mystic strangeness which you absolutely breathed in the Egyptian Hall. In its somewhat dingy interior the most amazing things happened. The entertainment was refined, drawing-room variety, and always had something of the air of the feeling that you were at a children's party and that the conjuror had come to entertain you. For magic formed the greater part of the show. It was not all card tricks, plate spinning, rabbits, flags, miles of coloured ribbons and suchlike unusual things out of tall hats, though tall hats, borrowed from the profusion in the audience, underwent the strangest uses at the Hall and went back to their owners none the worse. There was a magic orchestra—with brass and an organ predominating, which, unseen though not unheard, brayed forth 'The Death of Nelson' and other heartening compositions, apparently without human aid and from the most unlikely places, such as mid-air and the back of the circle. There were, when the cinema began to peep in, what were popularly known as animated pictures or technically, the Bioscope. Here you saw moving pictures on the screen, the same idea as to-day, only in a very blurred and flickery form. Human beings moved at great speed and jerkily, apparently through torrential downpours, but quite recognizable for what they were. Processions were a great feature. The Lord Mayor's Show or one of the other pageants which so often filled the streets, for foreign royalties were many in those kingly days and came and went with frequence and regularity, providing Londoners with opportunities to see the Household Cavalry in full panoply as escort and nice little shows to brighten the streets. The animated pictures showed these. And other features. But the most popular and the most striking was the representation of a railway station. Here life went on as usual as you sat and watched. Then the scene became busier for a train was signalled. Still you watched, interested, amused and unsuspecting. Then, suddenly, the train was upon you, coming full at you, belching steam and smoke and apparently driving right amongst you, amidst screams of horror and excitement from the astonished audience. Even strong men turned pale at this novel experience, and children screaming mightily were tucked under motherly arms as the exit was sought in full flight. We got a lot of kicks then that nobody gets to-day.

The high spot of the Egyptian Hall show was the little play which Maskelyne staged at the end. It was an affair of pure mystery and trans-cendant magic, called *Will, the Witch and the Watchman*. The plot does not linger clearly in the mind, although witnessed many times in youth, for it mattered little—what did matter was the magic, the absolutely unbelievable things one saw with one's own eyes. There was a butcher (played by Maskelyne, who also doubled other parts), a witch and an old-fashioned watchman. And there was a life-sized monkey—human (not simian) life-size. Late Victorian and early Edwardian children were assured that it was a man dressed up—but in that home of mystery a frightful but pleasant doubt remained. The scene depicted a village green, in the middle of which, unaccountably, there stood a huge cabinet. For this was the great Cabinet Trick. One presumes, over the years, that it represented the Lock Up, hence the Watchman. But although people were locked up in it, and you could see all round and underneath, although inside, part of it was a cage, the power of the magic was such that they were out as soon as in, and in the meanwhile, vanished into thin air before your very eyes. Strange things happened in and around that cabinet—the witch was locked in—you saw it—but a second later, the doors being thrown open, she had turned into the monkey, whilst she herself reappeared in a state of freedom—the monkey meanwhile turning into the butcher, whom you had not seen go, and once more into the watchman. One remembers the monkey losing his tail, which, without visible means of support or transport, leaped all over the stage, whilst a thrill of delightful terror ran down the backs of all. Some of the more stupid children were terrified, but the majority were both terrified and delighted, the delight getting the upper hand, and there were always wails of woe when that unseen orchestra played the National Anthem, and the children were borne out, protesting, to the carriages which came to the Egyptian Hall shortly before five. It was a landmark of London which Edwardians mourn. There was a thrill before you went in, too, for next door was the shop of Rowland Ward, the taxidermist, and in the window an array of stuffed animals enough to please any child. A huge bear reared itself aloft, a stuffed but very ferocious lion had leapt on the back of a stuffed but very terrified horse which, with eyes wide and nostrils agape, galloped madly in suspended action, whilst the lion held on, its claws scoring bloodstained wounds on the horse's side. You saw all that for nothing before you went in to the Egyptian Hall, and got another peep coming out, if you were lucky.

The St. James's Hall was also in Piccadilly, its site being now covered by the Piccadilly Hotel. This was London's Home of Minstrelsy. Here the nigger minstrel entertainment held court, a form of show which has vanished to-day, although the Metropolitan Police Minstrels kept it gallantly and brilliantly alive long after the end of its professional days. The Moore and Burgess Minstrels packed the St. James's Hall for years, producing stars by the score—many great comedians graduated there, and there is one famous London manager to-day who wore a black face in the later days when the Moore and Burgess and Mohawk Minstrels, who originated in Islington, combined to sing the swan song of Burnt Cork ! The Nigger Minstrel show was refined, melodious and riotously comic. It was in traditional form. The boast—largely advertised —of the Moore and Burgess crowd was that they 'never sang out of tune or out of London.' The first part was true, the second not quite accurate. But they were, nevertheless, one of the most popular and regular features of London's entertainment. The curtain went up and there they were, rows of them, all with black faces, and shining eyes, seated in a great semi-circle, their instrumentalists behind them on a raised dais. In the middle sat 'Mr. Interlocutor,' the burnt cork equivalent of the old music hall Chairman. At the corners sat 'the cornermen,' the comedians who decorated their evening dress with frills to show that they were funny fellows and manipulated bones (the envy of every small Edwardian boy) and tambourines.

They cracked gags and cut capers, they asked the Interlocutor riddles, which he repeated, sonorously and slowly, and to which he never knew the answers, though quite a few of his audience did. But the audience joined heartily in the roars of laughter which greeted the answer, as the triumphant mischievous cornermen clacked their bones and banged their tambourines, and there was usually a black-faced, Eton-collared, white-gloved boy with a lovely alto, to sing a melancholy ditty (beloved of Victorians and Edwardians whose eyes got wet as they blinked at the solemnly staring black faces before them). Apart from the interruptions of the cornermen, the whole of the first half of the programme was tinged with gentle melancholy, but the choral singing was absolutely perfect, and can only be savoured to-day when 'The Kentucky Minstrels' take the air, for which all Edwardians—and all moderns too— owe a debt to the much maligned B.B.C.

In the second half things got lively, for this was a series of single turns of a lively nature, dancing, instrumental, an inevitable and not very funny stump speech and ending with a farce or extravaganza of the wildest, hilarious and most impossible absurdities. One called 'Rum 'Uns from Rome' remains in the memory, where two of the 'negroes' got mistaken for valuable ancient Roman statues—the Romans apparently being coloured men—with most amusing and knockabout results. We loved the Minstrels and one wonders if, in the midnight hour, sometimes there steals a burst of perfectly sung choral melody down the corridors of the great hotel from those minstrel ghosts who once revelled there.

Perhaps your taste ran to a Circus, which in later peace times you could only see for a brief Christmas period at Olympia or the Agricultural Hall. London in Edwardian days had permanent circuses—one at

o

Henglers, which came down to make room for the London Palladium. It was a ramshackle place, largely built of timber but it held the delight and glamour of the sawdust ring. It did more, for it was a versatile place and halfway through the performance it turned itself into a Water Show, with its arena flooded, where marvellous things happened, a funny family had excruciating adventures in a boat which they could not row and an enormously fat (inflated) policeman pursued them. They all fell in, of course, to the youngsters' extreme delight, and the very fat policeman ended as a very thin one. The other circus was the London Hippodrome, a much grander and imposing affair, which also went aquatic and where not only amazing circus turns of dexterity and daring were performed, but simply breathtaking spectacles were staged by a genius called Frank Parker. Townships were swept away by floods, packs of wolves pursued sledges driven with careering horses across snowclad plains—every boy's book of adventure came to life.

There was always, of course, Madame Tussauds, in Baker Street. Here you gazed, as you still can gaze, at the effigies of the famous and the infamous, quite deathlike in wax, yet amazingly lifelike as well, and all awake and staring. You could see Napoleon's carriage, you could see famous fairy tales, a Sleeping Beauty who actually breathed whilst an ardent if waxen Prince leaned over her in silent adoration. You could satiate your soul in horrors in the Chamber thereof, and see the actual relics of famous crimes and their perpetrators frozen into wax in the very act, although that cost a bit extra. You could gaze upon famous scenes of history waxenly arrested for your education, and many a father was plagued by curious children for further information. The scene was the death of Harold the Saxon on the stricken field of Hastings, the Norman arrow securely in his eye. Before it stood a stolid Cockney father and his excited but curious little boy, athirst for information, and you heard one of F. Anstey's delectable 'Voces Populi' take place before you. For the following happened :

Boy : Father, what's that the gentleman's got in his Heye ?

Father : A harrer.

Boy : Ooo shot the harrer, father ?

Father : The henemy, I hexpect.

Boy : Ooo was the henemy, father ?

Father : 'Ere w'ere's yer mother and the rest of 'em ? Gorn to tea, I expect. Carm on.

(Exit boy dragged off reluctantly and with longing glances at the scene of carnage behind him).

Things like that would enliven your visit, and you could, if you were from the country, ask the way of a most lifelike wax policeman or try to buy a catalogue from an equally lifelike and waxen lady attendant.

But perhaps you wanted something more gay and lively—and who should blame you ? If so, you went to a Music Hall. There were plenty, for in Edwardian days the halls were at their zenith, although the end was painfully near. You could go to the Tivoli in the Strand, to the Oxford in Oxford Street, to the London Pavilion in Piccadilly Circus. You would see all the stars, you would see Little Tich, George Lashwood, Chirgwin, Vesta Victoria, Vesta Tilley, Gus Elen, Harry Champion,

George Robey, Eugene Stratton, Cinquevalli, George Bastow, Harry Lauder—all that mighty array of unique and glorious talent, which would sing you the true folk songs of England. For the halls were entertainment of the people for the people by the people. The problems you all knew were those discussed, the rent, the landlord, the lodger, the kipper, the summer holiday, the mother-in-law, beer, the naughty boy and his grown-up equivalent who turned night into day, Gay Paree, and the delights of the seaside and the Strand. Marie Lloyd would show you the true spirit of London, Alec Hurley and Gus Elen the true meaning of the Cockney male. Harry Tate would demonstrate the delights of Edwardian motoring, and you would have your drink, smoke your pipe or cigar and spend three hours of unalloyed and truly English delight. The talent of the world was yours, foreign acrobats, Chinese jugglers, nimble Japs on the slack wire, bustling Americans, daring French soubrettes, it was all yours. But the core of it all was English to a degree, that England which had for its emblem the sturdy, bewhiskered figure of John Bull, not the short-sighted, patched and bowler-hatted Little Man. It was at the halls you learnt your patriotism, were told you had a Navy, a British Navy, which kept your foes at bay, that a Little British Army went a damned long way, that the Soldiers of the Queen (or later the King) always won, and that you couldn't beat the boys of the bulldog breed, who made Old England's name. And you believed it all. You were right, it has been since proved true.

Maybe, you wanted something a little more refined and yet varied? There was the London Coliseum for your money. Built by that great man, Sir Oswald Stoll, mammoth entertainment was supplied, first as something in the nature of a Circus and afterwards as a variety theatre or music hall with the accent on the music. Here you could meet— and did meet—the Vicar without the least embarrassment on either side. Edwardian London catered for the whole of London, you see.

There were many other halls, including the Metropolitan, still retaining a lot of atmosphere, the Holborn Empire, which flew the flag until the Germans bombed it to pieces, and the Middlesex, grown out of the Old Mogul. In the later Edwardian years this place became almost Parisian. It imported the Ba-Ta-Clan Revue direct from what was still known, by people who had not been there, as the Gay City. This was a sensation, for the bright particular·spot was 'The Girl in the Muff,' a handsome, comely and well developed young Frenchwoman who apparently wore nothing else. From behind that muff she glanced at you enticingly from posters, and you went there to find to your astonishment—and delight—that the posters were more than justified. The near nudity of the beach and the bathing pool and even the Hyde Park Lido was unknown then, and this suggestion was most exciting. All the Edwardian men went along, although they did not take their sisters, sweethearts or wives.

London was as theatre and music hall conscious then as it is cinema conscious to-day. Every suburb had its own playhouse, often a palatial theatre, its own music hall, an Empire or a Palace mostly, or just known by its local name like the Granville or the South London. In the halls you saw the West End stars, in the theatres you saw the best of the touring companies, sometimes George Edwardes' own, but more often George Dance's. Transport had not then learnt to burrow underground and the West End was quite a distance, so suburban Londoners went to their own theatre at their own price, and enjoyed it. Some of the theatres were small affairs, like the old Parkhurst, in the Holloway Road, where Camden Road joins it. Here shows were small and prices matched it, but even there you always got its own pantomime every Christmas. The Parkhurst was one of the first playhouses to succumb to pictures and there, for threepence, sixpence and ninepence you could see John Bunny, Max Linder and all the unnamed stars of the early films, including Lieutenant Daring, R.N., whose adventures were serialized but complete. To-day he is a big man in the boxing world. Talking of suburban pantomimes, which every suburban theatre staged at Christmas, the old Grand Theatre, Islington ran pantos equal to any in the West End. Indeed people came from all quarters to see them. For years Harry Randall was the chief comedian, who afterwards succeeded Dan Leno at Drury Lane. Artists like Tom E. Murray, Hebe Bliss, Alexandra Dagmar, Cliff Ryland, Charles E. Stevens and other great ones were with him. There, too, Lottie Collins had danced 'Ta-Ra-Ra-Boom-De-Ay.' If Randall was not a Dan Leno (and how could he be) at least he was a fine comedian who sang fine songs. One of his panto songs at the Grand recalls the days of catchwords and of George R. Sims, for it was called 'Tatcho,' a much boosted hair restorer invented or sponsored by 'Dagonet' himself. And Randall had another song with the true music hall swing :

> "You 'ave to 'ave 'em
> Whether you want 'em or not
> You 'ave to 'ave 'em
> That's what touches the spot
> Pluck up, buck up,
> Troubles will end or mend you
> Open your mouth and shut your eyes
> And see what somebody sends you."

That was true music hall and therefore true pantomime. You can see for yourself how wide the implication, it didn't matter what it was, which of the many ills that flesh is heir to, you 'ad to 'ave 'em. But in true music hall style, it bade you be of good cheer and Micawberlike, wait for something to turn up. It is the epitome of music hall and its tune was as true as its words.

Visiting stars came to the Grand, Islington, for flying matinées and for a week's visit, Irving amongst them. Improved transport, easy access to town and the pictures have slain the suburban theatre—all but a few. But one of the oldest and best, The King's, Hammersmith, still carries on very successfully, and for over forty years has been true to its Christmas pantomime tradition. A salute to this brave theatre which keeps alive the spirit of Edwardian days.

But if it was 'Life' you wanted, Leicester Square was the place for you. That was magic ground. There stood the heart of night time naughtiness enshrined in its twin palaces of variety and ballet, the Empire and the Alhambra. The Empire was unique, it vanished such a little while ago, although the name remains. But the glory has departed before the majestic opulence of the cinema. Yet the Empire was opulent too. It draped itself in Imperial purple, its deep, soft carpets bore crowns. Its walls and its stairs were of marble, its attendants were knee-breeched. You looked at its golden stage, where golden girls in wonderful costumes formed a rainbow of colour as they clicked into formation after formation in a ballet, seen through a haze of cigar smoke. You saw Genee, the unequalled. You saw Wilhelm's perfection of design, you saw Katti Lanner's mastery of terpsichorean art. And you saw the best male dancer this country—maybe the world—ever had. He was a little man with a rather wistful face and a sweet smile. His name was Fred Farren. Here was the great pantomimist. He played 'Pan' in one ballet, he knew little of the classics, yet caught the character of 'Pan' which he described as the 'creature who was always watching.' How right he was—for the woodland god of the glade was assuredly ever watchful and missed nothing. He created many parts, all of them superbly. But he astonished Edwardian London the most when, with a dancer called Ida Crispi, he performed the Apache Dance. Farren showed how the Parisian of the underworld got his name. He showed that cold, bitter ferocity and savageness which had the tang of the Red Indian in it, that impassive cruelty which transformed itself into dance. There were scores, nay hundreds of other Apache dancers when the craze grew. It remains to-day. But there has never been another to expound it like Freddie Farren. Alas, that rheumatism was to cripple those agile limbs—but the pain and suffering and disappointment never dulled that quick intelligence, that kindly nature, that great heart of the little genius.

There was, of course, the Empire Promenade, behind the Circle. That was what you really went for. Here you could walk up and down, glance at the stage, or sit at a table and have your drink, and watch the most amazing procession of glorified Vice pass by. The women of the Empire promenade have no counterpart to-day. It may be a good thing, it surely is. But the sights of London are the poorer for it. These women were astounding in their professional magnificence. With the slow but dignified gait of caged tigresses, they promenaded up and down, or sat at tables to be entertained by men. They drank with you, they laughed and talked with you, but they seldom accosted you and never importuned. You knew what they were there for, and they knew that you knew. Many drove up in their broughams. All were amazingly costumed. They were the great courtesans of their time. And their time is over. Some of them married men they met at the Empire and, astounding as it may seem, made good wives and mothers. There is always the paradox in life. There were no roaring choruses at the Empire and no noise (except on Boat Race Night)—it was the highest class of its kind in existence and it was known as 'The Cosmopolitan Club of the World.' Soon it will have its own history written—and what a tale that will be.

The Alhambra, on the other side, flanking the Empire and the Square, was not quite so high class, not quite so surprising, nothing like so regal or exclusive. Its promenade, behind the stalls, and its women, were not so wonderful nor so glamorous. Yet its exotic, oriental air, its large bars, its lounges and its distinct allure had its own habitués too and it was an extremely enticing place as well. It shared with the Empire the fact that it was the home of ballet and its ballets were lovely. In Edwardian times both houses were to take to Revue, and to lose much of their individuality. But Edwardian men of all ages loved them both and frequented them nightly. You met your friends, you had your drinks, you had adventure and excitement—that was enough. And on a summer night, when you approached the Alhambra from the West, across the Square, along by the hedged and locked garden, and saw the crescent moon ride the sky between the Eastern cupolas which shone dull gold in its silver light, you doubted very much if East and West did not meet, after all. If they did, it was at the Alhambra.

All around you lay adventure—male adventure. Here were the great cafés, the bars, the resort of the demi-monde, of sportsmen, of men with money to spend and women to spend it for them. If it was racing men you wanted, then the Queen's Hotel was the place to meet them. Professional backers rubbed shoulders with the jockeys and got information—which may or may not have been accurate, for jockeys' tips are notorious. They wasted their bodies to 'make the weight' in the Turkish Baths adjoining the Alhambra, in the hottest room of which a street bookmaker once took cover from the police and nearly died from staying too long therein. Or they went to the other baths in Jermyn Street, that curious thoroughfare where still a glimpse of Regency London tinges the air and where, in Edwardian days, retired butlers let rooms to men-about-town. Jermyn Street has gone 'commercial' but there is still a faint air of cravats and beavers and quizzing glasses, of Inverness capes, tall hats and canes to be savoured. It is still a masculine street in a feminine age.

But in the Square there was 'The Café de L'Europe,' its entrance still there but used as a cigarette kiosk, its name borne by a most respectable restaurant. Here you went downstairs to a German lager beer hall, where lager was not the only drink served, but lots of it, and English beer as well, was consumed. German waiters hurried about carrying an unbelievable number of foaming glasses which they never dropped or spilled. They took your order without seeming to hear it above the din and clatter, and served you with great celerity. Women, of the class known as 'unfortunates,' filled the place, but did not seem to realize their misfortune. Stuck on the wall midway to the ceiling was a string orchestra faintly heard amidst the hullaballoo, everyone talked at once, everyone shouted, quarrels were as rife as love-making and laughter—and from time to time there came a sudden hush as a police inspector and a sergeant walked through, but noise broke out again as soon as they had gone. Across the road, now bombed away, was The Provence. On the floor level it appeared to be an ordinary London pub, but downstairs in its basement was the first storey of hell. For there the women were of a lower type and the men also. Bullies, pimps, prostitutes, criminals—all the lower life of the half-world went there. Fights were frequent. Drinks were as often flung in faces as poured down throats, broken glasses, bottles, hat-pins were as often weapons as nails and fists, and the police had a busy time. Arrests were many and every arrestee was followed by a dangling wake of friends or enemies as he or she went between two stolid London 'bobbies' (as Edwardians called them) across the Square to Vine Street. And around the corner, in Bear Street, on the first floor this time, was a room called 'The Cosy.' It was much too cosy for modern minds or feelings. The room was small and always packed with femininity of the street and their followers. The close air was full of patchouli, and other highly flavoured scents which carried on a determined struggle with the aroma of hot humanity and alcohol. It was unwise to have anything of much value about you if you went to 'The Cosy.' Watches had a way of being missing when you came out. You did not carry a wallet, of course, for your money was in gold and silver in your trousers pocket, not easy to steal. But other portable property left you speedily in 'The Cosy.'

There was the Leicester Lounge, again upstairs, but vanished now in the flood of milk bars, drapers and such-like establishments which have submerged what was once the most exciting centre of the whole city.

You went up quite a lot of stairs and into a very large lounge indeed. It was guarded by stalwart attendants in Royal Blue. Here again were the women, lower than the Empire or the Alhambra but above the Provence and the Cosy, on a par, maybe, with the Europe. More drinking was done at the Lounge than elsewhere, and it was a great place for the Saturday night West Enders, aglow with health and spirits after a football match—in which they had played themselves and not just looked on. They got obstreperous and indulged in horse play, more often than not. And then those attendants interfered, and down the many stairs, each of which had a brass nosing, went those revellers, to go home sadder, wiser and sorer men. But there was no ill feeling, it was all part of a night out in Edwardian days.

There was the Globe Restaurant, another haunt of the Ladies, where gay doings took place, where the lights frequently got turned out and where battles were waged, in good part, with whatever happened to be on the tables at the time.

And away up Regent Street was Verreys', much more select and respectable, with its air of the First Empire, where you got good food, good wines and, on the whole, good company. If you were not out for a dash, but felt a little tired and wanted to sit down for a bit, have a drink and listen to an orchestra, Edwardian London gave you that too. For you went to Frascati's. There, around the fringe of the great central floor, you could have anything you wanted to eat, or just a drink, whilst the respectable middle classes (in the main) ate either à la carte, or devoured an immense banquet for seven and sixpence. The orchestra was good, there were bright lights, good food, good service, good drinks, and an air of leisure and peace which was quite delightful, if not truly West End. It had a dash of Paris, and it drew many foreigners. If you liked Turkish coffee, then a dark-faced individual in full Turkish attire, who perambulated the place, made and served you an excellent cup from his travelling café. And all the while the band played. . . .   ᶜ

But in the summer, after a day at work, Londoners wanted fresh air and amusement thrown in. They got it. They got it in full measure, with a witchery of magic, at either the White City or Earl's Court. These places were joyous. They were just what Edwardians wanted. And they were places of great beauty and charm on a velvet night in June, July or August. We did not indulge in daylight saving then, we enjoyed our evenings too well. The slow dimming of the sunlight in London, in those days, had a peculiar charm and peace which seems lacking to-day. Now nightfall seems to come with a clap, but then we had the delight of twilight—about which George Lashwood sang to us so perfectly. Maybe it is age which robs the senses of this keener perception of time, maybe the nights are not so gay—maybe, and most likely, London has changed as it has always been changing. But the appeal of the last attempt of this kind, at Wembley, was not the genuine thing at all. It was too vast, too unfriendly, too far away. There was no magic, no intimacy, no soft glow at Wembley. It was of the chromium and electric age. It turned night into day. Earl's Court and the White City were wiser, they glorified and beautified the darkness. Their lights were an adjunct to it, not a deterrent. They were lovely when they existed and are lovely memories still.

Earl's Court was the senior, and the best in many ways. It had a homelier air, it was a true Cockney, it was intimate. The exhibition it housed might be Hungary, India, Savage South Africa, what you will, that did not matter very much to the Edwardian night birds. There was much that was interesting, no doubt, and there is also no doubt that these exhibitions were very good for business between the commercial firms of the country. But it was as a pleasure garden, and at nightfall, that we liked Earl's Court. By day it was slightly garish, you saw the canvas scenery, the plaster and the joins, but at night, all that vanished to be replaced by sheer delight. You could go into the great Empire Hall, where Imre Kiralfy staged such impressive and truly wonderful pageants. They were terrific things, and the pageants at the Albert Hall to-day, which draw such throngs, are pale efforts compared to Kiralfy's. For he made it all real. If it was India, then he held the glorious East in fee. You saw Indian history in its barbaric splendour unroll before you. Not scores but hundreds of Mohammedans stormed Somnath in 1024, banners waved, spearmen struggled, armed horsemen charged in veritable hordes and cities went up in flame amidst the screams of pillaged citizens. English traders came before the Great Mogul—and the original scene could not have been more brilliant or rich—save that the gold and jewels would have been real.

The fierce Mahrattas, scimitars agleam, screamed, slew and burned ; a Hindu Paradise, with flooded arena, and hosts of dancing girls, formed before our very eyes. English troops embarked for the Mutiny and fought their battles all over again, and the thing ended with a pageant within a pageant of the blessing of the British Raj upon the Empire's pearl.

Or, if it was a naval exhibition, the battleships, cruisers, destroyers, all perfect scale models, manœuvred, shelled, attacked, blew up, sank and faithfully reproduced bombardments and naval battles.

In Savage South Africa the Matabele Impis gathered, danced and went to war, whilst Major Wilson and his gallant few made their historic last Stand with truly startling realism. This was better than the films, for it was real flesh and blood—and it was all historically correct down to the last dagger, the last helmet and boot button.

But the great man who created Earl's Court, Harold Hartley, whose main business was mineral water making, was the benefactor of his time.

He gave us true nights of gladness. For when you entered the great Court from the street you stepped into a different world—at night. Water glistened before you, great palaces were outlined in twinkling gaslight, and down the Water Chute dashed yelling, excited people, to bound with great splashes over the waters of the lake, and go and do it all over again. And if the Redskins who guided the chutes were from the Wild West of Hammersmith, that did not matter at all. You could glide over that lake on little swan boats, propelled by a white-clad attendant who pedalled the boat along whilst you and your girl, like a male and female Lohengrin, sailed through the gold-flecked waters and saw the lights in each other's eyes. You could sit and have a drink at an open air restaurant whilst a military band discoursed waltzes or the popular musical comedy selections, and take the air and your refreshment at your ease and at moderate prices, and if the waiter wore a straw hat with his evening dress, who cared? For this was London on a summer night in the secure days of good King Edward the Peacemaker. You went through a long corridor, really a bridge over the Metropolitan Railway, where dark men in frock coats and fezzes, often real Armenians, offered you the treasures of the Orient, and dark-haired houris—smacking rather of Whitechapel—offered you perfumes of the East and miniature bricks which, if stored with your handkerchiefs, administered at first a pungent perfume, but finally smelt like pepper.

But then you got to the Western Gardens, the true heart of Earl's Court. Above you towered the Great Wheel, one of the wonders of London. At night it was a thing of mystery, as it crept slowly round, a vast circle of points of light, with its brightly lit carriages hanging from their crossbars ; at day, a huge spider's web of iron bars, of satisfying strength and ingenuity. It was an adventurous trip which every Londoner took at least once in his life. From certain quarters of London you could not escape the Great Wheel—it dominated the approaches from the West and South West, you spied it afar off—and you got a thrill, for it signified the romance of London, where such things as this monster were possible. Around the Western Gardens were the fun fairs, the switchback which thundered up and down with never-ceasing loads perpetually yelling with excitement, the shooting galleries and many more attractions—and bars. But in the centre, away from the fringe of hectic fun, was the principal bandstand, with its Guards' Band, and the Welcome Club. Here, if you were a member, you sat on a velvet lawn under well-grown trees, had food or drinks deftly served by expert waiters, and watched the less fortunate people outside the fence. Its membership was smart and distinguished. Evening dress was the rule, not the exception. The great Lord Roberts, V.C.—our beloved Bobs— was President. Royalty visited it. That Welcome Club was indeed one of London's best night spots. But the younger people and the poorer people, who could not afford membership (which according to present ideas was next to nothing) did not worry about being outside that white fence, for they were inside Earl's Court and inside Fairyland. For, when dusk fell, an army of men with poles, on the end of which blazed burning tow, hurried around and lit the fairy lamps. These little cut glass containers, of all hues, were everywhere—in the bushes, in the trees, amongst the beautiful blooms in the plenteous flower beds, hanging from the buildings—and inside each was a powerful nightlight. This once lit, the glass receptacle shone like a jewel and it became what its name implied—a fairy lamp. And amidst the myriad of these fairy jewels, which gleamed red, amber, blue, yellow, green and white everywhere, decking the night with beauty, round and round the bandstand, up and down the paths, went the lads and lasses of Edwardian London, romance in their heart, laughter on their lips, their eyes aglow—for they were part of an era which was good to live in, although they knew it not. But they did know that it was a summer night in London, at Earl's Court, and that joy was all around them. And, not wanting better than that, they made the most of it—and remember it with gratitude still.

The White City lay out at Shepherds Bush. You got to it by the Tuppenny Tube, another of London's Edwardian wonders. It was larger, bigger, brighter, and altogether more grand than Earl's Court. By day it shone white, by night it glittered like a diamond. It was so well lit that it showed floodlighting to an age which knew nothing about it. It had no Great Wheel, but it had the Flip Flap, two gigantic fingers of steel which from a flat position rose to describe a perfect half-arc and descend again on the other side. Each carried aloft a carriage packed with Londoners having a foretaste of flying, for that was the feeling it engendered. It was far more venturesome, it was faster, and it looked far more dangerous than the Great Wheel. It was the flying age casting its shadow before. But it was never a landmark like the Wheel, nor did it ever catch the imagination to such an extent. Architecturally, the White City was much better than Earl's Court. Its Court of Honour transported you to India, where white palaces, seemingly a lacework of stone, surrounded a great lagoon. At one end was a minaret, which housed a band, and before it a cascade fell and splashed over a bed of coloured glass, which at night time lit up with a lovely effect. A canal wandered away into the night, and flowed between grassy banks decked with flowers, shrubs and trees, above which were white walls. To glide along its still, inky waters at night, in a silent electric launch, with the strains of 'The Gondoliers' in your ears from a bandstand as you passed by, whilst across your path lay bands of white brightness and golden glory from the innumerable lights, and overhead the full moon touched the white buildings into a sheen of silver, was to come very near to Paradise. To be young then, to have half a sovereign to spend (it would last you the whole day, and do things well), to have the girl of your choice with you, and to let the night slide by in that setting was to know and experience something the restless, racing, mechanical-bound youth of to-day will never know. It may have been simple, but it was a very lovely thing indeed. One day such leisure, such simplicity, such opulence of time, life and pleasure—and money—may return, and the world will be a better place.

The White City had its Club, its restaurants, its shows, its bands, its exhibitions. It had opened in 1908 as 'The Franco-British Exhibition.' It was a huge, overwhelming success, despite the fact that it was not ready on the opening day and many a silk dress and dainty shoe was spoiled in the mud and debris and by the inclement weather. But it got itself ready in a very short space and then the weather smiled. The

Entente Cordiale, the keystone of Edwardian diplomacy, was at its height. This was the Edwardian Exhibition *par excellence*, and as an exhibition, apart from its pleasure side, it was terrific. French people crowded over—it was almost another Great Exhibition of 1850, only between two great and friendly nations. To many people, it never changed its name as the years went on. It remained the Franco-British. But to most it became the White City, a name which the Londoners themselves gave it, and a name which was the perfect description. For it was a city in size and it was white. To-day the White City means dog racing, and no more. To the Edwardians it meant entrancing nights in beautiful surroundings, nights gay with laughter, music, youth and love. The Edwardians had the better of it.

But in this tour around London we have got away from the actor-managers and the theatres. Well, there remains but one more place we need visit. To see Edwardianism at its grandest, its richest, and its most powerfully plutocratic, to see the finest carriages, the best cars, the richest people, the smartest people, the holders of old titles and the clutchers of new ones, you had to go to Covent Garden Opera House, the Royal Opera House, Covent Garden, our last place of call. The Opera lasted only during the London season—sometimes there was a winter season but it was never so grand as that of the real season—the high time of Court and Society. It is a gala night, perhaps Melba is singing.

The great building is aglow, its gas cressets blow in the summer breeze above its high pediment, the odd little glasshouse perched on its portico is a pool of light, every window gleams, and a rich yellow flood pours out from under its covered carriage drive. One by one, in endless procession, the carriages roll up Long Acre or up Bow Street from the Strand, cockaded coachman with rug-covered knees, cockaded footman with arms folded and white buckskin legs, sitting stiffly to attention. Inside are handsome, moustached men, in tails and white waistcoats ; lovely—or at least smart, and sometimes great—ladies in their full array of trains, low necks, and silks and satins, enough material in each dress to make many to-day. And on their arms, their fingers, their corsages, around their necks, gleam a fortune of jewels—rubies, emeralds, sapphires, diamonds, pearls in ropes and dog-collars. And on their elaborate coiffures glitter diamond tiaras, for every woman in those days was a queen and behaved accordingly—or as nearly as she could. There was no equality, it was only being loosely and loudly declaimed by a band of social outcasts called Suffragettes—or the Wild Women—or the Shrieking Sisterhood. Women ruled men, and knew it. Equality did not appeal to the late Victorians or early Edwardians *en masse*. They sat on their pedestals and relied on their menfolk, who realized their duty and their responsibility—and mostly did it. These women did not foresee the day when that equality would reign supreme. They did say sometimes that when women had some say in the affairs of the world there would be no more war. The Blitz of 1940 was undreamt of, of course. Yet that was a woman's war as well as a man's, and it was the worst yet. But all that was in the future—which nobody could foresee. Those carriages, brought to a halt by the press and congestion of hundreds like them, slowly but at long last dropped their people at the door of the Opera House. They entered the vestibule, some to pass the evening-dressed, white-gloved attendants at the stalls and stall boxes entrances, others to pass up the grand staircase to their boxes in the tiers. Few of them cared much for music, few of them understood it ; indeed, few Londoners of that time were lovers of classic or operatic music. Those who did were perched away in the gods, up at a dizzy height, or hanging in the slips, unable to see much, but they could follow in their scores with trembling and pleasurable reverence. The Opera was a place to be seen at, so one wore one's best—clothes, jewels, air and smile. Lorgnettes flashed as their users turned about to see who was there, men levelled opera glasses at fair women in their glory. It was a rich, glittering, wonderful night such as to-day cannot offer. Once, indeed, that Shrieking Sisterhood disturbed its holy ritual by yells of "Votes for Women" and showers of leaflets falling —sometimes in solid packets—on tiaraed heads. The Edwardian opera-goers that night, male or female, had little sympathy with the Cause.

But that was a solitary happening—and as a rule nothing untoward occurred to interrupt the social occasion. But the conductor entered to polite applause, he poised his baton, it fell and the myriad strings flickered like rushes in the breeze and a river of melody arose from that mighty orchestra pit as the picked players in the land began the overture.

But we are nearing the end, and the curtain has fallen. If you were a young Edwardian man, without a carriage, but with youth and desire for life and love, your night had not ended. You dashed out of the theatre in which you happened to be sitting and you joined the throng around the stage door. Some were there to gaze at the actresses and actors as they came forth, before making a rush for that last bus or train. But you, a young man, were in a class apart, in a world of your own. You had an appointment with one—the word 'date' in that respect was unknown—to take her out to supper. She was probably a lady of the chorus, or a lady of the ballet. It did not matter, she was an actress, she was on the stage, she was therefore only semi-human and semi-divine, for she belonged to another race and another world. You waited impatiently, a smile already on your face, your eyes alive with anticipation. And then she came. Out of the door, the Stage Door, she came. She looked the part, she did not look just like any other girl —and to-day almost every girl looks like every other girl. She had individuality, she had a distinction, a little something, a little glow—a little overdone in the matter of cut and smartness maybe but altogether charming, delightful, admirable—and above all an actress. She had a large hat, a long skirt, and as she lifted it you saw dainty, high-heeled shoes. She smiled at you adorably, and you with your hat in your hand, your overcoat open and your white waistcoat agleam, whisked her into a hansom, or later a single cylinder taxi, and knew that you were the envy of every other young man in sight; for you were taking an actress out to supper. So perhaps you went to Romano's, perhaps you went to Kettners, perhaps you went to Rules—but perhaps, if you were very lucky indeed, perhaps the most perfect night of all Edwardian nights lay before you. Perhaps you were taking her to the Covent Garden Opera House—not to see tiaraed people gaze at each other in a fully lit house ; oh, no, but to a Covent Garden Ball. For those were the real nights of gladness for late Victorian and early Edwardian youth. To take a pretty little actress to a Covent Garden Ball, after an evening at the theatre. Life held no more than that.

For on certain nights, when the opera was over, when the high and mighty had departed, then Romance took over Covent Garden. Miracles happened. 'The stalls vanished as if by magic, a polished dance floor appeared and, as if from nowhere, and into the Opera House, like a crowd of carefree Arcadians, dashed the young Edwardians, yes, and the middle-aged ones too, for a Covent Garden Ball. All wore fancy dress or dominoes, and the majority were young, though some men of more mature years came to recapture their youth, and mostly succeeded. Then lights were really bright, and these people, who knew nothing of war or its perils, who had money in their pockets which would go five times as far as it would to-day, let themselves go with pleasure and danced the whole night away. Champagne popped and fizzed, pretty mouths munched sandwiches of caviare, or foie gras, or ate chicken or salmon mayonnaise in boxes where duchesses had so short a time before sat in splendid dignity. Kisses were freely given, or stolen adventurously, vows were made, hearts beat and fluttered, assignations were whispered—and always the dance went on and laughter rang everywhere. Up and down the staircases they ran, in mad, happy chases, in and out of the dancers on the floor, across the stage and amongst the musicians—and still the waltzers revolved, or the lancers made them scream with delight as the strong young males lifted the dainty girls off their feet. Valse cotillon, polkas, waltzes again, a barn dance, then a few quiet moments in the back of a box, to kiss and be kissed, to embrace, to vow eternal adoration. Who cared for to-morrow? It would be as to-day, as yesterday. The world was rich, secure, and prosperous. Nobody dreamed of war. Love and laughter were the watchwords, and the melody of the strings, the haunting magic of the waltz. Those Covent Garden nights were all too short, if only they could have lasted for ever. And then, in the rosy light of a summer morning, whilst the men in the market were busy at work, they would see the tired but happy young folk, in the motley of London's gaiety, come out of the great theatre, which had seen so much in so many years, get into cabs, and linked in embrace depart for home in a mist of sleep, to part to meet again that night, when work was done, to tumble into bed and dream of a night which had been wholly of their era, for their descendants knew them not. The youths went to work unjaded, for the tonic of joy kept them alert—and there was the night to look forward to again ; the girls to sleep and dream until the day failed and dusk came with the stars and the gas lamps, for another round of frolic in the 'eighties, the 'nineties and the Edwardian nineteen hundreds which seem so far away but which are so near in terms of time. 'That perhaps was the best Edwardian memory of all.

And the older folk woke in the morning with memories of that play they had seen, that great piece of acting, that fine bit of singing or dancing. How pleasant it had all been. What a nice play, what clever people, how smart the house, what pleasant hours had been spent before that curtain fell and they had left that Theatre, that Edwardian actor-manager's theatre, and got into their carriages at eleven.

INDEX